A THEORY OF NARRATIVE

A THEORY OF NARRATIVE

F. K. STANZEL

Translated by Charlotte Goedsche

With a preface by Paul Hernadi

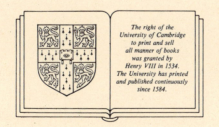

The right of the
University of Cambridge
to print and sell
all manner of books
was granted by
Henry VIII in 1534.
The University has printed
and published continuously
since 1584.

CAMBRIDGE UNIVERSITY PRESS

Cambridge

London   New York   New Rochelle

Melbourne   Sydney

Published by the Press Syndicate of the University of Cambridge
The Pitt Building, Trumpington Street, Cambridge CB2 1RP
32 East 57th Street, New York, NY 10022, USA
10 Stamford Road, Oakleigh, Melbourne 3166, Australia

Originally published in German as *Theorie des Erzählens* by
Vandenhoeck and Ruprecht, Göttingen, West Germany, 1979 (2nd revised
edition, 1982) and © Vandenhoeck and Ruprecht, Göttingen, 1979

First published in English as *A Theory of Narrative*.
English translation © Cambridge University Press 1984

First paperback edition 1986

Printed in Great Britain by
Redwood Burn Limited, Trowbridge, Wiltshire

British Library cataloguing in publication data

Stanzel, F.K.
A theory of narrative.
1. Narration (Rhetoric)   2. Hermeneutics
I. Title   II. Goedsche, Charlotte
III. Theorie des Erzählens. *English*
809'.923   PN212

ISBN 0 521 24719 5 hard covers
ISBN 0 521 31063 6 paperback

Library of Congress catalogue card number: 83–15262

CONTENTS

Contents

Contents

Contents

PREFACE

The prominent Austrian scholar Franz Karl Stanzel published his first book, *Die typischen Erzählsituationen im Roman*, in 1955. This pioneering exploration of what Wayne Booth later called *The Rhetoric of Fiction* (1961) was based on close readings of selected passages from British and American novels (primarily Fielding's *Tom Jones*, Melville's *Moby-Dick*, James's *The Ambassadors*, and Joyce's *Ulysses*). Perhaps because Stanzel, now professor of English at the University of Graz, had studied at Harvard as well, the critical framework of the book was nearly as Anglo-American as it was 'Germanic.' Yet non-German readers had to wait almost two decades for the English version (*Narrative Situations in the Novel*, 1971), and Stanzel's even more internationally oriented second book, *Typische Formen des Romans* (1964, 10th edn 1981), has so far remained untranslated.

It is all the more fortunate to have his latest and most advanced study, *Theorie des Erzählens* (1979, 2nd, revised edn 1982), available in English without undue delay. As the reader will soon discover, this book integrates various literary and critical traditions into an impressively unified examination of the ways and means whereby novels and shorter narrative works have, since the Renaissance and especially in the last three centuries, evoked fictive worlds to the imagination of their responsive readers. Despite Stanzel's continued attention to minute textual detail, the chief ambition of the present book is appropriately announced in its title as theoretical. Stanzel attempts, above all in chapters 3 and 7, to delineate a comprehensive typology of all conceivable narrative structures.

Such an undertaking may provoke scepticism or outright hostility among a few readers. Some may even glorify their aversion to any systematic study of literature by invoking the authority of a couple of lines from a time-honored dramatization of academic advising: 'Gray, my dear friend, is all theory / And green the golden tree of life.' It should of course be noted that it is not Goethe and not even Faust who speaks the often-quoted words to a disoriented Freshman. The early badmouther of theory is none other than the Devil. Blinded by the excessively colourful rhetoric – is life's tree green or golden? – the young student remains so deficient in 'theory' (the word's Greek root, *thea*, means 'act of seeing') that he cannot see through Mephisto's disguise and fancies to have been counselled by Professor Faust himself.

It is far less pardonable for latter-day admirers of Goethe and of other Romantic classics to take the shrewd verbal masquerade at face value. Why attribute all grayness one perceives to theory rather than to one's blurred intellectual vision? Like his younger English contemporaries, Blake and Coleridge, Goethe was always straining his mental eyes to see – not abstract generalities, to be sure, but 'the universal in the particular,' that is to say, the 'natural forms' (whether of flora, fauna, or human culture) in the prodigious manifold of individual phenomena. In a note appended to his collection of late poems, *West-östlicher Divan* (1819), he called narration one such *Naturform* of literature and even pleaded for the systematic study of particular works and genres as either homogeneous or interactive manifestations of 'natural forms' of this kind.

Our views of nature and of its primal forms are, of course, products of culture. Indeed, every theory (whether it makes us envisage the 'natural forms' of nature or culture) emerges at a specific point of human history. This is why all theorizing appears to have been partial in both senses of the word when new theories, based on new or newly perceived phenomena, reveal its limitations and characteristic bias. But the inevitable historicity of theoretical endeavours also explains why there are propitious times for certain kinds of theory.

In the fourth century BC, for example, Aristotle could assert that the gradual development of Greek tragedy 'stopped on its attaining to its natural form' (*Poetics*, Chapter IV). As we now realize, his high point of theoretical observation was just one of several comparable summits in the historical development of drama. All the same, it did provide Aristotle's sharp eyes with an overview not only of the actually broken paths leading up to his observation post, but also of some as yet untravelled neighbouring areas. How else could so many of his theoretical generalizations, based exclusively on ancient Greek literature and theatre, have proven to be eminently applicable to literary and dramatic works of other nations and periods? Many centuries later, it may well be that European and American fiction as we know it has realized its potential with respect to what Aristotle would have called its means, manner, and objects of mimesis – the 'means' being printed prose, the 'manner' narrative discourse, and the 'objects' verbal, nonverbal, and quasi-verbal (that is, mental) events. To the extent that it has, the time has also come for a theoretical survey of the novels and short stories of post-Renaissance Western civilization, and the present book may prove to be very helpful indeed in the study of narrative discourse for a long time to come.

According to Stanzel, the central task of a theory of narrative is to systematize the various kinds and degrees of 'mediacy' (*Mittelbarkeit*) that result from the shifting relationship in all storytelling between the story and how it is being told. In order to discover the fundamental possibilities of narrative mediation, one must inquire: 1. Does the narrator belong to the world of the story or does he/she abide in another postulated realm of existence? 2. Does the narrator directly convey information to the reader or does he/she filter it through the consciousness of one or several of the characters? 3. Does the narrator give the reader an external view of the narrated events or does he/she represent them, as it were, from within? There is considerable overlap between the respective answers elicited to this set of questions by the textual examples that Stanzel culls from well over a hundred representative novels and short stories. Yet his corresponding set of basic analytical categories – 1. person, 2. mode, and 3. perspective – provides a flexible framework within which those answers can be both distinguished and interrelated.

The present refinement of Stanzel's first tripartite typology of authorial, first-person, and figural 'narrative situations' owes a great deal to his cautious recourse to some binary oppositions that have emerged from the pertinent inquiries of the last hundred years: scenic versus proper narration (Otto Ludwig), objective versus subjective narration (Friedrich Spielhagen), tellers versus reflectors (Henry James), panoramic versus scenic presentation (Percy Lubbock), narrating self versus experiencing self (Leo Spitzer), progressively evolving versus retrospective temporal orientation (Roman Ingarden), narrative perspective 'with' versus 'from behind' the fictive characters (Jean Pouillon), telling versus showing (Norman Friedman), reliable versus unreliable narrators (Wayne Booth), texts with speakers versus texts without speakers (Lubomír Doležel), homodiegetic versus heterodiegetic narration (Gérard Genette). In a similarly productive fashion, Stanzel has assimilated the results of the thoroughgoing study, by Dorrit Cohn and some other critics, of the interior monologue and free indirect discourse. This splendid pair of relatively recent narrative devices challenges the universal validity of the Platonic and Aristotelian distinction between the 'poet's own speech' and the speeches of the represented characters (*The Republic*, Book III, and *Poetics*, Chapter III). No one, of course, 'speaks' the words in which interior monologues render a character's thoughts, feelings, and perceptions *as if* they were orally expressed by that character; and free indirect discourse allows the narrator actually to 'say' what, as the reader is made to realize, a character has said, written, or meant on some (more or less clearly defined) fictive occasion. These two techniques have thus enlarged the spectrum of mimetic possibilities registered by classical rhetoric and poetics, but Stanzel's typological circle (see p. xvi) accommodates them in its spacious conceptual order. Typologically as well as historically speaking, the interior monologue and free indirect discourse turn out to be approximations of the camera-eye narrative method of the French *nouveau roman*, some consideration of which concludes Stanzel's circumnavigation of the vast continent of storytelling.

The embarked reader may look forward to a pleasant voyage of discovery. Unlike more adventurous flag-carriers of what is sometimes called narratology, Stanzel steers clear of the coral reefs of metalinguistic neologisms, as well as the self-referential whirlpools of profound speculation. But there will be brief stretches of rough sailing, mainly because the translator seems to have been anxious not to immobilize our vessel by anchoring it too securely to a foreign idiom. Take the crucial phrase used by Stanzel to describe his project as the study of how novels and short stories 'render the mediacy' involved with the ubiquitous narrative relationship between the telling and the tale. While *Mittelbarkeit* is not a household word in the Danube valley either, its not quite English equivalent makes uncanny spectres of Latinate erudition (not to mention shades of Hegelian dialectic) hover over the Thames and Mississippi rivers. More important still, the German verb translated here as 'render' is *gestalten* and connotes the act of in-forming inchoate matter by giving salient shape (*Gestalt*) to it. One is tempted – but no faithful translation could presume – to circumscribe what the familiar German word also means in its present context as 'making literary virtue out of linguistic necessity.'

The adjective 'epic' may serve to illustrate the conceptual rather than purely linguistic difficulty that Stanzel's readers sometimes face if they are unfamiliar with the German critical tradition. In English, the word's connotations chiefly point to the *serious* and *consequential* events narrated in *monumental* works like the *Iliad* or *Paradise Lost*. In German, however, *episch* and the corresponding noun *Epik* have long been used to refer to any kind of *fictional narrative*, whether grave or lighthearted, whether long or short, whether in verse or prose; Goethe, for example, designated his three natural forms of literature as *episch*, *lyrisch*, and *dramatisch*. Problems of this kind (none of them too serious) are most likely to surface whenever Stanzel draws on or takes issue with important German scholars whose work is insufficiently known or totally neglected in the English-speaking countries (e.g., Käte Friedemann, Robert Petsch, Wolfgang Kayser, Käte Hamburger, Eberhard Lämmert, Harald Weinrich, Johannes Anderegg, and Karlheinz Stierle, to name a few in rough chronological order).

Clearly, the reader of any translation must tread lightly on the semantic field of routine verbal associations and remain open to less 'self-evident' connotations suggested by the notes, prefatory remarks, and (above all) each key term's conceptual context. Considered in this way, Stanzel's work should prove highly stimulating not only for students of the Euro-American novel and short story; readers interested in non-narrative literary genres may be especially prompted to elaborate on structural and stylistic affinities between scenic presentation and drama, between the interior monologue and certain kinds of lyric poetry, or between the discourse of personalized narrators and what is perhaps the most typical form of the essay. Those interested in nonliterary or not primarily literary narratives (from motion pictures through autobiography and dream summaries to news reporting and historiography) will also find Stanzel's astute observations about some segments of the typological circle eminently useful. Sociolinguists, anthropologists, and cultural historians could in turn profit from familiarizing themselves with the present study for reasons I wish to suggest by way of conclusion.

The increasing significance of mental events among prose fiction's 'objects of mimesis' surely parallels some post-Renaissance developments in Western life and consciousness. Two of these come readily to mind: the gradual eclipse of transcendence by secular humanism and the increasing stress on the private self as a motivating force of all public behaviour including economic and political life. At the same time, the verbal 'means of mimesis' available to writers of novels and short stories in the Germanic,

Romance, and Slavic languages have played a comparably important role in the evolution of what are rightly perceived as the
modern West's most distinctive literary genres.

Not only have the European vernacular languages retained much
closer ties than, for instance, Arabic and Chinese between their
spoken and written versions, their elaborate yet streamlined
systems of grammatical tense, mood, voice, and person also force
storytellers to invoke, in virtually every sentence, the temporal and
mental relationship between the teller and the tale. Furthermore,
Indo-European languages make us perceive every speech act in a
clearly articulated network of specific references to the speaker or
writer (first person), listener or reader (second person), and those
objects or partially objectified human beings that are usually absent
from the scene of narrative speech as well as from the respective
scenes of almost all writing and reading (third person). Thus certain
linguistic features, already present in Sanscrit, ancient Greek,
Latin, and the medieval predecessors of the major European
languages but largely absent in many other tongues, seem to have
been awaiting – if not, indeed, helping to bring about – those social
and psychological conditions which the short story and the novel
have emerged in the West to reflect and to illuminate. All
languages, cultures, and historical periods have, of course, evolved
more or less varied forms of narration to enable men and women to
verbalize and exchange the products of their memory and imagination. Students of languages, cultures, and periods other than the
ones whose narrative techniques have been examined by Stanzel
may, therefore, gain new insights into their subject matter by
establishing the extent to which his categories for the critical
analysis and interpretation of modern Western prose fiction are
relevant to their respective areas of inquiry.

Paul Hernadi

ACKNOWLEDGEMENTS

For the virtues of the present version of this book I am much indebted to some critics of the original German edition (1979). I have especially benefited from Dorrit Cohn's review in *Poetics Today* 2 (Winter 1981), which includes a detailed comparison of my theory of narrative with Gérard Genette's *Narrative Discourse*.

I wish to thank Charlotte Goedsche for the conscientious translation of a study which bears indelible marks of having been originally conceived and written in German. In carrying out this difficult task she was helped by Thomas Leech and Ingrid Buchegger on a number of occasions. To Ingrid Buchegger I am also very much indebted for a scrupulous reading of the manuscript and the proofs. Since, however, the final revision of the English text was my own work I myself take the responsibility for its short-comings. I am grateful to Monika Fludernik for compiling the two indices of the book and to Gerlinde Herfs for the expert typing of the final manuscript. Most of all I owe a great debt to Terence Moore of the Cambridge University Press for his interest in this book and for his support during the process of translation and publication.

F.K.St.

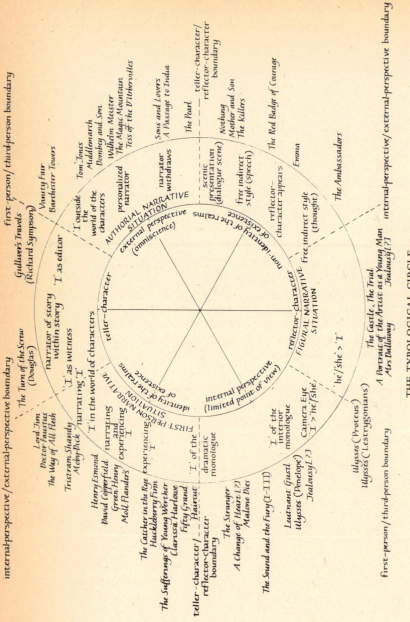

THE TYPOLOGICAL CIRCLE

internal-perspective/external-perspective boundary

first-person/third-person boundary

teller-character/reflector-character boundary

internal-perspective/external-perspective boundary

first-person/third-person boundary

The Turn of the Screw (Douglas)

Gulliver's Travels (Richard Sympson)

Vanity Fair
Barchester Towers

Tom Jones
Middlemarch
Dombey and Son
Wilhelm Meister
The Magic Mountain
Tess of the D'Urbervilles

Sons and Lovers
A Passage to India

The Pearl

teller-character/
reflector-character
boundary

Nothing
Mother and Son
The Killers

The Red Badge of Courage

Emma

The Ambassadors

'I' outside the world of the characters

personalized narrator

narrator withdraws

AUTHORIAL NARRATIVE SITUATION

external perspective (omniscience)

scenic presentation (dialogue scene)

free indirect style (speech)

reflector-character appears

free indirect style (thought)

non-identity of the realms of existence

'I' as editor

narrator of story within story

'I' as witness

teller-character

reflector-character

FIGURAL NARRATIVE SITUATION

internal perspective (limited point of view)

identity of the realms of existence

FIRST-PERSON NARRATIVE SITUATION

'I' narrating

Lord Jim
Doctor Faustus
The Way of All Flesh

Tristram Shandy
Moby Dick

Henry Esmond
David Copperfield
Green Henry
Moll Flanders

narrating 'I'

'I' narrating and experiencing

'I' of the dramatic monologue

teller-character/
reflector-character
boundary

The Catcher in the Rye
Huckleberry Finn

The Sufferings of Young Werther
Clarissa Harlowe
Fifty Grand

The Stranger
A Change of Heart [?]
Malone Dies

'I' experiencing 'I'

Hautval

'I' of the interior monologue

Lieutnant Gustl
Ulysses (Penelope)
Jealousy [?]

The Sound and the Fury (I–III)

'he/she' > 'I'

Camera Eye
'I' > 'he/she'

reflector-character

The Castle, The Trial
A Portrait of the Artist as a Young Man
Mrs Dalloway
Jealousy [?]

Ulysses (Proteus)
Ulysses (Lestrygonians)

INTRODUCTION

But first I wish to acknowledge that after Shakespeare and Spinoza it was Linné who influenced me most. Linné's influence was due to the conflict he caused in me. When I essayed to absorb his acute, ingenious differentiation, his pertinent and practical but often also arbitrary laws, there arose discord inside me; in the innermost recesses of my being I felt that that which Linné had attempted to forcibly keep asunder must be striving for union.

Goethe, 'History of My Botanical Studies'

When the original, German version of *Narrative Situations in the Novel* was published in 1955,[1] the study of narrative was in its Linnaean period. The order of the day was the classification of narrative types and the introduction of the most lucid nomenclature possible; only a comprehensive survey of the variety and profusion of narrative forms could make them accessible for systematic theory. At the same time we needed to learn fully to appreciate a narrative mode which, characterized by figural narrative situation, interior monologue, segmentation, etc., had become more and more common since the turn of the century. For even in the 1950s, some people, if only a few, still concurred with the negative verdict of older critics and scholars about such innovations.[2]

When these goals were attained, those involved in narrative research could turn their attention to other questions. The decisive change here was that these new questions had in part been formulated by other disciplines – text linguistics, speech act theory, communication theory, and others. A glance at any recent bibliography, for instance the selective bibliography by Wolfgang Haubrichs which was published in 1976,[3] reveals that today a large portion of narrative research consists of contributions from disciplines which either did not even exist as such in 1955 or which were not involved with literary criticism at that time. Because of this an inventory of the research findings to date for the whole area of

1

narrative theory is well beyond the scope of the present study. The investigation at hand has a more circumscribed goal, one which can perhaps be achieved without unduly foreshortening the problems to be discussed. It is essentially a further development and differentiation of narrative typology on the basis of the 1955 work.

As a result of the considerable extension of narrative research mentioned above, my work[4] has received positive as well as negative comments from representatives of several disciplines outside the field of literary criticism: text linguistics, linguistic criticism, communication theory, etc. For this reason, my investigation in this book will have to touch upon the conclusions and arguments of the above disciplines, in spite of the limits I have set to myself. This dispersion of reactions to the original version of *Narrative Situations* reveals to what extent the topics which in 1955 were still primarily a concern of narrative theory have begun to develop way beyond the field of literary criticism. Consequently one feature of the new situation is its openness. Almost every single question of narrative theory is also present in a context with larger questions of the intellectual situation of our culture. Thus the question as to whether literature, especially narrative works, is within the grasp of a systematic theory, is no longer of interest merely to literary critics but rather should be considered one aspect of larger, comprehensive attempts to understand the intellectual and social factors of our culture. When Yury Lotman and his associates describe culture as 'aggression of regularity against the sphere of the unregulated,'[5] and when Umberto Eco expects semiotics to yield a 'logic of culture,'[6] then one can begin to glimpse the larger context into which an attempt at a theory of narrative, a systematic presentation of the most essential elements of narration and their structural interrelations, must be integrated.

The fact that the study of narrative discourse has become an interdisciplinary issue has not only increased the number of recognizable facets of the object under investigation. It has also helped to refine the instruments with which narrative texts can be analysed. Every differentiation of the working concepts – this is generally true of all research – increases the number, the variety and the variability of the recognizable forms and phenomena. In reference to the concepts employed in *Narrative Situations* this means that these concepts must be revised in the light of current work in narrative theory if they are to remain functional. The original goal of a comprehensive and systematic classification of the primary narrative forms having been attained, we can attempt to come to terms with the 'recalcitrance' of individual narrative works better than was possible before. In other words, the theory of narrative may now approach more closely the concrete reality of narrative texts. In 1955 my chief concern was with the presentation of three basic narrative situations as ideal types rather than the detailed description of combined and intermediate forms capable of infinite modulation. My foremost intention in the work at hand is further to differentiate the concept of the narrative situations and, at the same time, to make it more dynamic.

Throughout this study my attempt to lead narrative theory beyond a rather coarse labeling of forms and works will be seen as accompanied by a no less important effort, which may at first seem opposed to the former. Under the surface of the recalcitrance of the individual works I am also trying to discern new contours which connect the individual work to other works through various correspondences, links, systems and structural patterns. In this respect, my work applies the method of structuralism, which has left its mark upon recent literary criticism, as well as upon linguistics, more than any other method. The typological circle in its new, more strictly formalized design (see the diagram on p. xvi), will help graphically to elucidate the relationships, correspondences and contiguities between different structures of narration.

1

MEDIACY OF PRESENTATION AS THE GENERIC CHARACTERISTIC OF NARRATION

By definition narrative art requires a story and a story-teller.

(Scholes and Kellog, *The Nature of Narrative*)

Whenever a piece of news is conveyed, whenever something is reported, there is a mediator – the voice of a narrator is audible. I term this phenomenon 'mediacy' (*Mittelbarkeit*). Mediacy is the generic characteristic which distinguishes narration from other forms of literary art. In earlier studies of narrative theory, the comparison of the mediate, indirect form, narration, with the direct form, drama, centred the discussion of mediacy upon the question of whether the reader's illusion was inhibited by the intrusion of a personalized narrator. In Germany, Friedrich Spielhagen and his followers had demanded 'objectivity,' that is, immediacy of presentation in the novel, as is the case in drama.[1] As early as 1910 Käte Friedemann countered by establishing that the mediacy of narration is by no means inferior to the immediacy of drama, but instead constitutes a sort of analogue to our experience of reality in general: ' "the narrator" is the one who evaluates, who is sensitively aware, who observes. He symbolizes the epistemological view familiar to us since Kant that we do not apprehend the world in itself, but rather as it has passed through the medium of an observing mind. In perception, the mind separates the factual world into subject and object.'[2]

The three *narrative situations* distinguished below must be understood first and foremost as rough descriptions of basic possibilities of rendering the mediacy of narration. It is character-istic of the *first-person narrative situation* that the mediacy of narration belongs totally to the fictional realm of the characters of the novel: the mediator, that is, the first-person narrator, is a character of this world just as the other characters are. The world of the characters is completely identical to the world of the narrator. I

4

shall discuss the consequences this has for the interpretation of the first-person narrative in the chapter on 'person.' It is characteristic of the *authorial narrative situation* that the narrator is outside the world of the characters. The narrator's world exists on a different level of being from that of the characters. Here the process of transmission originates from an external perspective, as will be explained in the chapter on 'perspective.' Finally, in the *figural narrative situation*, the mediating narrator is replaced by a reflector: a character in the novel who thinks, feels and perceives, but does not speak to the reader like a narrator. The reader looks at the other characters of the narrative through the eyes of this reflector-character. Since nobody 'narrates' in this case, the presentation seems to be direct. Thus the distinguishing characteristic of the figural narrative situation is that the illusion of immediacy is superimposed over mediacy. Many of the novels published in recent decades employ the figural narrative situation. The significance of this type of narration for the interpretation of a novel will be dealt with mainly in the chapter on 'mode.'

The mediacy of narration thus forms the basis for the distinction among the three narrative situations in such a way that in each narrative situation a different element (person, perspective, mode) of the mediacy complex is dominant. What determines the nature of a particular narrative situation is, above all, the first person as a character in the novel in the first-person narrative situation, external perspective in the authorial narrative situation, and reflector-mode in the figural narrative situation.

In keeping with its significance as the generic characteristic of narration, the term mediacy or the corresponding concept in generic theory has received attention in most of the recent literature – of the most diverse schools – on the theory of the novel.[3] For Käte Hamburger mediacy ('statement structure') is the characteristic which distinguishes first-person narration from third-person narration.[4] In Johannes Anderegg's distinction between a 'reporting model' (*Berichtmodell*) and a 'narrating model' (*Erzählmodell*) of the literary process of communication, the existence of a mediator or 'transmitter' in the former is the major distinguishing factor.[5] Mediacy ('narrative transmission') is also the essential point of departure in linguistically oriented descriptions of narrative types, as for example that of Seymour Chatman,[6] which is based on the speech act theories of John Austin and John Searle. In his *Linguistics and the Novel*, Roger Fowler describes 'proposition' and 'modality' as those two aspects of the deep structure of the sentence which could also be identified in analogous form in the structure of the novel.[7] Modality simply denotes all those characteristics of narrative structure which derive from the mediacy of narration.

Mediacy, that is, the rendering of mediacy, is perhaps the most important starting point for the shaping of the subject matter by an author of a narrative work. Every effort to render the mediacy of narration enhances the literariness (Roman Jakobson)[8] of a novel or a short story, that is its very specific potential effect as a literary and aesthetic artifact. It is, therefore, not a coincidence that mediacy is, as a rule, rendered only minimally in the popular novel. In marked contrast to writers of popular novels, the authors of epoch-making works of narrative literature like *Don Quixote*, *Tristram Shandy*, *Madame Bovary*, *Ulysses* and so on, devoted a good portion of their innovative abilities especially to the rendering of the narrative process of the novel. Narrative achievements such as these also counteract, as it were, the apparent signs of exhaustion which no widely used medium can withstand for long. This was implied as early as 1921 in Victor Shklovsky's interpretation of *Tristram Shandy* as a literary antidote to the 'familiarization' of the novel's narrative form. Sterne 'defamiliarizes' the conventions of the narrative form by means of estrangement. It is 'characteristic of him to "lay bare" his technique,' as Shklovsky very aptly puts it.[9] According to him, Sterne uses the anomalies of the act of narration itself as an instrument for making the reader conscious of the mediacy of the novel. The narrative act is an important part of the plot, and thus dramatizes mediacy in a heretofore totally unheard of way. Sterne lets the reader witness the exciting vicissitudes in the writing process and it is this which ultimately produces the unique form of this novel by portraying in detail Tristram's apparent difficulty with the narrative act; an act which seems to be as impaired by the free association of the narrator's consciousness as by his physical well-being or discomfort.[10] James Joyce's *Ulysses* also belongs to this tradition of defamiliarizing the act of narration. This is especially emphasized in Robert Scholes's structuralistic interpretation of Joyce's novel: 'In reading it we learn how to read it'; that is, as we try to comprehend the unusual form which mediacy has taken on here, we as readers are transformed, we gain a new dimension of experience as readers: 'Our comprehension is exercised and stretched. We are led gradually to a method of narration and to a view of man (the two inseparable) different from those found in previous fiction.'[11]

The majority of novels and stories are located somewhere

between these epoch-making innovations and the more conventional narrative manner of most popular novels, that is, they lie somewhere within the range I have indicated. It is not unusual to find a decrease or increase in the extent of mediacy, born within a single work as well as in the works of an author taken as a whole. As a rule one can observe a certain decline, a relaxation of the intensity with which the narrative act is handled between the beginning and end of a novel, or between the early and late works of an author. The opposite process is also possible, although much rarer, as is shown for example by the development of the narrative style of Henry James and, of course, of Joyce. This phenomenon, which up to now has hardly been noted as a general problem of narrative art, will be discussed further in connection with the concepts 'dynamization of the narrative situation' and 'narrative profile.'

Terms like 'intensity,' 'relaxation of tension,' and 'entropy,' when used in reference to the rendering of mediacy in the narrative situations, must be explained here briefly. The range, extent or degree of creative energy required by the several types of literary production is difficult – if not impossible – to measure. The most common forms of narrative in a certain period, that is, the historical narrative norms, and the degree of deviation of a specific narrative work from these norms provide certain criteria for the assessment of the extent and the intensity of the creative energy expended. For the Victorian novel, this norm is to be found close to both the authorial narrative situation or the quasi-autobiographical form of the first-person narrative situation. As a result the adherence to this norm made the fewest demands upon a Victorian author. The qualification of the authorial narrative situation as 'the most lazy approach of the novel'[12] is thus appropriate for that period. It no longer holds true for authors of our time, however, since the narrative norm of the novel of the mid-twentieth century is not an authorial or autobiographical first-person narrative situation, but rather a narrative situation combining authorial and figural elements. I shall use the term 'prototype' for that narrative situation which to all appearances is the most widely used by the authors of a certain period. Accordingly we shall have to differentiate a prototype of the narrative situation in the Victorian novel and a prototype of the narrative situation in the modern novel, more specifically in the contemporary novel.

Since mediacy rendered in an unusual way can increase the complexity of the semantic structure of a narrative, exact correspondence of the narrative form with one of the three ideal types of narrative situations – if at all possible – is not necessarily desirable. The first reviewers of the German edition of *Narrative Situations in the Novel* frequently assumed such a desirability, a mistake which was perhaps fostered by imprecise wording in the original description of the function of the types. For the sake of clarity it must be emphatically stated that the narrative situations are conceived as ideal types and as such are in no way prescriptive.[13] According to Max Weber, it is the essence of the ideal type that it remain an abstraction which can never be realized by an actual work: 'The sharper and the more explicit the construction of the ideal types, that is, the more removed they are from reality, the better they serve, terminologically and classificatorily as well as heuristically.'[14] The recalcitrance of the work in part or as a whole to fit conveniently into a category is as much one of its essential features as conceptual consistency and comprehensiveness are essential features of the ideal type. Without subscribing to the shibboleth of deviation theory we can say that failure to match the ideal type in the rendering of the narrative situation can in certain cases enhance the 'poetic quality' or 'literariness' of that work more than the closest possible approximation to the ideal type could.

If one wishes to apply the deviation theory, that is, the theory that every work is a deviation from an existing literary norm or aims at the modification of such norms, to my typology, one must bear in mind that every work can be judged according to two systems of norms, that of the historical prototype of the narrative situation and that of the narrative situation as an ideal type. Deviation from the ideal type of a narrative situation generally occurs unconsciously, since the author as a rule is not familiar with the system of the typical narrative situations. Deviation from the prototype, however, may be interpreted as the conscious reaction of the author to the most common narrative model in popular literature.[15]

In recent decades deviation from all norms and conventions of narrative literature has been pursued to the extreme, mainly by some American authors – William Burroughs, John Barth, Thomas Pynchon, Kurt Vonnegut among others – who were followed by only a few, remarkably few, English authors.[16] In the course of this work I shall refer to some of their experiments which are of especial interest. As a whole, however, these experiments cannot yet be classified according to narrative theory. The situation is somewhat different for the French *nouveau roman*. Robbe-Grillet's attempt at a complete reification of represented reality by freezing the mediator optically (for instance by reducing a character to the function of a camera eye) in his novel *Jealousy* (*La Jalousie*) could be interpreted as an extreme solution to the rendering of mediacy. More will be said about the narrative situation of *Jealousy* in Chapter 7.

1.1 Mediacy and point of view

The terms which have led narrative criticism to the problem of mediacy again and again since the end of the nineteenth century are 'point of view' and 'narrator' or 'personalized narrator.' Point of view is a precise term, but it has by no means been consistently applied. First, one must distinguish between the general meaning 'viewpoint,' 'attitude toward a question,' and the special meaning 'standpoint from which a story is narrated or from which an event is perceived by a character in the narrative.' As the definition of the special meaning reveals, the term point of view in narrative terminology is used in two contexts which are distinct in narrative theory: to narrate, that is to say, to transmit something in words; and to experience, to perceive, to know as a character what is happening in the fictional space. Because of this, Kristin Morrison, who called attention to the fact that point of view has been used inconsistently since Henry James and Percy Lubbock, differentiates a 'speaker of the narrative words,' in my terminology a teller-character in an authorial or a first-person narrative situation, and the 'knower of the narrative story,' that is, a figural medium or reflector-character.[17] The actual difficulty is that the two functions of point of view can overlap. This happens especially frequently where authorial and figural elements of the narrative situation of a novel appear in close association. In this case the perception of the represented reality takes place from the standpoint of a figural medium, but the voice of an authorial narrator can still be heard in the transmission of the figural perception, and his point of view can consequently be registered by the reader, too, although only quite vaguely. James provides numerous examples of this in his novels and stories. The form of a dual perspective of 'knower' and 'sayer' like this which has attracted the most attention is called 'free indirect style.'[18] I shall have occasion to examine this form of narration repeatedly in later chapters of this book.

The early works on the point of view theories of James, Lubbock, Jean Pouillon, Cleanth Brooks and Robert Penn Warren, Norman Friedman, and Robert Weimann have already been reviewed so often in the literature on narrative criticism that it is not necessary to discuss them here.[19] The further development of the point of view theories by Gérard Genette, Lubomír Doležel, Seymour Chatman and others will be discussed in more detail below.[20] For now it will suffice to mention that there are several cross connections between the point of view theories which explain mediacy in terms of perspective, the estrangement theory of Shklovsky, and the concept of *skaz* developed especially by Russian literary criticism. *Skaz* in this sense means a form of narrative perspective, above all in first-person narratives, which is stylized after oral recitation. A full treatment of the concept has been undertaken by Boris Eikhenbaum and Irwin R. Titunik.[21] Shklovsky's estrangement theory is a point of view theory, too, insofar as it refers to perspectival means of estrangement. Shklovsky's definition that 'art exists that one may recover the sensation of life; it exists to make one feel things, to make the stone *stony*'[22] can most easily be met by transferring the point of view from a 'speaker of the narrative words' to a 'knower of the narrative story,' from the report of a narrator to the perception experienced by a fictional character. The estranging effect of the experience of unfamiliar perceptions, however, can generally no longer be attained in the modern novel by the use of allegory or an allegorical fable (Shklovsky cites Tolstoy's story 'Kholstomer,' in which the events are presented from the point of view of a horse in the manner of Swift). However, it can be attained by concentrating on the point of view of characters from the fringes of society. The number of outsiders, of outcasts and déclassés who are entrusted with this function in the modern novel – Joyce's Leopold Bloom, Kafka's Josef K., Bieberkopf in Döblin's *Alexanderplatz, Berlin,* Meursault in Camus's *The Stranger* (*L'Etranger*) – is remarkably large. Focussing on a mentally ill or debilitated person's manner of seeing and experiencing – Benjy in *The Sound and the Fury* or Chief Bromden in Ken Kesey's *One Flew Over the Cuckoo's Nest* – is an extreme form of the tendency toward estrangement. In all these cases it is precisely the complete shift of the point of view into an outsider which produces the estrangement by causing the reader to see a reality which is familiar to him with entirely 'other' eyes.[23]

1.2 Mediacy and the figure of the narrator

A fundamental feature of our experience of reality is also true of fictional narrative: every apprehension of reality is dependent upon more or less accurate presuppositions or a prior understanding of this reality. This is revealed in an especially striking way when the characters' or the personalized narrators' perceptions are presented entirely from their own perspective and in their uncorrected subjectivity. As early as 1910 Friedemann had fully grasped this fundamental fact when she said that it is the narrator who, as 'the one who evaluates, who is sensitively aware,' conveys to us a picture of the world as *he* experiences it, not as it really is.[24] This basic principle of narration is still sometimes neglected nowadays in criticism. For example, the Dickens critic Philip Collins complains that Esther Summerson in Dickens's *Bleak House* is not perceptive enough to become the first-person narrator of one-half of this novel.[25] One can indeed raise a number of objections to Esther Summerson as a narrator. But if we wanted to exchange her for someone like Dickens himself, we would fail to recognize the essential character of the structure of the novel *Bleak House*, namely the contrast between a panoramic omniscient perspective and a subjectively limited one. If we tried to assimilate the individual personality of a fictional narrator to the personality of the author for the sake of the clarity and reliability of the narrative, we would relinquish the most important use which the mediacy of narration has: to reveal the biased nature of our experience of reality. Not infrequently does such a narrator become simply the mouthpiece of the author. The novel and, to a lesser degree, the shorter narrative forms have constantly had to defend themselves against this tendency toward authorial essayistic writing. This tendency is already conspicuous in Moll Flanders, whose moralistic retrospection is very often expressed in the voice of Defoe rather than in that of the penitent protagonist.[26] And it can still be found in later novels. Thus in a novel by George Orwell a character who is at first quite distinct from the author suddenly turns into an undisguised mouthpiece of the author as he expatiates upon British imperialism in India or Burma.[27] A quite different example is Robert Musil, whose *Man Without Qualities* (*Der Mann ohne Eigenschaften*) was interpreted by the first reviewers as 'figuralized essay,' assuming a great degree of identity between the character Ulrich and the author Musil. But Musil made clear how very much the mediatization of the essayistic content through Ulrich mattered to him: 'But I can say what I want to say only in the novel, through the medium of events and characters.'[28] In contrast to Orwell, one cannot therefore reproach Musil with 'dilettantism,' by which Anderegg means an author's failure to transform his own image of reality into the fictive frame of reference of a character or a narrator.[29] Cases like these, in which the novel is used as a vehicle for the direct propagation of an idea or an ideology of the author, miss the specific function of point of view and personalized narrator as devices of narrative composition, which Friedman with reference to Mark Schorer describes very accurately as follows:

If Lubbock was concerned with the point of view as a means to a coherent and vivid presentation, Schorer takes it one step further by examining 'the uses of point of view not only as a mode of dramatic delimitation, but, more particularly, of thematic definition.' A novel, he says, normally reveals a created world of values and attitudes, and an author is assisted in his search for an artistic definition of these values and attitudes by the controlling medium offered by the devices of point of view; through these devices he is able to disentangle his own prejudices and predispositions from those of his characters and thereby to evaluate those of his characters dramatically in relation to one another within their own frame.[30]

It is clear that this kind of definition of the function of point of view and the role of the personalized narrator pertains more to the modern novel than to the earlier one, since from around the turn of the century the demands of authors, critics and readers have fundamentally changed as regards the degree of perspectivization and mediatization in the narrative. Most novels of the Victorian period are still narrated aperspectively, that means, Victorian authors pay little attention to the question of spatial perspective in the description of an interior or of scenery. Parallel to this, perspectivization in the broader sense – the delimitation of the characters' attitudes and value judgements, especially the protagonists', from those of the narrator, especially the authorial narrator – is usually quite hazy, too. This is no longer true of most modern novels. We can thus differentiate two styles in the history of the novel, a perspectival and an aperspectival manner of narration. These styles are perhaps represented most clearly by the aperspectivism of the earlier novels of Dickens or Thackeray and the perspectivism of the later James or of Joyce and Virginia Woolf. Interpretations of earlier novels often pay insufficient attention to this historical change from aperspectivism to perspectivism. The possibilities which the perspectival narrative style makes available for the rendering of mediacy are fundamentally different from those of the aperspectival narrative style. Applying the criteria and standards of perspectivism to a work which has been aperspectivally conceived can have a certain heuristic value for the theory of interpretation, but one must be aware of the historical inadequacy of such a point of departure. It will thus be necessary to define the terms perspectivism and aperspectivism more precisely in the chapter on perspective.

While some Anglicists in Germany and English and American critics concerned with narrative theory prefer to use the concept of point of view in the analysis of the mediacy of narration, German speakers and Germanists prefer the concept of the personalized narrator. This results in differences in emphasis and in a slightly different definition of the phenomenon. A few further remarks must thus be added to the discussion of the narrator. The differentiation of the figure of the authorial narrator from the author is still a relatively recent accomplishment in narrative theory – it began to become accepted around the end of the 1950s:[31] the authorial narrator, as we meet him in *Tom Jones* or *The Magic Mountain* (*Der Zauberberg*), for instance, is, within certain limits, an independent character who has been created by the author (just as the other characters of the novel have been) and with whose own peculiar personality the reader and critic are confronted. Only if an attempt to distinguish between authorial narrator and author has proved impossible can the two be considered to be identical. However, even today an authorial narrator frequently will be identified simply as the author especially in literary histories. (Literary histories frequently preserve superannuated terms of literary criticism in other matters as well.)

The distinction between author and authorial narrator has made available to the novel a very important dimension of meaning, in which the narrator functions as the mediator between the author and the reader and between the story and the reader. Who is this narrator and what mediating functions does he fulfill?

'Who narrates the novel?'[32] Narrative criticism written in German has dealt very intensively with this question and offers many answers to it, some of them contradictory. In the course of this discussion critics have again and again taken recourse to that ambiguous phrase of Thomas Mann's, 'the spirit of narration' ('der Geist der Erzählung'), and by so doing have often caused confusion. The spirit of narration, according to Mann, is first of all to be regarded as the actual ('eigentliche') narrator in a novel. Mann uses this term in the introduction to his novel *The Holy Sinner* (*Der Erwählte*), intentionally giving an ambiguous answer to the self-posed question as to who is narrating in this novel. It is, according to Mann, the spirit of narration with whom the narrated story originates:

He is ethereal, bodiless, omnipresent, not subject to distinctions of here and there . . . So spiritual is this spirit and so abstract, that grammatically one can only speak of him in the third-person . . . And yet he can also draw himself together to a person, namely to the first, and can embody himself in someone who speaks in this first-person . . . 'It is I. I am the spirit of narration, who, sitting in his present place, namely in the library of the monastery of St Gall in Allemannenland . . . narrates this story . . . I am Clemens the Irishman, ordinis divi Benedicti, a visitor here who has been brotherly received and envoy of my Abbot Kilian of the monastery of Clonmacnois, my house in Ireland.'

Er ist luftig, körperlos, allgegenwärtig, nicht unterworfen dem Unterschiede von Hier und Dort . . . So geistig ist dieser Geist und so abstrakt, daß grammatisch nur in der dritten Person von ihm die Rede sein . . . kann . . . Und doch kann er sich auch zusammenziehen zur Person, nämlich zur ersten, und sich verkörpern in jemandem, der in dieser . . . spricht: 'Ich bin es. Ich bin der Geist der Erzählung, der, sitzend an seinem derzeitigen Ort, nämlich in der Bibliothek des Klosters St. Gallen in Alamannenland . . . diese Geschichte erzählt . . . Ich bin Clemens der Ire, ordinis divi Benedicti, zu Besuch hier als brüderlich aufgenommener Gast und Sendbote meines Abtes Kilian vom Kloster Clonmacnois, meinem Hause in Irland.'[33]

As the many ellipses reveal, the details essential to this study were excerpted at the expense of the many-layered structure of the original text. Reinhard Klesczewski has shown to what extent the use of the term spirit of narration is permeated with irony in this and also in other works by Thomas Mann,[34] a fact which was not always taken into account sufficiently when the concept was subsumed into narrative theory, for instance by Wolfgang Kayser; though this is not the case with Hamburger. Both Kayser and Hamburger appeal to Mann's spirit of narration in their theories, in which they dispute the assumption that the (authorial) narrator is a character whose personality (personal history, experiences, views, judgements) could be the subject of interpretation.[35] Kayser's objection is aimed primarily at the notion that the narrator of a novel is comparable to a person who reports, or tells or informs us of something in daily life: 'The narrator of the novel – that is not the author, that is also not the created figure who often confronts us in a very familiar manner. Behind this mask stands the novel, the novel which narrates itself, and the spirit of this novel, the omniscient, omnipresent and creating spirit of this world.'[36] And as proof of this view Kayser refers to the passage quoted above from the novel *The Holy Sinner*. It is surprising to see that Kayser, who was one of the first to distinguish the personalized (authorial) narrator from the author and thus to make the narrator accessible to interpretation,[37] here abandons this figure by reducing it to a vague metaphor. This is precisely the point at which his argument meets that of Hamburger. Hamburger denies the existence of the narrator as a character in the third-person novel much more emphatically than does Kayser: 'There is no such thing as a fictive narrator . . . or indeed as a "figure created by the author" (Stanzel). There is also no such fictive narrator in cases where this impression might be awakened by interspersed first-person flourishes such as "I," "we," "our hero," and the like . . . *There is only the narrating poet and his narrative acts.*'[38] Thus according to Hamburger, Friedemann 'merely appears to be correct'[39] when Friedemann speaks of the role of the narrator as the one who 'evaluates, who is sensitively aware, who observes,' just as the descriptions of the personalized narrator are altogether only 'sometimes more, sometimes less adequate *metaphorical pseudo-definitions*.'[40] Hamburger replaces the personalized narrator with the concept 'narrative function': 'the act of narration is a function, through which the narrated persons, things, events, etc., are created: the *narrative function* . . . The narrative poet is not a statement-subject. He does not narrate about persons and things, but rather he narrates these persons and things . . . *Between the narrating and the narrated there exists not a subject-object relation, i.e., a statement structure, but rather a functional correspondence.*'[41] For Hamburger, Thomas Mann's spirit of narration thus becomes a sort of allegory of the narrative function, that is to say, of the act of the impersonal narrative production and transmission of a story – it 'is nothing other than the narrative function itself.'[42]

The contradiction between Hamburger's position and that of all those theorists of narrative for whom the narrator assumes a tangible personality is clear from novels like *Tom Jones*, *Vanity Fair*, *Père Goriot*, *War and Peace*, Thomas Mann's *Buddenbrooks*, Wieland's *Agathon* and Jean Paul Richter's *Flegeljahre*. This cannot be simply a difference of terminology but can only be accounted for as a fundamental difference in the inception of the argument.[43] Spirit of narration and narrative function belong to another conceptual level than the expression personalized narrator. Terms like spirit of narration, narrative function and to a certain extent Wayne C. Booth's 'implied author,'[44] too, necessarily refer to factors which for the sake of brevity I shall sum up with the term 'the deep structure' of a narrative work. The only thing that this expression has in common with that used in transformational generative grammar is that the factors of a narrative structure to which it refers can be made visible only with the help of theoretical operations. In contrast to deep structure, the 'surface structure' of an incident of narrative transmission is directly evident to the reader. Hamburger's fundamental thesis '*Epic fiction is the sole epistemological instance where the I-originarity (or subjectivity) of a third-person* qua *third person can be portrayed*'[45] is a pronouncement about the deep structure and as such is valid for the whole genre of narrative literature. (This deep structure is of course actualized differently in the figural narrative than, for example, in the authorial.) All designations of tangible agents of transmission, be they first-person narrator, personalized or omniscient narrator, authorial narrator, figural medium or reflector, refer, on the other hand, to another stratum, namely to the surface structure, which is visible to the reader without any theoretical operations.

The excerpt from the introduction to the novel *The Holy Sinner* which was quoted above is a masterpiece of the literary metamorphosis of a critical concept. The spirit of narration, which belongs to the airy heights of abstraction, is suddenly made a completely tangible person who presents himself as the narrator in his Here and Now to the reader. According to my terminology, a phenomenon of deep structure has been transformed into a manifestation of surface structure. Understandably, these transformations confused several narrative theorists. In theoretical discussions, it is better for the sake of conceptual clarity to keep these two strata and their respective terminologies separate. By doing so, some contradictions between Hamburger's theory of the narrative function and my typology of the narrative situations using the notion of a personalized narrator resolve themselves surprisingly quickly. The two theses are not incompatible with each other: Hamburger's thesis is valid for the realm of the genesis, the conception and the production of a narrative (that is the formation of a different, namely a fictional, reality), while the typology of narrative situations is valid for the realm of the transmission of that which is produced by the narrative function with the help of a narrator.[46] It is advisable to keep this methodologically important distinction in mind during the following discussion. The criterion by which the various types of narrative situations are distinguished, namely the mediacy of narration, refers exclusively to the surface structure of narrative. All those narrative elements and the system of their coordination which serve to transmit the story to the reader belong to the surface structure. The main representative of this transmission process is the narrator, who can either perform before the eyes of the reader and portray his own narrative act, or can withdraw so far behind the characters of the narrative that the reader is no longer aware of his presence. These phenomena do not stand opposed to each other in separate blocks – here the personalized narrator who performs audibly and visibly before the readers and there the invisible, unpersonalized stage manager behind the scene. Rather, they form a continuum densely populated with intermediate and transitional forms.

This is also true of the distinction between first-person narration and authorial third-person narration. Both have a personalized narrator in common, yet one who appears before the reader at quite different degrees of presence and of proximity to the fictional world of the characters. The path of transmission between the two narrative situations is open and marked by several intermediate stages. Accordingly we may assume that a continuum of narrative forms exists here, too: at one end we find a narrator who belongs entirely to the characters' world (first-person narrative situation) and at the other end a narrator whose world is distinct from that of the characters (authorial narrative situation). These circumstances are presented schematically in the diagram of the typological circle (see p. xvi).

We can now conclude that while the authorial narrator and the first-person narrator can be differentiated according to their position in regard to the represented world of the characters, they cannot be distinguished according to their relationship to the apparatus of narrative transmission. Both are representatives of the rendered mediacy of the narrative and have nothing directly to do with the production of the work, with the act which generates the fictional world (plot, scene, characters *and* narrator) as fictional images. Both the first-person narrator and the authorial narrator are elements of the surface structure of the narrative. They originate in that primal motivation of all narration, to make the fictional world appear as reality. Booth coined the term 'rhetoric of dissimulation' for this process of obliterating the fact that the fictional worlds originate in the author's imagination.[47]

It is perhaps clear now why such a broad discussion was provoked by Hamburger's thesis that a narrative function, not a narrator, is discernible in an authorial narrative situation, while a personalized narrator is discernible only in a first-person narrative situation. With this thesis the argument shifts from the stratum of deep structure to that of surface structure. The concept narrative function belongs to the realm of deep structure, to that realm with regard to which, among other things, the question must be clarified as to how fiction originates in general, how the genesis of a fictional narrative text is different from that of a nonfictional report; the concept 'first-person narrator' as Hamburger understands it,[48] belongs, on the other hand, to the descriptive repertoire of the surface structure, where the process of narrative transmission is made visible for every reader. This shift from one level of argumentation to another had far-reaching results which were not fully eliminated by the concept 'fluctuation of the narrative function,' which Hamburger emphasises more strongly in the second edition of the German version of *The Logic of Literature* after numerous critics had objected to her thesis that no narrator figures in the third-person narrative.[49] Like many other theses in this controversial book, this mistake has consequently proved fruitful to narrative theory, turning the discussion to the distinction suggested here between two structural strata. This distinction can also be of use where the results of linguistic narratology are to be correlated with the results of literary narrative theories.

At this point I should like to note that the earlier debate about the narrator, about his right either to intrude in the narrative or to make the reader believe that he has withdrawn completely from the narrative, belongs exclusively to the realm of the surface structure of narration, where the narrative is transmitted to the reader just like Kayser's often-quoted prognosis of over two decades ago: 'The death of the narrator is the death of the novel.'[50] Joseph Warren Beach's well-known dictum about the narrator in the modern novel also belongs here: 'Exit Author. In a bird's eye view of the English novel from Fielding to Ford, the one thing that will impress you more than any other is the disappearance of the author [= narrator].'[51] Neither of these statements thus has anything to do with Hamburger's deep structural thesis that there is no person-alized narrator in the genre of epic fiction.[52] This must be stressed here because it may not have become sufficiently clear in the detailed discussion of Hamburger's *Logic*.

Since the days of Spielhagen it had been vehemently debated whether the narrator of a novel or short story should be allowed to speak personally or whether he should as much as possible desist from intruding. In German narrative theories of the 1950s the question was finally answered by affirming both possibilities. It was at last realized that these are two different narrative modes of quite equal validity.[53] In English narrative criticism and theory, however, the question still seems to be somewhat a matter of contention. Booth devotes three chapters of his highly regarded and frequently reprinted book *The Rhetoric of Fiction* to arguing against the various dogmas which resulted from the discussion of the objectivity of presentation. Booth vigorously rejects the excessive demands of the 'objectivists' and 'neutralists' who wish to see every trace of a personalized narrator in novels and short stories erased.[54] Apparently the discussion of the narrator's role took a somewhat different course in England and America than it did in German speaking countries. The German discussion of the 'intrusion' of the narrator was at the beginning conducted more vehemently and uncompromisingly, for example by Spielhagen and his opponents, than in England and America. In his historical survey of this discussion, John R. Frey could, therefore, speak of the 'forced nature of so much of the German controversy' in comparison with the temperate 'common-sense approach' of most of the English and American contributions.[55] It seems, though, as if the more turbulent earlier course of the German discussion had the result that nowadays the equal rights of the two narrative styles, one with a personalized narrator and the other objective, dramatic, or 'narrator-less,'are hardly a subject of debate any more in German narrative theory, while in English criticism one still finds impassioned comments both for and against. As late as 1967, for example, the *Times Literary Supplement* devoted a whole page to an author's eloquent lament that, especially at American universities, the critical climate was still not favorable to a personalized narrative style.[56] In 1970, Bernard Bergonzi took up this grievance, perhaps not entirely by coincidence in a chapter entitled 'The Ideology of Being English,' to champion the cause of personalized narration. Bergonzi then summarizes the situation as follows:

The reaction against the dogmatic banishment of the author [Bergonzi means the narrator!] was inevitable, and it seems to have been started independently by several different critics in the late fifties; there was Kathleen Tillotson's inaugural lecture at London University, *The Teller and the Tale*, and the late W. J. Harvey's *The Art of George Eliot*; and, most magisterially, Wayne C. Booth's *The Rhetoric of Fiction*. All these critics advanced much the same arguments: a novel is a narrative as well as an object, that is to say, it is a tale that has been told; even the most rigorously impersonal and dramatised piece of fiction was written by *someone*.[57]

Aside from the fact that the debate is viewed as an internal matter of English and American theorists of narrative, the last sentence of this passage is of special interest for our purposes. In it Bergonzi, too, underscores the mediacy of all narration. When Bergonzi then continues by stating that 'even the most . . . dramatised piece of fiction was written by *someone*,' however, he too shifts his argument from the surface structure level to that of the deep structure of the work's conception and genesis. Once again we see how the discussion can be confused by confounding the two systems of reference. In every word of the printed page of a novel the narrative function leaves its trace, 'written by *someone*.' The process of production, the genesis of a narrative text (deep structure) must, however, as was stated above, be distinguished from the process of transmission, 'a tale that has been told' (surface structure). It is not legitimate to treat these two statements as parallel: 'a tale that has been told' and '[a] piece of fiction [that] was written by *someone*' as has been done by Bergonzi – the first referring to the narrator, the second to what Hamburger calls the narrative function.

The narrative strategies of the surface structure are, of course, connected to the deeper levels of the narrative text via language and its norms, but they are not totally determined by it. The mediacy of presentation of the narrative text provides latitude for the author in which he can design an appropriate form for the transmission of each story. It goes without saying that the act of conception and the act of shaping the agents of narrative transmission are intimately connected and occur at much the same time. It is thus very seldom that the rendering of mediacy clearly occurs after the act of conception of the story; something which can be shown, for example, with the aid of James's *Notebooks* as I shall show in the next chapter. Separating the two processes is, however, absolutely necessary for methodological reasons.

Point of view and narrator are thus the two most important concepts for the critical and theoretical analysis of the transmission process in a narrative. Both aim at one and the same generic epic phenomenon, mediacy, but emphasize distinct elements of that phenomenon. Point of view theories stress especially the necessity of separating the views of the narrator and the characters ('to disentangle . . . prejudices and predispositions'[58]); narrator theories, on the other hand, stress the relativity and the modality of the narrative statement. Every perception, every expression of a narrator's thought originates from a standpoint which not only can be defined more or less accurately according to its spatial and temporal distance from the action, but also according to the degree of its insight into the external and internal events. The stance of omniscience is thus no exception, because there is hardly a work in narrative literature in which it is maintained consistently from beginning to end. Mediacy of narration, as exemplified by the personality of the narrator, thus manifests very vividly how the dialectic unity of content (story) and form (rendered mediacy) is to be understood: 'Form [is the] relativizing externalization of the content.'[59]

With this I have returned to the point of departure of my considerations about mediacy as the generic characteristic of narration, namely to Friedemann's pronouncement about the narrator as the symbol that we do not apprehend the world in itself, but rather as it appears through the medium of an observing mind.[60] The terms point of view and narrator both refer to this central fact of narrative theory, but stress different aspects of it, namely point of view that of perspectivization and the narrator that of the modality of the narrative.[61] Perspective and modality will be considered further in later chapters.

One more explanation is necessary before continuing with the topic. The systematic theory which is being developed here concentrates mainly on the formal aspect of narration. It goes without saying that the formal process of narration which is analyzed here is rooted along with the person of the author in a historical, social and political context which in turn affects the transmission as well as the several phases of conception of fiction.[62] I thus concur with Robert Weimann's demand that the discussion be broadened to the 'totality of those attitudes of the author which have been realized in the work.'[63] The present study, however, cannot meet Weimann's demands apart from occasional references because of the limits of space.

The next chapter will focus on mediacy as it appears in synoptic versions of narrative text. This chapter, though logically a first step in the development of the genre-specific concept of mediacy, has a more specialized character than most of the other chapters of the book. The reader chiefly interested in the elaboration of the main theory is advised to skip Chapter 2 and continue with Chapter 3, in which a new definition of the narrative situations is being attempted.

2
ZERO GRADES OF MEDIACY: SYNOPSIS, CHAPTER HEADING, OUTLINE

I shall now consider synopses or summaries, outlines or sketches and notes from the author's pen, and synoptic chapter headings with a view toward mediacy. A common element shared by all three kinds of texts is that mediacy has not yet or only partially found expression in them. They thus represent texts which approach the zero grade of mediacy. In contrast to formalist and structuralist attempts to reconstruct a model for 'narration minus mediacy' with the aid of concepts such as *fable* (versus *sujet*) or *histoire* (versus *discours*),[1] my method has the advantage that it is not based on theoretical hypotheses, but rather on concrete textual examples.[2]

2.1 The synopsis: story without narrator

'There are few works of art which are not ridiculous or meaningless in synopsis (which can be justified only as a pedagogical device).'[3] This quotation is characteristic of the attitude of literary criticism toward the much used literary tool of the summary.[4]

It is astonishing that so far narrative criticism and the theory of interpretation have almost entirely neglected the synopsis as a means of illuminating those components of the narrative process which determine the specific form of mediacy in a narrative text.[5] The meaning of a novel can, of course, be determined only by a consideration of the interaction of content and narrative process in the sense of 'form as the relativizing externalization of the content.'[6] In many cases, however, the extent to which the narrative form affects the content can be best brought to light by a radical reduction, a synoptic rendering of the story. Especially revealing in this respect are those passages of a narrative text which require the most radical changes in such a reduction.

Reading several summaries of well-known novels in one of the common reference works, such as the *Concise Oxford Dictionary of English Literature*, confirms at once what I asserted above: it is characteristic of the summary that it says nothing about the form of mediacy, that is to say the form in which a story is narrated. At most there may be an allusion to mediacy in the case of an epistolary novel. But in the case of novels such as *Emma*, *Vanity Fair*, *David Copperfield*, *Hard Times*, and *Tess of the D'Urbervilles*, which seem to be entirely different from each other as regards the narrative form, the *Concise Oxford Dictionary of English Literature* tells the reader nothing at all about this difference. It is true that a development has recently begun even in the summaries found in reference works. Although the classic type of summary is still used in reference works such as the *Concise Oxford Dictionary*, in other reference works, for example, the much-used *Student's Guide to 50 British Novels* or *Daten der englischen und amerikanischen Literatur von 1890 bis zur Gegenwart*,[7] a brief description of the novel's narrative form is frequently added to the synopsis. One can conclude from the increasing number of summaries of this type that the mere repetition of content is no longer regarded as sufficient, even for a very brief description of a narrative.

The recent rise of the summary from semirespectability in literary criticism is partly due to the recognition of the fact that it is rendered in the present tense in almost all languages. Hamburger distinguishes this present tense from the historical present, which constitutes a genuine rival tense to what Hamburger terms the 'epic preterite,' which is the past tense commonly used in narration. Hamburger introduced the term 'reproducing present' for the present tense used in summaries. As it is also used in drama summaries, this tense could be called the 'synoptic present,' as well. Hamburger describes the synoptic or reproducing present of the summary as an 'a-temporal tense of statements about ideal objects.'[8] Roy Pascal extended this discussion to the more-detailed chapter headings in the earlier novel. These headings, which are frequently in the present tense as well, offer a microsummary of the chapter in question (for instance, 'Mr Pickwick journeys to Ipswich and meets with a romantic adventure'). Pascal also deals with authors' notes made before or during the writing of a novel, which are also, as a rule, in the present tense. According to Pascal, the fact that the reported events occur over and over again whenever a reader reads the narrative, accounts for the present tense in summaries. In conclusion, he states: 'The present tense in this context has not so much a temporal as a generalizing function, and seems to be similar to that used in such statements as "emotions are dangerous" or "men have a habit of falling in love", etc.'[9] I should add that such statements of universal validity can never be 'narrated,' but in a narrative they can become the subject of a narrator's or a character's direct speech possibly in a generalizing or gnomic commentary. As direct speech they do not belong, strictly speaking, to the narrated but to the mimetic part of a text. If they are reproduced in indirect speech or in free indirect style, on the other hand, they immediately forfeit the claim to universal validity and become no more than the subjective opinion of a fictional character. Such an opinion can be 'narrated,' which means that it will no longer be expressed in the present tense but in the past: 'He knew that emotions were dangerous,' 'She accepted the situation as it was: men had a habit of falling in love.' This calls attention to an important difference between a statement which is synoptically presented and one which is narrated in the strict sense of that word. Although approaching the question from a different direction, Harald Weinrich seizes upon this difference when he relates the synoptic present to the tenses of the 'discussed world' (*besprochene Welt*) rather than to those of the 'narrated world' (*erzählte Welt*).[10] According to Weinrich, the distinguishing feature of the tenses of discussion is that they do *not* narrate.[11] In my terminology this means that they report a story without mediacy, that is, directly. The views of Hamburger, Pascal and Weinrich thus agree in one essential point: there is no narrating in a summary; rather, something is being established in a factual or general way – content or subject matter is being referred to or, as Weinrich puts it, 'discussed' (*besprochen*). Therefore, a summary can disregard the nature of the narrative process of a story. In other words, the present tense in a summary is an indication that the summary presents story-minus-mediacy or story-without-narrator.

There is further proof for his thesis. As soon as the summary of a story becomes the subject of the narrative in a novel, the past tense appears.[12] The 'Black Notebook' of Doris Lessing's novel *The Golden Notebook* contains the summary of a novel which the main character of the 'Black Notebook' story line, Anna Wulf, wrote on a slip of paper and then pasted into the 'Black Notebook.' The synopsis is entirely in the present tense, as one would expect in a summary.[13] The 'Yellow Notebook' of the same novel contains the synopsis of a story taken from a French women's magazine. Here, however, the summary becomes part of the narrative. Ella, a kind of persona of Anna Wulf, negotiates with a representative of the French women's magazine for the purchase of this story. She already knows that this story is not suitable in its present form for the English periodical which she represents:

For form's sake, she began explaining to Monsieur Brun how the story would have to be adapted for England. It concerned a young and poor orphan, sorrowing for a beautiful mother who had been brought to an early death-bed by a callous husband. This orphan had been reared in a convent by some good sisters. In spite of her piety, she was seduced at the age of fifteen by the heartless gardener.[14]

Ella's report of the content of this story is entirely in the past tense because it is now part of the narrative – it does not matter whether it is a verbally rendered report (Ella retells the content) or the reflection of the content of the story in Ella's mind. The past tense can, therefore, be understood as an indication of the mode of mediacy. It is used here for the same reason as in the example: 'He knew that emotions were dangerous.' The past tense is a signal that a reference is being made to facts which are now no longer a matter of bare contents, but of narrated views, thoughts and opinions of fictional characters.

The past tense in Lessing's narrated summary is comparable to that which David Lodge uses in his critical study of the modern novel, *The Novelist at the Crossroads*, to summarize the content of Julian Mitchell's 'non-fiction novel' *The Undiscovered Country*. Lodge explains his use of the past tense as follows: 'To have used the present tense in which one customarily summarizes fiction would have been to give the whole game away,'[15] referring to the contradictory basis of the 'non-fiction' novel, 'fiction disguising itself as far as possible as fact.' Lodge evidently means that a summary in the present tense would have classified the summarized 'non-fiction' novel as 'fiction' right from the start. In fact, it is only in the summary of *fictional* works that the present tense stands in opposition to the past tense; only there does its use indicate fictionality, albeit fictionality with the zero grade of mediacy. The synoptic present (in opposition to the past tense) is, therefore, the only syntactical sign which reveals that the narrative text summarized is fictional.

The synopsis represents the zero grade of mediacy of narration only as long as no narrative elements are included. The story reported in this form is still open to any kind of transmission (narrative situation). This is not the case with the retelling of a narrative which uses the past tense. Here we are not confronted with the zero grade of mediacy but with a reduced grade of mediacy. In prose paraphrases of dramatic texts such as Charles and Mary Lamb's *Tales From Shakespeare*, mediacy is even added to the paraphrased text. In the teaching of literature, the summary often approaches a form of abbreviated paraphrase, into which individual narrative elements have been assimilated. There seems to be a preference for those narrative elements which, when viewed separately, do not conclusively determine the narrative situation, for example, the past tense and temporal adverbs (excluding, of course, those which indicate the temporal orientation of a reflector-character.) However, the first-person form is always excluded from this kind of summary, because its use would anticipate the form of transmission to be employed in the act of full narration.

2.2 The use of synopsis and paraphrase in the teaching of literature

Contrasting a synopsis (summary) and a paraphrase of a novel or a short story sheds new light on the essence of the narrative as a literary genre. We can start with a comparison of synopses and paraphrases of a specific work of fiction found in various reference works. Such a comparison will show that there are quite diverse methods for summarizing the content of a narrative. These include the classic form of a summary, which uses the present tense and makes no reference to the narrative process, as well as the summary followed by a separate characterization of the narrative form. There is also a third type which we have not yet mentioned, namely a combination of summary and paraphrase. It is this type which is especially instructive from a didactic viewpoint, since it demonstrates that some narratives simply cannot be reduced to a synoptic statement of their story or subject because the narrative process itself is an essential part of their content. This is evident, for example, where the synoptic present tense has to be replaced by the past tense because the time structure of the narrated events would otherwise have to be changed entirely. This is the case when a narrative deviates substantially from the linear chronology of the story. Also, the temporal division between the main story and the preliminary phase depicting prior events often necessitates such a combination of a summary in the present tense and a paraphrase in the past tense. The resulting change in tense is especially conspicuous at the beginning of synopses, but it can also occur within them. The present tense is used to summarize the main story, while the past tense is used to retell the prior events. The question as to what extent writers of synopses are influenced by the actual time structure of a novel and by the narrative situation while determining this temporal zero point has as yet received little attention. I must, therefore, content myself with an illustration of a case in point. The following is an excerpt from the summary of *Tristram Shandy* in Abraham Lass's *A Student's Guide to 50 British Novels*:

Immediately after Tristram's conception, which occurred sometime between the first Sunday and the first Monday of March, 1718, Tristram's father journeyed from Shandy Hall, the ancestral estate, to London, a trip his sciatica had hitherto prevented him from making . . .

On the night Tristram is born, his father and his Uncle Toby are comfortably debating some complicated and endless issue before a cheerful fire. When Susannah, the maid, informs them of the impending birth, they send for a midwife and for Dr Slop.[16]

The first events, Tristram's conception and his father's journey to London, are narrated at the very beginning of the novel; his birth, in the third book. Whereas the first two events are paraphrased very briefly in the past tense, the circumstances of the birth are presented in the synopsis in the present tense. Lass and others are compelled to employ this method because of Sterne's extraordinary multi-dimensional narrative style, which vigorously resists a reduction to the two- or one-dimensionality of a synopsis. The tricks and subterfuges which writers of synopses have felt compelled to employ because of the overt mediacy in this novel deserve additional study.

The past tense also appears frequently when a story within a story has to be summarized, as for example in a summary of Gottfried Keller's *Die Leute von Seldwyla*:

In S. there lives in modest circumstances a widow with her two children, the charming Esther and the two-year older Pankraz. Pankraz, a plain looking and serious boy, is a loafer . . . Pankraz disappears from S. without a trace. After fifteen years he suddenly returns as a French colonel and tells his mother and sister his story. At the time he had travelled to Hamburg, was in New York and then went to India as an English soldier . . . fell in love with the colonel's capricious daughter, the beautiful Lydia. At first she seems to return his affection.

In S. lebt in bescheidenen Verhältnissen eine Witwe mit ihren beiden Kindern, der anmutigen Esther und dem zwei Jahre älteren Pankraz. Dieser, ein unansehnlicher und ernster Knabe, ist ein Müßiggänger . . .

Pankraz verschwindet spurlos aus S. Erst nach 15 Jahren kehrt er plötzlich als französischer Oberst zurück und erzählt der Mutter und seiner Schwester seine Geschichte. Zu Fuß ist er damals bis Hamburg gewandert, war in New York und kam dann als englischer Soldat nach Indien . . . verliebte sich in des Obersten kapriziöse Tochter, die schöne Lydia. Sie scheint zunächst seine Neigung zu erwidern.[17]

The ultimate return of the synopsis of the story within a story to the present tense shows that the past tense is employed primarily to identify the narrative character of the story within a story. A paraphrase temporarily takes the place of the synopsis, because the latter would fail to distinguish the two narrative levels. It would be interesting to examine at what point the paraphrase of such a story within a story returns to the present tense of the general synopsis.

Lass structures his synopsis of Emily Brontë's *Wuthering Heights* in a very similar manner:

Mrs Dean tells him that years before Mr and Mrs Earnshaw lived at Wuthering Heights with their daughter, Catherine, and their son, Hindley. Returning from a trip to Liverpool one day, Mr Earnshaw brings back with him a filthy, ragged, dark-complexioned orphan boy.[18]

Here the past tense can also be interpreted as marking the division into main story and summary of prior events. This division is not made arbitrarily by the author; it seems to depend on factors such as time structure, narrative situation (which in turn determines the time structure), and distribution of summary narrative and scenic presentation. In addition, the occurrence of the present tense at the beginning of the first sentence (the next verb is in past tense) would not be compatible with the adverbial phrase 'years before.'

Temporal orientation in a synopsis by means of adverbs of time poses a difficult problem indeed. Again, thorough investigations have not been carried out. One would have to examine, for instance, to what extent the two basic means of temporal orientation are manifested – by the prevailing narrative situation (temporal centre of orientation in the narrative present of a narrator or in the experiencing present of a character of the novel) or by the use of certain temporal adverbs or adverbial phrases such as 'yesterday,' 'today,' 'tomorrow,' or 'the day before,' 'this day,' or 'the next day.' As a rule, 'today,' 'tomorrow' and similar adverbs referring to the temporal experience of a fictional character seem appropriate in a vivid paraphrase but inappropriate in a synopsis. Weinrich ascertained that when the 'narrative characteristics of the work . . . are to be summarized as well' (which means we are not dealing with a synopsis but with a paraphrase in the historical present) then the 'narrating temporal adverbs reveal a certain ambivalence which is – together with other characteristics – constitutive of the genre "summary." '[19] Weinrich's classification of reporting and narrating temporal adverbs should be examined once again with a view to the two basic means of temporal orientation sketched above. The use of the temporal adverbs beyond the characterization of the 'and then' nexus should probably be regarded as an infiltration of narrative elements into the summary.

In the interest of completeness, I should mention the practice of interspersing the synopsis with explicit quotations and expressions from the narrative text. This can occur very subtly, almost imperceptibly, and is comparable to the phenomenon of stylistic contagion in which narratorial language assumes certain stylistic features of the language of the fictional characters. I will deal with this in a later chapter. A contagion of the synopsis by the narrative text is quite obvious when the summary attempts to interpret and illustrate a narrative, as for example in *Kindlers Literaturlexikon*,[20] but it can also be found in the conventional summary. Sometimes an adopted expression is identified as a quotation, as in the following passage from a summary of *Vanity Fair* which alludes to the famous title of Chapter XXXVI 'How to live well on nothing a year':

Egged on by Dobbin, however, George defies his father's will and marrie, Amelia, and the couple honeymoon in Brighton. There they meet Rawdon and Becky, who are deeply in debt as a result of living handsomely on 'nothing a year.'[21]

The death of George Osborne in the Battle of Waterloo is reported later in the same summary. Here the synopsis follows the narrative text very closely but does not quote it directly:

Meanwhile, George, after only six weeks of marriage to the docile but unexciting Amelia, has made overtures to Becky Sharp. The Battle of Waterloo interrupts his adulterous plans, however, and at the battle's end, George Osborne lies *dead with a bullet through his heart*.[22]

Thus the synopsis continually takes over stylistic elements from the narrative text. One could, therefore, speak of an authorialization through which the synopsis stylistically approaches the narrative text. Tracing such authorial elements, that is to say stylistic deviations from the norm of the purely reportive prose of the summary, is an exercise which can sharpen the eye and the stylistic feeling for authorial statements in the narrative text itself.

2.3 The zero grade of mediacy in *The Notebooks of Henry James*

An author's first outline of the plot of a narrative usually shows the story in a form still lacking narrative mediacy. Like plot synopses, outlines are, as a rule, in the present tense, for which the designation 'reproducing present' seems inappropriate. Rather, the tense of a plot outline such as this seems more closely related to the present generally used in diaries for the recording of perceptions and impressions: on the whole, notes of this kind frequently appear together with an author's diary-like memoranda. Published diaries of novelists, for example, those of Albert Camus or Max Frisch, furnish much evidence of this practice.

The Notebooks of Henry James, on which the following remarks are primarily based, are especially interesting because they consist of diary entries, notes, sketches and a detailed working synopsis for a novel (*The Ambassadors*). The first notes for the tale 'The Lesson of the Master' is characteristic of the way in which James entered a sudden or provocative idea for a narrative ('a suggestive germ') in the *Notebooks*:

Another came to me last night as I was talking with Theodore Child about the effect of marriage on the artist, the man of letters, etc. He mentioned the cases he had seen in Paris in which this effect had been fatal to the quality of the work, etc. – through overproduction, need to meet expenses, make a figure, etc. And I mentioned certain cases here. Child spoke of Daudet – his *30 Ans de Paris*, as an example in point. 'He would never have written that if he hadn't married.' So it occurred to me that a very interesting situation would be that of an elder artist or writer, who has been ruined (in his own sight) by his marriage and its forcing him to produce promiscuously and cheaply – his position in regard to a younger *confrère* whom he sees on the brink of the same disaster and whom he endeavours to save, to rescue, by some act of bold interference – breaking off the marriage, annihilating the wife, making trouble between the parties.[23]

The situation in which the author hit upon this idea is reported in the past tense, the content of the 'suggestive germ' in the present tense and the corresponding present perfect. This first note about the basic situation in 'The Lesson of the Master' contains no information whatsoever as to how the recorded situation could be narrated. Sometimes James indicates which form of mediacy is to be used in the narrative when recording the first provocative idea for a story. Thus he writes at the end of the note on 'The Turn of the Screw': 'The story to be told – tolerably obviously – by an outside spectator, observer.'[24] More often, the narrative form which James is contemplating during the early stages of conception is only implied in the note. The note for 'The Liar,' for example, shows fairly clearly that James at first intended to present the recorded event from the point of view of the liar's wife.[25] In the tale, however, the point of view is that of a third person who was not mentioned at all in the note. It is in fact the later introduction of this new mediator which raises the question of the identity of the real liar in the story. Because of this alteration, the original idea undergoes a radical change which has significant implications for the interpretation of the story. It is an extraordinarily illuminating piece of evidence that the meaning of a suggestive germ recorded in the *Notebooks* can undergo such a substantial change in the course of the development of a specific narrative medium. In the chapter on mode I shall deal with several problems of interpretation resulting from the particular kind of mediacy introduced in 'The Liar' and 'The Turn of the Screw.'

James's entries in the *Notebooks* for the novel *The Ambassadors* are particularly interesting because they document two different stages of composition. There is the short first notation of the novel's basic idea (a man who has passed the zenith of his life becomes aware that he has missed the opportunity for self-realization) and a detailed synopsis ('scenario') of the entire novel, which James prepared for his publisher before completing the manuscript.[26] Thus three genetic stages of the narration of the novel *The Ambassadors* are available: first notation, detailed synopsis (scenario) and final text. Although the scenario of *The Ambassadors* is the only detailed synopsis which seems to have been preserved, several others are known to have existed. Of these, James once wrote to H. G. Wells: 'Those wondrous . . . preliminary statements (of my fictions that are to be) don't really exist in any form in which they can be imparted.'[27] Obviously they lacked the form of finality which a text attains when it is completed for transmission to the reader. If we designate the condition of the narrative material in its earliest stage, perhaps the first rough sketch of the plot, as the zero grade of mediacy, then the detailed synopsis, the scenario of *The Ambassadors*, is already a transitional form in the direction of mediacy as it is realized in the narrative situation of the final text. It seems to be characteristic of the zero grade of the notes that the author is still preoccupied with the 'materials' of the content, the characters, scenes and locations of the future novel: 'It touches me – I can see him – I can hear him,' James is talking of the main character, Lambert Strether, 'I seem to see his story, his temperament, his circumstances, his figure, his life.'[28] This total preoccupation with the material, the fable or *histoire*, anticipates Tzvetan Todorov's 'aspect du récit' with respect to the genesis of the work. Todorov defines this concept as 'la façon dont l'histoire était perçue par le narrateur.'[29] The essential point is that the perspective in which the story will be presented to the reader later is still largely undetermined. Another characteristic feature of the first notation is that various elements of the content are not yet fixed:

He may be an American – he might be an Englishman . . . It might be London – it might be Italy – it might be the general impression of a summer in Europe – abroad. Also, it *may* be Paris . . . I can't make him a novelist . . . But I want him 'intellectual,' I want him *fine*, clever, literary almost: it deepens the irony, the tragedy.[30]

The present tense in the notes thus signifies a presence in the sense of a 'tabular' present:[31] at this stage of conception the author still feels free to alter the characters and the elements of the plot ('He may be an American'). This exchangeability ends abruptly with the transposition into the past tense, into that mode of mediacy which is the familiar convention of realistic narration. It is one of the functions of narrative rhetoric which comes into play at this point to obliterate the traces of the former variability of characters and plot as much as possible, a process which is very well described by Booth's term 'rhetoric of dissimulation.' To be sure, certain authors of the realistic tradition (Fielding, Trollope) occasionally treat this practice ironically by implying in the novel that their characters continue to be subject to their creative omnipotence and disposition. Other authors, including James, have felt that an ironic attitude like this on an author's part impairs the reader's illusion.[32] In the modern novel, however, the conventions underlying this type of realistic conception are being questioned more and more frequently, for example, by coupling the topic of variability with a description aiming at realism. Thus John Fowles offers three possible variants for the conclusion of his novel *The French Lieutenant's Woman*, and in Kurt Vonnegut's science fiction the fictional world is often very consciously denied any finality. This openness is especially striking in his *A Breakfast of Champions*. In Flann O'Brien's extraordinarily experimental novel *At Swim-Two-Birds*, the topic of variability is very consciously carried to its absurd reversal: some characters demand the power of disposition over the author of the story within a story in this novel.[33]

James's detailed synopsis of *The Ambassadors* can be placed halfway on the road from conception to composition of the final text. This scenario also reveals – and this is the point – that mediacy is not bestowed on the material in one operation, but rather is added gradually to the story as it is conceived in the author's imagination. There seems to be a process of interaction between story and narrative form which extends over a rather long period. In this process, the determining components of the final narrative situation, that is to say, narrator or reflector, perspective, narrative tense, etc., are introduced step by step. At least this description seems to apply to authors who use narrative forms as consciously as does James. I shall describe this process in more detail by means of two excerpts from the *Notebooks*.

The first example, James's brief plot outline for 'The Friends of the Friends' in the *Notebooks*, illustrates how the process of conception may reach a stage where the figure of the narrator becomes vaguely visible, together with the main features of the plot and the rough contours of the characters. It is especially interesting in this context that this narratorial 'I' (in the final version, the first-person narrator is a woman) seems to emerge step by step from the author's 'I.' Consequently it is often difficult to tell whether the personal pronoun of the first person singular still refers to the author or whether it already refers to the fictional first-person narrator, as the following quotation illustrates.

I am doing for Oswald Crawfurd – in 7000 words – the little subject of the 2 people who never met in life . . . They perpetually *miss* each other – they are the buckets in the well. There seems a fate in it. It becomes, *de part et d'autre*, a joke (of each party) with the persons who wish to bring them together: that is (in the small space) with *me*, mainly – the interested narrator. They say, each, the same things, do the same things, feel the same things. It's a JOKE . . . *Chance* must bring the meeting about . . . The LAST *empêchement* to the little meeting, the supreme one, the one that caps the climax and makes the thing 'past a joke', '*trop fort*', and all the rest of it, is the result *of my own act*. I prevent it, because I become conscious of a dawning jealousy because something has taken place between the young man (the man of my story; perhaps he's not in his 1st youth) and myself. I was on the point of writing just above that, something takes place just before the last failure of the 2 parties to meet – something that has a bearing on this failure. Well, what takes place is *tout simplement* THAT: I mean that he and the narrator become 'engaged'.[34]

James also proceeds in this manner in his notes or sketches for several other stories.[35] This tendency is very instructive and gives us insight into the mystery of the process of conception, but has so far been scarcely noticed in James criticism.[36] The case illustrated here, in which the narrative situation of a story's final version is anticipated, can naturally be expected only in the outline of a story which is ultimately narrated in the first person. The second example illustrates how a narrative situation can be anticipated for a story which is presented ultimately in a figural third-person form.

The synopsis of *The Ambassadors* already contains several passages of dialogue.[37] Only parts of these dialogues were later used by the author, and then only in expanded form. There are also passages in which dialogue is jotted down in a kind of free indirect style. What is especially conspicuous here is the present tense, which, generally speaking, is an unusual tense for free indirect style. It is evidently the present tense of the summary. Passages such as these, in free indirect style, represent an intermediate stage between an author's résumé of individual characters' speech or thoughts, and a reflectorization of speech or thoughts as they occur in a character's consciousness, in this case Lambert Strether's, the reflector-character of the finished novel. The question arises as to whether one is already dealing with Lambert Strether as the reflector-character that he becomes in the final narrative situation of the novel, or with the author in the process of conception as the 'centre of consciousness.' A quotation from the synoptic version of a scene between Strether and Maria Gostrey illustrates this. Maria Gostrey, as confidante or *ficelle*, is assigned the role of Strether's conversation partner. In keeping with this function only an outside view of Maria Gostrey is presented. In her opening conversation with Strether about the background and special circumstances of his mission which took him from Woollett, Massachusetts, to Paris, part of the exposition is presented in retrospect. The very delicate relationship between Strether and Mrs Newsome, the wealthy widow in New England who has sent him on his mission, plays an important role here. Should he be successful in his mission, a marriage between Strether and Mrs Newsome can be expected. In the novel, this conversation between Maria Gostrey and Strether is rendered predominantly in direct speech and is very much drawn out; in the synopsis it is compressed predominantly in free indirect style in the present tense:

She [Maria Gostrey] even urges with exaggeration, almost with extravagance, his not disappointing a person who has made such an effort for him. Of course she's in love with him, Mrs Newsome; but for many women that wouldn't have availed – the proceeding would have been too unusual. She herself, she, Miss Gostrey, would really like to know the person capable of it: she must be quite too wonderful. She will be, at all events, clearly, this heroic lady, his providence. Rich, clever, powerful, she will look after him in all sorts of charming ways, and guarantee and protect his future. Therefore he mustn't let her back out. He must *do* the thing he came out for. He must carry the young man home in triumph and be led to the altar as his reward. She gives the whole thing a humorous turn but we get from it all we need.[38]

This free indirect style, which prevails in the entire quotation with the exception of the first and the last sentence, suggests the author rather than the character as its source, as is the case in comparable passages of the novel *The Ambassadors*. It is not yet clearly Strether's consciousness in which these words of Maria Gostrey's are reflected – rather, at the same time it is also the author and writer of the synopsis who is summarizing Maria Gostrey's speech in this way. This conclusion seems to follow from the 'authorial' sentences with which the quotation is introduced and closed. It is also revealed by a comparison with similar passages of the same synopsis in which this form of free indirect style summarizes the thoughts and attitudes of those fictional characters, for example Mrs Newsome, of whom a direct inside view is never offered in the novel. The following quotation discloses Mrs Newsome's apprehensions regarding her son Chad's refusal to leave Paris and return to New England:

She has her theory of the *why* – it's all the dreadful woman. The dreadful woman looms large to her, is a perpetual monstrous haunting image in her thoughts, grotesquely enlarged and fantastically coloured. Details, particular circumstances have come to her – they form, about the whole connection, a mass of portentous lurid fable, in which the poor lady's own real ignorance of life and of the world infinitely embroiders and revolves. The person in Paris is above all a *low* person, a mere mercenary and ravening adventuress of the basest stamp. She would have gone out herself long since were it not that the same highly nervous conditions that prompt and urge also dissuade, deter, detain. She is a particularly intense and energetic invalid, moreover, but still an invalid, never sure of herself in advance.[39]

In spite of an occasional occurrence of free indirect style, what is reported here in the synopsis is not so much an anticipation of the rendering of Mrs Newsome's thoughts, but rather the author's summary of Mrs Newsome's attitude towards her son's problem. In the novel this attitude must be inferred from Strether's conversation with Maria Gostrey. In the scenario we are thus still dealing more with a text which 'discusses' a subject than with a narrating text in the sense of Weinrich's distinction.[40] A passage such as this one demonstrates how fragile the distinction is between a discussing and a narrating text. If we were to assume that in the first quotation it is no longer the synopsis author but rather Strether in whose consciousness Maria Gostrey's speech is reflected, then we would be dealing with a figural narrative situation, that is to say the presentation would be mediated (despite the present tense) and the text would no longer be a synopsis but a narrative. However, if we consider the author of the synopsis as the bearer of the consciousness which contains these thoughts, then the first quotation becomes a discussing text just like the second.

Thus the point of view of the observation and the presentation of the action in the *Ambassadors* synopsis is not yet fixed, but the tendency toward reflectorization of the narrative situation through Strether can already be observed. To be sure, these beginnings are not yet as pronounced as the consistent execution of the figural narrative situation with Strether as the reflector-character would lead us to expect. After James submitted his synopsis to the publishing house, the publisher's reader who reviewed it did not refer at all to the character of Strether in his (negative) appraisal.[41] We must assume, therefore, that he was not at all aware of the importance of Strether's later narrative function. In the synopsis, in fact, all characters are still introduced authorially, that is to say, they are presented by the author and not, as is the case in the novel, from Strether's point of view. From the very beginning of the synopsis, on the other hand, Strether is more privileged in terms of inside views than is any other character. There are also several indications that a certain situation in the novel is to be explored and presented from Strether's point of view.[42] Because of James's preference for reflector-characters in his later years, the question of whether Strether was to become the main bearer of the point of view of the novel as first-person narrator or as figural reflector would not have been raised at all had the author not alluded to such deliberations in the Preface to this novel, which was written somewhat later.[43] There is no clear indication in the synopsis that James while writing the summary ever considered the possibility of making Strether the first-person narrator. On the other hand, the evidence mentioned above suggests that Strether had already been selected for a reflector role at a very early point although perhaps not yet for the entire novel. One can also assume that the author's inclination to summarize dialogue and thought complexes in a kind of free indirect style in his working synopsis reflects already his preference for the figural narrative situation so prominent in his later novels.

With regard to narrative theory, the most important result of the preceding discussion is the observation that the final form of mediacy in a narrative is by no means always established at the beginning of the process of conception and composition. One may assume instead that the narrative situation is the result of a rather lengthy gestation period especially in the case of self-conscious authors who are always mindful of the exigencies of narration during writing.

2.4 Synoptic chapter headings

Detailed chapter headings summarizing the contents of chapters are quite common in earlier novels. (I shall not deal with nominal titles like 'Podsnappery' or participial ones like 'Cut Adrift,' for these are leitmotifs or have a symbolic rather than a synoptic function.) Many of the detailed chapter headings contain one or more sentences with a finite verb form. As a rule they are in the present tense, in accordance with the use of tense in the summary. This 'rule' is frequently broken, however: in some earlier novels, present and past tense seem to occur randomly. This variation of tense is crucial as regards my contention that one of the functions of the past tense is to designate the mode of mediacy. If this thesis is correct, it could perhaps help to explain the alternation of the two tenses. Up until now, neither narrative theory nor linguistics has studied this phenomenon in detail.

To begin with, let us consider all sentence titles, that is, chapter headings with finite verb forms, in which the verb refers to the narrative act or to the act of reading.[44] These are especially frequent in Fielding's works:

In which the author himself makes his appearance on the stage. (*Tom Jones*, Bk. III, Ch. VII)

Which concludes the first book; with an instance of ingratitude, which, we hope, will appear unnatural. (*Tom Jones*, Bk. I, Ch. XIII)

In these examples the present tense corresponds to the temporal arrangement of the authorial narrative situation, in which the zero point of time is represented by the moment of the act of narration of the narrator; therefore, the authorial commentary referring to this act is in the present tense. This authorial present tense emphasizes the absence of mediacy characteristic of the narrator's address to the reader and consequently cannot be used as evidence for my thesis. Those sentence titles in which the verb does not refer to the narrative act but rather to the action of the characters are, on the other hand, more revealing. If one disregards the historical dimension of the problem for the time being – the development of chapter titles is as yet an unwritten chapter in the history of the novel[45] – one can roughly distinguish two types of synoptic chapter headings: a type of discussing chapter heading in the present tense and one of narrating chapter heading in the past tense. It is very important in this connection that these two types are distinguishable not only by tense, but also by the absence or presence of words and stylistic elements signalling narration.

First, I shall present some examples of discussing chapter headings which may be taken as the norm of synoptic chapter headings according to my thesis. These are synopses in that they sum up or discuss the subject matter or material (*fable, histoire*) out of which the narrative (*sujet, discours, récit*) is formed. They do not refer, therefore, to the process of structuring a fictional text of this material:

Agathon is saved from a dangerous adventure by Ciclian pirates and sold as a slave in Smyrna. (*Agathon*, Pt. I, Bk. I)

Agathon wird durch Ciclische Seeräuber aus einem gefährlichen Abenteuer gerettet, und in Smyrna zum Sklaven verkauft. (*Agathon*, 1. Theil, 1. Buch)

Mr Pickwick journeys to Ipswich, and meets with a romantic Adventure with a middle-aged Lady in Yellow Curl Papers. (*The Pickwick Papers*, Ch. XXII)

As I mentioned above, chapter headings of the narrating type contain, as a rule, a signal revealing that we will be dealing with narration: the heading itself draws the reader's attention to the mediacy of narration. The past tense is thus used instead of the synoptic present. Chapter headings like these are not micro-synopses but microparaphrases:

Relates that Mr Jones continued his journey, contrary to the advice of Partridge, with what happened on that occasion. (*Tom Jones*, Bk. XII, Ch. XII)

Honourably accounts for Mr Weller's Absence, by describing a Soirée to which he was invited and went; also relates how he was entrusted by Mr Pickwick with a Private Mission of Delicacy and Importance. (*The Pickwick Papers*, Ch. XXXVII)

The narrative formula 'relates how,' which signals narration, retains this signaling function even when shortened to 'how.' The stereotypical chapter heading in earlier novels beginning with 'How/Comment/Wie' is followed, almost without exception, by the past tense. Most chapter headings in *Gargantua and Pantagruel* begin with *Comment* and consequently are almost always in the past tense:

Comment Pantagruel trouva Panurge, lequel il ayma toute sa vie. (*Pantagruel roy des Dipsodes*, Ch. IX)

Victorian narrators proceed similarly. In *Vanity Fair* all sentence titles belong to the discussing type with two important exceptions:

How Captain Dobbin bought a Piano. (Ch. XVII)

Who played on the Piano Captain Dobbin bought. (Ch. XVIII)

The heading of Chapter XVIII must be classified either as a narrating heading, because, 'Who,' just like 'How,' implies a relating and thus refers to the narrative process; or it must be interpreted as a perseverance of the narrative model of the preceding chapter heading. Such a perseverance seems likely because both headings refer to one and the same object. Moreover, it can be said in general that there exists a certain tendency towards the continuous use of a heading type, above all in novels with many chapters, as for example, in the work of Rabelais. This perseverance of a certain type of chapter heading in a novel makes it difficult to ascertain whether there exists a correlation between the type of chapter heading and the narrative situation prevailing in the respective chapter. Only a historical description of the development of this narrative convention could clarify this point.

Even a very general survey of the history of this convention reveals a development: from the detailed heading encountered in Fielding's novels to a nominal and then numerical title. The chapter heading finally disappears completely in the modern novel. One can also observe a distinct change in the use of this narrative convention within the work of individual authors. Dickens's novels contain a great variety of forms, and his chapter headings become increasingly functional within the narrative. In *The Pickwick Papers* the chapter headings are still very detailed; distinct examples of both types can be found, as well as instances of perseverance. In *David Copperfield* the headings are already much shorter. All the sentence titles are discussing according to tense, since they are in the present, but they are narrating according to the form of the personal pronoun (first person). In the later novels, beginning with *Bleak House*, the chapter headings become shorter and shorter. *The Old Curiosity Shop* and *Great Expectations* have no chapter headings at all: the chapters are merely numbered. The development of this convention in Dickens is by no means entirely linear, however. *Dombey and Son* is an especially interesting exception. Out of the sixty-two chapter headings in this novel, thirteen contain one sentence with a finite verb form. Twelve of these are in the present tense, and only one (!) is in the past tense, namely the title of Chapter XVI: 'What the waves were always saying.' There is a difference between the content of this heading and that of the twelve in the present. The headings in the present tense refer to an external process; the past tense heading, on the other hand, refers to a process of the inner world, a figural perception, namely that of the dying Paul Dombey. Since the perspective of perception here has to reveal the subjectiveness of the experience denoted in the heading, the past tense signifying mediacy of narration was therefore retained in the heading. A heading in the synoptic present would have concealed this important circumstance. How concerned the author was to characterize the special content of this chapter heading can be seen from the fact that there are three elements which denote this title as belonging to the narrating type: the introductory 'What' which implies a 'relates,' the past tense and the reinforcement of the past tense by means of the progressive form.

The example from *Dombey and Son* exhibits the beginnings of a transition in the rendering of mediacy in a chapter heading in the direction to a figural narrative situation. (It is very revealing of the narrative situation in Dickens, by the way, that this move towards the figural narrative situation appears in a chapter with a great death scene.) In *David Copperfield*, on the other hand, there are chapter headings which retain the first-person reference to the hero (dictated by the first-person narrative situation of the novel), although these occur with decreasing frequency in the second half of the novel. This raises two problems. First, why has the first person, characteristic of rendered mediacy, been retained contrary to general usage, which requires that the first person be transposed into the synoptically neutral third person? Second, since the past tense would be more in keeping with mediacy, which is signalled by means of the first person, why is the present tense used instead? Both problems are mentioned only in passing; they cannot be solved here. With regard to person, *Gulliver's Travels* may serve as a comparison. In the chapter headings of this work, the first person of the narrative is replaced by 'the Author' and the third-person reference:

The Author giveth some Account of himself and Family; his first Inducements to travel. He is shipwrecked, and swims for his Life; gets safe on shoar in the Country of *Lilliput*; is made a Prisoner, and carried up the Country. (Ch. I)

The transposition of the narrating first person to the third person used in synopses accords with the prevailing use of the present tense in the chapter headings of *Gulliver's Travels*. These headings were allegedly added by the (fictional) editor of the work, Richard Sympson. Since it is he who addresses the reader in the chapter headings, it is possible for him to include Gulliver's narrative act in his summary without the heading thereby becoming a narrative. Pascal has already called attention to this: 'In these headings the events are seen in another perspective, they are resumed by the author as editor (not as storyteller).'[46] Swift's method with regard to chapter headings in his first-person narrative seems to have corresponded with the general practice of the eighteenth century.[47] Thus, the heading of the first chapter of Robert Paltock's quasi-autobiographical first-person narrative *The Life and Adventures of Peter Wilkins* (1750), which begins with the words: 'I was born at *Penhale*, in the Country of Cornwall,' reads as follows:

Giving an Account of the Author's Birth and Family; the Fondness of his Mother; his being put to an Academy at sixteen by the Advice of his Friend; his Thoughts of his own Illiterature. (Ch. I)

The heading of the second chapter of the same novel shows that the two types of headings distinguished above could also appear in conjunction with one another:

How he spent his Time at the Academy; an Intrigue with a Servant-Maid there; she declares herself with Child by him; her Expostulations to him; he is put to it for Money; refused it from Home, by his Friend, who had married his Mother; is drawn in to marry the Maid; she lies-in at her Aunt's; returns to her Service; he has another Child by her. (Ch. II)

Before one can interpret the heading of the first chapter of *David Copperfield*, 'I am born,' as being intentionally ironic as Casparis suggests,[48] one would have to find out whether Dickens thereby violated a convention which was still known at that time. In this connection, it is necessary to consider the extent to which the reader notices or at least senses the tension resulting from a contamination of a discussing element (present tense) by a narrating element (first-person form).

In *Henry Esmond* the situation is especially complex because of the variation between first-person/third-person reference throughout. In the chapter headings references to the hero are all in the first person ('I go to Cambridge, and do but little good there'), while the headings of the books always refer to him in the third person. The use of the first person in the chapter headings consequently emphasizes the first-person basis of this narrative and thus confirms again at the beginning of almost every chapter the norm from which the third-person reference which prevails in the narrative deviates. The headings of Chapters II and III of the first book reveal, by the way, the beginnings of a continuous synopsis of the content which is interesting in this context:

Relates how Francis, Fourth Viscount, arrives at Castlewood. (Ch. II)

Whither in the Times of Thomas, Third Viscount, I had preceded him as Page to Isabella. (Ch. III)

The present tense of the heading of Chapter II contradicts my thesis, but can perhaps be explained as a phenomenon of perseverance or analogy: all the other sentence titles of the novel are synoptic and are, therefore, in the present tense in accordance with my thesis. The 'Whither' with which the heading of Chapter III begins is more striking. Since the place of reference can only be inferred from the end of the narration of the second chapter, one can conclude that the author wrote this chapter heading after the chapter was already written and without much regard for the connection with the end of the preceding chapter. The use of the perfect tense in the heading of Chapter III is also striking. The perfect tense actually does not seem to correspond to the discussing tense, that is, the present which is used in all the other chapters. This inconsistency is resolved when the title of the second chapter is transposed according to the rule formulated above. According to this rule, narrative references like 'Relates' make the heading a narrating title in which the past tense is consequently to be expected:

Relates how Francis, Fourth Viscount, arrived at Castlewood – Whither in the Times of Thomas, Third Viscount, I had preceded him as Page to Isabella.

Comparison of this chapter heading with the heading of the sixteenth chapter of *Dombey and Son* suggests that Thackeray was less sensitive with regard to the implications of the shifts in narrative tenses than Dickens. On the other hand, Thackeray's perception of the effects to be achieved by means of first/third-person opposition seems to have been more differentiated than that of Dickens. This, too, would be worth a closer examination. The fundamental significance of the two narrative categories 'tense' and 'person,' to which Hamburger and Weinrich have emphatically called attention, would have to be included in such a study.[49]

The analysis of chapter headings in the novel must be extended to a greater number of works before a conclusive explanation of the phenomenon can be given. Although this phenomenon is extremely interesting in respect to the theory of the novel, it has up to now received little notice. Only tentative conclusions may be drawn on the basis of the evidence submitted. Chapter headings in the form of sentences in the present tense must be classified with the synopsis, that is to say with discussing texts. In this case the mediacy of narration is not operative in them. Chapter headings with a verb in the past tense, usually combined with references to the mediacy of narration, belong to the narrating texts. The transition from one type of heading to the other in a novel is quite common. The combination of both types within one heading is also possible, although rather rare. The classification of a heading as belonging to the narrating type depends primarily upon the past tense, which once more functions here as an expression of the mode of mediacy. Whether the first person shifts to the third person or not also plays an important role. I hope I was able to demonstrate in at least one case that the oppposition between narrator and reflector can be of consequence in narrating chapter headings. The body of texts examined here, although still very limited, already furnishes sufficient evidence for the conclusion that the sentence titles of chapters common in earlier novels can provide an explanation of how – in a single work – texts with the zero grade of mediacy can be changed into texts with various degrees of rendered mediacy by the addition of certain narrative elements. Both conclusions will have to be considered in a future 'grammar' of narrative art. The discussion of synopses of entire novels and of plot outlines from an author's notebooks yielded results which match those gained from an investigation of chapter headings. In all three areas the past tense proved to be a clearly recognizable signal for the mode of mediacy. Furthermore, it has become evident that the subject matter is structured step by step by the narrative elements which are primarily responsible for the rendering of mediacy in a novel. A very intimate interplay seems to take place between content and form. This dialectic is not merely a product of the finished work, but rather a state characteristic of the process of production. Narrative theory will have to pursue this problem further; only a rough sketch could be given here. The proposed solutions are intentionally formulated in a tentative way. Their main goal is to prompt a more detailed investigation of these phenomena, which have so far received little attention.

2.5 Addendum and excursus: the change of tense in picture stories

After concluding this chapter I became aware of an important contribution to this topic. In his article 'Thesen zu den Tempora im Deutschen' Otto Ludwig calls attention to the fact that the 'change from present tense to past tense . . . is evidenced in the narrating captions of picture stories.'[50] Numerous examples can be found in Wilhelm Busch to illustrate that the text describing a situation in the picture is in the present tense, while the action which is no longer depicted is reported in the past tense. In addition to Busch, to whom Ludwig refers, several examples of this kind can also be found in *Struwwelpeter*:

> Little Pauline was home alone, / Her parents were out . . .
> And Minz and Maunz, the cats, / Raise their claws.
> They threaten with their paws: / Father has forbidden it!

> Paulinchen war allein zu Haus, / Die Eltern waren beide aus . . .
> Und Minz und Maunz, die Katzen, / Erheben ihre Tatzen.
> Sie drohen mit den Pfoten: / Der Vater hat's verboten![51]

In *Struwwelpeter*, as in Busch, this change is determined by a number of other factors (forced rhyming, traditional narrative formulae, and the like). Consequently, the regularity of the change of tense in these picture books is relatively slight.

In his explanation of the change of tense Ludwig does not

consider the possibility of underscoring the distribution of roles among the characters in a narrative poem by means of tense change, which would be tantamount to a rudimentary perspectivization. In the popular ballad 'Der Unglücksschuß,' cited by Ludwig, the report depicting the actions of the pursuers (hunter, dog) is thus in the past tense, while the report referring to the pursued (little deer, girl) is in the present tense. The narrator's commentaries, moreover, are likewise in the past tense. Ludwig's explanation that the present tense appears where the narrator employs scenic presentation[52] is not entirely convincing, since the difference between the passages in this ballad with scenic presentation and reportorial narration is not at all clearly defined. On the other hand, Ludwig's explanation of the past tense as a signal for 'mediation'[53] is a welcome corroboration of my thesis that the past tense in narration denotes above all the mode of mediacy.

The change of tense as a signal for a change of perspective was also noted by W. J. M. Bronzwaer in W. B. Yeats's poem 'Leda and the Swan.'[54] While the octave and the first tercet of this sonnet contain a description of the copulation of Leda and the swan in the present tense, the last tercet contains a question which the speaker of the poem asks himself about the significance of the incident described. The perspective of the passive observer, emphasized by the 'tabular present' of the description, becomes the perspective of one directly affected, in which the past tense seems to establish a relationship of personal concern between the observer and the described event more forcefully than could be expressed, for instance, by a first-person reference. This cursory glance at tense change in lyric poetry has shown that some of my observations about narrative literature seem to be valid beyond the realm of the epic genre.[55]

3

A NEW APPROACH TO THE DEFINITION OF THE NARRATIVE SITUATIONS

'Bitzer,' said Thomas Gradgrind. 'Your definition of a horse.'

'Quadruped. Graminivorous. Forty teeth, namely twenty-four grinders, four eye-teeth, and twelve incisive. Sheds coat in the spring; in marshy countries, sheds hoofs, too. Hoofs hard, but requiring to be shod with iron. Age known by marks in mouth.' Thus (and much more) Bitzer.

'Now girl number twenty,' said Mr Gradgrind. 'You know what a horse is.'

(Dickens, *Hard Times*)

Since 1955, the year of the publication of the original German edition of *Narrative Situations in the Novel*, narrative criticism has advanced to the extent that the theoretical foundations of the narrative situations which I presented at that time no longer suffice today. The present state of the discussion in this field requires, on the one hand, a thorough re-examination of the theoretical assumptions which served as a point of departure and, on the other hand, a formalization of the method employed in the delineation of those types of narrative situation. I shall try to meet both demands in this chapter, insofar as these are in keeping with the scope and the aim of this book. In doing so I shall evaluate some provocative and critical arguments advanced in the debate sparked off by the original *Narrative Situations*.[1]

One of the most frequently raised objections to the concept of narrative situations asserts that these types schematize the narrative action in a way which fails to do justice to the particularity and complexity of the individual narrative work. It was not my intention to restrict the multiplicity of narrative possibilities to a limited number of categories by means of the typology of the narrative situations. This point must be emphasized more clearly here than it was in earlier discussions.[2] In previous applications of this typology emphasis was placed on determining the predominance of one of the three narrative situations in a novel, for instance, 'the authorial novel.' Since the narrative situation of a novel is constantly subject

46

to modification, from chapter to chapter or from paragraph to paragraph, it is also necessary to give special attention to the sequence of modifications, transitions, and overlappings of the narrative situations between the beginning and the end of a work. The adaptation of the typological model to the particularity of the individual narrative text will be termed for short the 'dynamization' of the narrative situations.[3] It will be described in detail in the second section of this chapter.

In another section of this chapter I shall describe those formal forces which counteract the dynamization of the narrative process. They can be observed above all in the realm of the popular novel and tend to counteract the awareness of mediacy. These phenomena are summed up by the concept 'schematization' of the narrative situations.

3.1 The constitutive elements of the narrative situations: person, perspective, mode

Mediacy as the generic characteristic of narration is a complex and multi-layered phenomenon. In order to use this generic characteristic as the basis for a typology of the forms of narration, it is necessary to break down this complex into its most important constitutive elements.[4] The contours of the latter have already become visible in the preceding discussion about the various degrees of rendered mediacy. They will now be defined more exactly.

The first constitutive element is contained in the question 'Who is narrating?' The answer may be: a narrator who appears before the reader as an independent personality or one who withdraws so far behind the narrated events that he becomes practically invisible to the reader. The distinction between these two basic forms of narration is generally accepted in narrative theory. The following pairs of terms are usually applied: 'true' and 'scenic narration' (Otto Ludwig), 'panoramic' and 'scenic presentation' (Lubbock), 'telling' and 'showing' (Friedman), 'reportorial narration' and 'scenic presentation' (Stanzel).[5] While the concepts proposed for the narrative mode of a personalized narrator are relatively unambiguous, the terms designating scenic presentation conflate two techniques which often occur in conjunction but which must be distinguished in theory. One of these is the dramatized scene consisting of pure dialogue, dialogue with brief stage directions, or dialogue with very condensed narratorial report. This procedure is well illustrated by Hemingway's short story 'The Killers.' The other technique is the reflection of the fictional events through the consciousness of a character in the novel without narratorial comment. I call such a character a reflector to distinguish him from the narrator as the other narrative agent. Stephen in Joyce's *A Portrait of the Artist as a Young Man* has this function. Because of this ambiguity I should like to introduce another distinction. Narration can be considered to be effected by two kinds of narrative agents, narrators (in a personalized or unpersonalized role) and reflectors. Together these two comprise the first constitutive element of the narrative situation, the *mode* of narration. By mode I mean the sum of all possible variations of the narrative forms between the two poles narrator and reflector: *narration* in the true sense of mediacy, that is, the reader has the impression that he is confronted by a personalized narrator, as opposed to direct or immediate *presentation*, that is, the reflection of the fictional reality in the consciousness of a character.

While the first constitutive element, mode, is a product of the various relations and reciprocal effects between the narrator or reflector and the reader, the second constitutive element is based on the relations between the narrator and the fictional characters. Again, the multiplicity of possibilities is delimited by two polar positions. Either the narrator exists as a character within the world of the fictional events of the novel or else he exists outside this fictional reality. In referring to this situation I shall also speak of the identity or non-identity of the realms of existence of the narrator and the fictional characters. If the narrator exists in the same world as the characters, he is a first-person narrator according to traditional terminology. If the narrator is existentially outside the world of the characters, we are dealing with third-person narration in the traditional sense. The time-honored terms first-person and third-person narration have already caused much confusion, because the criterion of their distinction, the personal pronoun, refers in the former to the narrator, but in the latter to a character in the narrative who is *not* the narrator. In a third-person narrative, for example in *Tom Jones* or in *The Magic Mountain*, there is also a narratorial 'I.' It is not the occurrence of the first person of the personal pronoun in a narrative outside the dialogue, which is decisive, but rather the location of the designated person within or outside the fictional world of the characters of a novel or a story. The term *person* will be retained nevertheless, as the distinguishing attribute of this second constitutive element because of its succinctness. The essential criterion of the second constitutive element, however, and this cannot be overemphasized – is not the relative frequency of occurrence of one of the two personal pronouns 'I' or 'he'/'she,' but the question of the identity or non-identity of the realms of existence to which the narrator and the characters belong. The narrator of *David Copperfield* is a first-person narrator because he exists in the same world as the other characters of the novel, Steerforth, Peggotty, the Murdstones and the Micawbers; the narrator of *Tom Jones* is a third-person narrator or an authorial narrator because he exists outside the fictional world in which Tom Jones, Sophia Western, Partridge and Lady Bellaston live. The identity and non-identity of the realms of the narrator and the characters are fundamentally different prerequisites for the narrative process and its motivation.

While mode focuses the reader's attention primarily on his relation to the process of narration or presentation, the third constitutive element, *perspective*, directs the reader's attention to the way in which he perceives the fictional reality. The manner of this perception depends essentially on whether the point of view according to which the narration is oriented is located *in* the story, in the protagonist or in the centre of action, or else *outside* the story or its centre of action, in a narrator who does not belong to the world of the characters or who is merely a subordinate figure, perhaps a first-person narrator in the role of observer or a contemporary of the hero. In this way an internal and an external perspective can be differentiated.

The opposition internal perspective–external perspective embraces an additional aspect of the mediacy of narration different from the other constitutive elements, person and mode, namely, that of the orientation of the reader's imagination within the time and especially the space of the narrative, or, in other words, that of the regulation of the spatio-temporal arrangement with respect to the centre or the focus of the narrated events. If the story is presented from within, as it were, then the perceptive situation of the reader is different from when the events are seen or reported from outside. Accordingly, there are differences in the ways in which the spatial relations of the characters and things in the represented reality are treated (perspectivism–aperspectivism), as well as in the restrictions placed on the knowledge and experience of the narrator or reflector ('omniscience'–'limited point of view').[6]

Narrative theory in the past has dealt with the state of affairs described by the opposition internal perspective–external perspective in diverse ways. Eduard Spranger, a psychologist, essentially anticipated my opposition more than half a century ago with his distinction between 'reportorial perspective' and 'inside view perspective.'[7] Later, Erwin Liebfried termed perspective the most important factor in the differentiation of narrative texts.[8] On the other hand, in the work of Pouillon, Todorov, and Genette,[9] what I call perspective is subordinated to other components, specifically to those which coincide largely with my concepts of mode and person. A basic clarification is perhaps in order here. From the point of view of narrative theory, a typology or taxonomy of the forms of narration is conceivable on the basis of *one* distinctive feature, as well as two, three or more such criteria. However, the number of basic constitutive elements affects the practicability of these categories. The greater the number of constitutive elements included in a typology, the more narrowly the space is circumscribed in which the individual work must find its place. This precision is an advantage and a disadvantage at the same time. The advantage lies in the greater accuracy of definition provided by a typology or taxonomy of the narrative forms which is based on several constitutive elements; the disadvantage lies in the danger of greater constraint on attempts to classify the individual work as a type, because of the relative narrowness of the categories. The triadic basis proposed here as a basis for the three narrative situations has proven itself in practice, as is evidenced by its application in numerous studies of narrative theory over the last twenty years.[10] It will thus be retained in spite of the fact that most of the recent typologies of narrative theory are designed either as monadic (Hamburger) or, more frequently, as dyadic (Brooks and Warren, Anderegg, Doležel, Genette).[11]

Dorrit Cohn has proposed the elimination of the constitutive element perspective from my typology, suggesting that it coincides essentially in its content with the constitutive element mode.[12] I cannot agree to this suggestion for several reasons, one of them being that this elimination could also remove one very important advantage which my system has over dyadic or monadic ones. This advantage lies above all in the fact that the triadic arrangement brings out very clearly the character of the system as a continuum of forms, while the dualistic character of the monadic and dyadic system always leads to more abrupt differentiation by confronting one form group with another directly.[13] The character of the system as a continuum also finds reinforcement in the design of the system according to ideal types. This design aims more at the revelation of exemplary possibilities than at the clear delimitation of narrative categories. It is to be hoped that in the light of these circumstances the new definition of the term perspective in this edition, occasioned above all by Cohn's criticism, will establish that the constitutive element perspective cannot be fully equated with the constitutive element mode.

The narrative situations are thus constituted by the triad mode, person and perspective. Each of these constitutive elements permits of a great number of actualizations which can be represented as continua of forms between the two extreme possibilities. In recent structurally oriented literary criticism inspired by Saussure and Jakobson, the description of this kind of continua of forms is based on the concept of binary oppositions.[14] The concept of binary opposition rests on man's inclination to recast phenomena which present themselves to perception as a great number of variants of a basic form, differing only slightly from one another, into an opposition of two clearly distinct forms. This can be observed in language, but it also occurs in other spheres of intellectual activity in which it is necessary to classify a wealth of perceptions with minimal variations. The binary opposition is thus a particularly congenial system of classification for a narrative theory based on the fact that concrete narrative texts exhibit an immense profusion of modifications and modulations of certain basic forms. Thus each of the formal continua corresponding to the three constitutive elements can be comprehended as a binary opposition of two discrete concepts. For my three constitutive elements and their corresponding formal continua, the binary oppositions are as follows:

Formal continuum mode: Opposition narrator–non-narrator (reflector)
Formal continuum person: Opposition identity–non-identity (of the realms of existence of the narrator and the characters)
Formal continuum perspective: Opposition internal perspective–external perspective (perspectivism–aperspectivism)

Each of the three oppositions will be described in detail in one of the following chapters.

The constitution of the three narrative situations on the basis of the three constitutive elements and their corresponding binary oppositions expands and refines the description of the authorial, figural and first-person narrative situations undertaken for the first time in 1955 in the original edition of *Narrative Situations in the Novel*.

I shall review now some descriptions of narrative forms more thoroughly, because their design was evidently stimulated by *Narrative Situations*, and because they offer solutions that deviate from my system of the narrative situations.

In his contribution to the Festschrift for Roman Jakobson, Doležel attempted a strictly structural classification of possible narrative forms. The derivation of Doležel's narrative types cannot be repeated here in detail. He distinguishes first of all texts with a speaker and texts without a speaker. Texts with a speaker are divided according to whether the speaker is a narrator or a (non-narrating) fictional character. A narrator can be active or passive with regard to the event and the narrative process. Only in the last instance is a distinction also made between first- and third-person pronominal references to the narrator or the fictional character. Two of Doležel's basic oppositions are constitutive elements of the narrative situations, namely, personalized–unpersonalized narrator (mode) and third- and first-person narration (person). It is essential for Doležel's system that these two criteria of classification are used successively, following the linguistic tree diagram.[15]

Doležel accords perspective only implicit consideration. For Leibfried, however, it constitutes the most important criterion of classification: Leibfried distinguishes 'internal perspective,' the perspective of the narrator who takes part in the action, and 'external perspective,' the perspective of a narrator who is not involved in the action.[16] This very important distinction is somewhat obscured, however, by Leibfried's choice of Jean Paul Richter's *Flegeljahre* as an example, a novel in which it is very difficult to distinguish external and internal perspective, as well as third- and first-person reference. Since Leibfried presumes that the concept narrative situation denotes only perspective,[17] his critical attempt to develop the concept of the narrative situation further is somewhat one-sided. Leibfried holds that neither the third- and first-person opposition nor the distinction between narrator and non-narrator (reflector) is a valid criterion for classifying types.[18] It is thus understandable that Leibfried asks whether the figural narrative situation could be a mere variant of first-person perspective.[19] As the diagram on p. 56 shows, the figural narrative situation is contiguous to those forms of the first-person narrative situation in which the narrating self has completely withdrawn, but not to those forms of first-person narration characterized by a personalized narrator. These forms are more closely related to the authorial narrative situation than to the figural narrative situation.[20]

Another systematic presentation of narrative forms which

furthered the discussion was offered by Wilhelm Füger.[21] Under-lying Füger's approach are the oppositions between external and internal perspective and between first- and third-person form. In addition he distinguishes three degrees of insight or states of consciousness of the narrator. The narrator can be better, equally well or less fully informed than the remaining characters in the novel or the reader. Like Doležel, Füger uses the tree diagram as the foundation for his system. The advantages of this model are its logical stringency and the precision of the distinctions which are possible. Füger defines twelve types, one-third of which are almost exclusively hypothetical. A classification system which is so finely subdivided is surely more useful to narrative theory than to the study of interpretation. A disadvantage of this model is that traditionally related types are often far removed from each other within the system represented by the tree diagram. Thus, for example, Füger's type 10a (a figural narrative situation with authorial elements) is far removed from type 4a (an authorial narrative situation in which figural elements can emerge). On the typological circle these two forms are directly adjacent. Another disadvantage of Füger's system of presentation is that the transi-tions between the individual types cannot be taken into account.

It is clear that no systematization of narrative forms can meet both the demands of theory and of interpretation equally – the demands of conceptual order and consistency, on the one hand, and of suitability to texts and applicability in interpretation, on the other. Füger and Doležel decided in favour of distinctness of classification. In the redefinition of the narrative situations which follows, however, I shall try to find a middle course between a systematic theory and a practical model for interpretation.

Chatman, a representative of the linguistically oriented New Stylistics, has already sought such a middle course with his feature analysis.[22] Chatman undertakes a systematic description of the forms of 'narrative transmission,' by which he means essentially the forms of rendered mediacy in narration. He, too, proceeds from the question of the presence of a narrator and postulates various degrees of awareness of the narrator's presence on the part of the reader. In doing so, he makes use of Austin's speech act theory.[23] By 'discourse feature' Chatman means 'a single property of the narrative discourse, for example, the use of the first-person singular or the use or non-use of time summary.'[24] Chatman emphasizes explicitly that these narrative elements can be combined randomly with one another and can therefore be examined and described individually as well. Friedman, Booth, and most English and American critics of the novel share this view. Chatman seeks to set it off by confronting it with the typological method applied in *Narrative Situations*. The confrontation clearly reveals the advantages and disadvantages of both methods. The descriptive method of feature analysis permits the closest possible approach to the text, since the formal analysis can concentrate entirely on the idiosyncratic combination of narrative forms in a text. The result is a table of the various degrees of the narrator's presence in the narrative, a table which is highly informative for purposes of interpretation. Feature analysis cannot, however, reveal the correspondences and the interdependence of the individual narrative elements, that is, narrative structure in the broadest sense. This approach is tantamount to the renunciation of any aspirations toward an analysis and classification of more complex and interdependent forms within a broader systematic context. It would, therefore, be desirable if both methods could be recognized as complementary approaches with different emphases: feature analysis stresses the exact description of the individual narrative elements in their respective particularity, while systematic narrative theory attempts to clarify the correspondences and connections between the separate narrative phenomena. When Chatman establishes, for example, that 'in narrative, speech and thought are significantly different actions,'[25] this important finding is ultimately of no consequence, because within the scope of feature analysis there is no systematic frame to which it can be attached. One of my constitutive elements of the narrative situations, mode, that is, the opposition teller-reflector, however, offers a theoretical reference point for the description of both modes of presentation, of which one is oriented toward speech, the other toward thought.

The systematic classification of the individual features also has consequences for the interpretation of narrative texts. Thus Chatman, until recently one of the few American critics acquainted with the concept of free indirect style, correctly perceives that a sentence such as 'John sat down' is not merely the description of a purely external event, but can also imply a certain degree of awareness of this action, especially if it occurs in the proximity of free indirect style.[26] Substituting a word (for example 'lounged' instead of 'sat'), however, is hardly a sufficient manner of testing whether an outside or an inside view prevails in a narrative sentence of this kind. Much more important is the larger context in which such a sentence appears. If a definite authorial narrative situation prevails, then only an outside view suggests itself as an interpretation of the sentence 'John sat down.' If, on the other hand, a figural narrative situation prevails, then the interpretation of this sentence as a description of internal experience is also possible. Feature analysis thus demands the framework of a comprehensive and systematic narrative theory.

In conclusion, I wish to point out a misunderstanding on Chatman's part which was probably caused by an imprecise formulation in the text of the original version of *Narrative Situations* (1955). It is of interest with regard to the redefinition of the narrative situations. Chatman assumes that person, mode and the presence of the narrator in the fictional world comprise the three constitutive elements of the narrative situation.[27] Person and identity of the realms of existence (presence of the narrator *in* the fictional world), however, are only two different terms for one and the same constitutive element. This point has been discussed above in detail. The element perspective is missing in Chatman's list.[28]

My theory of narration based on the narrative situations distinguishes itself from all of the theories discussed here principally by the fact that it projects a triadic system in which all three constitutive elements are taken into account *in the same way*. In each of the three narrative situations another constitutive element or pole of the binary opposition associated with it attains dominance over the other constitutive elements and their oppositions:

Authorial narrative situation–Dominance of external perspective (aperspectivism)
First-person narrative situation–Dominance of the identity of the realms of existence of the narrator and the characters
Figural narrative situation–Dominance of the reflector mode

If the narrative situations are systematically arranged in a circle according to the correspondences existing among them so that the opposition axes belonging to the narrative situations intersect this circle at equal intervals, the resulting diagram will clearly illustrate the coordination of the narrative situations and their relations to the poles of the opposition axes. The diagram on p. 56 shows the dominance of one oppositional element but also the participation of the contiguous oppositional elements, which exercise a secondary effect on the narrative situation. Thus, for example, the figural narrative situation is distinguished primarily by the dominance of a reflector-character and secondarily by the internal perspective, on the one hand, and by the non-identity of the realms of existence, that is, third-person reference (to the reflector-character), on the other.[29]

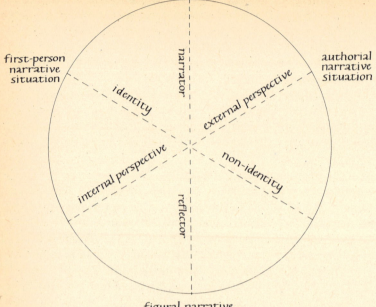

figural narrative
situation

After this theoretical foundation of the narrative situations, I shall now examine three texts to see whether the above-mentioned oppositions actually denote essential differences in the rendering of mediacy in a narrative text and thus affect the structure of the narrative. If the oppositions do denote differences in mediacy, then a change in one of these elements would also produce a change in the meaning of the narrative. Otherwise these differences could be regarded as stylistic variants. For methodological reasons I shall begin with the best known and most obvious constitutive element, person. Perspective and mode will follow.

3.1.1 Opposition I (person): first-person reference– third-person reference

As the main character of the narrative, Holden Caulfield, the first-person narrator of J. D. Salinger's *The Catcher in the Rye*, is situated in the middle of the world represented in the novel. The identity of the realms of existence of the narrator and of the rest of the characters is thus established and maintained in spite of the tendency of this first-person narrator to address his remarks directly to the reader. One can share David Goldknopf's amazement about the possibility of this kind of communication: 'Someone *inside* the novel is talking to someone *outside* the novel. This strikes me as a remarkable, almost hair-raising phenomenon.'[30] However this astonishing phenomenon may be explained (I shall return to it later), it does not alter the fundamental fact of the identity of the realms of the first-person narrator and of the rest of the (fictional) characters in the novel.

Holden begins his narrative as follows:

If you really want to hear about it, the first thing you'll probably want to know is where I was born, and what my lousy childhood was like, and how my parents were occupied and all before they had me, and all that David Copperfield kind of crap, but I don't feel like going into it. In the first place, that stuff bores me, and in the second place, my parents would have about two haemorrhages apiece if I told anything pretty personal about them. They're quite touchy about anything like that, especially my father. They're *nice* and all – I'm not saying that – but they're also touchy as hell. Besides, I'm not going to tell you my whole goddam autobiography or anything. I'll just tell you about this madman stuff that happened to me around last Christmas before I got pretty run-down and had to come out here and take it easy.[31]

If one tries to transpose the first-person narrative into a third-person narrative, that is, to abolish the personal union between main character and narrator and to introduce a narrator situated outside the fictional world of the characters (non-identity of the realms of narrator and characters),[32] one encounters great difficulty immediately. If the objective of this transposition is an authorial third-person narrative like *Tom Jones* or *Vanity Fair*, then the role of the first-person narrator, Holden Caulfield, must be assigned to two characters, namely, a character of the scene of the action and a narrator situated outside of the fictional reality. For such a narrator, however, Holden's juvenile, simplified system of values would be just as inappropriate as his style, which is saturated with teenage slang. If the style were transposed into that of an adult, a hiatus would be created between the narrator and that which is narrated. The absence of such a hiatus is a very significant feature of the original text. If, on the other hand, the objective of the transposition is a third-person narrative like *A Portrait of the Artist* (figural narrative situation), then Holden Caulfield would have to be eliminated as narrator. There would only remain the reflector-character Holden, with whose thoughts and emotions we would become very well acquainted, although Holden would not narrate them himself. With this change, the compulsive nature of the narrative act and the confessional character of the narrative – essential features of this first-person novel – would be lost. In this way the connection between experience and narration, which is given by the identity of the realms of the narrator and of the represented reality, cannot be severed without seriously interfering with the structure of meaning of the novel. The severing of this connection is, however, a prerequisite for a transposition of a first-person into a third-person narrative.

3.1.2 Opposition II (perspective): internal perspective– external perspective

The opposition internal perspective–external perspective can be illustrated with the aid of a passage from Joyce's *A Portrait of the Artist as a Young Man* which depicts Stephen's going to confession. Stephen is waiting in front of the confessional in a state of great psychological and moral tension:

The slide was shot to suddenly. The penitent came out. He was next. He stood up in terror and walked blindly into the box. At last it had come. He knelt in the silent gloom and raised his eyes to the white crucifix suspended above him. God could see that he was sorry. He would tell all his sins. His confession would be long, long. Everybody in the chapel would know then what a sinner he had been. Let them know. It was true. But God had promised to forgive him if he was sorry. He was sorry. He clasped his hands and raised them towards the white form, praying with his darkened eyes, praying with all his trembling body, swaying his head to and fro like a lost creature, praying with whimpering lips.[33]

In the first part of this passage Stephen functions as a reflector-character. The reader perceives objects of the outer world through Stephen's eyes and at the same time is granted a direct insight into Stephen's inner state, his thoughts and his extremely agitated state of mind. The first part of the passage, concluding with the sentence 'He was sorry,' presents an internal perspective and contains a representation of the inner world. It can be transposed without difficulty into a first-person form, like *The Catcher in the Rye*, for example, which also employs an internal perspective. The last sentence of the quotation resists such a transposition, however, because of the predominance of external instead of internal perspective and of the representation of the outer instead of the inner world. In this sentence the voice of a narrator, too, becomes somewhat more audible than in the first part of the quotation, where the transmission proceeds from a reflector. The fact that the parts of the quotation with internal and external perspective behave so differently when a transposition is attempted indicates that the difference between the two perspectives is a matter of structure rather than style.[34]

3.1.3 Opposition III (mode): narrator-reflector

Stephen Dedalus also functions as a reflector-character in the first three chapters of *Ulysses*. In the following passage, Mr Deasy, the headmaster of the school where Stephen teaches, has just handed Stephen a letter concerning foot and mouth disease and asked him to deliver it to the editor of a Dublin newspaper. At Mr Deasy's request Stephen skims this letter:

– I have put the matter into a nutshell, Mr Deasy said. It's about the foot and mouth disease. Just look through it. There can be no two opinions on the matter.
  May I trespass on your valuable space. That doctrine of *laissez faire* which so often in our history. Our cattle trade. The way of all our old industries. Liverpool ring which jockeyed the Galway harbour scheme. European conflagration. Grain supplies through the narrow waters of the channel. The pluterperfect imperturbability of the department of agriculture. Pardoned a classical allusion. Cassandra. By a woman who was no better than she should be. To come to the point at issue.
  – I don't mince words, do I? Mr Deasy asked as Stephen read on.
  Foot and mouth disease. Known as Koch's preparation. Serum and virus. Percentage of salted horses. Rinderpest. Emperor's horses at Mürzsteg, lower Austria. Veterinary surgeons. Mr Henry Blackwood Price. Courteous offer a fair trial. Dictates of common sense. Allimportant question. In every sense of the word take the bull by the horns. Thanking you for the hospitality of your columns.
  – I want that to be printed and read, Mr Deasy said.[35]

Between Mr Deasy's remarks, which are quoted in direct discourse, appear passages containing phrases from Deasy's letter reflected in Stephen's consciousness as he reads silently. This leads to a peculiar fragmentation of the letter. Special attention is given to the numerous stylistic clichés, to Mr Deasy's extravagant formulations and to several quite arbitrarily chosen bits of information taken out of context. If one were to put the content of this passage into the mouth of a narrator-character, its meaning would be very significantly changed. The emphasis of the altered passage would no longer be on the subjective impressions which the letter creates in the consciousness of the reflector-character, Stephen, but rather on the actual content of the letter. This experiment in transposition shows that substituting a teller-character for a reflector-character can result in a decisive change in the narrative statement. Consequently, it has been shown that the opposition narrator–reflector signifies structurally opposite forms of the rendering of mediacy in a narrative.

3.1.4 The typological circle

Having demonstrated the structural significance of the three oppositions of person, perspective and mode which underlie the narrative situations, I shall proceed to the arrangement of the narrative situations as illustrated by the diagram of the typological circle. As I have already stated, the points corresponding to the ideal types of the three narrative situations are located at one of the poles of each of the three axes of the typological circle which represent the three oppositions. (See diagram of typological circle, p. xvi and the diagram on p. 56.)

Compared with simple dyadic or simple monadic systems, a number of advantages result from the triadic arrangement of a system such as this:

Each narrative situation is defined by three constitutive elements (person, perspective, mode). The concept is thus determined more comprehensively according to generic theory than are the types of a monadic system based on a single opposition.

The triadic structure of the typology permits the arrangement of the types in a circle. The circular form reveals the closed nature or inclusiveness of the system, on the one hand, and its essentially dialectic character, on the other. The secondary constitutive elements of each narrative situation involve the suspension and in this sense the resolution of the oppositions which define the other two narrative situations. In the first-person narrative situation, for example, the contrasts in mode and perspective between the authorial and the figural narrative situations are suspended.

The arrangement of the narrative situations on the diagram of the typological circle makes it possible to illustrate the systematic locus of all conceivable forms and modifications of the main types. In this sense the typological circle can be regarded as an inclusive continuum. This continuum incorporates the unlimited number of variations of the main types and the modifications which approach each of the two contiguous types.

The typological circle connects ideal types or ahistorical constants[36] – the three narrative situations – with historical forms of narration, which can be described as modifications of the ideal types.

It is appropriate here to emphasize once more that ideal types are not literary programs, for the realization of which authors are awarded a prize by critics. In their function for criticism, the narrative situations are comparable to trigonometric surveying points, by which the narrative landscape with its immense variety of topographical phenomena and forms can be charted and described. The older criticism of the narrative situations often assumed erroneously that the main types of the narrative situations were normative prescriptions or at least amounted to a schematization of the narrative possibilities consisting of three categories. Such objections have been raised less frequently in recent years. Nevertheless, I wish to state once more that the objective of this typology is not to restrict the multiplicity of narrative possibilities, but, on the contrary, to bring them into view.

Between the ideal types of narrative situations as ahistorical constants and the historical forms of narration, as recorded in the history of the novel and the short story, there exists one more very revealing connection. Of the six narrative situations which could have been established at the six poles of the three oppositions, only three were actually realized. These three types are those which have been developed most frequently in the history of the novel. This approach is advantageous in that the vast majority of the works can be readily classified in terms of one of the three types of narrative situations. Consequently there remain only relatively few novels which are situated near the unrealized but theoretically possible positions. This decision in favour of the majority of those typical forms which have developed historically can be revised at any time, should the future development of the novel demand it. Such a revision of the typological circle could become necessary, for instance, if certain tendencies of representation in the novel, which appeared at first only sporadically after Joyce, should continue to become more frequent and widespread. One example of such a tendency is the extremely rigorous execution of internal perspective in the form of interior monologue, as exemplified in Beckett's novel trilogy *Molloy*, *Malone Dies* and *The Unnamable*. It is conceivable that interior monologue could attain the rank of an important narrative situation in the next decades. Such a narrative situation would have to be located at the internal perspective pole of the perspective axis. The other two as yet unrealized positions also have a good chance of becoming historically 'occupied,' considering the present tendency to develop new narrative forms.[37] More will be said about this in the detailed description of the typological circle in Chapter 7.

The diagram of the typological circle thus reveals a close relation between the system of narrative situations and the history of the novel and the short story. For example, if one entered all novels recorded in the history of the novel in the appropriate places on the typological circle in chronological order, one would find that until shortly after the turn of the century only certain portions of the typological circle were 'colonized,' specifically the sectors in which the positions of the first-person narrative situation and the authorial narrative situation are located. The sector representing the figural narrative situation, on the other hand, does not begin to fill until after the turn of the century, slowly at first, but then – after Joyce – more quickly. As I have already mentioned, this tendency continues in the most recent development illustrated by Beckett's works, by those of the *nouveau roman* and by the Americans Barth, Pynchon, Vonnegut, among others. Seen in this light the diagram of the typological circle looks like a program for the structure of the novel which is being gradually realized, as it seems, by historical developments of the novel. Without the cognitive device of the typology and the system of interrelationships among individual narrative forms which the typology reveals, this correspondence between the general system and the particular historical form would scarcely be so evident.

Finally, the diagram of the typological circle also offers an approach to the modification of the theory of norms and deviation. Because of the arrangement of the forms of transmission of a story on the typological circle, a deviation from one type is always concurrently an approach toward the type of another narrative situation. The operations which Jacques Dubois and his collaborators perform on the norm of narration illustrate this point. Insofar as such operations as detraction, adjection, immutation, transmutation[38] relate to elements of the narrative transmission of a story, they amount to shifting the locus of a narrative on the typological circle away from one narrative situation and toward another. The model norm–deviation[39] is thus replaced by a new one, namely the concept of a closed continuum of transformationally generated forms, in which, strictly speaking, there can no longer exist a norm and a deviation from this norm, but only a continuous motion from form to form in either direction along the typological circle. What appears as deviation according to the norm model turns out, on the basis of my model, to be a historically consistent step in the further realization of the structural potentialities of this genre.

3.2 Dynamization of the narrative situation

From the way in which the typology of the narrative situations has recently been applied in the interpretation of narrative works, it is evident that narrative theory has finally outgrown its Linnaean age, during which the classification of 'species' and forms was its principal objective. Our primary attention is no longer directed toward finding out which narrative situation prevails in a narrative, but rather toward the particular profile or, to replace the spatial metaphor with a temporal one, toward the rhythmical pattern resulting from the succession of various narrative situations or from various modulations of a specific narrative situation. By dynamization I mean the extension of this study to include the variations of the narrative situation during the course of the narrative process in a novel or a short story. A certain regularity is discernible in the recurrence of individual phenomena, a rhythm as it were, in the variation of the narrative situation in individual works. Presumably, this rhythm is structurally determined. I shall now describe some of these structural determinants which to all appearances are connected with the narrative situation.

The changing focus of recent narrative theory sketched above has a very revealing parallel in a shift of interest and emphasis which can be observed especially in English novel criticism of the last few decades.[40] For some time, those critics of the novel interested in questions of form and structure occupied themselves chiefly with works written with great formal consistency, such as the novels of the older James or those of Faulkner, Hemingway, Virginia Woolf and of course Joyce. Recently, however, critics of the novel interested in the theoretical aspects of form and structure are turning their attention more and more toward the 'large loose baggy monsters,' as James once called the great Victorian novels, which at first glance seem so lacking in form.[41] The consequences of this shift of interest are twofold. On the one hand, the text material of the Victorian novel, which overwhelms all formal categories, necessitates a modification of the apparatus of theoretical research. On the other hand, there are indications that under the seeming lack of form of so many Victorian novels a formal and structural regularity lies hidden which has not yet been studied sufficiently. It is probably no coincidence that one of the first comprehensive studies along this line was devoted to stories and novels by Tolstoy, Dostoevsky, Gogol and other Russian authors whose narrative vitality, like that of the Victorians, goes beyond most formal conventions. The work in question is Uspensky's *A Poetics of Composition: The Structure of the Artistic Text and Typology of a Compositional Form*. Uspensky, whose approach is related to the semiotic approach of Yury Lotman, makes the transition in narrative point of view (*točka zreniya*) the key point of departure of his study: 'In the transition from one point of view to another, from one manner of describing to another, there must be a harmony, an order, peculiar to the particular work, which eventually would allow us to define the inner rhythm of the work in question.'[42] It is primarily this fundamental statement which is important in this connection. One must not forget that circumstances in the Russian novel seem especially suited for this approach because here, as Johannes Holthusen and Wolf Schmid have shown, the conditions which made possible, or better, necessitated the above-mentioned shift of interest in the novel of Western literatures are not present to the same extent. According to Holthusen and Schmid, the strictly consistent execution of a specific narrative situation is found far less frequently in the Russian novel than in the French, Anglo-American or German novel.[43] Recently, however, a tendency has become apparent in the novels of Western literature as well to suspend the lines of demarcation which Flaubert, James and their successors had often drawn very conscientiously between the personal and impersonal form of narration, that is, between the point of view of the narrator and that of a character of the novel. Jean Ricardou has already attempted to define this phenomenon with the aid of the concept 'narrateur flottant,' as has Barth with that of 'viewless viewpoint.'[44]

The variation of the narrative situation in the course of the narrative process in a novel is connected with a number of factors, of which two are especially significant: the organization of the content, that is to say, of the story and the structure of the novel, its composition as a complex of certain basic narrative forms; and the distributive sequence of these forms. The systematic analysis of the structure of a narrative, its composition of basic motifs and archetypal myths, was greatly stimulated by structuralists such as Vladimir Propp and Claude Lévi-Strauss. The results of this approach, as interesting as they are, cannot yet be correlated with my line of questioning, but hopefully this will some day be possible. Consequently I shall concentrate on the relation between the novel's composition as a complex of basic narrative forms and the variation of the narrative situation. Eberhard Lämmert's *Bauformen des Erzählens* describes structural forms which are discernible in the time structure of a narrative.[45] Since they are already relatively complex, however, Lämmert's forms are unsuitable for my approach, which aims first of all at the rudimentary correspondences between structural forms and narrative situation. I shall thus have to go back to earlier critics such as Robert Petsch, who, in his pioneer work of 1934, *Wesen und Formen der Erzählkunst*, distinguished the following basic forms: report, description, picture, scene and dialogue.[46] Even today they still provide a helpful point of departure for an inquiry into the forms of which a novel is composed and how these forms are distributed over the entire structure of the novel and in what sequence. Later narrative critics have added to Petsch's list or have omitted one concept or another. Thus Helmut Bonheim's list of four contains three of Petsch's basic forms: description, report and dialogue (speech). Bonheim's fourth category, comment, is included in Petsch's concept 'report.'[47] For a novel theory based on mediacy as the generic characteristic of narration, these elementary forms can be divided into two categories, namely specifically narrative forms (report, description, comment) and non-narrative or dramatic forms (speech, dramatized scene). Dramatized scene consists essentially of dialogue interspersed with narrative elements which function as stage directions and as brief reports of the action. Depending on the predominance of narrative or non-narrative elements in it, the dramatized scene can be reckoned either to the narrative forms or to the non-narrative ones. This division of the longitudinal profile of a narrative corresponds to the distinction known to us since Plato between diegesis and mimesis and the definition of the epic poem as a hybrid of the two.[48] Mimesis, in the strict sense of direct or drama-like presentation, is possible in the novel actually only by means of dialogue. Strictly speaking, the dialogue scene is, therefore, a foreign body in the narrative genre, because in the novel a long quotation in direct speech must be regarded as an avoidance of mediacy, i.e., the mode of transmission by a narrator.[49] The occurrence of dialogue passages in the novel is thus largely independent of the respective narrative situation. 'Properly speaking, in literature pure mimesis is only possible where . . . behaviour is only linguistic . . . [T]he absolutely unmediated story or pure transcript or record . . . consists of nothing beyond the speech or verbalized thoughts of characters . . .'[50] This statement by Chatman is related to Hamburger's view that dialogue occupies an 'indigenous locus' in the mimetic narrative only, not in the indirect, first-person narrative.[51] This view is contradicted by the fact that on the level of the surface structure no significant differences are to be found in the ratios of narrative parts to dialogue passages in first-person narration and third-person narration.[52] These ratios themselves fluctuate greatly, as I shall show below. This fluctuation, however, is not caused primarily by the narrative situation or by the difference between epic fiction and first-person narration in Hamburger's sense. The novel is not a homogeneous genre but a mixture of diegetic-narrative and mimetic-dramatic parts. In the narrative parts, however, a gradual progression from the pronounced diegetic-narrative to the mimetic-dramatic can be noted. Free indirect style, indirect speech, speech report and largely dramatic scene are more closely related to the mimetic-dramatic than are a narrator's very compressed report of action and authorial commentary. The various forms by which consciousness may be rendered assume a special position in this series, because they disregard the boundary postulated here. Authorial thought report, the rendering of thought in a form analogous to indirect speech, as well as free indirect style are among the narrative forms, but interior monologue can also be regarded as a mimetic-dramatic form under certain conditions.

Diegesis, that is, narration in the true sense, and mimesis, as it is prevalent in long dialogue scenes, evoke different attitudes of spatio-temporal orientation in the reader, as was already described in *Narrative Situations*.[53] Between these two possibilities, however, there is presumably a broad transitional zone, in which the propensity of the individual reader's imagination determines whether he regards a particular text as an instance of an epic-indirect or a dramatic-direct presentation. All statements about the narrative profile or the narrative rhythm of a novel must, therefore, also take into account the indeterminacy of the reader, especially his tendency toward perseverance. Once the reader has assumed an attitude with its corresponding spatio-temporal orientation, he will maintain it until a conspicuous signal in the narrative text necessitates a change. This is also the explanation for the fact that when the narrative situation is only vaguely defined in parts of a text, as, for example, in large portions of D. H. Lawrence's *Women in Love*, these parts are not necessarily perceived by the reader as perspectivally ambivalent. When reading such passages, the reader maintains the assumed narrative attitude until he is induced to change it by a clear indication requiring a new orientation.

3.2.1 Narrative profile

The description of the dynamics of the narrative process with the aid of the narrative profile of a novel must begin with the relation of the narrative parts of the novel to the non-narrative parts, that is, to dialogue and dramatized scene; specifically, with their purely quantitative ratio and their distribution. Individual works differ considerably from one another. In parts of Walter Pater's *Marius the Epicurean*, dialogues comprise less than 10% of the text; in Henry Green's *Nothing*, 80–85%; and in Ivy Compton-Burnett's *Mother and Son*, 90–95% of the text. The novels of Henry Green and Ivy Compton-Burnett are, therefore, termed 'dialogue novels.' But their location on the typological circle approximately halfway between the authorial and the figural narrative situations is primarily determined not by the quantity of their dialogues, but rather by the narrative prerequisites for the pervasiveness of those dialogues, namely the withdrawal of the authorial narrator and, at the same time, the absence of figural presentation. Dialogue as a non-narrative structural element of a narrative cannot, by itself, decisively determine the classification of a work on the typological circle.

The works mentioned are extreme cases. More representative of the average for novels and stories are the ratios of narrative parts to dialogue in the novels of D. H. Lawrence. In *Sons and Lovers* dialogue comprises nearly 50% of the text in the middle chapters, at the beginning and towards the end somewhat less. In *The Rainbow*, dialogue amounts to only 15%, but increases to 40% again in *Women in Love*. The decrease in dialogue at the beginning and end of a novel is characteristic of Lawrence, and can be explained by the exposition and conclusion of the action. Another characteristic of the distribution of dialogue passages in Lawrence is their scattered occurrence and their limitation to relatively short narrative units. By comparison, Trollope's novels, in which dialogue amounts to 50% or more of the text, tend to be divided into larger, monolithic blocks of narrative and dialogue.

In analyzing the profile of the narrative process, however, it does not suffice to register the alternation between diegetic-narrative and mimetic-dramatic parts of a narrative. The overlapping of these two structural elements in indirect speech and in free indirect style, on the one hand, and in the narrative function of some dialogues and monologues, on the other, is also important. In some authors, such as Dickens, Hardy, and Lawrence, parts of a dialogue tend to fuse with the narrative report in the form of free indirect style or summary.

This phenomenon occurs with particular frequency in Hardy's *The Woodlanders* and *The Return of the Native*. It can also happen that in a dialogue situation the speech of one partner is rendered in direct speech, while that of the other is presented in indirect speech or reported in summary. The quantitative relation of indirect and direct presentation of speech is also relevant here. (The first belongs to actual narration, while the second belongs to mimetic-dramatic presentation.) Frequently indirect speech amounts to only a fraction of direct speech. Strangely enough, it hardly occurs at all in some novels, for example, in *Sons and Lovers*. This fact seems to contradict the assumption that indirect speech is the form of speech presentation most compatible with the report form of a narrative.[54] Free indirect style is a special case. Presentation of speech in free indirect style is relatively frequent in an authorial narrative situation as well as in a figural narrative situation. It often provides a smooth transition from reportorial narration to scenic presentation, thereby reducing the dynamics of the alternation of narrative forms in a novel.

For how long must a dialogue scene interrupt the narrative part of a novel in order to effect a change in the reader's attitude, to induce him to remove his centre of orientation completely from the act of narration and to transfer it to the action progressing before him? The answer depends largely on the disposition of the individual reader's imagination and cannot be generally stated. It is very difficult to specify any percentage figure here, too, because dialogue scenes with direct speech are frequently interspersed with passages in indirect speech or free indirect style, which recall or can recall the narrative process. In general we know much too little at this point about what goes on in the reader's imagination when he is led in his reading from a fairly long narrative passage to a fairly long dialogue passage and then back again to a narrative passage.[55] Finally, questions concerning the temporal meaning of the epic preterite, and the reader's temporal orientation in the fictional world have not yet been fully answered because no truly reliable, that is, verifiable information is yet available. A comparison with the media film and television might be of help here. Not infrequently borderline situations arise precisely in the filming of novels which, under certain circumstances, can explain the state of affairs in the novel itself. In the filming of Dostoevsky's *The Devils* for television, for example, action-scenes are projected onto the screen, which are

presented to the viewer *in actu* several times, while at the same time
the narrator as 'voice-over' narrates the event in the past tense of
the narrative report. Is the imaginative act of the reader determined
here by the mimetic-dramatic or by the diegetic-narrative manner
of presentation?

3.2.2 Narrative rhythm

If the profile of a narrative results from the sequence of narrative
and dialogue blocks, the rhythm of a narrative can be determined
from the succession of the various basic forms of narration which
comprise the narrative part of a work (report, commentary,
description, scenic presentation interspersed with action report)
and from their relation to the narrative profile. While the alternation
of narrative and dialogue parts largely takes place independently
of the narrative situation, the succession of the basic forms of
narration in a novel is primarily determined by the narrative
situation. Here the transitions from one narrative situation to the
other play a very important role. Narratives with considerable
alternation of the basic forms and with frequent transitions between
narrative situations have a strongly pronounced rhythm. Narratives
based on only one or two basic forms and on a consistently
maintained narrative situation, on the other hand, have a relatively
weak rhythm. This does not mean, however, that the literary
quality of works with a less pronounced narrative rhythm is in any
respect lower than that of works with a marked rhythm. The
narrative rhythm is not very distinct in either Schnitzler's narrative
'Leutnant Gustl,' which consists only of interior monologue, or in
Hemingway's story 'The Killers,' which proceeds almost exclusively
in scenic presentation. Yet these two narratives are certainly not
dull and without tension; on the contrary, the monotony of the
narrative process even contributes to the intensification or suspense
in these stories. In Kafka's *The Trial* (*Der Prozess*), too, with its
predominantly figural narrative situation, the narrative rhythm as a
whole is subdued. There are only inconspicuous shifts in the
narrative situations. These shifts, however, are very important
indeed for the interpretation as studies by Winfried Kudszus and
Walter H. Sokel have shown.[56] In the first chapters the figural
perspective of Josef K. is superimposed several times on that of an
authorial narrator who dissociates himself from the protagonist. As
Kudszus shows, the decrease in these authorial intrusions parallels
the increase of the hero's 'perspective solipsism.' A temporary

reversal of this tendency occurs in Chapter VI, with its authorial broadening of the point of view. In the second half of the novel, however, the authorial intrusions take on a new function (Kudszus terms it 'antifigural') which sets the stage for the destruction, first, of Josef K.'s awareness of reality and then of his person. A parallel is evident between the slow shifting of the narrative situation and the gradual inner process of the psychic exhaustion and the final disintegration of the protagonist's personality. Consequently the significance of the change of a narrative situation cannot always be gathered in general from the degree of the dynamics developed. On the contrary, every novel has its own standard which determines which deviation from the dominant narrative situation will be considered as 'unmarked' and which as 'marked' and thus significant of the novel's interpretation. The barely perceptible transitions from the figural to the authorial narrative situation which are so important for the interpretation of *The Trial* would be much less significant in the context of the very pronounced narrative dynamics of the beginning of *Anna Karenina*.[57]

The beginnings of *Vanity Fair* and *Buddenbrooks* are similar. A comparison of these books with a novel such as Trollope's *Phineas Finn* reveals an essential difference not only in the narrative profile, but also in the dynamics of the alternation of the basic forms of narration and of the narrative situation. Trollope's novel conforms much more closely to the authorial narrative situation established at the beginning, which is later interrupted basically only by the insertion of dialogue scenes of increasing length. In this way the narrative profile of this novel undergoes a certain levelling and its narrative dynamics have a subdued effect. Again, Dickens's third-person novels are contoured differently. Here the passages with report are less extensive than the scenes with dialogue and dramatized action. The narrative on the whole is more articulated throughout and alternates from one basic form to another more frequently than is the case in Trollope. Also, a large portion of the authorial action report is 'sight report,'[58] that is to say, the narrator confines himself mainly to the report of that which an invisible observer could himself perceive at the scene of the action. Thus in Dickens's novels the greater part of the narrative process clearly lies in the scenic presentation edited by an authorial narrator, into which dialogue passages are integrated.

Especially striking in Dickens are also the transitions from authorial outside view (external perspective) to figural inside view (internal perspective), which can almost always be explained thematically. The transition to an extended inner view with figural narrative situation is found most frequently in scenes of great inner pathos, especially in death scenes. Almost all the great death scenes and the narrative sections immediately preceding them have a tendency toward figural narrative situation. The classic example is the long illness and finally the death of the little Paul Dombey in *Dombey and Son*. As mentioned above, this tendency toward reflectorization extends here even to the heading of the chapter with the death scene.[59] Chapter LV of this novel contains a focalization of the narrative situation which is even clearer and more consistent in regard to perspective. The narrative is restricted almost exclusively to the rendering of Carker's thoughts and feelings. Carker is oppressed by presentiments of death and actually meets his fate at the end of this chapter. In comparison, the most famous death scene in Thackeray, the death of Thomas Newcome at the end of the novel *The Newcomes*, is reported entirely by means of an outside viewpoint, which of course results from the first-person narrative situation of this novel. As Fred W. Boege has shown, Dickens's interest in questions of the perspective of presentation seems to have grown steadily in the course of his development as a novelist.[60] One need only think of his last novel, *The Mystery of Edwin Drood*, the strictly figural beginning of which is most unusual for Dickens. In the case of Dickens, however, the change in narrative situation, especially the transition from authorial report to consistent figural presentation, is almost always determined by the content and is thus, to all appearances, not an intentionally employed narrative technique. An exception to this tendency is *Bleak House*, in which sections consisting of several chapters with clearly authorial narrative situation and sections of about the same length with unambiguous first-person narrative situation alternate with great regularity throughout the novel. These two narrative situations represent two different perspectives, namely, the panoramic one of the authorial narrator who is critical of the times, and the naive but sympathetic viewpoint of the first-person narrator, Esther Summerson, circumscribed by her domestic horizons. Perhaps the dynamics of this alternation do not entirely correspond to the narrative effort, since the regularity of the sequence excludes one important factor, namely surprise, from the very beginning, and also because this extravagant narrative apparatus is used only in part for a true perspectivization of the events involving two different points of view.

Typical of the first-person novels of the eighteenth and nineteenth centuries, as well as the authorial novels, is the constant alternation of passages in which report prevails and passages consisting of scenic presentation and dialogue. The recurrent narrowing of the perspective of the narrating self to the point of view of the perceptual horizon of the experiencing self is a specific characteristic of the first-person narrative situation. The transition is almost always gradual and thus usually not apparent to the reader. Yet it is precisely this change which is very important for the dynamics of the narrative in the first-person novel. Through it the tension between the two phases of the self in confrontation in a quasi-autobiographical first-person novel becomes part of the narrative structure. The dynamics of the modulations of this scheme diminish as the presentation is increasingly restricted to the point of view and the perceptual horizon of the experiencing self. Accordingly, they are greater in *David Copperfield* than in Salinger's *The Catcher in the Rye*, and they diminish further in a novel which approaches the form of interior monologue, as, for example, Faulkner's *The Sound and the Fury*.

In the novel with a predominantly figural narrative situation the dynamics of the alternation of basic forms and of narrative situations are reduced, since there is a tendency to retain the point of view of one character of the novel which inhibits the frequent change of the narrative situation. The most frequent modulation takes place in the direction of a stronger authorial narrative situation, but this transition is almost always smooth and inconspicuous, as, for example, in Kafka's *The Trial* and *The Castle*. In novels in which the figural narrative situation is maintained consistently, the structure of the process of narrative presentation becomes relatively stable, at times even monotonous, as a result of the fixation of the point of view in the figural medium, as, for example, in *Pilgrimage*, Dorothy Richardson's series of stream of consciousness novels. In novels of this type a pattern of rhythmical alternation can be produced through the alternation of dialogue and the rendering of consciousness. The alternation of figural inside view and dialogue in Joyce's *A Portrait of the Artist as a Young Man* has a rhythmical effect due to the constant shifting from external to internal events, from loud to soft, from dialogue and report to figural inside view. In the following quotation from this novel Stephen has dared to do the unthinkable. He complained to the headmaster about an undeserved punishment by a prefect. Upon his return his fellow pupils surround him full of curiosity:

The fellows had seen him running. They closed round him in a ring, pushing one against another to hear.

– Tell us! Tell us!

– What did he say?

– Did you go in?

– What did he say?

– Tell us! Tell us!

He told them what he had said and what the rector had said and, when he had told them, all the fellows flung their caps spinning up into the air and cried:

– Hurroo!

They caught their caps and sent them up again spinning skyhigh and cried again:

– Hurroo! Hurroo!

They made a cradle of their locked hands and hoisted him up among them and carried him along till he struggled to get free. And when he had escaped from them they broke away in all directions, flinging their caps again into the air and whistling as they went spinning up and crying:

– Hurroo!

And they gave three groans for Baldyhead Dolan and three cheers for Conmee and they said he was the decentest rector that was ever in Clongowes.

The cheers died away in the soft grey air. He was alone. He was happy and free: but he would not be anyway proud with Father Dolan. He would be very quiet and obedient: and he wished that he could do something kind for him to show him that he was not proud.

The air was soft and grey and mild and evening was coming. There was the smell of evening in the air, the smell of the fields in the country where they digged up turnips to peel them and eat them when they went out for a walk to Major Barton's, the smell there was in the little wood beyond the pavilion where the gallnuts were.

The fellows were practising long shies and bowling lobs and slow twisters. In the soft grey silence he could hear the bump of the balls: and from here and from there through the quiet air the sound of the cricket bats: pick, pack, pock, puck: like drops of water in a fountain falling softly in the brimming bowl.[61]

Here dialogue and scenic report alternate with the figural presentation of Stephen's thoughts and perceptions in such a way that the voices of his fellow pupils are pushed into the background while Stephen's thoughts claim the foreground of the presentation more and more. Thus the narrative as well as the thematic structure of the novel is reflected in this short excerpt: a finely articulated sequence of relatively short basic forms (dialogue, scenic report, figural rendering of consciousness) and the presentation of the outer world as the antechamber of the inner world, where all the experiences of the hero converge. Even the portrayal of the quiet autumn evening over the countryside (which is entirely appropriated to Stephen's consciousness by the distinctly figural narrative situation) is internalized by means of metonymy. The pleasant mildness of the air, the fragrance promising a fruitful harvest, the twilight of the approaching evening, all these elements of the portrayal of the countryside are an expression of the hero's state of mind at the moment of his triumph, of his first successful self-assertion. It would make little sense to simply list this paragraph under 'description' in an analysis of the basic forms of this novel. The most important function of this paragraph for the context would be overlooked, namely the metonymic character of this description revealing states of consciousness of Stephen, the reflector-character of the novel. It is an *experienced* description of a piece of the outer world which becomes the mirror of the hero's inner world. Thus the respective dominant narrative situation must always be taken into account when registering the basic forms of narration. Assertions concerning the effect of a certain narrative profile and of a certain narrative rhythm are, therefore, only meaningful when they are related to their specific function within the narrative context. This function, as a rule, will more often than not be dependent on the narrative situation.

3.3 Schematization of the narrative process: narrative patterns

There are some indications that the process of the conception of the narrative style and the rendering of mediacy by means of a suitable narrative apparatus do not progress uniformly but rather with varying degrees of intensity. The ultimate reasons for this might be sought in the physiological laws which at least partly govern or influence the creative productivity of an author. Sterne's Tristram Shandy was already aware of the interdependence of body and mind: '– rumple the one – you rumple the other.'[62] There can also be states of exhaustion in the mental domain in which the creative process takes place. It is, therefore, not surprising that a kind of leveling off of the narrative profile or a diminishing of the dynamics of the narrative process can be detected as we progress toward the end of a novel. This tendency is particularly apparent in longer works. It is astonishing that, although occasional observations refer to this phenomenon, it has not yet been studied systematically. Understandably a leveling off like this will become evident sooner in a novel with a prominent profile and more pronounced dynamics of the narrative process such as *Vanity Fair* or *Anna Karenina*, than in a novel with a relatively inconspicuous profile and limited dynamics such as Ivy Compton-Burnett's *Men and Wives* or Kafka's *The Castle* (*Das Schloss*). The leveling off of the profile and the diminishing of the narrative dynamics in longer stories and novels suggests that the rendering of mediacy demands of the author a high degree of exertion and intense application of his creative imagination to the narrative act. Frequently such concentration cannot be maintained with the same intensity over an extended period of time. This phenomenon deserves a careful investigation comparing various authors. The kind of narrative situation must also be taken into account, since presumably not every narrative situation demands of the author the same degree of concentration. This study should also examine differences between the popular novel and the literary novel in this respect.

A leveling off or neutralization of narrative profile and rhythm can become evident not only in an individual work, but also in the works of an author taken as a whole. To all appearances there is a certain leveling off of the narrative profile and a diminishing of the narrative dynamics in the later novels of those great Victorian writers with very extensive complete works, such as Thackeray and Trollope. One must always reckon with the possibility of the reversal of this tendency in an individual work, however. The degree of leveling off also varies from author to author. The later works of Trollope and Thackeray reveal a greater leveling off than do those of Dickens, for example. In Dickens a leveling off of the profile is often evident within individual works. This phenomenon is connected apparently with the time pressure under which the later installments for serialization were often written. In *David Copperfield* this diminution of narrative dynamics is probably also related to the altered objective of the author in the second half of the novel. Here Dickens no longer concentrates his energies on David's life story but offers a kind of tour through a gallery of characters. In addition to the nature of the quasi-autobiographical first-person narrative situation, the gradual approach in time of the narrating self to the experiencing self seems to reinforce this effect. Such reasons, however, can hardly explain the evident leveling off of the profile in a relatively short narrative such as *A Christmas Carol*. Here, a narrator appears at the beginning whose numerous self-manifestations and emphatic narrative gestures lend great dynamics to the narrative. Later the personal appearance of this narrator fades noticeably. This leveling off can be observed in the decrease in the number of first-person references to the narrator from six just on the first page to none in the seven pages of the last chapter apart from the almost ritual closing phrase: 'God bless Us, Every One.'

A narrative pattern can also result from the stereotyped recurrence of a certain contour of the narrative profile. The profile which levels off toward the end of a story is such a pattern. A certain regularity in the alternation of narrative parts and dialogue passages can also be considered a pattern of the narrative process if it is no longer interrupted by variations of this sequence pattern. The authorial-figural slope, the tendency to shift from an authorial to a figural narrative situation, which can be observed with particular frequency in the transition from the exposition to the main part of a narrative or at the beginning of a chapter can likewise be included here. This schematization of the narrative opening is encountered in a large number of novels. An authorial-figural transition of this kind is discernible in the first chapters of Kafka's *The Trial*. It is also a determining factor for the structure of the narrative process in several stories in Joyce's *Dubliners* and is especially evident in 'A Painful Case' and in 'The Dead.' In Joyce this narrative pattern is actually an expression of an idiosyncrasy in the objective of his creative phantasy, the inclination of his imagination to turn away from the outer world to the inner world, from the recording of surface phenomena to the epiphany, to the intellectual penetration of this surface in order to reveal its underlying meaningfulness or symbolism. The snowfall at the beginning of 'The Dead' is presented by an authorial narrator as a meteorological phenomenon. At the end of the narrative, however, it is reflected by the figural medium, Gabriel, as part of an experience of intense awareness, whereby the snowfall becomes the internalized image of his emotional state. It is reasonable to ask whether one can still speak of a narrative pattern in such a case. An attempt to answer this would lead directly to the problem of deviation theory. Lack of space prohibits exploring this possibility.

Without using this concept himself, Helmut Bonheim recently came upon the problem of narrative pattern in an analysis of the basic forms of narration, which he calls 'narrative modes,' namely 'speech,' 'report,' 'description' and 'comment.'[63] In various American short-story authors he identifies distinct preferences for a certain sequence in which these basic forms appear and recur. Such recurring models can also be considered patterns, especially if their formation is very stereotyped. Bonheim acknowledges the difficulty confronting 'mode-chopping,' as he himself once terms his method in a mildly ironical tone. The great intermixing of modes in most literary texts makes such an enterprise difficult. However, if one does not wish to stop with a descriptive classification and quantification – surely an indispensable preliminary – then it is necessary also to consider the narrative situation which extends over and in part also determines the sequence of basic forms or modes. Thus little would be said about the structure of meaning of the passage from *A Portrait of the Artist as a Young Man* quoted above if one were satisfied with merely registering the modes and their sequence without simultaneously showing that, as part of a figural narrative situation, they contribute toward the formation of Stephen's experience and perception. Viewed in this light, the last paragraph of the quotation is not simply a description of an evening countryside, that is, description according to Bonheim's list, but the metonymic presentation of an inner experience of the hero, for which the technical term description no longer seems entirely appropriate.

3.4 Dynamization and schematization: summary

My analysis of the fluctuations and modulations which the narrative situation reveals in the course of a longer narrative has disclosed two opposing tendencies, one toward dynamization and the other toward schematization of the narrative process. Under dynamization are grouped together all phenomena in the rendering of mediacy which animate the process of transmission to the reader in the course of a narrative, which diversify it and thus counteract the monotony which could result from the excessive perseverance of a certain narrative situation. Schematization, on the other hand, denotes just that kind of perseverance or the recurrence of certain sequential patterns in the succession of basic narrative forms. Narrative patterns, such as the general leveling off of the narrative profile toward the end of a longer narrative, are a result of schematization.

It would be wrong, however, to conclude that dynamization of the narrative process is always exclusively the result of creative productivity and that schematization is always exclusively the consequence of creative entropy, that is, of the exhaustion of the creative productivity of an author. These two tendencies must be considered in their mutual interdependence. The alternation of dynamic and schematized parts of a narrative is a characteristic feature of the structure of the literary narrative text, in contrast perhaps to the factual text in a textbook, the non-fictional prose text of technical books, of a patient's medical record or of a police report. Such texts are, as a rule, more uniformly structured. This peculiarity of the literary narrative text reflects a fundamental formal law of aesthetic creations, specifically the structural composition marked by the alternation of artistically tense and relaxed elements.

These considerations have implications involving the relationship between the literary novel and the popular novel. Do the arrangement of dynamic and schematized parts as well as their ratio differ noticeably in these two forms? Differences in the reader's attitude in the face of dynamic and schematized narrative parts are another aspect of this topic. In my previously published analysis of the concept 'complementary story,' it already became evident that the reader, too, experiences a kind of alternation of systolic and diastolic phases in his attitude toward the story while reading a longer narrative work:

In the long novel, too, the act of communication between narrator and reader is a sequence of questioning or estrangement, of assertion or confirmation of the reader's field of reference. The length of a novel alone and the resulting duration of the reading does not, for purely physiological reasons, allow the reader to remain in a continuing state of consternation over the questionableness of the banality of his own field of reference the entire time. The role of the reader has the characteristic quality which Weinrich calls 'serenity,' by which he means a space of freedom which the reader enters in view of the negativity of the world (from the point of view of the author). In addition to this quality, the reader's role also implies the freedom of his imagination to add the banality and the stereotyped nature of reality . . . to the text of the narrated story to form an interlinear version, as it were.[64]

Here a vast field is still open to narrative criticism. Only the edges of it have been studied so far, and a closer investigation is essential.

4

THE OPPOSITION PERSON: IDENTITY AND NON-IDENTITY OF THE REALMS OF EXISTENCE OF THE NARRATOR AND THE FICTIONAL CHARACTERS (FIRST- AND THIRD-PERSON REFERENCE)

> Someone *inside* the novel is talking to someone *outside* the novel. This strikes me as a remarkable, almost hair-raising phenomenon.
>
> (David Goldknopf, *The Life of the Novel*)

In recent years narrative criticism has received some new and powerful stimuli from linguistics. It in turn has furnished text linguistics with several new and important concepts and questions. Egon Werlich's *A Text Grammar of English* contains an entire chapter on 'Point of View,' and the chapter 'Text Form' has sections about 'The narrative,' 'The report,' 'The news story,' etc.[1] Fowler recently defined the operational basis common to both disciplines as follows:

I shall maintain that [narrative] texts are structurally *like* sentences (as well as being constructed out of sentences). That is to say, the categories of structure that we propose for the analysis of individual sentences (in linguistics) can be extended to apply to the analysis of much larger structures in [narrative] texts.[2]

Fowler actually cites concrete examples for part of this interesting and daring hypothesis. Some of his assertions, however, still need to be scrutinized and discussed in detail. He contends, for example, that 'characters and incidents in fiction may closely resemble the stock of predicate-types and noun-types [as deep-structure elements of language].'[3]

The use of the concept opposition, which has been widely accepted in linguistics since Saussure, also reflects an understanding of the functioning of language common to both narrative criticism and linguistics:

When we compare signs . . . with each other, we can no longer speak of difference; . . . two signs . . . are not different but only distinct. Between them there is only *opposition*. The entire mechanism of language . . . is based on oppositions of this kind.[4]

In the following description of the elements which constitute the narrative situation, I shall, therefore, analyze these elements by contrasting the respective structurally significant pairs. For methodological reasons I shall begin with the most obvious opposition, that of person. I shall then deal with the oppositions perspective and mode in the following chapters.

4.1 Previous approaches to first- and third-person narration

To date, narrative criticism has not provided a generally accepted answer to the question of whether an essential, structurally based difference exists between first-person narration and so-called third-person narration. This failure is somewhat surprising. For a long time older views of first-person narration stood in the way of an accurate understanding of the peculiarity of this type of narration in contrast to third-person narration. One of these views, for example, asserted that the 'I' of a first-person narrator was largely identical with the author. This view evolved especially in conjunction with the interpretation of the great *Bildungsromane* in the first person, such as *David Copperfield* and Gottfried Keller's *Green Henry*, which actually suggested an identification of this kind. On the other hand, Spielhagen, the determined advocate of objectivity in the novel, maintained that the closest realization of his program was precisely that form of narration which, in the opinion of the nineteenth century was the most subjective, namely, the first-person novel. Spielhagen believed that in the first-person novel the author first changes his 'I' into a 'he': 'When the He changes back again into an I, it can, of course, no longer be the old, empirical, naive, limited and narrowminded "I." It must be a new, fiction-alized "I", artificially freed from its autobiographical limitations.'[5] In this twofold transformation of the subjective authorial 'I' in the first-person novel, Spielhagen saw the fusion of 'the objective and the subjective' in Schiller's sense of these terms. For Spielhagen and many of his contemporaries, this fusion was tantamount to the solution of the narrative problem. How easily the concepts objective and subjective can be reversed, however, became evident in the work of the first German theorist of the first-person novel. Kurt

Forstreuter writes about the difference between first- and third-person narration: 'The great difference is that in the third-person form each value judgement and interpretation can claim objective validity because it originates with the author, while the judgement of the first-person narrator is dependent on his person and is thus in no way binding for the reader.'[6] Apart from the subjective/objective problem, an important postulate is implied here. For Forstreuter, the first-person narrator is no longer mainly a mouthpiece for the author, but rather an independent fictional character. This recognition of the fictionality of the first-person narrator preceded the recognition of the fictionality of the third-person narrator.[7] The fictionality of the authorial third-person narrator was not generally recognized until the mid-1950s. The realization that the first-person narrator and the authorial third-person narrator were both fictional teller-characters and consequently similar in a very decisive point led critics to minimize the difference between first- and third-person narration. The fact that many still embrace this view today is probably at least partly due to its being shared by two well-known contemporary theorists: Wolfgang Kayser and Wayne C. Booth. As I have already mentioned, Kayser advanced narrative theory considerably by his definitive clarification of the distinction between the narrator of a novel, be it a first-person or a third-person novel, and the author. It was precisely this important point, however, which hindered his perception of the actual differences between third- and first-person narration. Since the narrating self is a narrator-role created by the author, Kayser believes that this narrating self is not identical with the fictional character whose life history is narrated in the first person, but instead an embodiment of the author's narrative function: 'The first-person narrator of a novel . . . is not at all the direct continuation of the narrating character. There is more to him. His narrator guise as an elderly hero is only a curious role behind which something else is hidden.'[8] It is significant that this sentence was not formulated in reference to David Copperfield or Heinrich Lee (*Green Henry*), but to the first-person narrator of *Moby-Dick*, in whom a tendency toward the authorialization of the narrator-role is in fact discernible. Kayser, therefore, does not admit the analogy between the first-person narrator and the 'grandfather who tells his grandchildren about his youth,' an analogy which forces itself upon most readers of first-person novels: 'We do not fail to recognize that Thomas Mann spins short threads between the narrated and the narrating Krull . . . but even here we do not think in the category of an individual having reached a final stage in his development and by no means do we unite the young and the old Felix Krull.'[9] That is a very astonishing statement; it ignores the thematic emphasis placed on the personal development of the protagonist and his ultimate identification with the narrator in the quasi-autobiographical first-person novel.[10] Consequently, Kayser's theory fails to do justice to the essential structural principle of the quasi-autobiographical form of the first-person novel as it is to be found in *David Copperfield*, *Green Henry* and Thomas Mann's *Felix Krull*: the tension between the older, matured and more sensible 'I' as narrator and the 'I' as hero, still completely engrossed in his existential situation. There is a certain irony in the fact that the same theorist who finally established the autonomy of the authorial narrator as a fictional character also endeavored to deprive the first-person narrator of a substantial part of his autonomous personality, the existential continuity between the narratorial 'I' and the 'I' of the hero of the story. One reason for Kayser's view is presumably that in many first-person novels the bond between the narrating self and the experiencing self, especially in its early stages, is very tenuous. Another reason is that novelists often characterize the narration of past events as personal recollections of the first-person narrator only in a very perfunctory manner. Both tendencies can be seen, for example, in Adalbert Stifter's *Der Nachsommer*.[11] The fact that some authors fail to realize the full potential of a certain narrative form does not necessarily imply that this aspect of the narrative form is unimportant for the genre in general.

The thesis of the essential similarity between first- and third-person narration often also involves a too-narrow conception of the first-person narrative process, if it attempts to confine the story of the first-person narrator to what he has experienced himself and what he can still remember. In other words, a first-person narrator not only remembers his earlier life, but can also re-create phases of it in his imagination. His narrating is, therefore, not strictly confined to the horizon of experience of the experiencing self. David Copperfield, for example, demonstrates this point repeatedly in the first chapters of his story.[12]

Booth considers the difference between first- and third-person narration to be structurally meaningless for a different reason. In his influential *Rhetoric of Fiction*, he arrives at the following conclusion: 'Perhaps the most overworked distinction is that of person. To say that a story is told in the first or third person will tell us nothing of importance unless we become more precise and describe how the particular qualities of the narrators relate to specific effects.'[13] The last clause, which seems at first glance to involve a substantial restriction of the previous contention, merely states a methodological truism valid for any literary classification. Booth prefers to emphasize the opposition 'dramatized'– 'undramatized narrator,'[14] by which he means basically the difference between a personalized and a nonpersonalized narrative form. His demonstration that the distinction between a personalized and a nonpersonalized narrative form can be observed in first- as well as in third-person narrators in no way proves that one opposition is more fundamental than the other. In the typology presented in this book both appear as fully equal constituent elements: person and mode.[15] Booth's negation of the distinction which the category person entails is obviously connected with two very pronounced tendencies in his *Rhetoric*. Booth's work exhibits a thoroughly understandable aversion to the simplified instructions for the use of first- and third-person forms which are to be found in manuals of creative writing as well as a perhaps less acceptable mistrust of any kind of systematic literary criticism,[16] a mistrust which until recently found much stronger expression in English than in German publications.

If there is a structural difference between first-person and so-called third-person narration, then it must be possible to define its place in a system of forms based on narrative theory. The discussion above of a passage from *The Catcher in the Rye* suggests the direction which such an investigation must take. Before proceeding with this argument, however, I would like to survey the preferences of a number of authors in this respect.

4.2 Some examples of authors' preferences

Some authors very clearly prefer one of the two narrative forms. Defoe, for example, prefers first-person narration, whereas Fielding favours authorial third-person narration. Presumably such preferences have not merely stylistic, but also structural reasons. Such reasons are clearly evident where authors, after careful consideration, have rewritten a novel or parts of it, changing from one form to the other. Jane Austen's third-person narrative *Sense and Sensibility* was first conceived in the first-person form of an epistolary novel; Gottfried Keller's *Green Henry* is a classic example of a transposition from the third-person to the first-person form, although this transposition was undertaken with hesitation and despite many misgivings; Kafka transcribed the first chapters of the novel *The Castle* from the original first-person version to a figural third-person form. There is evidence that many authors experience difficulties when having to choose between first and third person.

Joyce Cary reports the unsatisfying result of his transposition of a chapter of *A Prisoner of Grace* from the first to the third person.[17] Finally, there is the testimony of the author who made the deliberate choice of point of view the first commandment of narrative art, Henry James. He declared that the decision between first and third person repeatedly led him to examine thoroughly the peculiarities of these two forms of presentation. In the preface to his novel *The Ambassadors*, James writes that he had indeed considered using the first-person form in this novel, but that he had ultimately rejected it because of the 'looseness' and the 'terrible fluidity of self-revelation' which is inherent in it.[18] Strictly speaking, James is objecting here not only to first-person narration but also to the lack of formal sophistication often found with a more personalized style of telling, be it in the first- or third-person form. In his later phase as an author, James preferred the nonpersonalized form of the figural narrative situation to forms of personalized narration. In his case the decision against first-person narration is, therefore, also a decision in favour of a more impersonal way of narrating.

Many other authors beside James have racked their brains regarding the choice between the first- and third-person form, or else they have declared themselves emphatically for or against the former. I infer that this decision was for them not a question of stylistic decorum, but of the structure of the narrative. There is as yet no historical survey of the opposition of first- and third-person form from the standpoint of novelists; some quotations have already been made available by Richard Stang, Eberhard Lämmert and others.[19] In addition, the monographs dealing with first-person narration by Forstreuter, Romberg, Margit Henning and others may be consulted.[20]

The opposition between first- and third-person narration and the underlying opposition of the identity and non-identity of the realms of existence of the narrator and the fictional characters is still an area of immediate interest for contemporary authors. Several of them have found in this aspect of narration a broad field for innovations which are as ingenious as they are daring. In the English and American novels, the unusual first-person narratives by Beckett, *Molloy*, *Malone Dies*, and *The Unnamable*,[21] set a standard for such experiments. The most important works of this kind in the German novel were studied by P. F. Botheroyd.[22] Botheroyd analyzed three first-person novels whose significance is based to a large extent on the fact that their themes acquire their true definition only through the unusual use of first-person form: Günter Grass's *The Tin Drum* (*Die Blechtrommel*), Uwe Johnson's *The Third Book About Achim* (*Das dritte Buch über Achim*), and Max Frisch's *Mein Name sei Gantenbein*. Most of the other works of these three authors could also be cited as evidence that first-person narration occupies an exceptional position in contemporary fiction. In these first-person novels the structural assumptions behind the opposition of first and third person are foregrounded with such consistency that the first-person form can today already pass for a synonym of 'complex,' and 'difficult.' This is illustrated by Max Frisch's dictum: 'But how can estrangement be abstractly depicted as a concept, if not by means of a first person?'[23]

4.3 The filming of first- and third-person narratives

A comparison of stories or novels and the films based on them also yields very convincing arguments for the importance of the distinction between first- and third-person form. First-person narratives confront film directors with problems of transposition to the film medium that are entirely different from those of authorial third-person narratives. The motion-picture camera is capable of presenting spatial perspective much more sharply focused and with greater ease than the literary narrative; however, the camera is confronted with considerable difficulties in the detailed reproduction of the subjectivity of a fictional character as it emerges within a first-person narrative. Overcoming these difficulties almost always requires substantial changes and adaptations. For this reason Stanley Kubrick had Thackeray's first-person novel *Barry Lyndon* rewritten as an authorial third-person narrative for its filming. In the process the statement structure of the literary original is often handled rather arbitrarily, as, for example, when Barry's utterances in reference to himself are simply put into the mouth of an authorial voice-over commentary, that is, the commenting voice of a person not visible on the screen. The following example illustrates how the meaning of such a commentary can change. When the adventurer and soldier Barry has become weary of his liaison with the German Lischen, who had looked after him when he was wounded in battle, he tries to soothe his conscience with the following train of thought which is quite characteristic of his personality: 'A lady who sets her heart upon a lad in uniform must be prepared to change lovers pretty quickly, or her life will be but a sad one' (Chapter V). As Barry's thought is expressed in the film by the impersonal voice-over, it receives an entirely different significance than in the novel: Barry is exonerated of his cynicism and the utterance becomes the universally valid piece of practical wisdom of a disinterested observer. A similar method was employed in the filming of Ken Kesey's first-person novel *One Flew Over the Cuckoo's Nest*. Here again the first-person perspective was abandoned, resulting in a grave distortion of the novel's message. Most films or authorial third-person narratives, on the other hand, stay much closer to the literary original, as, for example, Ken Russell's film of D. H. Lawrence's *Women in Love*, Rainer Werner Fassbinder's film *Fontane: Effi Briest* or Eric Rohmer's film version of the Kleist novella *The Marquise of O–*. This last film illustrates how the director, in his endeavor to recreate the literary text as authentically as possible, counteracts the tendency towards immediacy in the film medium with the aid of narrative elements signaling mediacy. So, several times Rohmer fades in individual sentences from Kleist's narrative text into the film happening on the screen, a method which is also used successfully by Fassbinder in *Fontane: Effi Briest*. A hint at mediacy is attempted in a similar manner when the voice of a narrator can be heard, as voice-over, throughout a film. It is striking how frequently this narrative element has been employed recently. Thus the voice of a narrator is audible, as was already mentioned, in *Barry Lyndon* and in *Fontane: Effi Briest*. In the television film of Dostoevsky's *The Devils* (produced by German and Austrian national television) the first-person narrator is heard at exceptionally great length. This narrator himself, however, never appears in the film as the narrating self but always exclusively as the experiencing self, that is to say, as a character involved in the action. The director's efforts to allow the viewer to perceive the mediacy of narration in the film even go as far as to attribute to a first-person perspective several film scenes which are reported in the novel without being explicitly associated with the first-person narrator, for example, the duel between Stavrogin and Gaganov (Part II, Chapter III).[24] For this purpose the first-person narrator is made Gaganov's second in the film, whereas in the novel it is Drozdov. In the novel the first-person narrator is not present in person at the duel. This is also characteristic of many other scenes which the narrator portrays as if he himself had been an eyewitness to them.

The first-person narrator does not then narrate from his immediate recollection, rather, he allows the events to arise out of his imagination. Cases like these, in which the limits of first-person perspective are exceeded, can be observed relatively frequently in the novel of the nineteenth century. It is striking that the film refrains from making use of this licence of the first-person narrative situation in *The Devils*.

From the connections between novel and film which have been touched upon here it becomes apparent that analyses of films based on novels can be useful in elucidating specifically narrative peculiarities. The literary criticism of the 'Gutenberg era,' which according to McLuhan is now approaching its end,[25] will in the future have to concern itself to an increasing degree with the change which a literary text undergoes when it is rendered in an essentially nonverbal medium. Several general studies of the problematic nature of transposing literature into film are already available,[26] but the problem of transposing certain literary narrative structures and narrative situations into other media has not yet been sufficiently studied.

4.4 A new approach to the opposition person

The preceding considerations raise the question of whether the differences between first- and third-person narration can be explained by narrative theory. The attempt at founding this structural difference in narrative theory must proceed from the opposition of the identity and non-identity of the realms of the narrator and of the characters in a fictional narrative. The distinctive features of first-person narration on the one hand, and third-person narration on the other, derive from this opposition.

There have already been a number of attempts to formulate a theoretical foundation of this distinction.[27] Hamburger's *Logic of Literature* presents the most exhaustive critical support for a view that this opposition is an essential feature of the genre of prose fiction. She holds that a categorical boundary divides two fundamentally different types of narration from each other: 'epic fiction' is third-person narration produced by an impersonal 'narrative function,' and 'feigned reality statement' is the personal report of a first-person narrator. Almost all the phenomena of narration which Hamburger discovered or redefined in her *Logic of Literature* are located at this genre boundary – they are to be placed on one side or the other of the boundary, or else they undergo a change when crossing it. These phenomena include the meaning of the epic preterite (the past tense used in fiction), the function of the verbs of inner action, free indirect style, the realm of the personalized narrator and that of the impersonal narrative function, and so on. Because of the thorough and extensive discussion which Hamburger's theory has undergone in past years, it would be superfluous to deal with the questions she raised. Hamburger's line of reasoning cannot be accepted without qualification for the reasons indicated on p. 14ff. My most important objection concerns her attempt to eliminate the personalized narrator from the third-person form of epic fiction, in which, as she believes, only an impersonal narrative function is operative. Her theory is not fundamentally changed by the modification of this thesis through the concept of the 'fluctuation' of the narrative function introduced in the second German edition of *Logic*. According to Hamburger, there are not two narrators in different roles facing each other at the third- and first-person boundary of the novel, rather there is one impersonal narrative function, which usually cannot be associated with the notion of a personalized teller-character, and one first-person narrator who appears in person and of whose Here and Now in the narrative act the reader is made aware at all times. Hamburger thus concludes that genuine narration takes place exclusively in first-person narration: a personalized narrator reports what he experienced or observed at a previous point in time, or what he has learned about it. The epic fiction of third-person narration, on the other hand, is characterized by mimetic, impersonal presentation produced by the above mentioned narrative function. Accordingly the essential difference between third- and first-person narration lies in an opposition which can be expressed by the following terminological pairs: mimesis–diegesis, impersonal–personal narration, fiction–illusion of reality statement. As set forth above this opposition can claim a certain validity as a sort of deep structure of narration. On the level of surface structure, however, on which narrative phenomena are being analyzed and described in the present study, this opposition cannot be maintained for the important reason that a personalized narrator also appears in third-person narration, namely the authorial narrator. The criterion which Hamburger applies to all forms of third-person narration is valid only for the impersonal variants of the authorial narrative situation and for the figural narrative situation itself, in other words, for the distinction between personal and impersonal narration but not for the first-/third-person distinction.

In an article reviewing current narrative theory, Wolfgang Lockemann partially adopts the results of Hamburger's theory, but attempts a different line of reasoning on particular points.[28] In so doing he touches upon precisely those aspects which are important for my argument. Proceeding from the first sentences of Goethe's *Wilhelm Meister: The Years of Apprenticeship (Wilhelm Meisters Lehrjahre)*, Lockemann shows that a difference in the 'credibility' of a narrated statement exists for the reader, depending on whether this statement is made in the third-person form or in the first-person form. An additional, very essential difference between third- and first-person form is indeed being addressed here. The first-person narrator is by definition an 'unreliable narrator,' to employ Booth's terminology.[29] The unreliability of the first-person narrator is not, however, based on his personal qualities as a fictional figure, e.g., character, sincerity, love of truth, and so on, but on the ontological basis of the position of the first-person narrator in the world of the narrative. The presence of such a narrator in the world of fictional characters and his endowment with an individuality which is also physically determined leads to a limitation of his horizon of perception and knowledge. For this reason he can have only a subjective and hence only conditionally valid view of the narrated events. This conditional credibility alone does not suffice as a criterion, however, because some authorial third-person narrators – Lockemann overlooks this point[30] – are only conditionally credible, since they, too, are to be considered fictional characters created by the author and equipped with a certain individual personality. Only the unrestricted omniscient narrator would have to be excluded from this qualification of the narrator's role. For all practical purposes, however, there is no narrator who is omniscient throughout a novel. Almost every authorial narrator who at first presents himself as omniscient will sooner or later have to be subject to a limitation of his horizon of knowledge, or he will be temporarily deprived of the ability to make a final evaluation of a character or an event. This phenomenon can already be seen in Fielding's novels. Reliability is, therefore, a problem of the dramatized narrator in general, that is to say, of both the authorial narrator and the first-person narrator who reveal their personality.

The real difference between third- and first-person narration does not lie in this aspect of credibility or in the degree of certainty of the respective narrative form, although here, too, gradual differences between the two forms of narration become discernible.[31] The limited credibility of a third-person narrator is due to reasons essentially different from those involved in the limited credibility of a first-person narrator. These reasons point to the structurally most important feature distinguishing first- from third-person narration.

The main difference between a personalized first-person narrator and an authorial third-person narrator lies in the fact that the former belongs to the represented reality, the fictional world in which the characters live; the latter does not. The first-person narrator is distinguished from the authorial third-person narrator by his physical and existential presence in the fictional world. In other words, the first-person narrator is 'embodied' in the world of the characters.[32] The authorial third-person narrator may also say 'I' in reference to himself, but he is embodied neither inside nor outside the fictional world. Personal features can, of course, become visible in an authorial narrator, as well, that is why the criterion of credibility is applicable to him, too – but these personality features are not linked with the notion of his physical existence and corporeality. The situation is quite different in the case of the first-person narrator, in particular the first-person narrator of the 'classical,' i.e., the quasi-autobiographical novel. This first-person narrator is very concretely an embodied self, that is to say, his corporeality is part of his existence as an experiencing subject. The first-person narrator of Thomas Mann's *Confessions of Felix Krull, Confidence Man: The Early Years*, is unmistakably an embodied narrator of this kind. The physical condition of this narrating self is emphasized right at the beginning of the novel when the narrator complains that his great weariness interferes with the writing of his autobiography:

As I take up my pen at leisure and in complete retirement – in good health, furthermore, though tired, so tired that I shall only be able to proceed by short stages and with frequent pauses for rest – as I take up my pen, then, to commit my confessions to this patient paper in my own neat and attractive handwriting, I am assailed by a brief misgiving about the educational background I bring to an intellectual enterprise of this kind. But since everything I have to record derives from my own immediate experience, errors, and passions, and since I am therefore in complete command of my material, the doubt can apply only to my tact and propriety of expression, and in my view these are less the product of study than of natural talent and a good home environment.[33]

The weariness of this embodied narrator must be understood as an immediate consequence of the life-history of the protagonist who sets out to tell it himself. It signals an existential connection between the experience of the protagonist and the narrative process, between the experiencing and the narrating self.[34] In an authorial narrative a similar self-characterization of the narrator would remain an autobiographical flourish pointing to a vacuum. In Sterne's *Tristram Shandy*, the physical condition and the corporeality of the narrating self even become the central themes of the narrative. In this way *Tristram Shandy* could be described as an embodied narrator's attempt at the impossible task of writing a conventional novel under such a bodily burden.[35] Compared with *Tristram Shandy* and *Felix Krull*, the narrators of *Tom Jones* and Thomas Mann's *The Magic Mountain* remain unembodied, although they may say 'I' not less frequently than the above-mentioned first-person narrators, and their intellectual physiognomy may become clearly discernible to the reader. Here, then, lies the decisive difference between first- and third-person reference in narration. It is not the personality (first-person narrator) and the impersonality of the narrative process (narrative function) which is decisive, as Hamburger believes, but rather the degree of embodiment, of physical presence of the narrator who says 'I.' In the quasi-autobiographical first-person novel, this corporeality characterizes the experiencing as well as the narrating self. As the portrayal of the narrating self is reduced, the degree of the embodiment of the narrating self also decreases. In its place the embodiment of the experiencing self becomes all the more prominent.

4.5 The spatio-temporal deixis in first- and third-person narratives

The distinction made above between first- and third-person narrative extends to deeper levels of the structure of a narrative. This can be shown by examining the spatio-temporal deixis, that is the function of those words, mainly pronouns and adverbs, which help the reader to orient himself in the time and space of the fictional world in first- and third-person narratives. It can be illustrated by the sentence which was already used as an example by Karl Bühler and was then cited again by Hamburger in order to demonstrate the deictic peculiarity of the structure of fiction. Bühler used the example of a hero of a novel who is reported to be in Rome. After having communicated this information about the hero's whereabouts the narrator could continue with 'there' or 'here' to refer to the hero's place, depending on whether or not the narrator's point of view is to be transferred to the site of the action: ' "There" he trudged around the Forum the whole day, there . . . "Here" could be used just as well.'[36] Hamburger disagrees because an explanation like this presupposes a personalized narrator with his own spatio-temporal orientation. In the case of a fictional narrator (third-person narration), Hamburger argues, only the orientation system of the character(s) of the novel will be a decisive factor, but not that of the narrator or of the narrative function. But Hamburger's explanation is refuted when she uses the quoted example in order to demonstrate that ' "there" is nothing other than "here" referred to the fictive figure, the fictive I-Origo [the spatio-temporal orientation] of the person in the novel. This immediately becomes apparent when one combines a deictic temporal adverb with "there": "Today he trudged around there the whole day" is just as acceptable as "Today he trudged around here . . ." '[37] 'There,' a deictic adverb indicating distance, seems incompatible with 'today,' a deictic adverb indicating nearness or closeness in the context of an authorial third-person narrative. They are compatible, however, in the context of a first-person narrative: 'Today I trudged around there the whole day.' One reason for this fact is the corporeality of the first-person narrator, his physical presence at the site of the event to which the statement refers. This corporeal presence so emphatically determines the spatio-temporal orientation that an independent, autonomous system of orientation is established around this embodied 'I' and it is possible to combine distant and close deixis within this system of orientation. Because of his lack of corporeality, an authorial third-person narrator cannot readily establish a system of orientation that functions in a similarly autonomous way. He must, as it were, decide from sentence to sentence and clearly signal to the reader whether he would like to have his centre of orientation displaced and shifted to agree with the spatio-temporal frame of reference of a character of the novel, or whether it is to remain in the indefinite temporal and spatial distance suggested by the authorial narrative process. The narrative deixis functions differently again in connection with figural narrative situation. This difference will be discussed in connection with the opposition teller-reflector.[38]

4.6 The 'embodiment' of the narrator and the motivation of the act of narration

The contrast between an embodied narrator and a narrator without such bodily determination, that is to say, between a first-person narrator and an authorial third-person narrator, accounts for the most important difference in the motivation of the narrator to narrate. For an embodied narrator, this motivation is existential; it is directly connected with his practical experiences, with the joys and sorrows he has experienced, with his moods and needs. The act of narration can thus take on something compulsive, fateful, inevitable, as in the case of the first-person narrator of *The Catcher in the Rye*. The motivation to narrate can also originate, however, in the need for an organizing overview, in a search for meaning on the part of the matured, self-possessed 'I' who has outgrown the mistakes and confusions of his former life. Here, too, the motivation to narrate is in the end existentially determined by the narrator's existential situation, although a greater distance is involved, because in first-person narration the narrative process is always connected with the experience of the self of the narrator. The narrative process and the narrator's experience form an entity; in other words, the reader is constantly invited to keep in mind this existential unity of the experiencing self and the narrating self. Thus the consummation of the life of a first-person narrator is only attained with the completion of the narrative act. For example, the narrative act of the governess haunted by ghosts in Henry James's first-person narrative 'The Turn of the Screw' is the last act of the self-dramatization of this character and hence the direct continuation of the role which the governess plays in the story's plot.

For the third-person narrator, on the other hand, there is no existential compulsion to narrate. His motivation is literary–aesthetic rather than existential. The authorial narrator of *Tom Jones* or of *The Magic Mountain* can sympathize with the fate of his hero, he can feel affection for him or harbor antipathy toward him. In certain cases this attitude can also influence the narrative process (as a rhetoric of fiction in Booth's sense), but it does not motivate the narrator to narrate in an existential sense. From this fact it can further be deduced that a role change, perhaps from that of the omniscient Olympian to that of the invisible eye- and earwitness at the scene of the event or vice versa, is much easier to achieve for an authorial narrator than for an embodied first-person narrator, who is tied inextricably to a physical body which he cannot discard when it becomes inconvenient, a situation dramatized in the first-person narrators of Beckett's *Molloy* and *Malone Dies*.

Generally speaking, most of this escapes the reader's attention. He cannot, however, escape the very specific suggestive effect from the existential motivation of an embodied narrator. The innovations of modern authors in the realm of first-person narration even encourage an awareness on the part of the reader of this aspect of the narrative situation. Sterne has, of course, already led the way. *Tristram Shandy* provides a paradigm of the existential subjection of the first-person narrator by his corporeality:

No – I think, I said, I would write two volumes every year, provided the vile cough which then tormented me, and which to this hour I dread worse than the devil, would but give me leave.[39]

Max Frisch makes precisely this identity between the narrator and the experiencing subject the starting point of the search for identity of his first-person narrator. His novel *Mein Name sei Gantenbein* can also be read as an account of the process by which a 'book-I,' at first incorporeal, almost authorial, tests experimentally, as it were, which embodied narrator, Enderlin, Gantenbein or Svoboda, is best suited to fill his largely anonymous and abstract narratorial 'I' existence with that human substance which would ensure an existentially as well as aesthetically satisfying totality of being. In the narrative *Montauk* by the same author, both a non-embodied narrator and an embodied narrator are present and attempt to capture the elusive personality of the main character, who is designated by both the first- and the third-person pronouns.

4.7 Some consequences for interpretation

In some of his *Tales* Henry James exhibits a tendency to waver between the conventions of the first- and of the third-person form. This tendency is in contrast to his novels, in which he very consciously selects and consistently carries through the authorial or the figural third-person form. In the tale 'The Real Thing,' the main character is the first-person narrator of the story. He is a painter using models for a series of illustrations of novels. This first-person narrator reports his experience with a very distinguished-looking elderly couple who would like to be hired as models, apparently because of financial difficulties:

I liked them – they were so simple; and I had no objection to them if they would suit. But, somehow, with all their perfections I didn't easily believe in them. After all they were amateurs, and the ruling passion of my life was the detestation of the amateur. Combined with this was another perversity an innate preference for the represented subject over the real one: the defect of the real one was so apt to be a lack of presentation. I liked things that appeared; then one was sure.[40]

The reservations which the painter had about the couple who sought employment with him are relativized by the first-person form of the narrative in a way which would not be possible in a third-person form. First of all, the narrative distance plays a part here, that is to say, the temporal and psychological distance from which the narrating self now reports the considerations and feelings which the experiencing self had at the time. The past tense 'was' in 'the ruling passion of my life was the detestation of the amateur' and 'Combined with this was another perversity' signifies for the narrator, and therefore also for the reader, real past time and keeps the present time of the first-person narrator free from these views. This observation is corroborated by the uncommonly crass expression employed by the painter for one of the views which he has overcome: 'perversity.' In any case, the choice of this word must be credited to the narrating self, who thereby emphatically dissociates himself from his previous conception. From this the reader must conclude that the narratorial 'I' has undergone a change since the time of the reported events, resulting in a revision of his conception of life and art. All of this is of far-reaching significance for the interpretation of the narrative, especially of the painter's attitude toward the above-mentioned couple. The conclusion becomes clear only if the existential prerequisite of the narrative act, the corresponding change in the views of the first-person character as a human being and as an artist (to which references are found several times in the course of the narrative) is included in the interpretation of the tale. If this tale were written in the third-person form, the narrative distance would remain unmarked and insignificant, as is revealed by a short experiment in transposition. The past tense 'was' itself would not mean that these views had been abandoned. Only the differing views of the main character, namely of the painter, and those of an authorial narrator could be contrasted, and such a contrast would be significantly different in its implications from the confrontation of various views in the consciousness of *one* person.

Let us compare this passage from a first-person narrative with a similar passage from a third-person narrative by the same author. 'The Pupil' tells the story of a private tutor, Pemberton, and his pupil, Morgan, the sickly youngest child of an American family overshadowed by increasing economic difficulties, who just manage to survive as tourists in Florence, Venice, Nice and Paris. Pemberton, who never receives a fixed salary for his services, considers himself sufficiently compensated by the fascinating personality of his precocious and intelligent charge, with whom he explores Paris:

They learned to know their Paris, which was useful, for they came back another year for a longer stay, the general character of which in Pemberton's memory today mixes pitiably and confusedly with that of the first. He sees Morgan's shabby knickerbockers – the everlasting pair that didn't match his blouse and that as he grew longer could only grow faded. He remembers the particular holes in his three or four pair of coloured stockings.

Morgan was dear to his mother, but he never was better dressed than was absolutely necessary.[41]

The fact that Pemberton's later recollections of these days in Paris are unexpectedly mentioned in a third-person narration is of little relevance for the interpretation of the tale. The narrative distance here remains insignificant, although it is strongly emphasized by the change in tense from past to present. (The 'today' also denotes the narrative present of the authorial narrator.) The reason that the narrative distance is not significant lies in the third-person form of the narrative. The third-person form does not connect the narrative act with Pemberton's existential situation beyond the end of the story marked by Morgan's sudden death. Pemberton's later recollections of this episode, elected by the authorial narrator in a seemingly arbitrary way, are almost irrelevant for the narrative's meaning. If this passage is transposed into the form of a first-person narrative, then a significance is acquired by the statement that the first-person narrator now remembers – during the narrative process – the impression that Morgan's appearance made on him at that time. It is no longer an episode chosen at random, but receives a certain relevance by virtue of its preservation and selection in the memory of the first-person narrator.

Despite the artistic care with which James as a rule wrote his narratives, it is plausible that Pemberton's recollection is actually a remnant of an earlier stratum of composition, in which the narrative was still conceived in the first-person form with Pemberton as the first-person narrator. (Of the ten narratives written immediately before and after 'The Pupil,' it is striking that five are written in the first-person and five in the third-person form.[42]) This thesis is supported by the fact that the same phenomenon is also to be found in several other third-person narratives by James.

It is unusual in third-person narratives that a later recollection of an experience is anticipated, but it is generally common in first-person narratives. Compare the following passage from 'The Lesson of the Master':

He still, whenever he likes, has a vision of the room, the bright red sociable talkative room with the curtains that, by a stroke of successful audacity, had the note of vivid blue. He remembers where certain things stood, the particular book open on the table and the almost intense odour of the flowers placed, at the left, somewhere behind him.[43]

This narrative peculiarity can also be attributed to a tendency to neutralize the difference between first-person narration and authorial or figural third-person narration. By granting one of his characters the privilege of reminiscing from a point in time subsequent to the conclusion of the narrated events, an authorial narrator brings this character close to a first-person narrator. The privileged character regards individual episodes of his experience from a temporal distance corresponding to that of a first-person narrator. Bringing the time of the action up to the narrative present at the conclusion of the narrative also aims in the same direction. Here the narrative tense usually changes from past to present, a practice which is very common in earlier first-person as well as authorial third-person novels. At the end of 'The Lesson of the Master' the present tense employed in presenting the experience of the main character, the young novelist Paul Overt, refers to the same moment in time as the narrative present of the authorial narrator: 'Paul doesn't yet feel safe. I may say for him, however, that . . .'[44] The third-person narrative is brought closer to the first-person narrative by the technique of providing main characters of third-person narratives with that conditioning of their reminiscence typical of first-person narrators. The authorial narrator in such passages also approaches the world of the characters by allowing his narrative present to become simultaneous with the time in which the experience of the characters is concluded. There is apparently no analogue to this tendency in James's novels. An assimilation of an authorial narrative situation to a first-person narrative situation was very frequently undertaken by Victorian authors in a much more conspicuous form, for example, in the Pumpernickel episode in Thackeray's *Vanity Fair*. It will be dealt with more thoroughly at a later point.

In summary, the essence of the difference between first-person narration and third-person narration lies in the manner in which the narrator views the events of a story and in the kind of motivation for the selection of what is narrated. Everything that is narrated in the first-person form is somehow existentially relevant for the first-person narrator. For this existential relevance to the first-person narrator, there is no corresponding and similarly effective dimension of meaning in third-person narration other than the approaches mentioned above to first-person narration. The narrative motivation of an authorial narrator is literary–aesthetic, but never existential.

Until now, narrative theory has hardly paid attention to this aspect of the difference between first- and third-person narration. David Goldknopf's concept of the 'confessional increment,' of a kind of intensification of meaning resulting from the nature of the confessional form seems to come closest:

The 'confessional increment' means simply this: everything an I-narrator tells us has *a certain characterizing significance* over and above its data value, *by virtue of the fact that he is telling it to us*. This added significance may be minor, of course, depending on what he tells us. For example. 'He was born nineteen years ago in San Diego, California,' and 'I was born nineteen years ago in San Diego, California,' are almost equivalent, because there is nothing especially noteworthy about a person telling us when and where he was born. The meaning of both statements is largely confined to their factual content. But if the informant is a woman, and the age is forty, and the place has a slightly lurid connotation – for example, Las Vegas – the confessional increment begins to operate . . . Assume that an author tells us 'He was born nineteen years ago in San Diego, California. His mother was a whore.' An I-character giving us the same data becomes the *kind* of person who calls his mother a whore. And in our liberal age that becomes a much more important characterizing element than the lineage itself . . . this increment is the most valid reason for using an I-narrator.[45]

Goldknopf's concept of the 'confessional increment' essentially denotes that aspect of first-person narration for which I have coined the term embodied narrator: both concepts describe the existential conditioning of the first-person narrative act. Thus Goldknopf's thesis leads essentially to the same result as my considerations, although his argument runs in a direction opposite to mine. For Goldknopf, the narrative act determines the 'I'; for me, the 'I' determines the narrative act. In both cases, however, the inter-dependence of the narrating and the experiencing self is of decisive significance for the interpretation. The view of Goldknopf, who is both a narrative theorist and novelist, is all the more important as a corroboration of my thesis, as it was formulated expressly in opposition to Booth's view of the triviality of the difference between the first- and third-person form of narration.[46]

4.8 The alternation of first- and third-person pronominal reference

I would not like to be the I which experiences my story. (Max Frisch, *Mein Name sei Gantenbein*)

The *he* is an *I* kept at a distance. (Jacques Dubois and others, *Rhétorique générale*)

In many first-person novels the narrating self seems to resist its total identification with the experiencing self. An aversion to the disclosure of one's own past mistakes and confusion provides only a superficial explanation, although first-person narrators like to avail themselves of it, as, for example, W. Somerset Maugham in his *Cakes and Ale*: 'I wish now that I had not started to write this book in the first person singular . . . it is not so nice when you have to exhibit yourself as a plain damned fool.'[47] The actual cause of this resistance lies deeper and is connected with the embodiment of the experiencing self from which the narrating self, oriented toward the intellectual faculties of remembrance, imagination and cerebration, strives to distance himself. The narrating self is often reluctant to admit openly to this attempt at distance but it is nevertheless noticeable. The most pointed form which such an attempt can take is the variation in pronoun from 'I' to 'he' with reference to the earlier self of the first-person narrator. This corroborates the diagnosis by Dubois and his colleagues: 'The *he* is an *I* kept at a distance.' This tendency of the first-person narrator is also exposed in other ways. In *David Copperfield*, for example, the first-person reference is almost never abandoned, but the first-person narrator often presents his recollection of certain episodes and scenes from his earlier life in the present tense instead of in the usual narrative tense, the past. For this the designation 'historical present' is not quite appropriate, for only rarely in this novel is the present tense used to animate the development of a recollection by presenting it as if it were taking place at the moment.[48] This present tense frequently produces a kind of tableau-effect: the recollected scene is imagined as if it were a picture at some distance presented for quiet and reserved observation. This, too, results in an increase in distance: The 'I' on the tableau is nearly a 'he.' The most revealing passage from *David Copperfield* in this connection is the beginning of the forty-third chapter ('Another Retrospect'):

Once again, let me pause upon a memorable period of my life. Let me stand aside, to see the phantoms of those days go by me, accompanying the shadow of myself, in dim procession. Weeks, months, seasons, pass along. They seem little more than a summer day and a winter evening. Now, the Common where I walk with Dora is all in bloom, a field of bright gold; and now the unseen heather lies in mounds and bunches underneath a covering of snow. In a breath, the river that flows through our Sunday walks is sparkling in the summer sun, is ruffled by the winter wind, or thickened with drifting heaps of ice. Faster than ever river ran towards the sea, it flashes, darkens, and rolls away . . .

We have removed, from Buckingham Street, to a pleasant little cottage very near the one I looked at, when my enthusiasm first came on . . . What does this portend? My marriage? Yes!
   Yes! I am going to be married to Dora! . . .

Still I don't believe it. We have a delightful evening, and are supremely happy; but I don't believe it yet. I can't collect myself. I can't check off my happiness as it takes place. I feel in a misty and unsettled kind of state; as if I had got up very early in the morning a week or two ago, and had never been to bed since. I can't make out when yesterday was. I seem to have been carrying the licence about, in my pocket, many months.[49]

4.8.1 The alternation between first- and third-person pronominal reference in *Henry Esmond*

In the history of the English novel Thackeray's *Henry Esmond* (1852) provides the most interesting example of the consistent alternation of first- and third-person pronominal reference.[50] In this novel the change of pronominal reference occurs already in the transition from the book title to the chapter heading and from the chapter heading to the narrative text:

Book II
Contains Mr Esmond's Military Life, and other Matters Appertaining to the Esmond Family.

Chapter I

I am in Prison, and Visited but not Consoled There.

Those may imagine, who have seen death untimely strike down persons revered and beloved, and know how unavailing consolation is, what was Harry Esmond's anguish after being an actor in that ghastly midnight scene of blood and homicide. He could not, he felt, have faced his dear mistress, and told her that story.[51]

This state of affairs is quite complicated. Perhaps this is one reason why the change of pronominal reference in *Henry Esmond* has not yet been explained satisfactorily. Another reason, presumably, is that until now Thackeray criticism has been rather consistent in its assumption that Thackeray was not following any specific artistic intention in this experiment which is so striking to us today. From this point of view, a detailed analysis of this peculiarity did not seem necessary. Thus Geoffrey Tillotson, for example, writes of 'strange vacillations in *Esmond* between first and third person,'[52] but does not discuss them further. James Sutherland also fails to respond to this problem in his otherwise very interesting study of Thackeray.[53] John Loofbourow restricts himself to the important point that Thackeray's source for the first-person narrator's reference to himself in the third person must be sought in the contemporary literature of memoirs.[54] A further attempt to take the characteristic alternation of first- and third-person pronominal reference into account in the interpretation of this novel was not made until Wolfgang Iser.[55] Iser explains the transition from 'I' to 'he' as the endeavor of the author and his narrator to bring 'two things to the fore: first, the relative and temporary nature of the standpoints which conditioned earlier attitudes and events; second, the fact that in the meantime the faculty of conscious self-assessment must have developed considerably, since now it can view its own past with such detachment.'[56] This covers the main effect of the alternation of pronominal reference: the detachment of the first-person narrator from his own earlier experiences.[57] One aspect of this phenomenon has been completely ignored, however. The variation in the use of the pronouns not only occurs in reference to the experiencing self which appears as Harry, Henry Esmond, Mr Esmond, Captain and later Colonel Esmond, but also in reference to the narrating self. When the narrating 'I' is transformed into a 'he,' the narrator is assuming a role which dramatizes the contrast between the *vita activa* of Esmond the soldier with the *vita contemplativa* of Esmond the narrator. This technique often places the narrating self in an

101

ironic position. The distancing of the narrator from the experiencing self now extends also to the narrating self:

Seeing that my lord was bent upon pursuing this quarrel, and that no entreaties would draw him from it, Harry Esmond (then of a hotter and more impetuous nature than now, when care, and reflection, and grey hairs have calmed him) thought it was his duty, to stand by his kind generous patron . . .

Esmond's good-luck again attended him: he escaped without a hurt, although more than a third of his regiment was killed; had again the honour to be favourably mentioned in his commander's report; and was advanced to the rank of major. But of this action there is little need to speak, as it hath been related in every gazette, and talked of in every hamlet in this country. To return from it to the writer's private affairs, which here, in his old age, and at a distance he narrates for his children who come after him.[58]

It seems that the transposition of pronouns referring to the narrating self into the third person always takes place in connection with the transposition of pronouns referring to the experiencing self, almost as a continuation of it.

The change of pronominal reference which is more important in our context affects the experiencing self, not the narrating self. In regard to the 'I'/'he' alternation on the level of the experiencing self, the transition from 'I' to 'he' seems to be possible at any time. This is quite understandable, since a shift to a temporarily less intimate, more detached observation of one's own self belongs to the tradition of autobiography and memoirs. This deviation from the narrative norm of the first-person narrative cannot simply be retracted whenever desired, however. The return from 'he' to 'I' presupposes a certain degree of reflectorization of the narrative situation, and takes place most frequently when an inside view is offered of Esmond in a kind of figural narrative situation, perhaps the description of an observation, or an impression, or a detailed presentation of his thoughts and feelings. For example, the transition from 'he' to 'I' at the end of the thirteenth chapter of the second book, where Esmond's visit to his mother's grave is related, is preceded by a detailed description of the cemetery from Esmond's point of view as well as of the thoughts which the sight of the grave evokes in him. The same transition takes place in the scene in which Esmond, having returned to Castlewood after a long absence, finds himself alone for the first time with Lady Castlewood, his future wife. This decisive passage is preceded by an account of Esmond's memories and feelings during the sleepless

night. The next morning he is perusing family documents found in
the room adjoining his, when Lady Castlewood appears:

Next Esmond opened that long cupboard . . . There were a bundle of
papers here . . .

This was the paper, whereof my Lord had spoken, which Holt showed
him the very day he was arrested, and for an answer to which he would
come back in a week's time. I put these papers hastily into the crypt whence
I had taken them, being interrupted by a tapping of a light finger at the ring
of the chamber-door: 'twas my kind mistress, with her face full of love and
welcome. She, too, had passed the night wakefully, no doubt; but neither
asked the other how the hours had been spent. There are things we divine
without speaking, and know though they happen out of our sight. This fond
lady hath told me that she knew both days when I was wounded abroad.
Who shall say how far sympathy reaches, and how truly love can prophesy?
'I looked into your room' was all she said; 'the bed was vacant, the little old
bed! I knew I should find you here.' And tender and blushing faintly with a
benediction in her eyes, the gentle creature kissed him.[59]

The quotation begins with a third-person reference. Esmond's
thoughts and memories are reported in a manner which approaches
free indirect style and, therefore, a figural narrative situation: 'This
was the paper . . .' This figural inside view provides the prerequisite
for the return from third-person to first-person reference: 'I put
these papers . . .' But the unexpected return to third-person
reference in the last sentence, which again produces distance, is
especially striking: the 'I' literally takes refuge in the 'he' from the
onrush of his feelings. Esmond receives this late, first kiss from the
woman whom he has adored for such a long time not as 'I' but as
'he.' This return to the more detached third person does not take
place completely without warning, however. Before the quotation
in direct speech there appear statements which are identified as
belonging to the narrating self by their gnomic character and by the
present tense. The distancing actually takes place in two steps.
First, the narrating self frees itself from the experiencing self, then
the reference to the experiencing self is shifted to the third person to
achieve an even greater distance.[60]

The alternation of the pronominal references becomes even more
complex with the frequent use of 'we,' first for Esmond and his
companions, then for the experiencing self, and finally for the
narrator or the narrating self. A more detailed analysis of this
phenomenon would provide further important information about
the function of the opposition of first- and third-person narration in
general. It is clear, however, that the return of the reference from

'he' to 'I' is almost always preceded by a reflectorization of the narrative situation. This is especially important for my topic, because it anticipates a finding which will be substantiated later, namely, that the alternation of third- and first-person reference in connection with a teller-character (for instance in an authorial narrative situation) has a different function than in connection with a reflector-character (in a figural narrative situation).

The results of these deliberations about the variation of pronominal reference indicate that the change from 'I' to 'he' mainly occurs for the purpose of distancing the narrating self from the experiencing self. This change of reference can take place at almost any time within the context of a narrative, since this possibility is already inherent in the narrative distance between the narrating and experiencing self. The change from 'he' to 'I' that is to say, the return to the conventional personal reference of the first-person narrative, presupposes, on the other hand, a certain reflectorization of the narrative situation. Whether the change from 'I' to 'he' or from 'he' to 'I' is more significant and more conspicuous to the reader must still be examined in a more thorough analysis than has been possible here. Such analysis must also include the change of pronominal references in Thackeray's other novels, above all in *Pendennis* and *The Newcomes*.

The fact that criticism has shown relatively little interest in such questions until now is due in part to the widespread assumption that Thackeray had little interest in structural questions. Some critics base this assertion on the way in which the author revised *Henry Esmond*.[61] However, there is a difference between the change which Thackeray made in the course of writing and in the course of revision. The addition of the editor's apparatus beginning with the third book belongs to the later category while the alternation of first- and third-person pronominal reference, which was already included in the original design of the novel, belongs to the former. It is an essential part of the novel's structure that deserves close consideration.

4.8.2 The alternation of the first- and third-person pronominal reference in the modern novel: *Herzog, Montauk, Mein Name sei Gantenbein*

Alternation of pronominal reference has appeared with increasing frequency in the novels of the most diverse modern authors. The following list contains only some of the best-known English and

German novels or stories with alternation and is by no means complete: Joseph Conrad, *Under Western Eyes*; Robert Penn Warren, *All the King's Men*; Saul Bellow, *Herzog*; Margaret Drabble, *The Waterfall*; Kurt Vonnegut, Jr, *A Breakfast of Champions*; Günter Grass, *The Tin Drum*; and the novels of Max Frisch, in which up to *Montauk* one can recognize not only an increasing frequency of the phenomenon, but also an increasing complexity of meaning attached to it.[62] In *Mein Name sei Gantenbein* new first-person subjects originate from the narratorial 'I,' and then place the former 'I' at the distance of the third person. One could also say that the narratorial 'I' tries out various roles as an experiencing self: 'I am trying on stories like clothes.'[63] The availability of alternate first-person roles alone places the novel in the third-person category, even though the third person does not always establish itself grammatically. The power of controlling the fictional characters is a privilege which is reserved only for the authorial narrator. A first-person narrator is existentially dependent upon his embodied 'I.' A first-person narrator such as the 'I' of *Gantenbein*, who nevertheless claims this power of disposition, moves one step closer to the position of an authorial narrator. It is very revealing that the structural difference between first- and third-person narration is particularly prominent where changes of pronominal reference and authorial disposition over the fictional world are combined. Within certain limits it is possible for an authorial narrator to alter the fictional reality he is narrating. Victorian authorial narrators of serial novels occasionally spared a fictional character from his impending fate in response to readers' pleas by changing this fate at the last minute. A first-person narrator who attempts something similar jeopardizes the fictional basis of his own position. Since he himself is part of the fictional world, an embodied being in the world of the characters, any attempt to change the narrated reality is equivalent to ironizing the basis of his own existence. The paradox of this situation seems to stimulate modern authors who, like Vonnegut, prefer to go against the grain of the accepted practice of narration. The change of reference in the exclamation of the first-person narrator of *Slaughterhouse-Five* at the sight of one of the characters of the novel: 'That was I. That was me. That was the author of this book,'[64] can surely no longer be adequately described in terms of objectivization and distancing. Here the ultimate incompatibility of the narrative structure of first-person narration with that of third-person narration becomes the subject of the novel, a topic which is treated in an even more radically paradoxical fashion in Vonnegut's *A Breakfast of Champions*.

In dealing with the variation in pronominal reference in the modern novel one must distinguish between the aspects of content and form. With regard to content, this alternation is obviously connected with the psychology of the split personality. Psychologically speaking, ego awareness and the splitting of personality are problematic not only in pathology. The change from first- to third-person and vice versa can be found in the language of the child, especially in the development phase of 'Vorichlichkeit,' the state of mind of a child when it is not yet conscious of itself as an individual, but also in the socially or psychologically motivated role-playing of adults. The alternation of first- and third-person references of a patient to himself is a symptom of multiple personality in adults. It is highly probable that, as Botheroyd, too, suspects, the increase in the frequency of changes in pronominal reference in the modern novel is an expression of the growing identity problem of modern man.[65]

The formal aspect, which is of primary interest in our context, gains an additional topical interest from this background. Once again it becomes evident here that literature, as an aesthetic artifact, and reality are not always subject to the same laws. The change of first- and third-person reference in literature seems to be more significant in a narrative dealing with external events than in connection with the rendering of consciousness. In *Henry Esmond* this change is accomplished more easily in connection with the presentation of thoughts, observations, and so on, of the first-person character than elsewhere. In the rendering of consciousness (by means of a figural narrative situation or an interior monologue), the opposition first- and third-person generally loses all structural significance. This can be demonstrated by the fact that in such passages the pronominal reference can alternate constantly between 'he' and 'I' without any consequence for the meaning of such passages. In other words, the opposition first- and third-person is unmarked here. The peculiar lack of semantic significance of the variation of pronominal reference within the rendering of consciousness can also be observed today in novels which adhere fairly closely to the conventional narrative style. A revealing example is Bellow's *Herzog*, a novel in which the figural narrative situation predominates:

The telephone rang – five, eight, ten peals. Herzog looked at his watch. The time astonished him – nearly six o'clock. Where had the day gone? The phone went on ringing, drilling away at him. He didn't want to pick it up. But there were two children, after all – he *was* a father, and he must answer. He reached for the instrument, therefore, and heard Ramona – the cheerful voice of Ramona calling him to a life of pleasure but metaphysical, transcendent pleasure – . . .

Please, Ramona, Moses wanted to say, you're lovely, fragrant, sexual, good to touch – everything. But these lectures! For the love of God, Ramona, shut it up. But she went on. Herzog looked up at the ceiling. The spiders had the mouldings under intensive cultivation, like the banks of the Rhine. Instead of grapes, encapsulated bugs hung in clusters. I brought all this on myself by telling Ramona the story of my life – how I rose from humble origins to complete disaster. But a man who has made so many mistakes can't afford to ignore the corrections of his friends.[66]

The reason for the inconspicuousness with which third-person reference becomes first-person reference lies in the fact that the rendering of the content of consciousness here, as in many other modern novels, takes place in the absence of a personalized narrator: the bearer of consciousness himself functions as the reflector-character into whose thoughts, perceptions and feelings the reader seems to have direct insight. As soon as the 'he thought' of a personalized narrator fails to appear, the content of what has been thought can be formulated in the first as well as in the third person. The first person corresponds to the rendering of a spoken utterance in direct speech, the third person corresponds to indirect speech. The difference between direct and indirect quotation loses its significance, however, when no narrator is present to function as the mediator of the indirect quotation. In the rendering of consciousness, therefore, the distinction between 'direct and indirect presentation of thoughts' or 'first' and 'third person' with reference to the bearer of consciousness becomes irrelevant. Under these conditions the change from one category to the other is no longer noted by the reader.

This neutralization of the various forms of representation of the inner world can sometimes be observed even in an authorial narrative situation, though only on the condition that the authorial narrator restricts himself in such a passage to reporting thoughts and describing the inner states of a fictional character. The following passage from Lawrence's *Women in Love* reveals Gudrun's feelings for Gerald, who is sleeping next to her in a mountain inn somewhere in Tyrol:

'Oh, my dear, my dear, the game isn't worth even you. You are a fine thing really – why should you be used on such a poor show!'

Her heart was breaking with pity and grief for him. And at the same moment, a grimace came over her mouth, of mocking irony at her own unspoken tirade. Ah, what a farce it was! She thought of Parnell and Katherine O'Shea. Parnell! After all, who can take the nationalization of Ireland seriously? Who can take political Ireland really seriously, whatever it does? And who can take political England seriously? Who can? Who can care a straw, really, how the old patched-up Constitution is tinkered at any more? Who cares a button for our national ideas, any more than for our national bowler hat? Aha, it is all old hat, it is all old bowler hat!

That's all it is, Gerald, my young hero. At any rate, we'll spare ourselves the nausea of stirring the old broth any more. You be beautiful, my Gerald, and reckless. There *are* perfect moments. Wake up, Gerald, wake up, convince me of the perfect moments. Oh, convince me, I need it.[67]

Here the first-person form of interior or silent monologue (with and without quotation marks) alternates with the third-person form of free indirect style ('Ah, what a farce it was!') and of authorial reporting of thoughts ('She thought of Parnell'). The transition from past to present tense is almost as inconspicuous and unmarked as the change from first- to third-person pronominal reference. The past tense is the narrative tense of authorial reporting of thoughts and of free indirect style, the present tense that of interior monologue. The present also appears here in sentences which, in conformity with the context, are free indirect style rather than authorial reporting of thoughts: 'After all, who can take the nationalization of Ireland seriously?' In such sentences the use of the present tense imparts to the figural thought formulated in it a status similar to that of authorial commentary with its claim to general validity.[68] In Lawrence this 'gnomic present'[69] within free indirect style almost always appears where the political, moral or philosophical views of the authorial narrator or author coincide with those of a character in the novel.

In one of Max Frisch's later novels, *Montauk* (1975), the variation in first- and third-person pronominal reference seems to be used throughout as unmarked, a usage in a way characteristic of passages presenting consciousness. This usage produces a very peculiar tension between the presence of a personalized first-person narrator and the figural narrative situation with its third-person reference to the same person who is the narratorial 'I' of the first-person segments. This kind of variation manifests itself early in the novel. At first one kind of pronominal reference is maintained within one segment of the narrative; later variation becomes more and more frequent and seemingly arbitrary, until finally the shift can take place within one and the same sentence:

MAX, YOU ARE A FORTUNATE MAN
says Lynn, when once again, in order not to be silent for miles on end, he tells the story of how in 1963 I was given Marlene Dietrich's guest apartment.[70]

To all appearances, the author is striving for a deliberate foregrounding or estrangement of the norms which govern the use of the narrative element person. 'Estrangement' must be understood here in the original meaning with which Shklovsky introduced this concept.[71] A narrative with a personalized narrator traditionally employs either first- or third-person pronominal reference throughout a story. Here the reader's expectation, based essentially on experience with conventional narrative texts, remains conspicuously unfulfilled. Such estrangement makes the narrative text more difficult to comprehend, challenging the attentiveness of the reader. At the same time the central theme of the novel finds expression through narrative form: the difficulties of the main character in finding the distance to himself, that is, to his momentary experience and to his recollection of earlier experiences, which would permit a solution to his problem of identity:

Now, years later, I can see, but not recognize myself: she is in the Bircher Benner Clinic in Zurich, and he goes there to visit her.[72]

'I' and 'he' in this sentence refer to one and the same person. The author does not succeed, perhaps does not seriously try, to shift the 'I' for a period of time to that distance which would permit it to become a 'he' as in *Henry Esmond*. The impossibility of such a distancing becomes more and more obvious in the increasing confusion produced by the hectic variation in pronominal reference toward the end of the novel. This confusion is intensified by other narrative elements which also contribute to the estrangement of the narrative form, for example, the intermingling of forms of direct and indirect speech or direct and indirect presentation of thought within a sentence:

For example, *he says that I have* never in my life been inside a brothel.[73]

That question – whether one thinks of one's readers while writing – is asked at every university. *I, he thinks, have* never thought of my readers as barefooted, for instance.[74]

The statement from *Gantenbein* quoted above, 'I am trying on stories like clothes,' applies not only to the content of the stories, but also to the manner in which these stories are narrated. The 'simplistic narrative stance,'[75] by which the main character of the novel in *Montauk* first of all means the possibility of narrating without inventing a story, is revealed as an impossibility, also in the sense of narrative theory.

The structural significance of the opposition between first- and third-person narration in conjunction with the presence of a personalized narrator must, therefore, be taken into consideration in any systematic presentation of the narrative forms. Booth's ignoring this opposition as 'the most overworked distinction' in narrative theory proves to be a mistake.

The presentation of the problems of narrative theory which were raised by modern first-person narratives have only been sketched in this chapter and cannot be dealt with thoroughly within the scope of this study. The fact that this narrative form possesses a particular fascination not only for the critic, but also for the author is confirmed last but not least by Beckett's defensive gesture in the last of his first-person novels. Here the experiment with this narrative form is carried to an extreme: 'But enough of this cursed first person, it is really too red a herring. I'll get out of my depth if I'm not careful.'[76]

Some additional aspects of first-person narration will be introduced in connection with the description of the typological circle in Chapter 7.

5

THE OPPOSITION PERSPECTIVE: INTERNAL PERSPECTIVE–EXTERNAL PERSPECTIVE

No longer a figure that leans and looks out of a window, scanning a stretch of memory – that is not the image suggested by Henry James's book. It is rather as though the reader himself were at the window, and as though the window opened straight into the depths of Strether's conscious existence. The energy of his perception and discrimination is there seen at work.

(Percy Lubbock about *The Ambassadors* in *The Craft of Fiction*)

5.1 The relation of the opposition perspective to the opposition person

The opposition person and perspective have in common the problem of the point of view from which something is narrated or perceived. The difference between them lies in the consequences which follow from the choice of the point of view. The aspect to which person attracts attention is the identity or non-identity of the realm where the narrator and his point of view are located with that realm in which the characters are at home. This has implications which especially concern the existential basis and motivation of the narrative act. These implications are decisive for questions of the 'reliability' of that which has been narrated. The opposition perspective, on the other hand, involves the control of the process of apperception which the reader performs in order to obtain a concrete perceptual image of the fictional reality. In addition to this regulation of the perception of fictional reality and the spatio-temporal orientation of the reader in this world, the concept perspective also influences the choice of certain areas and events of the fictional world for presentation.

The opposition perspective distinguishes between internal and external perspective. Internal perspective prevails when the point of view from which the narrated world is perceived or represented is located in the main character or in the centre of events. Consequently internal perspective is found in the quasi-autobiographical

111

form of first-person narration, in the epistolary novel, in autonomous interior monologue and where the figural narrative situation predominates in a narrative.

External perspective prevails when the point of view from which the narrated world is perceived or represented is located outside the main character or at the periphery of events. Narrative texts with an authorial narrative situation and those with a peripheral first-person narrator (*The Way of All Flesh*, *Lord Jim*) belong here.[1]

As always, certain problems in classification arise at the points of transition. Conrad's *Lord Jim* with its peripheral first-person narrator Marlow has already crossed the borderline in the direction of external perspective, because Jim is clearly the main character of the novel. In *Heart of Darkness*, however, the first-person narrator Marlow can in some ways be regarded as the real main character. Being at the centre of events, he dominates the story to a greater degree than does Mr Kurtz. Accordingly internal perspective seems to prevail in our reading of *Heart of Darkness*. Similar problems arise at the point of transition from the authorial narrative situation with external perspective to the figural narrative situation with internal perspective. Passages which present an inside view, the thoughts and emotions of characters in free indirect style, can appear within the framework of an authorial narrative situation. The extended appearance of such passages can temporarily give rise to an internal perspective. Emma's recurrent musing in Jane Austen's *Emma* illustrates this phenomenon. The withdrawal of the authorial narrator and the simultaneous increase in the length of the dialogue scenes and of passages with scenic presentation in which the point of view seems to be located in the centre of events can also lead to internal perspective, as in Hemingway's 'The Killers.' Cases like these also depend upon the inclination of the individual reader. A reader can orient his image of the narrated events either according to an imaginary vantage point at the scene of the events, or from the voice of the authorial narrator which is still audible here. In the first case he imagines the fictional events from an internal perspective, in the second case from an external perspective.

More importantly, the opposition internal perspective–external perspective serves to describe how the reader's apperception of that which is narrated is regulated by means of the spatial and temporal categories of perception. Internal perspective exhibits a certain affinity with the perceptual category of space, and external perspective a certain affinity with that of time. Consequently perspectivization in a spatial sense becomes more important with internal perspective than with external perspective. The relations between persons and things in space and their observation or description from a fixed point of view gain in significance as data for the reader. Also, the limitation of the range of knowledge or experience of the teller- or reflector-character (limited point of view) gains in relevance and significance, as well. External perspective on the other hand, is more bound to narration as a temporal art, that is, the spatial relations between persons and things and the limitations of the narrator's range of knowledge are, as a rule, not thematic or remain subordinated to the 'and-then' scheme which dominates this narrative manner.

In other words, only in the case of internal perspective does perspectivization become semiotically significant. Spatial relations and the perceptual limitation of knowledge about the narrated world then gain in significance for the reader. On the other hand, aperspectivism frequently gains the upper hand in the case of external perspective as a consequence of its affinity to the temporal dimension of the story, the spatial relations of represented reality declining in significance. In this sense the contrast between perspectivism and aperspectivism is also included in the opposition internal perspective–external perspective.

The distinction between the point of view of the 'knower' and that of the 'sayer'[2] is another aspect of narrative involved in the question of perspective. This distinction seldom presents difficulties in connection with an internal perspective because it is applicable only to the quasi-autobiographical form of first-person narration. In this case it is equivalent to the distinction between the narrating self ('sayer') and the experiencing self ('knower'). It is often more difficult, however, to draw a line of demarcation between the 'knower' and the 'sayer' in a narrative dominated by external perspective. Aschenbach in Thomas Mann's *Death in Venice* is the 'knower' for the greater part of the representation of the external and internal world. His viewpoint does not always coincide with that of the 'sayer,' the authorial narrator, however. To be more precise, these two views diverge more and more in the course of the narrative, posing some very difficult problems for the interpreter.

Here the concept of 'focus' has to be introduced because it can, perhaps, provide a means of describing such phenomena more concretely. The focusing of a part of the represented reality directs the reader's attention to the thematically most important element of the narrative or of a part of the narrative. Therefore focusing can be defined as the foregrounding of a certain thematic aspect by means of narrative perspective. For example, the sharp focusing of the presentation of a room directs the reader's attention to the thematic relevance of the spatial relations between persons and things in this room. Shifting the greater part of presentation either to the narrating or to the experiencing self in a first-person narrative situation is also to be understood as focusing. Focusing is also evident in external perspective – perhaps in connection with an authorial narrative situation – if the attention of the reader is temporarily directed more to the narrative process itself than to the narrated events. Likewise, the episodic prominence of a minor character in a scene is a kind of focus. When an authorial narrator, making use of his privilege of omniscience, offers an inside view of only one character's thoughts and feelings, this technique is also a form of focusing. This kind of focusing is often used to regulate the reader's sympathies in regard to the characters. Finally, focus can also be observed in the rendering of consciousness. The focus of a reflector-character and by implication that of the reader can be directed chiefly either to the perception of events in the external world or to his own inner world. The focus of the rendering of the consciousness of Stephen Dedalus in the 'Proteus' episode of *Ulysses* is directed predominantly toward events in Stephen's mind, while the focus of the rendering of Leopold Bloom's consciousness in the 'Lestrygonians' episode of the same novel is directed predominantly toward events of the outer world, namely Bloom's perceptions on his walk through Dublin.[3]

The emphasis of this concept of focus differs somewhat from Genette's wider concept of focalization. Genette's focalization[4] coincides basically with the concept perspective developed above. Of the three kinds of focalization which Genette distinguishes, 'internal focalization' (Genette's example: James's *The Ambassadors* and *What Maisie Knew*) corresponds to internal perspective; the two other kinds of Genette's focalization are 'zero focalization' and 'external focalization.' Zero focalization implies omniscience on the part of an authorial narrator, while external focalization is illustrated by Hemingway's 'The Killers,' a story presented mainly in the scenic or dramatic mode.[5] The distinction between 'Who sees?' and 'Who speaks?' with Genette is not an aspect of focalization but of voice and mood.[6]

Two theories which dispute the necessity of a distinction between person and perspective with explicit reference to the original German version of *Narrative Situations* should also be discussed in this context. Lockemann denies the possibility of a separation of the two narrative aspects person and perspective. For him, as well as for Hamburger, the only fundamental distinction is that between 'third-person and first-person narration,' included here as the opposition person. In Lockemann's view authorial narrative situation and figural narrative situation are not distinctive narrative forms in spite of the difference in perspective. The former is characterized in my system by external perspective, the latter by the predominance of internal perspective.[7]

While Lockemann attempts to subordinate the opposition perspective to that of person, Leibfried attempts to subordinate the opposition person to that of perspective. The contrasting aim of these two theories is most clearly evident in their criticism of the figural narrative situation. Leibfried acknowledges the figural narrative situation merely as a variant of the first-person narrative situation, both exhibiting internal perspective, while Lockemann sees it as a variant of the authorial narrative situation, both being distinguished by third-person pronominal reference.[8] Strictly speaking, this divergence of views is not a contradiction of general principles but rather the logical result of different points of departure. Lockemann and Leibfried avail themselves of a point of departure which is based essentially on only one opposition, person in the case of Lockemann, perspective in the case of Leibfried. Their classification systems are, therefore, less exact in their defining functions than the triadic system presented here. No fundamental difficulties exist which would prevent reduction of the triadic system to the less differentiated systems of Lockemann and Leibfried. Such a revision would entail a significant limitation of the system's usefulness for interpretation, however.[9]

5.2 Perspective and the presentation of space

In *Laocoön* Gotthold Ephraim Lessing demonstrates that the real subject of literature, in particular narrative literature, is action.[10] As a temporal art its proper dimension is the succession of events. The vivid presentation of space, that is, the spatial juxtaposition of things in a narrative requires an additional effort, unnecessary in the narrative of successive actions, to overcome the narrative's inherent temporal emphasis.[11] While the temporal ordering of events is a necessary condition of the act of narration, perspectivization of a fictional space does not occur of its own accord – it requires an additional effort. Every genre of art, every medium can of course overcome its inherent tendency, but this always requires extra attention from both the producer and the recipient. In general literary perspectivization does not strive to achieve the visual sharpness of perspectivization in the graphic arts, since narrative perspectivization as a rule aims not at the discovery and presentation of the spatial interrelationship between objects but rather at the selection of the objects represented in terms of their semiotic importance and at the accentuation of meaning attached to particular objects. Narrated space, as Roman Ingarden has shown, is always a 'schematic structure' which is only partially determined. It contains many 'areas of indeterminacy'[12] which are blanks for the reader. Their realization or 'concretization' is left to a large extent to the reader's imagination. It is precisely in the case of the spatial perspectivization of a narrative scene that such indeterminate areas are very numerous, often posing the reader quite difficult questions of interpretation. Narrated space is frequently indeterminate just where film, a more spatially oriented medium than fiction, provides nearly total determinacy of the represented world. It would be wrong to regard this characteristic as a disadvantage of the literary medium; on the contrary, this generically determined property can even be seen as an advantage. John Fowles's experience with the filming of his novels led to an awareness of the advantage of the relative indeterminacy of narrated objects in comparison with their determinacy in film:

There are hundreds of things a novel can do that cinema can never do. The cinema can't describe the past very accurately, it can't digress, above all it can't exclude. This is the extraordinary thing in the cinema – you've got to have a certain chair, certain clothes, a certain decor. In a novel you can leave all that out. All you give is a bit of dialogue. It's this negative thing that cinema makers never realize. You don't have to 'set up' the whole screen. The delight of writing novels is what you can leave out on each page, in each sentence.[13]

Starting from Ingarden's theory of indeterminate areas in literature and its elaboration by Wolfgang Iser and some other German critics, narrative theory has recently begun to examine this topic further. In Russia Uspensky devoted his recent *Poetics of Composition* chiefly to a comparative study of perspectivization in literature and painting.[14] As a first result of these investigations, we state that a different norm is required to assess the inclusiveness in narrated space from that which can be applied to the presentation of space in a painting or film. This difference must be taken into account by the reader, for example, in deciding what significance can be attributed to the fact that a particular scene or setting is presented either in great detail or in a brief sketch. The importance of Hemingway's theory of omission for narration becomes evident only in the light of the genre-specific indeterminacy of the literary text.[15] The reader's willingness to put up with the schematic structure of the fictional world is probably connected to the fact that selection and reduction of data available is part of our everyday perceptual processes. Aldous Huxley discussed this aspect in *The Doors of Perception*.[16] More recently the psychology of perception has concerned itself with this problem. Robert E. Ornstein, among others, reaches the conclusion that our sensory organs must be treated not as windows open to the world, but rather as a system for data reduction which enables us to concentrate on those impressions and information important for biological and psychic survival.[17] Today we know some of the biological and psychological factors which control this data reduction in our perception of reality. But which criteria determine the selection of data in the course of the literary presentation of reality? This question will probably never be answered conclusively, since the laws governing the creative consciousness cannot be determined definitively. It is possible, however, to describe and analyze the results of the literary process of selection, or the fictional schematization of reality as it is revealed in the narrative text.[18]

5.2.1 Two models of spatial presentation in narration

Schematization and selection of the 'content' of fictional space is most conspicuous in descriptions of clearly delimited interiors which function as settings for fictional events. A first attempt at roughly sorting these spatial descriptions in fiction according to the degree of their perspectival schematization results in two kinds of descriptions: texts with distinctly perspectival spatial presentation and texts with aperspectival spatial presentation. Examples of strictly perspectival spatial presentation are found mainly in novels in which the narrator limits himself to an objective description of the setting of a scene. When such an approach is executed very strictly, it is usually designated as the 'camera eye'-technique. It can be found in Hemingway, Dos Passos, Christine Brooke-Rose, and of course in the *nouveau roman*. It is especially pronounced in Alain Robbe-Grillet's *Jealousy*. When a figural narrative situation prevails, the relatively strict perspectivization does not occur through an impersonal camera eye but rather through the consciousness of the reflector-character, such as Stephen in Joyce's *A Portrait of the Artist*. In the following quotation Stephen has been summoned by the headmaster of the Jesuit school he attends to discuss a very delicate subject, namely, the possibility of Stephen's entrance into the order. For this interview the headmaster has positioned himself in front of the window in such a way that Stephen can recognize only the outline of his figure, but not his facial expression. The perspectival fixation of the line Stephen–headmaster–window as a background contributes substantially to the thematic definition of this scene, which the reader perceives from Stephen's position within the room:

The director stood in the embrasure of the window, his back to the light, leaning an elbow on the brown crossblind, and, as he spoke and smiled, slowly dangling and looping the cord of the other blind. Stephen stood before him, following for a moment with his eyes the waning of the long summer daylight above the roofs or the slow deft movements of the priestly fingers. The priest's face was in total shadow, but the waning daylight from behind him touched the deeply grooved temples and the curves of the skull. Stephen followed also with his ears the accents and intervals of the priest's voice as he spoke gravely and cordially of indifferent themes, the vacation which had just ended, the colleges of the order abroad, the transference of masters. The grave and cordial voice went on easily with its tale and in the pauses Stephen felt bound to set it on again with respectful questions. He knew that the tale was a prelude and his mind waited for the sequel.[19]

The selection and the accentuation of certain details of the concrete inventory of the scene is intentional, as is the sharp perspectivization of the scene, the room, and the position of the characters in relation to each other. By means of the spatial alinement of the observer (Stephen) with the observed (Jesuit director) and with the bright window, the sharply-drawn outline of the skull of the Jesuit priest functions as an implicit commentary on the topic of abstinence in the life of the order: 'the waning daylight from behind him touched the deeply grooved temples and the curves of the skull.' The perspectivization also emphasizes the contrast between the darkness in front of the headmaster's face, which Stephen's eyes cannot penetrate, and the brightness outside the window, where a beautiful summer day is coming to an end. This contrast between the bright, cheerful world outside and the gloomy, serious mood in the priest's room is intensified at the end of the meeting. After having been shown out by the headmaster and leaving the house, Stephen sees a group of young people strolling through the streets, singing and stepping to the accompaniment of a concertina.[20] The sharp perspectivization of the scene in the headmaster's room from Stephen's point of view also results in the omission of details regarding the character's clothing and of the furnishing of the room. Since selection occurs here within the consciousness of the reflector-character Stephen, every detail which passes through this filter of consciousness gains in importance and relevance for his situation. In the filming of this same scene other details would most likely also appear in the picture, such as the furnishing in the room or the particular draping of the priest's cassock. This increased concrete definition of the scene in a film, however, makes it difficult for the viewer to select what is actually significant, unless the camera emphasizes the essential elements, for instance, by means of a close-up. In a literary narrative it is precisely the reduction and selection of details which effect their semiotic enhancement. The value of what has been selected increases even more when the choice of details is made by means of immediately experienced perspectivization, that is to say, through the perception of a reflector-character such as Stephen.

The process is very different when the room and the position of the characters in space are presented in interrelation. A comparison of the aperspectival presentation of the interview in the forty-fourth chapter of Dickens's *Bleak House* and Stephen's conversation with the director reveals significant differences. The first-person narrator of *Bleak House*, Esther Summerson, is called into the room of her guardian Jarndyce for a talk; immediately afterwards she receives a letter from him containing a proposal of marriage. In Esther's narration of this incident and of the subsequent meetings there is no hint of a perspectivization of the room and of the spatial relation of the two characters:

My guardian called me into his room next morning, and then I told him what had been left untold on the previous night. There was nothing to be done, he said, but to keep the secret . . .

On entering the breakfast-room next morning, I found my guardian just as usual; quite as frank, as open, and free. There being not the least constraint in his manner, there was none (or I think there was none) in mine. I was with him several times in the course of the morning, in and out, when there was no one there; and I thought it not unlikely that he might speak to me about the letter; but he did not say a word.[21]

This episode is not transmitted by a reflector-character as in *A Portrait of the Artist*, but by the first-person narrator, a teller-character. That is an important difference. Telling, the report of a narrator, has as a rule a certain affinity with aperspectivism, while showing, scenic and figural presentation through a reflector-character, has an affinity with perspectivism. A correspondence between the oppositions mode and perspective is quite evident here. The nature of temporal art comes to bear more strongly in narration when a teller-character is present and when external perspective dominates; on the other hand, it is weaker when a reflector-character and internal perspective are predominant.

Attempting to draw a sketch of a room described in fiction provides a quite reliable test for distinguishing perspectival and aperspectival spatial presentation. In a predominately aperspec-tival narrative, the interior of a room is never depicted in such a way that a graphic sketch can be made of it, even if the reader is given a more or less complete inventory of the objects in the room. The following quotation from Trollope's *Barchester Towers* is a charac-teristic example of the description of an interior in the Victorian novel. Two ecclesiastical dignitaries of Barchester, Dr Grantly and Mr Harding, make their first visit to Dr Proudie, the new bishop of Barchester, albeit somewhat reluctantly, because they are not entirely in agreement with the appointment:

His lordship was at home, and the two visitors were shown through the accustomed hall into the well-known room, where the good old bishop used to sit. The furniture had been bought at a valuation, and every chair and table, every bookshelf against the wall, and every square in the carpet, was as well known to each of them as their own bedrooms. Nevertheless they at once felt that they were strangers there. The furniture was for the most part the same, yet the place had been metamorphosed. A new sofa had been introduced, a horrid chintz affair, most unprelatical and almost irreligious: such a sofa as never yet stood in the study of any decent high church clergyman of the Church of England . . .

Our friends found Dr Proudie sitting on the old bishop's chair, looking very nice, in his new apron; they found too, Mr Slope standing on the hearth-rug, persuasive and eager, just as the archdeacon used to stand; but on the sofa they also found Mrs Proudie, an innovation for which a precedent might in vain be sought in all the annals of the Barchester bishopric![22]

This passage is particularly relevant, for here a room and its furnishings are placed at the focal point of the narrative. The changes which the new bishop and his wife have made in the reception room of the bishop's residence immediately catch the visitors' eyes. They find the new sofa – 'a horrid chintz affair' – particularly offensive. Not a single word is said about the location of this piece of furniture, however. The reader is given a rather complete inventory of the furnishings of the room, but no reference is made as to their arrangement. The concretization of this room in the reader's imagination is only possible insofar as the arrangement of the furniture in the room is perhaps assumed to conform to the floor plan of the typical Victorian reception room. The reader was apparently expected to be familiar with this floor plan, as are the two visitors who regard the parlor as 'the well-known room.' In any case, the spatial relations constitute an indeterminate area for the modern reader, since the narrated text itself contains no reference to this floor plan. Strictly speaking, the reader of this passage is not even called upon to orient himself in the room with respect to left, right, front, back, opposite, etc. This has far-reaching consequences for the kind of mental image he makes of the narrated space. He learns of a number of judgements regarding the taste and value of individual furnishing, but he arrives at no concrete impression, no experienced perception of the room itself. The individual pieces of furniture have a function similar to that of props on the stage. The bishop's throne is the place from which the bishop strives to rule the world of Barchester, and the sofa is the place from which Mrs Proudie strives to rule it. The attentive reader probably already anticipates conflicts between these two positions of power. Where does the chaplain, Mr Slope, fit into this contest of strength? He has taken up his position 'on the hearth-rug,' that is, at the fireplace. A modern writer would hardly neglect the opportunity to indicate the spatial relation of the bishop's chair, the sofa and the fireplace by means of a corresponding perspectivization, thereby making them semiotically significant. There are exceptions, but generally the aperspectivism of the Victorian novel excludes this level of implication.

The narrative situation of the quoted passage retains an authorial flavour, although the authorial narrator largely adopts the views of the visitors. External perspective and aperspectivism prevail. The aperspectivism of the quoted passage is not necessarily a consequence of the authorial narrative situation, however. A comparison with an equally authorial spatial description from Thomas Mann's *Buddenbrooks* supports this view:

Through a glass door opposite the window one looked out into the dimness of a pillared hall, while to the left of a person entering the room were the high, white folding doors leading to the dining room. Against the other wall, though, crackled . . . the stove.

Durche eine Glastür, den Fenstern gegenüber, blickte man in das Halbdunkel einer Säulenhalle hinaus, während sich linker Hand vom Eintretenden die hohe weiße Flügeltür zum Speisesaale befand. An der anderen Wand aber knisterte . . . der Ofen.[23]

In spite of the authorial narrative situation, a certain tendency toward perspectivization can be noted here: it seems as if the narrator shifts himself into the depicted setting. In this way the reader is also able to orient himself in the salon of the Buddenbrooks. With the aid of this passage, Hamburger tries to demonstrate how this orientation occurs. She believes that the real I-Origo of the reader is invoked, and he can then, 'with the aid of his own "tactile images," effect a mental picture of the spatial relationship of the room.'[24] This description is true only of a perspectival spatial presentation; in an aperspectival presentation the reader will not succeed in constructing a spatial image 'with the aid of his own "tactile images." ' The difference is revealed in a comparison of the passages quoted from *Barchester Towers* and *Buddenbrooks*. A transfer of the reader into the fictional reality, which Hamburger generally supposes to take place in third-person narration (epic fiction) is possible only when the spatial presentation takes place perspectivally. In the case of an aperspectival spatial presentation, the orientation within the room remains undetermined, and it will be undertaken by every reader on the basis of his individual imagination if at all.

5.3 Perspectivism–aperspectivism

The earlier novel exhibits a pronounced preference for an aperspectival narrative style. Almost all the important Victorians, Dickens, Thackeray, George Eliot and Trollope, as well as their contemporaries Balzac, Jean Paul Richter, Tolstoy, among others, narrate on the whole aperspectivally. A tendency toward perspectivism is first noticeable in the novels of Flaubert and Henry James, becoming the predominant stylistic trend in the twentieth-century novel. The causes of this increasing preference for the perspectival narrative style, evident since the end of the nineteenth century, are both literary and nonliterary. The literary causes can be found in the endeavors of Flaubert, Spielhagen, James and a few like-minded writers, to make the novel objective, impersonal, scenic.[25]

Perspectivism accommodates this intention inasmuch as it encourages the reader's illusion of being directly and vividly presented with fictional reality. Nonliterary causes should probably be sought in the impressionism of the late nineteenth century. The art theorist E. H. Gombrich shows that in the artistic as well as in the practical perception of the external world with its vast multiplicity of forms, an interaction occurs between the traditional patterns of perception and a correction which is constantly necessary, because of autoptic, that is individual visual experience. With the advent of impressionism, traditional patterns of perception decline more and more in importance and are supplanted by individual, subjective perceptions.[26] The reader of Trollope's *Barchester Towers* was probably still content with the imaginative pattern 'reception room in a manor house.' The post-impressionistic reader, on the other hand, expects a more detailed determination of the corresponding spatial image. This expectation has been reinforced not only by the graphic arts but also, after the turn of the century, by photography.

Perspectivism and aperspectivism should be understood as two historical stylistic trends which are of equal literary value. To keep this in mind is especially important in this connection, because the development of the novel in the course of the past hundred years has been affected decisively by the discovery of perspective as a dimension of literary presentation. As a result of this new emphasis, the perspectival narrative style has been granted a higher aesthetic value in the eyes of some literary critics. The creative potential of the novel has actually been expanded by perspectivism in a way which is unique in the entire history of the novel.[27] The historical development in this direction can hardly lessen the value of those great works written in the older, predominantly aperspectival narrative tradition, however. In the interpretation and evaluation of the individual novel one must note whether it is written in a more perspectival or more aperspectival style. The classification of a novel in terms of one of these styles reveals the extent to which the dimension of perspective can or must be included in critical interpretation.

In the previous discussion the term perspective and its derivatives have been used mainly in their spatial meaning or in their relation to the presentation of narrated space. For narrative literature, however, the figurative meaning of the term in the sense of view of a thing as it presents itself from the personal, subjective point of view of a novel-character or narrator is at least equally important. Perspectivization in this sense consequently means subjectivization. While narrative fiction appears to be at a certain disadvantage in regard to media such as painting, still photography, and film, it is superior in its potential for perspectivization in the sense of subjectivization. Compared to still photography and film, narrative is more diverse and more flexible in terms of perspectival subjectivization. Film, for example, can render a continuous first-person perspective only with difficulty. Similarly aperspectival presentation, when employed intentionally, becomes a privilege of the literary narrative, since the camera is forced to shoot exclusively in perspective. Against the background of the intentional aperspectivism in some modern novels (Burrough's *The Naked Lunch*, Barth's *Lost in the Funhouse*), it is clear why the aperspectivism of the older novel, considered for a time old-fashioned and primitive, seems to be gaining in topicality again. Moreover, both stylistic trends, perspectivism and aperspectivism, find their apologists in English novel criticism (as well as in German and French) as early as the 1920s, in English novel criticism, perspectivism is extolled in Lubbock's *The Craft of Fiction* (1921) and aperspectivism in E. M. Forster's reply to Lubbock in *Aspects of the Novel* (1927). Forster's oft quoted rejection of Lubbock's demand for perspectivization in the novel by means of a consistently executed point-of-view technique culminates in a spirited commitment to aperspectivism:

Now for the second device: the point of view from which the story may be told.

To some critics this is the fundamental device.

The whole intricate question of method, in the craft of fiction [says Mr Percy Lubbock], I take to be governed by the question of the *point of view* – the question of the relation in which the narrator stands to the story.

And his book *The Craft of Fiction* examines various points of view with genius and insight . . .

Those who follow him will lay a sure foundation for the aesthetics of fiction – a foundation which I cannot for a moment promise . . . for me the whole intricate question of method resolves itself not into formulae but into the power of the writer to bounce the reader into accepting what he says – a power which Mr Lubbock admits and admires, but locates at the edge of the problem instead of at the centre. I should put it plumb in the centre.[28]

Now that the perspectival demands of Henry James, Lubbock, and his followers, have made their impact on narrative criticism, it is possible to give deserved recognition to the other trend, aperspectivism, as a legitimate and equal alternative to perspectivism. This impartiality helps us develop a more helpful approach to the great novels of the nineteenth century. In English and American novel criticism, it is above all W. J. Harvey and Barbara Hardy (not to mention Booth) who have already taken pains to present authors of aperspectivally designed novels such as George Eliot, Meredith, Thomas Hardy, and D. H. Lawrence, as well as the great Russians of the nineteenth century in a more positive light.[29] Barbara Hardy writes in her introduction to *The Appropriate Form*:

I have tried to show that there is after all some sense in calling novels like *Middlemarch* and *Anna Karenina* large and loose, but that this largeness and looseness has a special advantage, allowing the novelist to report truthfully and fully the quality of the individual moment, the loose end, the doubt and contradiction and mutability. James was wrong to call such novels 'fluid puddings.'[30]

There is at the moment even a danger, especially in English and American novel criticism, that the pendulum could swing to the other extreme. As an example I could cite Scholes and Kellogg and their fundamental reservations about the perspectivism propagated by James.[31]

5.4 Internal perspective–external perspective

The choice of one of these two positions is generally determined in part by one's philosophy of life or one's ideology. This is stressed in most studies dealing with the problem of point of view, most emphatically, however, by Weimann, as was mentioned above.[32] More widely discussed has been Jean-Paul Sartre's statement that the presence of a personalized narrator in nineteenth-century fiction has had a conservative ideological influence on that fiction, glorifying the status quo of the political and social situation.[33] Lodge regards this problem from another standpoint, but he, too, ultimately postulates a close connection between narrative perspective and philosophy of life. Referring to the discussion of this question by Sartre, François Mauriac and Graham Greene, Lodge concludes that 'it is not difficult to establish a normative correlation between omniscient authorial narration and an explicitly Christian perspective on events; and, correspondingly, between limited narrators and a more secular, humanist perspective.'[34] The connections are probably still more complex and more difficult than Lodge suggests. The clarification of the narrative technique involved in perspectivization attempted here may be of use in throwing some light on these difficulties.[35]

The ideological and philosophical components of the opposition internal perspective–external perspective are thus connected, as Lodge indicates, with the limitations placed on the knowledge which the narrator possesses. Internal perspective necessarily results in a restriction of the kind and degree of knowledge (limited point of view) of the teller-character or the reflector-character. Omniscience always presupposes the external perspective of an Olympian authorial narrator. The latter has at his disposal unlimited insight into the thoughts and feelings of the characters. It is astonishing, though, that there are hardly any novels in which such omniscience is used throughout and for all characters, connections, causes, and so on. In the novels of Dickens and Thackeray, as well as in those of most other Victorians, for example, sections in which the authorial narrator reveals himself to be omniscient alternate with those in which he pretends to have only partial knowledge of the narrated events. This alternation of the degree of knowledge is generally accompanied by a parallel alternation of external and internal perspective. The recurring patterns of such alternation in a rather long story or in a novel can be quite significant in terms of ideological implications. A thorough study of this relationship has not yet been undertaken, however. Füger recently presented a contribution to the theoretical discussion of the basis of this question, the results of which will have to be taken into consideration in studies of this kind.[36]

The opposition perspective is a complex and many-sided phenomenon. From the profusion of related problems two will be examined in greater detail because of their general significance: the perspectival problem in the presentation of consciousness and the question of the demarcation between the narrator's commentaries and the view of the individual characters.

5.4.1 The presentation of consciousness

It is a genre-specific feature of narrative that the presentation of the consciousness of a fictional character can create the illusion of immediacy. In the words of Hamburger: '*Epic fiction is the sole epistemological instance where the I-originarity (or subjectivity) of a third-person* qua *third-person can be portrayed.*'[37]

Presentation of consciousness can, of course, be included in the first-person form of a narrative, too, at least to the same extent as in the third-person form which Hamburger calls epic fiction. The presentation of the thoughts, perceptions, feelings and the state of mind of the characters is within the domain of all narrative literature, but it is especially prominent in the novel. In this connection the generic characteristic of narrative plays a special role. Realistic presentation of consciousness seems to require the illusion of immediacy, that is, the apparent suspension of mediacy, more than does presentation of external events. The modern novel especially shows a very pronounced tendency to give the presentation of consciousness the semblance of immediacy, of the unedited and the spontaneous. This tendency explains why presentation of consciousness in the contemporary novel favours the use of the reflector-mode. Consequently, the presentation of internal experience is also a problem of narrative mode and will be included in the respective chapter. It is also connected with perspective, in the choice of the point of view of a narrative. The form of presentation of consciousness which corresponds to external perspective is the summary and analysis of internal experience provided by an authorial narrator. Authorial omniscience is a prerequisite of this technique. A peripheral first-person narrator, on the other hand, will have to motivate his knowledge of the thoughts of any character other than himself for the reader, perhaps by referring to appropriate communications and utterances of this person, or by drawing inferences about this person's inner world from his gestures and facial expressions and from reactions of the fictional character. When internal perspective predominates, such motivation is unnecessary. Interior monologue, free indirect style and figural narrative situation, that is, the forms of the reflector-mode and of internal perspective, suggest immediacy, that is, the illusion of direct insight into the character's thoughts.

Modern narrative literature has devoted more attention to the rendering of consciousness than any other aspect of represented reality and in doing so has developed a very differentiated collection of forms of presentation. For this reason the analysis of such techniques has also attracted the attention of numerous narrative critics. Dorrit Cohn's book *Transparent Minds: Narrative Modes for Presenting Consciousness in Fiction* is the most thorough study of this topic to date. It also deals in detail with the secondary literature in English, German and French on this topic. Cohn's study is especially important for the application of my theory, because she analyzes techniques employed in the rendering of consciousness which are compatible with third- and first-person forms of narration.[38]

Presentation of consciousness and inside view are effective means of controlling the reader's sympathy, because they can influence the reader subliminally in favour of a character in the story. The more a reader learns about the innermost motives for the behaviour of a character, the more inclined he tends to feel understanding, forbearance, tolerance, and so on, in respect to the conduct of this character.[39] This means of controlling sympathy probably has a stronger effect on the modern reader when it is elicited by the immediate presentation of consciousness rather than by authorial summary and analysis of the thoughts of a character. The question raised here cannot be decided on the basis of theory alone, to be sure, but would have to be clarified by psychological investigations of readers' reactions to these two techniques of inner world presentation. It is important that narrative criticism examine this area further.

If several characters in a novel at first appear to the reader to be equally important, an additional problem arises. The distribution of the presentation of inside views among the individual characters and their relative frequency for a certain character can result in a clear shift in the reader's sympathies to the character who is favoured by the presentation of inside views. In this way Gudrun is favoured over Ursula and Birkin, and even over Gerald, in the final part of *Women in Love*. This kind of subliminal wooing of the reader for Gudrun on the part of the narrator is all the more important because it compensates for the loss in sympathy resulting from Gudrun's behaviour toward her lover Gerald and the stranger Loercke. In order to be able to analyze the control of sympathy through the presentation of inside views in a longer novel, one must note which characters' thoughts and feelings are presented and whether one character is favoured quantitatively by the narrator. Margaret Drabble's triangle story *The Needle's Eye* illustrates this point. Until shortly before the end of the story the presentation of consciousness is limited to two of the three main characters, the wife estranged from her husband and her friend and legal advisor. Only once, and then only temporarily, does the narrator make known to the reader the husband's view of the circumstances, as reflected in his thoughts. This insight leads to a distinct change in the distribution of sympathy in favour of the husband.[40] One must not assume, however, that an author always consciously plans the distribution of inside views among his characters while writing a novel.[41] From a detailed analysis of the frequency and distribution of the presentation of inside views among the individual characters of a novel, conclusions can sometimes be drawn about the values and attitudes in an author's deeper layers of consciousness which are similar to those drawn from an analysis of imagery.[42]

A work in which such an analysis practically forces itself upon the critic is Jane Austen's novel *Sense and Sensibility* (1811), which deals with two dissimilar sisters. The title reflects the polar types of experience and behaviour characteristic of women at the end of the eighteenth century. 'Sense' is assigned to Elinor and 'sensibility' to her sister Marianne. Since it was very likely that Austen was expressing an unconscious personal conflict with the confrontation of the two sisters, it is revealing how unequally the presentation of inside views is distributed in this novel. The reader constantly receives insight into Elinor's thoughts and feelings (sense), but he is largely denied direct insight into Marianne's consciousness (sensibility). Such a strategy of presentation is all the more remarkable since it is precisely Marianne's mode of experience which represents a deviation from the norm of behaviour which was obligatory at that time for a woman in the social circles described. Austen's strategy of presentation even goes against the grain of the natural predisposition of the two sisters, whom Tony Tanner characterizes as follows: 'Marianne . . . "abhors all concealment," and Elinor . . . is willing to contain private feelings in the interest of preserving some order among the necessary social coverings.' It is not accidental that Tanner localizes the central problem of the novel in this issue: 'How much of the individual's inner world should be allowed to break out in the interest of personal vitality and psychic health; and how much should the external world be allowed to coerce and control that inner reality in the interest of maintaining a social structure which does provide meaningful spaces and definitions for the lives of its members?'[43] Austen's narrator strikingly enough intervenes personally more toward the conclusion than at the beginning and in the middle,[44] but fails to express an opinion explicitly on this central problem of the novel. On the other hand, Austen made her position regarding this question very clear by favouring Elinor over Marianne with the presentation of inner world. The thesis of such a partisanship could perhaps be put on a firmer foundation through textual criticism if the earlier version of the novel in epistolary form had been preserved. One may assume that the presentation of internal experience was more evenly divided between the two sisters in the epistolary form of the first version, provided that both Elinor and Marianne functioned as correspondents.[45] In any case, in Maria Edgeworth's *Letters of Julia and Caroline* (1795), which served Austen as the model for the story of the dissimilar sisters, both sisters are given the opportunity of expressing their thoughts and feelings. The particular strategy of presentation in regard to the presentation of inside views in *Sense and Sensibility* seems to have been chosen by Austen in opposition to the traditional form of the theme in contemporary literature, which increases the importance of this decision for the interpretation of the novel.[46]

5.4.2 Problems of demarcation between internal perspective and external perspective

The opposition internal perspective–external perspective calls our attention to a hermeneutic problem involving interpretation. When internal and external perspective are combined in the same work, it is usually difficult or even impossible for the reader to decide whether a certain passage exhibits the internal perspective of a fictional character or the external perspective of an authorial narrator. The reader's expectations and demands have changed very decisively in regard to the perspectival focus of presentation in the course of the last century. The historical dimension cannot be ignored, therefore, when considering this question. It is also no coincidence that the problem of demarcation became a subject of discussion at the beginning of this development, more than one hundred years ago. The debate created a sensation far beyond the realm of literature. In a lawsuit against Gustave Flaubert, the author of *Madame Bovary*, the public prosecutor contended among other things that a passage depicting Emma's thoughts after her first extramarital love affair amounted to a 'glorification of adultery.'[47] These thoughts are presented as part of Emma's consciousness. Flaubert's use of this technique enabled the defending counsel to refute the accusation directed against Flaubert with the explanation that the thoughts and phantasies are those of Emma and not those of the author. He employed the distinction between the views of a fictional character and the views of the novelist, or rather between internal and external perspective. Jauss formulates the situation as follows: '[the] censured sentences are not an objective observation of the narrator which the reader can believe, but a subjective opinion of the person whose feelings are characterized in this manner.' Jauss states that the artistic device employed by Flaubert for this purpose 'with virtuosity and with a consistent perspective' is free indirect style.[48] This is correct as a summary of the argument of the defense, but imprecise in terms of narrative theory. When a form of free indirect style is embedded in authorial narrative style, it usually combines both internal and external perspective. Roy Pascal has also defined it in this way in his book *The Dual Voice*. If Emma's thoughts appeared exclusively in free indirect style in the censured passage, the author or the narrator could not be completely exonerated from sharing the responsibility for the sentiments of these thoughts, because the author's or the narrator's implied presence would offer him the opportunity to dissociate himself from Emma's views. Nevertheless, the argument of the defense is pertinent, because free indirect style occurs here in the context of interior monologue or simulated direct speech,[49] which strengthens the internal perspective of the figural narrative situation in contrast to the mixture of internal and external perspective implied by the free indirect style. Emma looks at herself in the mirror:

But when she saw herself in the glass she wondered at her face. Never had her eyes been so large, so black, of so profound a depth. Something subtle about her being transfigured her. She repeated, 'I have a lover! a lover!' delighting at the idea as if a second puberty had come to her. *So at last she was to know those joys of love, that fever of happiness of which she had despaired! She was entering upon marvels where all would be passion, ecstasy, delirium.*

En s'apercevant dans la glace, elle s'étonna de son visage. Jamais elle n'avait eu les yeux si grands, si noirs, ni d'une telle profondeur. Quelque chose de subtil épandu sur sa personne la transfigurait. Elle se répétait: J'ai un amant! un amant! se délectant à cette idée comme à celle d'une autre puberté qui lui serait survenue. *Elle allait donc enfin posséder ces plaisirs de l'amour, cette fièvre de bonheur dont elle avait désespéré. Elle entrait dans quelque chose de merveilleux, où tout serait passion, extase, délire.*[50]

The determining factor is the impression of the immediate presentation of consciousness which is conveyed to the reader in this passage by a combination of several narrative techniques. These include the predominance of a figural narrative situation in the greater part of the novel, which limits the point of view to that of Emma. Where the narrative situation is authorial and the perspective external, one encounters passages which would have allowed the prosecutor to build a stronger case. In the fifth chapter of the third part, for example, the reader experiences through Emma's eyes one of her trips to the city, where her lover is waiting. The presentation is governed by internal perspective. The description of the appearance of the city as the carriage reaches the crest of a hill, however, displays external perspective. Here the unmistakable voice of an authorial narrator is heard, lending the description a poetic aura inappropriate to Emma, even in her emotionally excited anticipation of the meeting with Léon. In this poetic or imaginative intensification of the impression which the city makes on her, there is something which could perhaps be interpreted as authorial consent to Emma's conduct:

At last the brick houses began to follow one another more closely, the earth resounded beneath the wheels, the 'Hirondelle' glided between the gardens, where through an opening one saw statues, a periwinkle plant, clipped yews, and a swing.

Then on a sudden the town appeared. Sloping down like an amphi-theatre, and drowned in the fog, it widened out beyond the bridges confusedly. Then the open country spread away with a monotonous movement till it touched in the distance the vague line of the pale sky. Seen thus from above, the whole landscape looked immovable as a picture; the anchored ships were massed in one corner, the river curved round the foot of the green hills, and the isles, oblique in shape, lay on the water, like large motionless, black fishes. The factory chimneys belched forth immense brown fumes that were blown away at the top. One heard the rumbling of the foundries, together with the clear chimes of the churches that stood out in the midst. The leafless trees on the boulevards made violet thickets in the midst of the houses, and the roofs, all shining with the rain, threw back unequal reflections, according to the height of the quarters in which they were. Sometimes a gust of wind drove the clouds towards the Saint-Catherine hills, like aerial waves that broke silently against a cliff.

Enfin, les maisons de briques se rapprochaient, la terre résonnait sous les roues, l'*Hirondelle* glissait entre des jardins, où l'on apercevait, par une claire-voie, des statues, un vignot, des ifs taillés et une escarpolette. Puis, d'un seul coup d'œil, la ville apparaissait.

Descendant tout en amphithéâtre et noyée dans le brouillard, elle s'élargissait au delà des ponts, confusément. Le pleine campagne remontait ensuite d'un mouvement monotone, jusqu'à toucher au loin la base indécise du ciel pâle. Ainsi vu d'en haut, le paysage tout entier avait l'air immobile comme une peinture; les navires à l'ancre se tassaient dans un coin; le fleuve arrondissait sa courbe au pied des collines vertes, et les îles, de forme oblongue, semblaient sur l'eau de grands poissons noirs arrêtés. Les cheminées des usines poussaient d'immenses panaches bruns qui s'envolaient par le bout. On entendait le ronflement des fonderies avec le carillon clair des églises qui se dressaient dans la brume. Les arbres des boulevards, sans feuilles, faisaient des broussailles violettes au milieu des maisons, et les toits, tout reluisants de pluie, miroitaient inégalement, selon la hauteur des quartiers. Parfois un coup de vent emportait les nuages vers la côte Sainte-Catherine, comme des flots aériens qui se brisaient en silence contre une falaise.[51]

An author who condemns Emma's 'wrongdoing' in the manner demanded by the prosecutor in the historical trial would have put other notions and associations into the mouth of the authorial narrator. In a certain sense the transition of the presentation from internal perspective to external perspective contains a commentary by the author, although one which is barely perceptible. If one shared the prosecutor's moral indignation, this fact would provide more grounds for criticism on the basis of narrative theory than Emma's thoughts in front of the mirror. In the paragraph following the quoted passage, the authorial description of the sight of the city is directly connected to Emma's passionate expectation. Pascal, who also deals with this passage in his study of free indirect style, criticizes the transition from internal to external perspective and from figural to authorial perception in the portrayal of the journey, calling it an oversight of the author.[52] Such criticism presupposes a consistency in perspectivism which can hardly be expected in a novel of the mid-nineteenth century, particularly from *Madame Bovary*, one of the first novels with a predominantly figural narrative situation.

A little more than a hundred years after the case of *Madame Bovary*, an English court tried the case *Regina* v. *Penguin Books Limited*. The incriminated work was Lawrence's *Lady Chatterley's Lover* in its authentic, unexpurgated version. Lawrence's novel is a much more strongly aperspectival work than *Madame Bovary*. Not only do internal and external perspective alternate constantly, it is also very frequently impossible to distinguish between the views of the narrator, behind whom the author can be clearly perceived, and those of the two main characters, Lady Chatterley and Mellors. In the course of the trial, the defense and its imposing number of witnesses – almost all of them prominent figures in the field of literary criticism – could not, unlike Flaubert's attorney, refer to the fact that some of the passages incriminated by the prosecutor because of their obscenity reflect only the view or the experience of individual characters and not necessarily the author's view. This point proved very useful to the prosecution.[53] On the other hand, the prosecutor did not employ the most important argument which could have been introduced into the discussion about the literary rank of the novel as a qualifying factor, namely, the insufficient development of the main characters as independent fictional individuals. Here lies the real literary weakness of the novel: only very rarely does Lawrence attempt 'to disentangle his own prejudices and predispositions from those of his characters' through the person of his narrator.[54] Lawrence's narrative style in *Lady Chatterley's Lover* is primarily aimed at persuading his readers to accept as far as possible the sexual philosophy he proclaims, an undertaking which at that time was very risky and difficult. The difficulties which confronted the publication of the authentic text can be traced to a large extent to the fact that Lawrence chose an untimely form, namely, an authorial-aperspectival style, for the presentation of a topic which was so provocative. *Lady Chatterley's Lover* could have become an important modern novel if it had been written in a sharply figural perspective, perhaps employing the consistent presentation of Connie Chatterley's point of view. In that case, the form of the novel understood as the 'relativizing externalization of the content,' would have served the author as an artistic counterweight to the missionary one-sidedness of his own sexual ideology. In *Women in Love* Lawrence was much better able to channel the formal energy latent in the mediacy of narration to produce such a relativizing effect.

In contrast to Lawrence, Flaubert found a new way of viewing an old topic. This new technique involved perspectivization by means of a figural narrative situation. In Jauss's words, 'the novel was able to radicalize or to pose anew questions pertaining to conduct which made the initial cause of the indictment, the supposed lasciviousness, recede into the background during the trial.'[55] Lawrence's novel did ultimately receive the tolerance, if not the approval, of the court, but in this case the narrative form contributed only very marginally to the acquittal. The trial *Regina* v. *Penguin Books Limited* was not won by Lawrence, the author of the novel, but by Lawrence, the apostle and prophet of a new sexual code.

Even these brief remarks about the two lawsuits have perhaps demonstrated that the form of perspectivization in a novel can affect its thematic structure. In a novel with consistently internal perspective, the form of the narrative relativizes the 'validity' of the statement in a different way than in a novel with external perspective or with alternating perspectivization. The resulting problems of demarcation are also different. This point can be illustrated by an example intentionally chosen from a work which is not thematically compromising in any respect. In H. G. Wells's story 'The Country of the Blind,' Nunez, the involuntary intruder in the valley of the blind, considers himself far superior to the blind inhabitants of the valley because of his sight. The idea occurs to him to realize his superiority by subjugating the blind inhabitants of the valley. As he approaches the first blind men he encounters, the following thought goes through his mind:

All the old stories of the lost valley and the Country of the Blind had come back to his mind and through his thoughts ran this old proverb, as if it were a refrain –
  'In the Country of the Blind the One-eyed Man is King!'
  'In the Country of the Blind the One-eyed Man is King!'
And very civilly he gave them greeting.[56]

If 'very civilly' in the last sentence of the quotation is interpreted as authorial description, then those words describe the real state of affairs. Nunez's greeting, which is addressed to the inhabitants of the valley, is actually polite and sincere. If 'very civilly' still belongs to the internal perspective of the preceding sentences, however, then the accentuated politeness is a pretence, a trick to deceive the blind people regarding Nunez's real intentions. There is a similar demarcation problem in an important key passage at the end of the story. Nunez has succeeded in escaping from the valley of the blind. Exhausted, he is now resting on a ridge of the mountains surrounding the valley:

From where he rested the valley seemed as if it were in a pit and nearly a mile below. Already it was dim with haze and shadow, though the mountain summits around him were things of light and fire. The mountain summits around him were things of light and fire and the little detail of the rocks near at hand were drenched with subtle beauty – a vein of green mineral piercing the grey, the flash of crystal faces here and there, a minute, minutely beautiful orange lichen close beside his face. There were deep mysterious shadows in the gorge, blue deepening into purple, and purple into a luminous darkness, and overhead was the illimitable vastness of the sky. But he heeded these things no longer, but lay quite inactive there, smiling as if he were satisfied merely to have escaped from the valley of the Blind in .which he had thought to be King.
  The glow of the sunset passed, and the night came, and still he lay peacefully contented under the cold stars.[57]

Judging by the external circumstances, Nunez's escape was successful. Whether he can survive, and whether his regained freedom can be an adequate compensation for the renunciation of his love for the blind girl are questions central to the understanding of the story. Here the narrative gives no conclusive answer. The reason for the open conclusion must be sought in the kind of perspectivization the narrative exhibits. The beginning of the passage quoted provides an internal perspective from Nunez's point of view. This internal perspective blends into authorial external perspective with 'he heeded these things no longer.' Finally this authorial external perspective is underscored by the 'as if' comparison. At the same time, however, at this critical moment, insight into Nunez's thoughts is withheld from the reader. Thus it remains uncertain whether the shining of the 'cold stars' is still a perception experienced by Nunez, who is resting – a perception in the sense of an epiphany, similar to the conclusions in most stories of Joyce's *Dubliners* – or whether it is an authorial commentary on the irony of Nunez's fate. Nunez has indeed regained his personal freedom, but he is now deprived of life and the enjoyment of that freedom.

Problems of demarcation resulting from the perspectivization of the narrative can, therefore, raise important questions with regard to the interpretation of a story or a novel. The distinction between the two stylistic trends of perspectivism and aperspectivism, and between the two structural possibilities of internal and external perspective, provide a theoretical apparatus which can be used when attempting to solve similar problems of interpretation.

5.4.3 Subliminal perspectivization in Dickens

In the narrative literature of the nineteenth century the perspectival and aperspectival styles were generally not yet consciously differentiated. Flaubert's *Madame Bovary* was remarkably advanced in this respect. The English novel did not catch up with Flaubert until Henry James's later novels toward the end of the century. The problem of perspectivization had, of course, been a subject of discussion already before Flaubert and James. However, interest had centred on the first-person narrative (together with the epistolary and the diary novel), because of their tendency towards internal perspective. The difficulties that Thackeray, for example, experienced with his first-person life-history of the charming but morally reprehensible adventurer Barry Lyndon,[58] indicate that a sensitivity for the perspectivizing and relativizing possibilities of this narrative form was still hardly developed among the greater part of the Victorian reading public. Obviously it was still difficult for most Victorian readers to view the first-person internal perspective of the narrator Barry Lyndon with detachment. Thackeray was not sparing in providing indications of the limited ability of the narrator to present his situation objectively. In fact, hostile reception of the first-person novel by a portion of the contemporary public finally induced Thackeray to add some footnotes in the form of authorial commentary requesting the reader to view Barry's stories from a critical distance:[59]

The service about which Mr Barry here speaks has, and we suspect purposely, been described by him in very dubious terms.[60]

From these curious confessions, it would appear that Mr Lyndon maltreated his lady in every possible way.[61]

Readers who obliged an author to point with his authorial index finger to the moral weakness of his hero surely did not offer the author any incentive to employ more demanding techniques of perspectivization in a narrative. The Victorian reading public was, however, very heterogeneous, both socially and in regard to education. Consequently the presence of some readers capable of appreciating the beginnings of a more subtle, more indirect rendering of mediacy can be assumed. Again and again in Dickens, Thackeray, George Eliot and others, passages occur in which more-sophisticated forms of perspectivization are also employed. Such inchoate perspectivization, it is true, is mostly restricted to individual incidents or short sections of a novel, and provides episodic intensification rather than a consistent alinement of vision binding for the entire novel. Dickens comes closest to a consistent point-of-view technique when he makes a nonpersonalized narrator present an event as if he himself were present as an invisible witness.

The presentation of consciousness in the Victorian novel reveals a similar tendency. The point of view is sometimes confined to one fictional character, but never for very long. In Dickens it is mainly the characters destined to die on the open stage who are presented by means of a more detailed figural internal perspective.[62] One of the best known examples is the depiction of Paul Dombey's illness and his ultimate death in *Dombey and Son* (Chapters XIV and XVI). The opening scene in Dickens's last and unfinished novel *The Mystery of Edwin Drood* with its strictly internal perspective, is a special and very interesting case. One might be able to deduce from this perspectivization, particularly conspicuous at the beginning of the novel, that Dickens was experimenting with a new perspectival narrative style shortly before his death. It is supposed that he was influenced by Wilkie Collins's detective stories, in which the nature of the content necessitates a sharper perspectivization.

These observations about perspective in Victorian narrative

literature have proceeded from those forms of perspectivization characteristic of the modern perspectival novel. Works representative of the aperspectival stylistic trend defined at the beginning of this chapter also employ certain devices to control the reader's sympathies, which can, in a way, be traced back to perspectivizing narrative techniques. *A Christmas Carol* is a story which at first seems to be told entirely in the aperspectival style generally characteristic of Dickens. The conversion of the old miser, Ebenezer Scrooge, to the genuine Christmas spirit in Dickens's sense is effected by means of a series of visions of others' Christmas cheer. This story calls for a certain degree of perspectivization just because of its theme. In his imagination, the reader is expected to participate in the fun at Fezziwig's ball, in the festive contentment of the Cratchit family eating a Christmas goose and pudding, and in the merriment of Scrooge's nephew's family during a sociable game of forfeits. He is supposed to experience these events through the eyes of the old, misanthropic Scrooge. These are the impressions which penetrate Scrooge's emotional callousness. But here Dickens forgoes the internal perspective which would be more effective according to the theme. The point of view is not assigned to Scrooge but rather to an authorial narrator, who portrays these scenes of Christmas geniality with much gusto and the appropriate pathos. The reader is usually not reminded until the end of each Christmas vision that these visions are actually Scrooge's internal experience. Dickens was, in fact, just as interested in describing vividly the disarming joys of Christmas as an expression of his 'philosophie de Noël'[63] as he was in depicting Scrooge's conversion. The external perspective of the narrator and the prevailing aperspectivism are very much in keeping with the former intention.

If one considers the change of heart evoked in Scrooge to be the real theme of the story, the situation appears in a different light. The psychological motivation for Scrooge's introspection and conversion is very rudimentary. In the final analysis his conversion seems to be a miracle, similar to those which occur in a fairy tale. Behind the aperspectivism of the surface story of *A Christmas Carol* there are, nevertheless, the beginnings of perspectivization. This perspectivization is effective only subliminally. Parallel to Scrooge's conversion a process takes place in which the monster Ebenezer Scrooge becomes gradually reintegrated into a community of people who exhibit the spontaneousness and selflessness of the Christmas spirit. This process finds expression in an imperceptible shift of the point of view from which the joys of

Christmas are experienced from that of the authorial narrator to that of Scrooge.

In the first Christmas vision, the Ghost of Christmas Past presents the distribution of gifts for a large number of children. A somewhat older girl attracts the attention of the narrator. The authorial narrator keeps his admiration for this girl entirely to himself. This element is quite evident in the unusual accumulation of the personal pronoun in the first person singular. In his imagination the narrator mixes with the children who fall all over the older girl he admires – an erotic undertone is unmistakable – while they are playing a game and 'plunder' her like 'young brigands':

What would I not have given to be one of them! Though I never could have been so rude, no, no! I wouldn't for the wealth of all the world have crushed that braided hair, and torn it down; and for the precious little shoe, I wouldn't have plucked it off, God bless my soul! to save my life. As to measuring her waist in sport, as they did, bold young brood, I couldn't have done it; I should have expected my arm to have grown round it for a punishment, and never come straight again. And yet I should have dearly liked, I own, to have touched her lips; to have questioned her, that she might have opened them; to have looked upon the lashes of her downcast eyes, and never raised a blush; to have let loose waves of hair, an inch of which would be a keepsake beyond price: in short, I should have liked, I do confess, to have had the lightest licence of a child, and yet been man enough to know its value.[64]

Scrooge, whose conversion has scarcely begun, is not included in these thoughts and feelings. In the last chapter, on the other hand, when, after Scrooge has become a new man, a servant of his nephew opens the door for him at his Christmas visit, the reader learns directly, through a kind of free indirect style, or, if you like, incipient interior monologue, what thoughts the sight of the girl evokes in Scrooge:

'Is your master at home, my dear?' said Scrooge to the girl. Nice girl! Very.[65]

In the first scene, Scrooge would hardly have been capable of such an emotion. Now, however, since Scrooge has become more humane, the reader is given the opportunity of experiencing Scrooge's incidental but all the more human thoughts and feelings. This is especially obvious when the new Scrooge is moved to make the following, entirely unscrooge-like observation at the sight of the turkey, a truly splendid specimen of its species which he had ordered for the large family of his employee, Bob Cratchit:

'– Here's the Turkey. Hallo! Whoop! How are you! Merry Christmas!' It *was* a Turkey! He never could have stood upon his legs, that bird. He would have snapped 'em short off in a minute, like sticks of sealing-wax.[66]

The happiness which Scrooge's dinner visit at his nephew's family elicits is now described entirely from Scrooge's point of view:

'Why bless my soul!' cried Fred, 'who's that?'

'It's I. Your uncle Scrooge. I have come to dinner. Will you let me in, Fred?'

Let him in! It is a mercy he didn't shake his arm off. He was at home in five minutes. Nothing could be heartier. His niece looked just the same. So did Topper when *he* came. So did the plump sister, when *she* came. So did every one when *they* came. Wonderful party, wonderful games, wonderful unanimity, won-der-ful happiness![67]

Perspectivization is not only a matter of deliberate planning in the selection of the point of view, but can also take place in deeper levels of a narrative. In Dickens's *A Christmas Carol* perspectivization is a direct result of the altered attitude of the author and of his narrator toward the main character of the narrative. The gradual shifting of the centre of perception to the person of Scrooge is a direct consequence of the moral and emotional regeneration of this character in the course of the narrative. In contrast to narratives exhibiting a consistent point-of-view technique such a form of perspectivization has a more subliminal rather than a conscious effect on the reader. In fact, this kind of subliminal perspectivization is probably so effective precisely because the reader is not aware of it.

6

THE OPPOSITION MODE: TELLER-CHARACTER– REFLECTOR-CHARACTER[1]

The teller of a story is primarily, none the less, the listener to it, the reader of it, too.

(Henry James, Preface to *The Princess Casamassima*)

A beautiful infatuation this, always, I think, the intensity of the creative effort to get into the skin of the creature.

(James, Preface to *The American*)

The opposition mode is one of the three supporting pillars in the triadic system of narrative situations and is, therefore, closely related to the other two oppositions. The analysis of the opposition person already revealed that the semiotic significance of the change from third- to first-person reference depends on whether this change takes place in the domain of a teller-character or of a reflector-character. When consciousness is presented by means of a reflector-character, this change in reference is practically unmarked. Consequently it remains probably unnoticed by the majority of readers. The analysis of the opposition perspective also disclosed a connection with the opposition mode. There evidently exists a close correspondence between internal perspective and the mode dominated by a reflector-character, on the one hand, and between external perspective and the mode dominated by a teller-character, on the other. These relations and their structure are clarified by the diagram of the typological circle.

The opposition mode embraces the following two manifestations of mediacy, the generic characteristic of narration: overt mediacy of narration and that covert or dissimulated mediacy which produces the illusion of immediacy in the reader. During narration the pendulum constantly swings back and forth between these two poles. There are only a few works – as a rule, shorter ones – whose structure is not affected by this oscillation. There are a large number of works, however, in which the narrative mode is oriented in the direction of one of the two poles, in spite of the oscillation. In these works, the opposition mode is a distinctive feature of the narrative situation.

The distinction between two narrative modes, between an indirect one and a seemingly direct, that is, an immediate, scenic or imitative one, is one of the oldest discoveries of narrative theory. It forms the conceptual nucleus of Plato's contrast between diegesis and mimesis,[2] which was adopted and developed in classical and post-classical rhetoric.[3] The distinction between these two narrative modes was given a new lease of life in the course of the discussion of objectivity among critics interested in the theory of the novel at the end of the nineteenth century. Otto Ludwig's distinction between 'true' (*eigentliche*) and 'scenic' (*szenische*) narration[4] forms the basis for the terms suggested in *Narrative Situations*, namely 'reportorial narration' (*berichtende Erzählung*) and 'scenic presentation' (*szenische Darstellung*), which seems to have generally been accepted in German narrative criticism.[5] In English and American narrative criticism, the terms 'simple narration' and 'scenic presentation' or 'scene' (Lubbock), or 'telling' and 'showing' (Friedman), are also here to stay.[6] Anderegg's distinction between a 'reporting model' and a 'narrating model' has recently provided this opposition with a basis in communication theory.[7] More informative from the point of view of terminology are Anderegg's designations for the kinds of texts associated with these models: 'Ich-Du-Texte,' the narratorial 'I' addressing the 'you' of the reader, and 'Er-Texte,' where only third-person pronominal reference to a reflector-character occurs. These terms must be regarded as synonyms for the familiar terms first- and third-person narrative, as Anderegg himself points out.[8] Essentially they denote that contrast in narrative mode which is expressed in my theory by the opposition mode.

It is quite conceivable that a certain connection exists between the basic forms of narration included in the opposition mode and the basic attitudes or the ways of experiencing reality and art as defined in the oppositions 'abstraction' and 'empathy' by Wilhelm Worringer or 'conceptualism' and 'impressionism' by E. H. Gombrich.[9] The concepts reportorial narration or telling, abstraction and conceptualism have in common an oblique mode of perception and expression, which includes the aspects of compressed report, summarizing abstraction and conceptualization. The concepts scenic presentation or showing, empathy and impressionism refer to a direct mode which includes the aspects of scenic presentation of the event *in actu*, concretization of the idea, and immediacy of the impression. These correspondences are mentioned only to demonstrate that the opposition to be discussed here represents a concept whose relevance is not limited to the domain of narrative theory. In the present context the two differentiated basic forms must first of all be understood as different conceptions of the mediacy of all narration: personalization and impersonalization of the narrative process. Impersonalization attempts to awake in the reader the impression of the immediacy of the narrative presentation of an event and with it the illusion that that which is narrated is to be perceived, so to speak, *in actu*. The apparent paradox encountered here, the immediacy of the mediate, is also acknowledged by Anderegg, when he writes that in the 'Er-Text' 'communication institutes its own prerequisite by denying its own existence.'[10] It is perhaps especially revealing that precisely that pole of the opposition of the two basic forms of narration which is occupied by mimesis or scenic presentation resists simple definition, while the pole occupied by diegesis or reportorial narration hardly presents any difficulties. The definition of scenic presentation is problematic primarily because of the approximation of the dramatic process which this phenomenon involves. In discussing scenic presentation in a narrative, one must differentiate between narrative and non-narrative sections of the text, as explained in an earlier chapter.[11] Dialogues of characters without introductory verbs of the type 'he said,' etc., and without explanatory authorial 'stage directions' are non-narrative parts of the text, and as such are actually dramatic foreign bodies in a narrative. Strictly speaking, they must, therefore, be excluded from the concept scenic presentation. Scenic presentation as a narrative form always includes a certain amount of dialogue accompanied by introductory verbs, authorial 'stage directions' and at least some report of the action, even if extremely condensed. Such narrative utterances, reduced to impersonal formulas, do not, as a rule, destroy the reader's illusion that he is experiencing the narrated event directly, *in actu*, as it were. The illusion of immediacy, which arises here because the narrator does not make an appearance, has led to the use of the term scenic presentation also to designate those non-dialogue parts of novels, especially modern ones, in which the action is presented as it is reflected in the consciousness of a fictional character. We must, therefore, keep in mind that scenic presentation comprises two different phenomena capable of evoking the illusion of immediacy, namely, the scene with extensive dialogue and brief impersonal allusions to the context and the accompanying action, as well as the reflection of the fictional events in the consciousness of a fictional character. Scenic presentation in the first sense can occur in first-person narrative situation as well as in authorial narrative situation, when the narrator withdraws and the course of events is placed in the foreground. Scenic presentation as a reflection of the events in the consciousness of a fictional character, on the other hand, is the domain of the figural narrative situation.[12]

The confusing and in part contradictory terminological diversity in this area results especially from the difficulty of distinguishing the phenomena reportorial narration or telling from scenic presentation or showing. For this reason the opposition mode will be first described not in terms of the process of narrative transmission, but in terms of the agent of transmission, who generally can be identified more easily and more clearly. The opposition mode consequently refers to the contrast between transmission by a teller-character and transmission by a reflector-character, or between teller and reflector, for short.

A *teller-character* narrates, records, informs, writes letters, includes documents, cites reliable informants, refers to his own narration, addresses the reader, comments on that which has been narrated, and so on. This teller-character prevailed almost unchecked in the earlier novel: Cid Hamete Benengeli, Grimmelshausen's Simplicius, Robinson Crusoe, Clarissa Harlowe, Tristram Shandy, Goethe's Werther, the teller of *Tom Jones*, of Wieland's *Agathon*, of *Wilhelm Meister*, of *Vanity Fair*, David Copperfield, Heinrich Lee, Marcel, and many others up to Marlow,[13] Serenus Zeitblom in Thomas Mann's *Doctor Faustus*, Felix Krull and to the 'book-I' of *Mein Name sei Gantenbein* are teller-characters. By contrast, a reflector-character reflects, that is, he mirrors events of the outer world in his consciousness, perceives, feels, registers, but always silently, because he never 'narrates,' that is, he does not verbalize his perceptions, thoughts and feelings in an attempt to communicate them. The reader seems to find out directly, by direct insight into the consciousness of the reflector-character, about the events and reactions which are mirrored in this consciousness. In the contemporary novel the reflector-character has become a serious rival of the time-tested teller-character. Reflector-characters today exhibit just as extensive a diversity as that of the teller-characters of the great tradition: the two Emmas (Jane Austen's *Emma* and Flaubert's *Madame Bovary*) already have little in common aside from the accessibility of their inner world. The fact that Lambert Strether (*The Ambassadors*), Stephen Dedalus (*A Portrait of the Artist*), Arthur Schnitzler's Leutnant Gustl, Hermann Broch's Virgil (*Death of Virgil*), Josef K. and K. (*The Trial*, *The Castle*), Leopold and Molly Bloom (*Ulysses*), Mrs Ramsay (*To the Lighthouse*), Malone (*Malone Dies*) are all reflector-characters suggests the diversity of this role.[14]

The two lists of illustrative examples indicate that the function of the teller-character is common to authorial narrators of almost all kinds, as well as to the first-person narrators in whom the narrating self is clearly discernible. On the other hand, first-person narrators who are actualized only as an experiencing self, and who therefore restrict themselves to the reflection of experiences not overtly communicated, are reflector-characters. To these we must add all figural media, who represent the largest proportion of reflector-characters. While the concepts reflector-character and teller-character comprise phenomena of the first as well as of the third person, the concept 'figural narrative situation' is applicable only to the third-person form. This distinction is incorporated in the diagram of the typological circle, in which first- and also third-person forms are found on that half of the circle where the teller-character pole is located, as well as on that other half where the reflector-character pole is located. The figural narrative situation, on the other hand, is limited to that segment of the typological circle in the vicinity of the reflector pole, which lies in the domain of the third-person form.

Between those areas on the typological circle which are clearly dominated by one pole or the other, there are transitional zones on the third-person as well as on the first-person side where those narrative works may be located in which it is ambiguous whether the process of transmission is determined by a teller-character or a reflector-character. By and large the narratives in question consist primarily of dialogue with extremely brief reports of action and an occasional short rendering of consciousness. Hemingway's stories, such as 'The Killers' (third-person form) and 'Fifty Grand' (first-person form), approach this text model very closely. An unstable equilibrium between the teller- and the reflector-moment prevails in them. A single sentence clearly spoken by a teller-character – perhaps an authorial commentary, or, conversely, a longer passage attributing a perception exclusively to a character as reflector-character, or including the first-person narrator's thoughts as if in an interior monologue – would upset this equilibrium and would suggest the presence of either a teller-character or a reflector-character for the narrative as a whole. It is characteristic of Hemingway's stories of this type that the short and generally not very numerous narrative passages which interrupt the lengthy dialogues exhibit no features which are either distinctly authorial or figural. Demarcation problems occur here, too, quite frequently. For instance, it is occasionally unclear whether a certain description is intended as the perception of a reflector-character, that is, of a fictional character, or as part of the authorial report of a teller-character. In this respect, the reading of Hemingway's works demands careful attention. This subtlety is surely one reason for the diverse interpretations of many of Hemingway's stories.

6.1 Teller-characters, reflector-characters and transitional forms

If you think . . . that anything like a romance is preparing for you, dear reader, you never were more mistaken. Do you expect passion, and stimulus, and melodrama? Calm your expectations; reduce them to a lowly standard. Something real, cool and solid lies before you; something unromantic as Monday morning. (Charlotte Brontë, beginning of *Shirley*)

Mrs Dalloway said she would buy the flowers herself.
   For Lucy had her work cut out for her. The doors would be taken off their hinges; Rumpelmayer's men were coming. And then, thought Clarissa Dalloway, what a morning – fresh as if issued to children on a beach.
   What a lark! What a plunge! (Virginia Woolf, beginning of *Mrs Dalloway*)

The introductory discussion of the opposition mode revealed some characteristic features of teller-characters and of reflector-characters. The distribution of these features between the two depends primarily on their association with the narrative modes of reportorial narration or telling by means of a teller-character, and scenic presentation or showing by means of a reflector-character. The processes of transmission and reception differ according to whether they are governed by a teller-character or a reflector-character. A teller-character always functions as a 'transmitter,' that is, he narrates as if he were transmitting a piece of news or a message to a 'receiver,' the reader. Communication proceeds differently with a reflector-character. Since he does not narrate, he cannot function as a transmitter in the above sense. In this case the mediacy of presentation is characteristically obscured by the reader's illusion that he is witnessing the action directly – he feels he is perceiving it through the eyes and mind of the reflector-character. These differences between the two processes of communication have consequences for the interpretation of a narrative text, in that the narrative assumes varying degrees of credibility or validity depending on whether it is conveyed by a teller-character or by a reflector-character. Friedman already alluded to one reason for this phenomenon in his point-of-view theory. In telling, the account is explicit, generalized and purportedly complete; in showing, the account is implicit, specific and conspicuously incomplete, because it focuses not on the whole but on a part.[15] This difference can be expressed more concretely. The epistemological difference between a story which is communicated by a teller-character and one which is presented by a reflector-character lies mainly in the fact that the teller-character is always aware that he is narrating, while the reflector-character has no such awareness at all. Teller-characters such as Moll Flanders, Tristram Shandy, David Copperfield, Ishmael, Heinrich Lee, Felix Krull, Stiller, Siggi Jepsen (in Siegfried Lenz's *The German Lesson* (*Deutschstunde*)) and the authorial tellers of *Tom Jones*, Jean Paul Richter's *Siebenkäs*, *Père Goriot*, *Vanity Fair* and *Buddenbrooks* not only treat the narrative process thematically while narrating, but also continually reveal their awareness of the fact that they are in the presence of an audience, their readers. This obliges them to find a narrative strategy[16] or rhetoric appropriate to the audience as well as to their story. Every kind of strategic or rhetorical treatment of the story changes it, shifts accents of meaning, influences the selection of details, the arrangement of the parts and necessitates a net of cross references between that which has already been narrated and that which is still to come. These implications are not to be found when the story is presented by a reflector-character. Reflector-characters such as Emma Bovary, Lambert Strether, Stephen Dedalus, and Josef K. are never aware that their experiences, perceptions and feelings are the subject of a process of communication. The quality of their experience is not influenced by this process, and the validity or credibility of what is presented is not affected. This point does not mean, of course, that the author does not apply strategy or rhetoric in constructing the narrative. This strategy is not part of the transmission process (the surface structure), but rather of the process of production (the genetic deep structure).

In addition to the clear-cut, so to speak typical cases of this opposition, there are also numerous ambiguous, atypical cases which cannot readily be assigned to one pole or the other. Such hybrid forms are to be found on the third-person side of the typological circle at the transition from the authorial narrative situation to the figural narrative situation. The narrative situation of these works is marked by the coexistence of an authorial teller-character and a figural reflector-character. This coexistence usually presents itself within the narrative profile as a sequence: a section in which authorial narration prevails is followed by one in which figural narration is predominant. A very typical example of such a transition occurs in Chapter XXII of Jane Austen's *Emma* at the beginning of which the voice of an authorial narrator is distinctly heard:

Human nature is so well disposed towards those who are in interesting situations, that a young person, who either marries or dies, is sure of being kindly spoken of.
   A week had not passed since Miss Hawkins's name was first mentioned in Highbury, before she was, by some means or other, discovered to have every recommendation of person and mind; to be handsome, elegant, highly accomplished, and perfectly amiable: and when Mr Elton himself arrived to triumph in his happy prospects, and circulate the fame of her merits, there was very little more for him to do, than to tell her Christian name, and say whose music she principally played.[17]

After about a page of this reportorial narration in the teller-mode Emma takes over as reflector-character. The transition from the teller-mode to the reflector-mode is smooth, eased by the appearance of inconspicuous free indirect speech:

During this present short stay, Emma had barely seen him; but just enough to feel that the first meeting was over, and to give her the impression of his not being improved by the mixture of pique and pretension, now spread over his air. She was, in fact, beginning very much to wonder that she had ever thought him pleasing at all; and his sight was so inseparably connected with some very disagreeable feelings, that except in a moral light, as a penance, a lesson, a source of profitable humiliation to her own mind, she would have been thankful to be assured of never seeing him again. She wished him very well; but he gave her pain, and his welfare twenty miles off would administer most satisfaction.
   The pain of his continued residence in Highbury, however, must certainly be lessened by his marriage. Many vain solicitudes would be prevented – many awkwardnesses smoothed by it. A Mrs Elton would be an excuse for any change of intercourse; former intimacy might sink without remark. It would be almost beginning their life of civility again.[18]

Many of the modern novelists proceed similarly. In Muriel Spark's *The Prime of Miss Jean Brodie*, for instance, unmistakably reportorial narration of an authorial teller is closely followed by the figural presentation of the thoughts and perceptions of the reflector-character Sandy Stranger.[19] There is also a special case in which a teller-character approaches the role of a reflector-character. This technique will be discussed separately in the section 'Reflector-ization of the teller-character' (6.4). Scenic presentation consisting of passages of dialogue with brief impersonal authorial report similar to stage directions usually occupies a neutral position between the two poles of this opposition. A sort of unstable equilibrium obtains which can tip toward the pole of the teller-character or to that of the reflector-character when definite signs of one of the two modes appear.

Narratives on the first-person side of the typological circle which exhibit both a teller-character and a reflector-character are somewhat more problematic. Transitions in this area of the circle do not involve a shift from one person (the teller-character) to the other (the reflector-character), but simply a change in the role of the narratorial 'I' from that of the teller to that of the reflector. Such changes often occur in very subtle, gradual ways sometimes difficult to define. The more the narrating self of a first-person character withdraws, exposing the experiencing self directly, the closer this first-person character moves to the function of a reflector-character. This shift can best be observed when an author changes the narrative situation during the revision of a text to suppress the manifestation of the narrating self and bring the experiencing self into the foreground. Joyce revised 'The Sisters,' the first story in the *Dubliners*, in this way:

That evening my aunt visited the house of mourning and took me with her. It was an oppressive summer evening of faded gold. (Early version)

In the evening my aunt took me with her to visit the house of mourning. It was after sunset; but the window-panes of the houses that looked to the west reflected the tawny gold of a great bank of clouds. (Final version)[20]

In the revision of the text, the narratorial 'I' is moved closer to the position of a reflector-character by the transformation of the time-phrase 'That evening' to 'In the evening,' and by the replacement of a general, distanced, and evaluative description ('an oppressive summer evening of faded gold') with a more detailed account of what strikes the reader as the perception of an impressionable onlooker.[21]

A first-person character such as Molly Bloom, whose thoughts are rendered exclusively in the form of interior monologue, is no longer a teller-character but rather a reflector-character. The conditions which affect the interpretation of passages in the reflector-mode are also valid for interior monologue.[22] The situation is not always so clear, however. The first-person characters in Beckett's novels *Molloy*, *Malone Dies* and *The Unnamable*, for example, oscillate between the role of a teller-character and that of a reflector-character in a way which expresses their split personality structure. But when Beckett's first-person character in *The Unnamable* asks questions like 'shall I ever be able to go silent . . . what if I went silent?',[23] he identifies himself unequivocally, at least at this point, as a teller-character, since only a teller can feel threatened by such a fate. Being silent is not a problem for a reflector-character. On the contrary, the silence of a reflector-character can even be seen as an existential intensification of his experience. Reflector-characters frequently communicate most when they silently abandon themselves either to their perceptions of the outside world or to the reflections which these perceptions evoke.

6.1.1 The credibility of teller-characters

Never trust the artist, trust the tale. (D. H. Lawrence, 'The Spirit of Place,' in *Studies in Classic American Literature*)

The differences between teller-characters and reflector-characters allow us to draw some conclusions about their relative reliability as mediators of the fictional events. This problem has already been encountered in the description of the opposition person. To what extent can a narrator be considered a trustworthy and reliable reporter? In the chapter dealing with differences between first- and third-person narrators it was established that because of their existential motivation for narrating, first-person narrators are more likely to exhibit a certain bias in the rendering of their story than are authorial narrators. Generalizing and simplifying the situation somewhat, it could be said that all first-person narrators are biased by definition and are thus more or less unreliable as narrators. It is true that the veracity of an authorial narrator, too, insofar as he manifests himself as a personalized narrator, is not entirely above suspicion. As a rule, however, he can claim credibility as long as the reader receives no explicit indication that scepticism is appropriate.

In such a case the question of credibility is closely connected with the narrator's characteristic qualities – there are as many sincere and insincere or at least prejudiced and biased narrators as there are people with these traits – and also with the particular motivation of the narrative act. Comparing teller-characters with reflector-characters reveals another dimension of this problem: as narrators, teller-characters are constrained to present their story in such a way that it appeals to the listener or reader or at least awakens his interest. This demand involves a certain narrative strategy, as was noted above: the elements of suspense must be distributed with care, and the reader's sympathy for and criticism of the individual characters must be guided. For this reason the narrator inserts his interpretations and evaluations in the form of commentaries or employs a rhetoric which operates more subliminally, or gives several characters the privilege of communicating their innermost thoughts to the reader, while others are deprived of the privilege. In short, the presence of a teller-character can hardly avoid changing the content of the story, in the course of its composition and narrative presentation, whether the author is conscious of this effect or not. An interpretation must take changes and intrusions of this kind into consideration, because they are important elements of form which enable the author to modify the content of a story in a manner characteristic of narrative literature as the genre of mediacy.

Thanks to Booth's *The Rhetoric of Fiction*, the concept of the reliability of the narrator has become a permanent feature of both narrative theory and text explication. Booth distinguishes between reliable and unreliable narrators, defining them as follows: 'For lack of better terms, I have called a narrator *reliable* when he speaks for or acts in accordance with the norms of the work (which is to say, the implied author's norms), *unreliable* when he does not.'[24] I cannot deal here with the very difficult problem of whether such norms can be identified in a narrative work in the first place; a large part of Booth's book is devoted to just this problem. It is especially interesting in this context that Booth applies the criterion of reliability indiscriminately to both teller-characters and reflector-characters. This lumping together results from the fact that he does not as a rule distinguish between tellers and reflectors but rather includes both agents in his use of the term narrator.[25] Several other English and American narrative theorists and critics use the term narrator in this broad sense as well, as did Henry James in his Prefaces. Booth also follows James's example when he occasionally distinguishes between 'narrators,' 'reflectors' or 'third-person reflectors' and 'disguised narrators'[26] in the sense of the opposition teller-character–reflector-character, but he later discards this distinction and seems to consider it more a question of stylistic shading than of narrative mode. Following a description of Stephen's function as the reflector-character in *A Portrait of the Artist as a Young Man*, Booth writes: 'We should remind ourselves that any sustained inside view, of whatever depth, temporarily turns the character whose mind is shown into a narrator; inside views are thus subject to variations . . . in the degree of unreliability. Generally speaking, the deeper our plunge, the more unreliability we will accept without loss of sympathy.'[27] In keeping with this thesis, Booth then terms reflector-characters – Jane Austen's Emma, Strether, Paul Morel, Pinkie (*Brighton Rock*) and Gregor Samsa (from Kafka's *The Metamorphosis* (*Die Verwandlung. Erzählung*)) – 'narrators' and discusses their reliability. By obliterating the distinction between teller-characters and reflector-characters, and by applying the criterion of reliability indiscriminately to both categories, Booth obscures the structural significance of this distinction and reduces the usefulness of the otherwise very important criterion of reliability. The criterion of reliability could be more useful if limited to teller-characters, that is, to characters who make verbal statements and thereby address or intend to address an audience (Anderegg's 'Ich–Du-Texte'). Only in this case can the question of reliability, credibility and veracity be a meaningful topic of interpretation. The criterion of reliability, especially if it also means credibility, is irrelevant in regard to reflector-characters. One must instead distinguish here between lucid and torpid reflectors, depending on whether the respective reflector-character has keen or dim perception, between reflector-characters who tend to intellectualize their experiences, such as those found especially in the novels and stories of James, and reflector-characters who are intellectually dull, often only vegetating. The latter type is frequently found in the modern novel, for example the Bundren family in Faulkner's *As I Lay Dying* and an even more extreme case, the idiot Benjy in *The Sound and the Fury*.

6.2 The opposition mode and 'areas of indeterminacy' (Roman Ingarden)

The work of Roman Ingarden has greatly stimulated narrative theory and provided it with several important concepts. Of these, the concept of the 'areas of indeterminacy,'[28] which was taken up again recently by reader-response theories and reception criticism,[29] is especially relevant in our context, because teller-characters generate areas of indeterminacy of a different kind and with different frequency than do reflector-characters.[30] With the aid of the opposition teller–reflector, this thesis can now be formulated more accurately. Ingarden himself raised the question of whether the number of areas of indeterminacy is dependent on the form of a literary work, but he did not reach a conclusion. It is surely not a coincidence, however, that Ingarden, in his suggestion for further investigation, mentions two pairs of novelists, of whom one novelist shows a clear preference for teller-characters and the other for reflector-characters: Galsworthy and Joyce, Thomas Mann and Faulkner![31] The reader can understand the motivation which the teller-character provides for the process of selection in the narra-tive: the teller vouches for the 'completeness' of the proffered fictional information through the presence of his person in the narrative act. In the case of a reflector-character, the narrative process and the motivation for the selection of what has been presented are not made the subject of the narrative, so any explicit information about the criteria for the selection is withheld from the reader. The selection results primarily from the perspective of the presentation. Through the usually sharply focused perspective of a reflector-character, a section of the fictional reality is isolated and spotlighted in such a way that all the details important for the reflector-character become discernible. Outside of this sector, however, there is darkness and uncertainty, a large area of indeterminacy, which the reader can penetrate only here and there by drawing inferences from the illuminated sector. This mode of presentation lacks the higher authority which could inform the reader whether something relevant to the events presented exists outside of that sector of fictional reality illuminated by the perception of the reflector-character. For better or for worse, the reader is at the mercy of the reflector-character and his existentially limited knowledge and experience. Indeterminacy is not a question of communication here as it is in the case of a teller-character, but is experienced as a condition of the existence of a fictional character.

The narrative mode of a teller-character (telling) tends toward the conceptual summarizing of the concrete event in the form of a compressed report supplemented by commentary which explains or evaluates it. In the presentation by a reflector-character individual and concrete details which have not been reduced or abstracted dominate, just as they are experienced and perceived by that character. Consequently, these two narrative modes offer very different aspects of the story to the reader.[32] Just how the reader's concretization of the areas of indeterminacy and his actualization of the aspects which the text presents are affected by or determined at all by these differences is still largely unknown. The opposition teller-character–reflector-character can perhaps suggest a new approach to the further investigation of this problem.

The presence of a teller-character always draws the attention of the reader more strongly to the act of narrative communication than that of a reflector-character. As a rule, a teller-character explains explicitly why he selects or eliminates parts of the story or why he omits or abridges the description of a character, a setting or an event. When this is not the case, the reason for the abridgement or omission is usually implied in the manner of the teller's delivery. Owing to the continuous confirmation of this tacit agreement between the teller-character and the reader, the reader becomes confident that the teller-character will not allow him to remain uninformed about anything that is important for an understanding of the story. The reader's willingness to supplement that which has been narrated in his own imagination is reduced or suppressed by this narrative attitude, rather than stimulated. This, of course, holds true only for that type of teller-character whose reliability is indisputable. We are dealing here with a narrative convention which produces a very specific attitude of expectancy on the part of the reader. That is why many modern authors intentionally violate this convention. The authorial narrator of *The Prime of Miss Jean Brodie*, for example, often reports very arbitrary details from the later lives of his characters, but completely skips important periods in the characters' experience.

A reflector does not have any personal relationship whatsoever with the reader, and therefore is not accountable in any way for what is recorded by his consciousness and what is not perceived. The fixation and demarcation of the perspective can, of course, be interpreted as an explanation of the selection of a specific sector of represented reality. This does not give the reader any guarantee, however, that some thing or some event outside of the recorded sector of the represented world might not be of importance for the story. The areas of indeterminacy at the edge of a sector of fictional reality illuminated by a reflector-character consequently sometimes have a threatening or at least an ominous character:

The space outside of the sector illuminated by the spotlight of conscious-ness of a novel character is empty space, in which supposition, apprehen-sions, fears . . . can arise. It is not by chance that man's existential anguish and distress in the modern world is expressed most convincingly in the figural form of the novel. Kafka's novels provide especially striking examples of this correspondence between form and content.[33]

Kafka's transposition of the first-person form of the manuscript version of the first chapter of the novel *The Castle* into the third-person published form can be interpreted as the transformation of his hero K. from a teller-character to a reflector-character. As a reflector, K. is released from the reader's demand for an explana-tion of the countless inexplicable and mysterious circumstances which surround the hero here as in Kafka's other novels. Cohn's observation in reference to this transposition that 'the logic of self-narration demands self-justification – if not self-explanation,'[34] is valid in general for the contrast between a teller-character and a reflector-character. It is also valid for the teller-characters in the domain of the authorial narrative situation so long as the authorial narrator does not assume the role of the omniscient and omnipotent Olympian. Cohn's explanation of the reasons which led Kafka to rewrite the opening chapters of *The Castle* in the third rather than the first person is no less valid if one broadens the frame of reference of her interpretation from the opposition first-person reference–third-person reference to the opposition teller-character–reflector-character. Perhaps Kafka's revision of the original version of *The Castle* is best explained as a transposition on the teller/reflector-axis of the typological circle. The transposition of the original version (first-person form) to a figural narrative situation and the trans-formation of the main character K. from a teller-character to a reflector-character results in, among other things, a restructuring of the areas of indeterminacy, which underscores the general tendency of this novel to present the nameless ominousness of fate.[35]

6.3 Teller-characters and reflector-characters at the beginning of the narrative

The pronoun is one of the most terrifying masks man has invented. (John Fowles, *The French Lieutenant's Woman*)

The mode of transmission of a story is manifested most distinctly at the beginning of a narrative, because the process by which the reader's imagination is attuned to the actual mode of narration begins with the first word of the narrative.

The opening of a narrative is least conspicuous in an authorial narrative situation with a teller-character, because this beginning proceeds in analogy to the beginning of a non-fictional report. The teller-character usually announces his presence in the opening sentences of the narrative and conveys to the reader the preliminary information necessary for the understanding of the story, that is to say, he deliberately leads the reader to the threshold of the story. In the earlier novel, the chapter heading is included in this introductory process:

Chapter I

An Account of Mr Gamaliel Pickle. The Disposition of his Sister described. He yields to her Sollicitations, and retires to the Country

In a certain county of England, bounded on one side by the sea, and at the distance of one hundred miles from the metropolis, lived Gamaliel Pickle Esq; the father of that hero whose adventures we propose to record. He was the son of a merchant in London.[36]

An opening such as this one is meant to evoke the illusion that the teller-character, who introduces himself here as an agent of transmission, guarantees a narrative mode which at any time will provide the reader with all that is necessary of the best understanding of the events and characters, and if need be will also supply him with an appropriate interpretative or evaluative commentary by the teller-character.

Emma Woodhouse, handsome, clever, and rich, with a comfortable home and happy disposition, seemed to unite some of the best blessings of existence; and had lived nearly twenty-one years in the world with very little to distress or vex her.[37]

A summary introduction of this type does not preclude some retouching of the portrait later. Jane Austen's teller already hints at this possibility in Emma's case when he immediately adds a 'seemed' like a question mark to the list of Emma's numerous, indeed all too numerous, virtues. With this 'seemed,' the teller forgoes his omniscience for a moment, thereby suggesting a reflectorization of his role.

In a first-person narrative situation, the narrative opening proceeds as in an authorial narrative situation. The self, which functions here as a teller-character, introduces himself first as the reliable transmitter of a story, in which information important for the reader, such as the hero's name and ancestry, is made known at the first opportunity, somewhat according to the principle 'first things first.' A difference between the teller-character of an authorial narrative situation and that of a first-person narrative situation does exist, of course, in the existential bond of the first-person narrator and his motivation to the story and in the absence of such a bond in the case of the authorial narrator. This point was discussed earlier. The well-known beginning of Dickens's *Great Expectations* illustrates this aspect very effectively. Immediately after introducing himself as a teller-character and giving preliminary information about his name and his family, Pip begins to interweave his life as hero (experiencing self) and his role as teller (narrating self). What his phantasy infers from the inscription of his parents' tomb and from the shape of the stones marking his brothers' graves for want of other information about his family, is a fascinatingly imaginative sketch of the existential situation from which his origin derives. This passage has justifiably become famous:

As I never saw my father or my mother, and never saw any likeness of either of them (for their days were long before the days of photographs), my first fancies regarding what they were like, were unreasonably derived from their tombstones. The shape of the letters on my father's, gave me an odd idea that he was a square, stout, dark man, with curly black hair. From the character and turn of the inscription, 'Also Georgiana Wife of the Above', I drew a childish conclusion that my mother was freckled and sickly. To five little stone lozenges, each about a foot and a half long, which were arranged in a neat row beside their grave, and were sacred to the memory of five little brothers of mine – who gave up trying to get a living exceedingly early in that universal struggle – I am indebted for a belief I religiously entertained that they had all been born on their backs with their hands in their trousers-pockets, and had never taken them out in this state of existence.[38]

In the traditional, quasi-autobiographical first-person narrative there is no identity problem. Innovation in the modern first-person novel often begins at this point, however, and the identity of the first-person character becomes problematic. Today the provocative beginning of Frisch's *I'm Not Stiller* (*Stiller. Roman*), 'I'm not Stiller,' can already be described as a model of this kind of opening.[39]

Less conspicuous, but especially interesting in this context, is the occurrence of the first-person singular of the personal pronoun without the person to whom it refers introducing himself as in the following examples:

I had taken Mrs Prest into my confidence; in truth without her I should have made but little advance, for the fruitful idea in the whole business dropped from her friendly lips.[40]

I walked right through the anteroom without stopping.[41]

Although this self still remains indeterminate, there is no doubt about the subject to whom it refers: it is the teller-character, because, with the exception of direct quotations, only this character can appear in the first person singular at the beginning of a narrative. The importance of this statement becomes apparent as soon as we transpose a narrative opening such as this one into the third person: 'He walked right through the anteroom without stopping.' In contrast to the 'I' of the original text, which can only refer to the teller, the 'he' in the transposed text remains completely open with regard to its antecedent. To examine this problem more closely, we must first consider the beginning of narration with a reflector-character more thoroughly.

A narrative opening with a reflector-character lacks all those preliminaries which introduce the story to the reader. This beginning acquires its special accent from the fact that the first mention of the reflector-character almost always employs the personal pronoun 'he' or 'she' without its being defined more narrowly. Personal pronouns are 'sequence signals,'[42] which indicate that they have been preceded by information which determines their true meaning. At the beginning of a narrative, however, personal pronouns referring to the reflector-character lack an antecedent, except those cases where a pronoun refers to a character named in the title. Joseph M. Backus terms referentless pronouns which lack an antecedent, 'nonsequential sequence-signals.'[43] He has examined this kind of narrative opening in a large number of American short stories from Washington Irving to J. D. Salinger. Backus reaches the conclusion that this type of opening can be observed with striking frequency above all in Henry James, Jack London, Sherwood Anderson, Hemingway and Faulkner, as well as in many less well-known authors since 1925. He attempts to interpret this phenomenon primarily in historical terms, citing the influence of James and Anderson as models. He does not attempt to establish a relationship between this phenomenon and categories of narrative theory.

A correlation of this kind requires a re-sorting of Backus's material. First of all, those cases must be eliminated in which the referentless pronoun appears in an opening sentence which is the direct speech of a character, as for example in Nathaniel Hawthorne's story 'Egotism': ' "Here she comes!" shouted the boys along the street.'[44] The dialogue opening and the opening under consideration here have a certain abruptness in common, but strictly speaking the former is not narrative but scenic and therefore mimetic. Likewise, all those cases must be eliminated in which the personal pronoun appears in the first person singular (and in the corresponding second person). As mentioned above, an 'I' appearing at the beginning of a narrative always refers to the agent of transmission, that is, to the teller-character. (The 'I' at the beginning of an interior or silent monologue is a special case, and does not function as a teller-character, but rather as a reflector-character.)

If we exclude the cases mentioned, it is evident that almost all narratives which open with a sentence in which a personal pronoun 'he' or 'she' occurs as a nonsequential sequence-signal exhibit a predominantly figural narrative situation; the person to whom this personal pronoun refers is almost always a reflector-character. This fact also explains the striking frequency of this phenomenon in stories by James, Anderson, Hemingway, since all of these authors display a very pronounced preference for the figural narrative situation. This conclusion can be corroborated by an examination of English authors such as Joyce, Katherine Mansfield, or W. Somerset Maugham, and is illustrated by the following examples:

Eight years before he had seen his friend off at the North Wall and wished him good speed.[45]

She was sitting on the verandah waiting for her husband to come in for luncheon.[46]

Of course he knew – no man better – that he hadn't a ghost of a chance, he hadn't an earthly.[47]

A very clearly pronounced figural narrative situation prevails at the beginning of these three narratives. Behind the referentless personal pronoun stands in all three cases the reflector-character from whose point of view and through whose consciousness the story is transmitted to the reader. Instead of the narrative preliminaries, which otherwise introduce the setting, the time of the events, and the characters to the reader, it seems as if the reader is directly confronted with the action. (The order of the quotations reflects their increasing immediacy.) In each one the reader is obliged to place himself in the position of the reflector-character indicated by the referentless personal pronoun. It is really astounding that an introduction such as this one, which demands that the reader put himself in the position of a character of whom he knows next to nothing apart from his sex, does not cause the modern reader any difficulties. It is also surprising that up until now narrative theory has hardly taken notice of this phenomenon; after all, this usage is a feature of fictional narration, inconceivable in a nonfictional text (or at least not conceivable without the aid of some kind of extralinguistic pointer which would supply the pronoun with the necessary antecedent).

Narrative theory can approach this phenomenon by means of the distinction between a teller-character and a reflector-character and the difference in the mode of transmission which this opposition represents. In the case of a narrative beginning with a teller-character, the story is introduced to the reader by preliminaries. The teller also guarantees that all the information required to understand the story will be made available to the reader as he needs it. In the case of a narrative beginning with a reflector-character, the reader is obliged to forgo all preliminaries and to place himself in the position of the reflector-character, experiencing the narrated event *in actu*. The absence of a teller and of narrative preliminaries and the reference to the reflector-character by means of a pronoun which lacks an antecedent are the narrative conditions under which this transfer is most quickly and completely effected. In modern narrative literature this type of opening has apparently come to stay.

In this way a narrative opening with a personal pronoun as a nonsequential sequence-signal effects a reflectorization of the narrative situation from the first sentence on, perhaps even from the first word on. In English, the reflectorizing function of the referentless pronoun is frequently supported by the use of the progressive form instead of the simple form of the verb: 'She was sitting on the verandah.' By means of the past progressive form, the state or the course and duration of the action is stressed and the internal perspective emphatically underscored. Whenever the progressive form occurs at the beginning of a narrative together with a noun subject, it expresses initially only a durative meaning, as the following example from O. Henry's 'The Marionettes' shows:

The policeman was standing at the corner of Twenty-fourth Street and a prodigiously dark alley near where the elevated railway crosses the street.[48]

The reader does not know whether the policeman will become a reflector-character, or whether the authorial narrator will continue to determine the narrative mode. In any case the presentation exhibits an external perspective, the stylization of the description contains authorial features ('prodigiously'), and the panoramic view of the place description is authorial. Nevertheless, a reflectorizing element can be detected in the use of the expanded form of the verb. The observation of an event *in actu* is characteristic of a reflector-character.

Another linguistic phenomenon which reinforces the reflectorization effect of narrative openings with referentless pronouns is the so-called 'familiarizing article.'[49] W. J. M. Bronzwaer, who developed this concept, comments on the first sentence in Iris Murdoch's *The Italian Girl*, 'I pressed the door gently,' as follows:

In the first analysis, the I here refers to the implied author or the narrator. It is a purely instrumental pronoun, which can for that reason function as the initiator of the narrative. With the definite article in 'the door,' however, the I's involvement in the story is suddenly brought about: he is now talking about a door that is familiar to him. His response to the door – and later on in the opening paragraph to the house – is not that of a narrator; it is that of a character, a human being who has known this door from childhood and cannot help responding to it emotionally.[50]

Translated into the concept of my terminology, this means that the opening sentence already shifts the reader's I-Origo entirely to the experiencing self, whereby the opening 'I' approaches the role of a reflector-character. Let us now examine narratives with third-person reference. A figural narrative situation prevails throughout James's story 'The Liar.' In addition to a referentless 'he,' behind which the reflector-character stands, the beginning of this story contains several 'familiarizing articles':

The train was half an hour late and the drive from *the* station longer than he had supposed, so that when he reached *the* house its inmates had dispersed to dress for dinner and he was conducted straight to his room. [My emphasis.][51]

The reflector-character is not familiar with the setting and the objects introduced with the so-called familiarizing article. It is Oliver Lyon's, the painter's, first visit to this elegant country house. Nevertheless, the use of the definite article has a familiarizing effect. With the definite article, the reader familiarizes himself simultaneously with the perception of these objects through the reflector-character. His acceptance of their presence makes an introduction by the teller superfluous. The consequence is a nearly total transfer of the reader to Lyon's position in the action.

Reinhold Winkler, who has examined closely this use of the article in Hemingway, enlarges on this topic with reference to the two main characters in 'Hills Like White Elephants,' first mentioned as 'The American and the girl': 'What justifies the use of the definite article? To which pre-information does it refer? . . . We have no other choice than to postulate a kind of virtual context, i.e., to assume that the definite article refers to a part of the story which is not presented in the text – the history of the prior events ("Vorgeschichte").'[52] The knowledge of these events is stored, so to speak, in the consciousness of a character (usually a reflector-character), but in contrast to the beginning of a narrative with a teller-character, it is not 'retrieved' for the reader. When the reader puts himself in the position of the reflector-character, he is obliged to suspend his need for information whenever indeterminate details appear under the guise of the determined, in order to achieve an empathy with the reflector-character or evoke the scene of the action as completely as possible.

In contrast to James, the reflector-character in Hemingway cannot always be clearly discerned. It is not unusual in Hemingway for a collective 'they' or 'everyone' or an impersonal 'one' to appear in place of an individualizing 'he' or 'she' in the position of the referentless pronoun at the beginning of a narrative:

They brought them in around midnight and then, all night long, every one along the corridor heard the Russian.[53]

A narrative opening such as this is also not unusual in Mansfield:

The week after was one of the busiest weeks of their lives. Even when they went to bed it was only their bodies that lay down and rested; their minds went on, thinking things out, talking things over, wondering, deciding, trying to remember where . . .[54]

And after all the weather was ideal. They could not have had a more perfect day for a garden-party if they had ordered it.[55]

For these cases, the concept of the emphatic transfer must be modified. The reader's identification with a collective 'they' is not really conceivable. Chatman explains the beginning of 'The Garden

162

Party,' the latter of the above quotations, as follows: 'Indistin-
guishably the thought of one or all the family, or what one of them
said to the others, or a report of the consensus of their attitudes, or
the narrator's judgment – but which differs in no way from theirs.'[56]
Precisely because it is impossible to identify clearly a reflector-
character in narrative beginnings such as these, we must postulate a
teller-character who summarizes and reports, but who in some ways
acts as if he were a reflector-character. In 'The Daughters of the
Late Colonel' (first of the quotations from Mansfield), for example,
the antecedent for the subsequent 'they' is explained by the title.
The time-reference 'The week after,' however, remains indefinite.
This vagueness really cannot be reconciled with the narrative
manner of a conventional teller-character. Such an indefiniteness
very often signals the beginning of a reflectorization of a teller-
character. I will deal with this phenomenon in some detail later in
this chapter.

What Backus considers a characteristic feature of all narrative
openings with nonsequential sequence-signals holds true for narrative beginnings such as these with a referentless personal pronoun in
the plural: it is the function of nonsequential sequence-signals 'to
pique the reader's curiosity . . . to plunge the reader *in medias res* in
order to give him a sense of immediacy or involvement . . . to give a
story verisimilitude . . . to give an impression of anonymity or
ambiguity.'[57] Here the reader does not, in fact, share the experience
of an individual fictional character; instead he is transported to the
scene of the fictional events as if he were a witness or detached
observer. In this respect, these narrative beginnings are fundamentally distinct from those discussed above.

In conclusion it should be mentioned that to all appearances there
exists a structural connection between a narrative beginning with a
reflector-character or a reflectorized teller-character and an open
ending. In addition to their 'open' narrative beginnings most of the
narratives mentioned in this section also end with a situation in
which matters remain peculiarly up in the air. Very frequently this
situation is presented as the perception of the reflector-character.
This kind of narrative conclusion can, therefore, be found above all
in the works of those authors in whose narratives a figural narrative
situation prevails or a reflector-character functions as the agent
of transmission. This group includes James, Joyce, Mansfield,
Hemingway, and the many modern authors whose narrative style is
largely influenced by these writers.

6.3.1 The opposition mode and the distinction between 'emic' and 'etic' text beginnings

Text linguistics has already analyzed the abrupt pronominal narrative opening in terms of the theme/rheme arrangement, that is, as a problem of the thematic organization of the sentence. Precisely at the beginning of a narrative one can see the suspense which is generated by the first elements of a sentence or by the introduction of the sentence, the theme. This suspense is then resolved by the actual message, the rheme, in the following part of the sentence.[58] The problem of theme/rheme arrangement has scarcely been examined by narrative criticism. The question would be a very rewarding area for future research.

Another pair of concepts provided by text linguistics, the contrasting concepts 'etic' and 'emic,' has already been employed by Roland Harweg[59] to analyze pronominal narrative openings such as those analyzed in the previous section. These terms were first coined by Kenneth L. Pike[60] in analogy to the words 'phonetic' and 'phonemic.' According to Harweg, 'etic openings' are those 'which are merely determined "externally," extralinguistically and not structurally. Emic openings, on the other hand, are those which are determined internally and structurally.'[61] Harweg quotes the beginning of Thomas Mann's 'The Tables of the Law' ('Das Gesetz') as an example of an etic narrative opening: 'His birth was disorderly.' According to Harweg, the 'indeterminate pronominal reference' of an opening such as this one produces a certain 'uneasiness' in the reader, which could be counteracted if it were preceded by an explanation such as 'Once upon a time there lived a man . . .' From the point of view of narrative theory one cannot agree with Harweg that such a narrative opening evokes uneasiness in the reader, nor can one speak of a grammatical 'offensiveness' of such an opening.[62] One could perhaps speak historically of uneasiness. The generation of readers around the turn of the century was still accustomed to the earlier narrative style which included a teller-character and narrative preliminaries. These readers may have experienced an uneasiness of this sort upon first encountering narratives by James, for instance, but surely the modern reader no longer perceives a narrative opening of this kind as unusual. It is, rather, one of (at least) two basic possibilities of beginning a narrative. It is probably correct that a reader reacts differently in his imagination to a narrative beginning with a reflector-character, than to one directed by a teller-character, in which all necessary information is placed at the reader's disposal from the very first. The authorially rendered beginning of Kleist's tale *Michael Kohlhaas: From an Old Chronicle* belongs to this latter type; according to Harweg it can also be regarded as an example of an emic opening:

About the middle of the sixteenth century, there dwelt on the banks of the River Havel a horse-dealer named Michael Kohlhaas. The son of a schoolmaster, he was at once the most upright and most terrible of human beings.

An den Ufern der Havel lebte um die Mitte des sechzehnten Jahrhunderts ein Roßhändler namens Michael Kohlhaas, Sohn eines Schulmeisters, einer der rechtschaffensten zugleich und entsetzlichsten Menschen seiner Zeit.[63]

Thus an important aspect of my opposition teller-character– reflector-character is visible behind the contrasting concepts of emic and etic openings which originated in text linguistics. This agreement can be regarded as provisional proof that the distinction of the two narrative modes (teller-character and reflector-character) in narrative theory has a linguistic foundation.

Harweg also reaches another conclusion of interest in this context, which allows him to differentiate between nonfictional and fictional texts, or, as he terms it, between 'the practice of non-literary, more precisely: extraliterary texts,' and 'the practice of literary, or more precisely, fictional literary texts.' He states that etic openings, such as 'He got up from the table,' ('A Weary Hour' ('Schwere Stunde')) are 'not tolerated' in nonliterary texts.[64] In other words, narrative openings such as these are only possible in fictional texts. This finding furnishes further proof that the narrative modes located in the vicinity of the pole of the teller-character on the typological circle differ in linguistic structure also from those which are found in the vicinity of the reflector pole. Narrative openings directed by a teller-character do not differ from similar beginnings of nonfictional texts; on the other hand, narrative openings dominated by a reflector-character are only possible in fictional texts.

Harweg cites Thomas Mann exclusively. It might be objected that Thomas Mann's narrative style is generally not figural, but rather has very pronounced authorial features. When the opening sentences isolated above in quotation are read in context, it becomes clear immediately that a teller-character, not a reflector-character, dominates the beginning of the story. To prove this point the beginning of 'A Weary Hour' is quoted here at somewhat greater length:

He got up from the table, his little, fragile writing-desk; got up as though desperate, and with hanging head crossed the room to the tall, thin, pillar-like stove in the opposite corner. He put his hands to it; but the hour was long past midnight and the tiles were nearly stone-cold. Not getting even this little comfort that he sought, he leaned his back against them and, coughing, drew together the folds of his dressing-gown, between which a draggled lace shirt-frill stuck out; he snuffed hard through his nostrils to get a little air, for as usual he had a cold.

It was a particular, a sinister cold, which scarcely ever quite disappeared. It inflamed his eyelids and made the flanges of his nose all raw; in his head and limbs it lay like a heavy, sombre intoxication. Or was this cursed confinement to his room, to which the doctor had weeks ago condemned him, to blame for all his languor and flabbiness? God knew if it was the right thing – perhaps so, on account of his chronic catarrh and the spasms in his chest and belly. And for weeks on end now, yes, weeks, bad weather had reigned in Jena – hateful, horrible weather, which he felt in every nerve of his body – cold, wild, gloomy. The December wind roared in the stove-pipe with a desolate god-forsaken sound – he might have been wandering on a heath, by night and storm, his soul full of unappeasable grief. Yet this close confinement – that was not good either; not good for thought, nor for the rhythm of the blood, where thought was engendered.

Er stand vom Schreibtisch auf, von seiner kleinen, gebrechlichen Schreib-kommode, stand auf wie ein Verzweifelter und ging mit hängendem Kopf in den entgegengesetzten Winkel des Zimmers zum Ofen, der lang und schlank war wie eine Säule. Er legte die Hände an die Kacheln, aber sie waren fast ganz erkaltet, denn Mitternacht war lange vorbei, und so lehnte er, ohne die kleine Wohltat empfangen zu haben, die er suchte, den Rücken daran, zog hustend die Schöße seines Schlafrockes zusammen, aus dessen Brustaufschlägen das verwaschene Spitzenjabot heraushing, und schnob mühsam durch die Nase, um sich ein wenig Luft zu verschaffen; denn er hatte den Schnupfen wie gewöhnlich.

Das war ein besonderer und unheimlicher Schnupfen, der ihn fast nie völlig verließ. Seine Augenlider waren entflammt und die Ränder seiner Nasenlöcher ganz wund davon, und in Kopf und Gliedern lag dieser Schnupfen ihm wie eine schwere, schmerzliche Trunkenheit. Oder war an all der Schlaffheit und Schwere das leidige Zimmergewahrsam schuld, das der Arzt nun schon wieder seit Wochen über ihn verhängt hielt? Gott wußte, ob er wohl daran tat. Der ewige Katarrh und die Krämpfe in Brust und Unterleib mochten es nötig machen, und schlechtes Wetter war über Jena, seit Wochen, seit Wochen, das war richtig, ein miserables und hassenswertes Wetter, das man in allen Nerven spürte, wüst, finster und kalt, und der Dezemberwind heulte im Ofenrohr, verwahrlost und gottverlassen, daß es klang nach nächtiger Heide im Sturm und Irrsal und heillosem Gram der Seele. Aber gut war sie nicht, diese enge Gefangenschaft, nicht gut für die Gedanken und den Rhythmus des Blutes, aus dem die Gedanken kamen.[65]

Even the few indications of the fictional character's perceptions and feelings are subordinated to the authorial narrative situation of the first paragraph. Authorial external perspective prevails. Not until the second paragraph does this external perspective change to figural internal perspective. It is characteristic that free indirect style appears at the transition point: 'Or was this cursed confinement to his room . . . to blame for all his languor and flabbiness? God knew if it was the right thing.' After this the narrative situation indeed becomes figural, but occasional authorial intrusions and stage directions are audible to the end. Apart from the first paragraph 'A Weary Hour' is a narrative with a predominantly but not exclusively figural narrative situation. The fictionalized figure of Friedrich Schiller, functioning as the reflector-character, influences the presentation more than does the authorial teller-character, who only speaks up occasionally. By means of an etic introductory sentence the narrative opening anticipates the figural narrative situation which predominates in the story, but the indeterminate pronominal reference of the etic sentence is weakened at once by the voice of the teller. The presence of a teller-character need only be intimated to suggest to the reader that the indeterminacy of the narrative opening will be resolved at once. Thomas Mann actually utilizes an etic opening to withhold the information expected by the reader, namely, to whom this 'he,' the first word of the story, refers. This technique is especially effective in view of the solution which is gradually revealed: Schiller! In this way, however, the examples quoted by Harweg from Thomas Mann are not entirely characteristic of etic openings. More typical, perhaps, is the beginning of Maugham's story 'The Force of Circumstance,' quoted here at greater length:

She was sitting on the verandah waiting for her husband to come in for luncheon. The Malay boy had drawn the blinds when the morning lost its freshness, but she had partly raised one of them so that she could look at the river. Under the breathless sun of midday it had the white pallor of death. A native was paddling along in a dug-out so small that it hardly showed above the surface of the water. The colours of the day were ashy and wan. They were but the various tones of the heat.[66]

The teller remains entirely in the background at first, so that the person introduced by the personal pronoun 'she' can really become the reflector-character and a true internal perspective can be established. The reader perceives the introductory description of the landscape with the eyes and from the point of view of this reflector, that is to say, the reader already begins to empathize with the reflector-character before he really knows who this person is – as paradoxical as that may sound. The reader's situation is consequently somewhat different here than when he is reading the beginning of the Thomas Mann text quoted above. In the Maugham text there is at first no teller-character who could guarantee to the reader that the indeterminate pronominal reference of the first sentence will soon be resolved. On the contrary, the reader senses that he will have to find the resolution himself by concentrating on the implications of the narrative text and through empathy with the reflector-character.

Only a figural narrative situation implies a type of communication process which is normally impossible in nonfictional texts. At the beginning of 'A Weary Hour,' this process of communication is only temporarily simulated, as it were. Immediately afterwards a form of communication emerges which is conceivable in a nonfictional text, as well. The narrative opening of Maugham's text corresponds to Anderegg's narrating model. Only the first, short sentence of Mann's story gives the impression that the beginning of the text is constructed according to the narrating model, but the opening immediately turns out to belong to the reporting model, or stated in terms of the opposition mode, the communication process at the beginning of 'The Force of Circumstance' is dominated by a reflector-character. The beginning of 'A Weary Hour,' in contrast, exhibits a teller-character, despite the referential indeterminacy of the first word. Thomas Mann superimposed temporarily an earlier convention for beginning a narrative on a more recent convention. This technique results in a certain estrangement. The effect of this estrangement on the reader cannot, however, be described as uneasiness. Ordinarily it slightly increases the effect of an opening *in medias res*. Another related aspect of Thomas Mann's narrative art will be discussed in the next section.

6.4 Reflectorization of the teller-character in Katherine Mansfield, James Joyce and Thomas Mann

Only in the theoretical construction of the typological circle are teller-character and reflector-character located opposite one another as clearly distinct poles. In practice we frequently find these techniques in combination and alternation within the same text. This section deals with a special case of assimilation of a teller-character to a reflector-character which is of particular interest, the reflectorization of the teller-character. The example selected from Joyce's *Ulysses* represents an extreme. Mansfield's 'The Garden Party' and Thomas Mann's story 'Tristan' provide less striking, but all the more typical examples.[67] The analysis of the example from the story 'Tristan' refers to Harweg's text-linguistic explanation of the narrative situation in that story.[68] Here we have the rare opportunity of presenting a description of the narrative situation from the point of view of text linguistics side by side with a description from the perspective of literary criticism.

In order to clarify the process of the reflectorization of a teller-character, i.e., the transition from a teller-character to a reflector-character, it is necessary to summarize the narrative stance characteristic of a teller, and to contrast it with the stance of presentation characteristic of a reflector. In the interest of brevity and clarity the characteristic features are presented in the form of two parallel lists.

Teller-character	Reflector-character
Narrative preliminaries: explicit introduction and exposition oriented toward the reader	Abrupt or clipped opening, presupposition (the reader has to deduce the exposition)
Emic opening (Harweg)	Etic opening (Harweg)
The teller is master of the story – it can be grasped as a whole, it is orderly and makes sense	That which is presented is registered by the reflector at the moment of perception. He usually cannot grasp it as a whole, and its meaning is often problematic
Tendency toward abridgement in report form, toward conceptual abstraction and generalization	Tendency toward concrete particularity, toward impressionism and empathy
Authorial narrative situation as well as first-person narrative situation with dominance of the narrating self	Figural narrative situation and first-person narrative situation with dominance of the experiencing self; interior monologue
Communication process as in reporting model (Anderegg)	Communication process as in narrating model (Anderegg)
Selection criteria obvious, motivated by the personality of the teller	Selection criteria not obvious, areas of indeterminacy are existentially significant

Narrative distance is explicit, simple past tense has past meaning	Presentation of the action *in actu*, simple past tense loses its past meaning, in English the *in actu* impression is reinforced by the progressive form of verb
Deixis: There/Then I-Origo in the teller-character, can temporarily transfer itself into the presented scene	Deixis: Here/Now I-Origo in the reflector-character, emphasis of the Here/Now deixis through familiarizing article, referentless pronoun, etc.
External perspective and internal perspective, tendency toward aperspectivism	Internal perspective, tendency toward perspectivism
Opposition between third-person reference and first-person reference is marked	Variation between third-person reference and first-person reference in the rendering of consciousness is unmarked.

Reflectorization means the assumption by the teller-character of particular attributes of a reflector-character: strictly speaking this process begins when an authorial narrator declares, for example, that he is not familiar or not completely familiar with a certain situation.[69] Reflectorization of the teller is not marked, however, until additional and more conspicuous attributes of a reflector-character can be observed in a teller-character. These include a way of beginning without preliminaries, of the spatio-temporal perspective and the values of the fictional characters, assimilation of the teller's language to that of the characters, associative structure, and so on.

6.4.1 Katherine Mansfield, 'The Garden Party'

How reflectorization takes place in detail will be illustrated by a passage from Mansfield's story 'The Garden Party.' The news of the death in a workman's family living very near the Sheridan's mansion means for Laura that the garden party cannot take place as planned. Laura's sister Jose calls these scruples 'extravagant,' an opinion which is later shared by her mother and her other sister. In the middle of the conversation between Laura and Jose there is a lengthy expositional commentary which must be attributed to the teller-character, since it is not attributed to any of the characters in particular:

'But we can't possibly have a garden-party with a man dead just outside the front gate.'

That really was extravagant, for the little cottages were in a lane to themselves at the very bottom of a steep rise that led up to the house. A broad road ran between. True, they were far too near. They were the greatest possible eyesore and they had no right to be in that neighbourhood at all. They were little mean dwellings painted a chocolate brown. In the garden patches there was nothing but cabbage stalks, sick hens and tomato cans. The very smoke coming out of their chimneys was poverty-stricken. Little rags and shreds of smoke, so unlike the great silvery plumes that uncurled from the Sheridans' chimneys. Washerwomen lived in the lane and sweeps and a cobbler, and a man whose house-front was studded all over with minute bird-cages. Children swarmed. When the Sheridans were little they were forbidden to set foot there because of the revolting language and of what they might catch. But since they were grown up, Laura and Laurie on their prowls sometimes walked through. It was disgusting and sordid. They came out with a shudder. But still one must go everywhere; one must see everything. So through they went.

'And just think of what the band would sound like to that poor woman,' said Laura.[70]

Since this insertion supplies supplementary information for the reader, it must be regarded as part of a reader-oriented exposition by an authorial teller. The descriptive summary, the reference to a time when the Sheridan children were younger, and the summarizing character of the report of their impressions evoked later by their exploration of this impoverished section underscore the authorial narrative situation of this passage. This impression is reinforced by external perspective and Then/There deixis. All of this is part of the characteristic narrative stance of a teller-character. The subjective manner of the comment about Laura's objections, however, is incompatible with the stance of an authorial teller. 'That really was extravagant' is not only a verbal echo of Jose's opinion, but also implies a way of thinking which is characteristic of the other members of Laura's family and not of the teller. The following quotations must be interpreted in a similar way: 'True, they were far too near,' 'the greatest possible eyesore,' 'little mean dwellings,' 'nothing but cabbage stalks, sick hens,' 'It was disgusting and sordid.' These are not the words of a teller, who unwittingly discloses his own social prejudices and lack of understanding, but rather of someone who represents the Sheridans in his manner of thinking and feeling. The character in question is nameless, because he is not part of the fictional reality of the story. This anonymous reflector-character experiences these deliberations as an event in which earlier experiences and observations of individual members of the Sheridan family are reflected. Here/Now deixis and internal perspective predominate in such a way that the passage might be read as part of an interior monologue by a reflector-character on the problem occupying Laura and Jose at the time. In it the reflector-character reveals a bias which connects him with the Sheridans. An authorial teller would have to break the illusion of this bias by virtue of the external perspective available to him. It is part of a reflector's nature, on the other hand, to indulge his subjectivity to the full. Because the reflectorized teller has no existential basis in this story, he must be considered a transformation of the teller-character. Making an authorial narrator think and speak as if he were one of the characters of the story is called reflectorization. In the passage quoted from 'The Garden Party,' the reflectorized teller-character temporarily becomes the collective voice of the members of the Sheridan family other than Laura, in which their lack of humanity and social conscience is audible. The Sheridans' behaviour is evaluated indirectly by this reflectorized teller in a manner similar to that of a dramatic monologue. This lack of social empathy is accentuated by the fact that the attitude of the Sheridans toward the poor people living in miserable conditions in front of the doors of their mansion appears to be shared by an authority who is outside the fictional world of the characters and consequently has the same ontological status as an authorial teller. At the same time, one cannot overlook the irony arising from the discrepancy between the opinions of the self-effacing narrator, whose presence can be inferred in other parts of the story, and the opinions announced by the reflectorized teller-character coinciding with those of the Sheridans. In this provocative way, the author evokes perhaps an even stronger rejection of these opinions in the reader than if they had been presented merely by individual characters, such as Mrs Sheridan.

The reflectorization of the teller-character is a very characteristic feature of Mansfield's narrative style, which until now has hardly received notice from literary critics. Striking examples of it can be found in 'At the Bay,' 'The Garden Party,' 'The Daughters of the Late Colonel' and other pieces collected in the volume *The Garden Party and Other Stories*.[71] A reflectorization of the narrator can be found in various other modern prose writers as well, including Virginia Woolf[72] and Muriel Spark.[73] A comprehensive study of this interesting phenomenon in the modern novel has not yet been undertaken.

6.4.2 James Joyce, *Ulysses*

The reflectorization of the teller-character is in a way the continuation of a tendency from authorial to figural narrative situation to be observed in modern novels and stories.[74] This trend is especially evident in Joyce. During the process of reflectorization an authorial teller temporarily assumes certain characteristic qualities of a reflector-character, especially when he stops narrating and instead begins to reflect the fictional reality in his consciousness in the manner of a figural medium. The narrative attitude oriented toward the reader now changes into an attitude of reflection centred in the subject. This change has consequences which affect the structure of the narrative, the selection of the elements of the fictional reality to be presented, the spatio-temporal orientation, and especially the manipulation of the reader's sympathies.

In *Ulysses* an important function is assumed by segmentation,[75] that is, the separation of the text into sections with abrupt beginnings and endings. There are no preliminaries or transitions. Therese Fischer-Seidel distinguishes segments in *Ulysses* with 'figural' and 'extrafigural presentation.' She is primarily interested in the alternation of segments of these two kinds, which entails an alternation of internal perspective (especially Stephen's and Leopold Bloom's) and external perspective, that is, a perspective which cannot be attributed to these two characters. For this reason this pattern is a very important structural principle of *Ulysses*. Fischer-Seidel also notes that there are 'gliding transitions between the two segments' and a number of 'figural segments' cannot be attributed to a particular fictional character.[76] Here again the reflector-mode seems to have been superimposed on the narrator to whom most of Fischer-Seidel's extrafigural segments have to be attributed. In this way a reflectorization of the teller-character occurs here too.

The prelude to the 'Sirens' episode of *Ulysses*[77] can be regarded as a product of a reflectorized teller-character. This prologue is composed like a fugue of the chapter's most important motifs of gestures, sounds and phrases. The genesis of this prelude might be envisioned in the following way: after the author-narrator has conceived the contents of this chapter, he gives his imagination free rein with regard to the elements of this content: frequently recurring words and sentence fragments appear now to be recombined in free association, forming new units of motifs, sounds, and perhaps even of meaning. The force regulating this process seems to come from deeper layers of consciousness.[78] A montage of motifs of this kind cannot be interpreted as the work of a teller-character who organizes the material in the interest of the reader, but rather as a product of the unleashed phantasy of a reflectorized teller-character playing with elements of the fictional reality.

A reflectorization of the teller-character is evident in several other passages in the first half of *Ulysses*, although nowhere in as detailed and conspicuous a fashion as in the prelude to the 'Sirens' episode.[79] One of these passages is the first large segment of the 'Wandering Rocks' episode which shall be analyzed in greater detail now.[80] The 'Wandering Rocks' episode presents a montage of snapshots from Dublin's streets from about 3 p.m. to 4 p.m. on 16 June 1904 ('Bloomsday'), in which the main characters and almost all the secondary characters are recorded in the imagination of the reader at their respective locations on the city map. Here Joyce employs the technique of segmentation and creates a montage of sections rendering events which occur simultaneously at different places. This technique can also be regarded as an expression of the reflectorization of the narrative act, because the narrator abdicates his function of explaining, ordering, selecting and presenting the elements of his story for the reader, in favour of an authority who apparently permits himself to be guided largely by the chance occurrence of perceptions and by free association in his mind. Both of these are characteristic features of a reflector-character.

The first large segment of the 'Wandering Rocks' episode shows the Jesuit Father Conmee on the way to Artane, where he intends to make an appeal on behalf of the son of the recently deceased Paddy Dignam at the orphanage. This segment is opened by a sentence providing a brief exposition of the scene in the form of an authorial report. The second sentence already exhibits a figural narrative situation. Father Conmee's thoughts about his commission along with the free associations which follow are rendered directly. Father Conmee then meets a sailor with one leg, who limps through the streets begging and who will also be encountered by several other characters in this chapter. (This begging invalid is one of the coordinators who make the synchronism of the events in the nineteen large segments of the chapter visible.) Not until the third paragraph does the voice of the authorial narrator become audible again, when he conveys the thoughts evoked in Father Conmee by the sight of the begging invalid. He then continues:

He [Father Conmee] walked by the treeshade of sunny-winking leaves and towards him came the wife of Mr David Sheehy M.P.

– Very well, indeed, father. And you father?

Father Conmee was wonderfully well indeed. He would go to Buxton probably for the waters. And her boys, were they getting on well at Belvedere? Was that so? Father Conmee was very glad indeed to hear that. And Mr Sheehy himself? Still in London. The house was still sitting, to be sure it was. Beautiful weather it was, delightful indeed. Yes, it was very probable that Father Bernard Vaughan would come again to preach. O, yes: a very great success. A wonderful man really.

Father Conmee was very glad to see the wife of Mr David Sheehy M.P. looking so well and he begged to be remembered to Mr David Sheehy M.P. Yes, he would certainly call.

– Good afternoon, Mrs Sheehy.[81]

Several things are striking in the presentation of this encounter. The selection of the excerpts from the conversation between Father Conmee and Mrs Sheehy does not accord with the conventions of a dialogue rendered by a teller-character. Father Conmee's greeting is omitted, but Mrs Sheehy's reply to it is quoted in direct speech. The rest of the conversation between the two appears in free indirect style. It is striking that the consciousness which records this conversation, or, more accurately, the not entirely complete echo of the conversation, is not Father Conmee's, as would be expected, but that of a third person. This can be inferred, because Father Conmee is not designated simply by the personal pronoun 'he,' which would express an internal perspective presented from Father Conmee's point of view, but repeatedly by his title and name: 'Father Conmee was very glad.' This third person can only be the authorial teller, whose narrative behaviour is beginning to approach that of a reflector-character. The reflectorization is revealed here mainly by the fact that the conversation between Father Conmee and Mrs Sheehy is reproduced in fragments, as if it had been recorded only incompletely by the consciousness of a participant or of a third person, as well as by the fact that the omissions are not explained by the narrator. The teller-character thus suspends his narrative responsibility and reacts as a figural medium.

This process can also be observed in the following passage from the same segment of the 'Wandering Rocks' chapter:

Father Conmee stopped three little schoolboys at the corner of Mountjoy square. Yes: they were from Belvedere. The little house: Aha. And were they good boys at school? O. That was very good now. And what was his name? Jack Sohan. And his name? Ger. Gallaher. And the other little man? His name was Brunny Lynam. O, that was a very nice name to have.

Father Conmee gave a letter from his breast to master Brunny Lynam and pointed to the red pillarbox at the corner of Fitzgibbon street.

– But mind you don't post yourself into the box, little man, he said.

The boys sixeyed Father Conmee and laughed.[82]

Here, too, we find the report of a narrator, speech directly quoted, free indirect style, and the omission of individual parts of the dialogue without any explanation from the narrator. The sentence 'The boys sixeyed Father Conmee and laughed' is especially striking, however. The unusual composite 'sixeyed,' in which the perception that the three boys looked wide-eyed at Father Conmee is verbally condensed, again presupposes the presence of a consciousness which records the events as in the manner of a figural medium. Father Conmee cannot be the bearer of this consciousness, since the reference to him in this sentence indicates an external perspective, as did that in the preceding quotation. For this reason the passage must be attributed to a reflectorized narrator. The stereotyping of Father Conmee by means of a repetitive description can be explained in the same way. It immediately follows the passage quoted above: 'Father Conmee smiled and nodded and smiled and walked along.' Finally, a short segment not quoted here indicates the location and description of Mr Denis J. Maginni, who is at an entirely different place in the city at the time. The insertion of the segment involves an abrupt transition and must also be understood as a montage resulting from an association in the consciousness of the reflectorized narrator.

Another of Father Conmee's encounters on his way to Artane is presented directly after this passage:

Was that not Mrs M'Guinness?

Mrs M'Guinness, stately, silverhaired, bowed to Father Conmee from the farther footpath along which she smiled. And Father Conmee smiled and saluted. How did she do?

A fine carriage she had. Like Mary, queen of Scots, something. And to think that she was a pawnbroker. Well, now! Such a . . . what should he say? . . . such a queenly mien.

Father Conmee walked down Great Charles street.[83]

Father Conmee's first awareness of Mrs M'Guinness is rendered in free indirect style and is clearly presented from Father Conmee's point of view: 'Was that not Mrs M'Guinness?' The paragraph beginning with 'A fine carriage she had,' is also a figural presentation of Father Conmee's perceptions and thoughts. The case is different in the intervening paragraph, in which the twice-repeated reference to Father Conmee by title and name is conspicuous. Figural presentation would lead one to expect only the corresponding personal pronoun. With the peculiar transposition of the greeting 'How do you do?', it becomes apparent that we are dealing with a statement of the reflectorized teller-character in this passage. 'How did she do?' cannot be free indirect style,[84] or, if it is free indirect style, then it does not reflect Father Conmee's point of view, but rather that of a reflectorized teller. Because it is an idiomatic expression, the greeting 'How do you do?' is not subject to the changes normally necessitated by the conversion of direct speech into free indirect style or indirect speech, including the change in tense and the transposition of the personal pronoun. If an idiomatic phrase such as this one is transposed nevertheless, its meaning changes. In this case, an erotic allusion can be detected in the transformation of 'How do you do?' into 'How did she do?', which probably should not be attributed to Father Conmee's consciousness, but rather to that of the reflectorized teller. The erotic *double entendre* and the pun are additional evidence that the perspective of a figural metaconsciousness, namely the reflectorized teller, is temporarily superimposed here upon the internal figural perspective of a fictional character. These changes suggest a very subtle reflectorization of the narrative process, in which the consciousness of an authorial medium extends over the consciousness of the figural medium, Father Conmee. The effects are a kind of mimicry as well as a kind of ironization of the narrative situation. The behaviour of the authorial medium becomes assimilated almost completely to that of the figural medium, and also assumes the figural perceptions, thoughts and feelings to a great extent. Then suddenly it exposes the discrepancy between the two perspectives through an unusual verbalization or an unexpected association. Examples of this technique in the quotation above are the repetition of the expletive 'indeed' (four times) in the encounter with Mrs Sheehy, the simultaneous omission of entire parts of the dialogue, the lexical innovation 'sixeyed,' and the deformation in form and content of the idiom 'How do you do?' These and similar phenomena increase in frequency in the first part of *Ulysses* until they attain their greatest frequency in the 'Sirens' episode. The prelude to this episode may even be viewed as an independent text consisting entirely of such techniques.

The theory that the novel *Ulysses* can be interpreted as a kind of

Konzeptionsmonolog, the interior monologue of the author or of an authorial medium while his imagination is occupied with the composition of the story of 16 June 1904 in Dublin, is based upon phenomena such as the reflectorization of the teller-character. The term *Konzeptionsmonolog* (compositional monologue)[85] is naturally more a metaphorical than an exact description of that which is extraordinary in the narrative act of *Ulysses*, but it offers a hypothesis, by which the very diverse phenomena associated with the reflectorization of the teller-character in *Ulysses* can be subsumed under a unifying concept.

6.4.3 Thomas Mann, *The Magic Mountain*

It may be surprising at first that the concept compositional monologue applied to the analysis of *Ulysses* can be applied to Thomas Mann's work as well. Francis Bulhof undertook this interesting experiment in his study of the novel *The Magic Mountain*.[86] Bulhof explains the attributive use of some notions, motifs, peculiar formulations or stereotyped conversational phrases as idiosyncratic traits of more than one fictional character and perhaps also the narrator without any relevant communication having taken place between the persons in question. This phenomenon he terms 'transfiguralization.' Transfiguralization means the participation of an individual consciousness in a more comprehensive, superindividual consciousness or the removal of the boundaries separating one individual consciousness from another. In this context, the flowing of notions and motifs from the narratorial, that is, the authorial consciousness to the figural consciousness of a fictional character and vice versa is of special interest, because it offers a parallel to the process of reflectorization of the teller-character. Here, too, an authorial and a figural medium seem to share some of the content of their consciousness with one another. Bulhof discusses an example of this process in *The Magic Mountain*: 'Hans Castorp first hears some details about Clavdia Chauchat from Miss Engelhardt, one of which is that her husband is an official in "Daghestan, you know, way off in the east, on the other side of the Caucasus." The narrator appropriates these words in his commentary, without verifying their geographical accuracy. He reports that Clavdia left "for Daghestan, way off in the east, on the other side of the Caucasus." '[87] In the ironic repetition of Miss Engelhardt's words by the authorial narrator, which necessarily changes their meaning, there is a parallel to the distortion of the greeting 'How do you do?' to 'How did she do?' by the authorial medium in *Ulysses*. In both instances utterances by fictional characters are snatched up by the respective teller authority and reproduced in slightly altered form. This variation alters the original meaning and imbues the phrases with irony. The reader can see and recognize this process within the framework of the authorial narrative situation of the novel *The Magic Mountain*; in the predominantly figural narrative situation of the first part of *Ulysses*, however, this process is so completely merged with the process of composition that it can only be inferred.

The differences between the structural context in which these transfigural elements are embedded in each of these two novels make it seem perhaps inadvisable to interpret the *The Magic Mountain* as the expression of an authorial stream of consciousness or as a compositional monologue, as Bulhof does. Bulhof himself also qualifies this hypothesis by inserting a 'perhaps.'[88] A comparison of this particular aspect in these two works, essentially so different, is nevertheless meaningful. A phenomenon emerges in both works which invites two contrary explanations. Transfiguralization in *The Magic Mountain* and reflectorization of the narrator in *Ulysses* can be explained, on the one hand, as an expression of the suspension of the boundaries of consciousness between the individual characters, which immerse them in a transfigural, super-individual or collective consciousness. On the other hand, however, these phenomena can also be understood as the result, or better as the traces of an incomplete individualization of the characters by the author in the process of writing. It is as if a complete separation of the imaginative world of the author/teller from that of the fictional characters had not been achieved. The distinction between perspectivism and aperspectivism as styles of equal value makes us hesitate today to denote such a compositional peculiarity as an artistic deficiency. We must instead endeavor to isolate these phenomena in the text, in order to make them accessible to interpretation. These phenomena are primarily important, however, for an understanding of the internal process of conception and writing and for the understanding of the catalytic function which a teller- or reflector-character assumes in this process in the author's imagination. Presumably an author who sets out to write a narrative with a teller-character proceeds differently during the conception of this narrative than an author who plans to entrust the mediation of this story to a reflector-character. It would be a very rewarding study to examine this conjecture on the basis of more extensive textual material, especially with the aid of first drafts in notebooks and revisions of narrative texts.

6.4.4 The narrative situation in Thomas Mann's 'Tristan' from the perspective of text linguistics and narrative theory

Harweg's description of the narrative situations in Thomas Mann's story 'Tristan' according to text linguistics proceeds from the following observation: 'The communicative situation in which a fictional text is embedded is more complicated than that in which a nonfictional text is embedded.'[89] In the course of the analysis, however, this important realization apparently recedes somewhat into the background. The narrative situation in 'Tristan' is measured primarily against narrative models derived from non-fictional communication situations. It is not surprising, then, that the result of the analysis amounts to a series of 'corrections of Mann's text.'[90] This case is of fundamental interest for the 'communicative situation' between linguistics and literary criticism which is becoming more and more important. It will therefore be treated in somewhat greater detail, not so much as an attempt to correct the findings of text linguistics, but in order to suggest how the two disciplines can complement each other.

One prerequisite for a symbiosis of this kind is an acquaintance with the attempts at a solution proposed by scholars in the other discipline. Harweg narrows his basis from the very beginning when he ignores all modifications brought to bear on Hamburger's thesis of the epic preterite except those advanced by Weinrich.[91] That the past tenses very generally denote the 'irrefutably signaled relation of posteriority between the sender and the receiver of a fictional narrative,' as Harweg believes,[92] is just as untenable, when formulated in such a general way, as the general definition of the present tenses as signals of 'a relation of simultaneity between the sender and the subject matter.' The latter assertion can be refuted merely by referring to narratives written in the present tense such as Dickens's *Bleak House*, Joyce Cary's *Mister Johnson* or Franz Werfel's *The Song of Bernadette* (*Das Lied von Bernadette*), in which the narrative present tense by no means always describes an event which is presented *in actu*, in the manner of an interior monologue.[93] From the point of view of literary criticism, there-fore, these two assumptions, which form the theoretical basis for the two narrative models he employs, appear to be somewhat problematic. In Harweg's model of the written narrative, the narrator is 'in a relation of posteriority to the subject matter and in a relation of anteriority to his receiver.' Moreover, teller, receivers and subject matter are each located in different places in the narrative model. In the model of oral narration, the narrator is 'in a relation of posteriority to the subject matter and in a relation of simultaneity to his receivers.' Moreover, the oral narrator is situated 'at the same locations as the receivers, but at a different location than the subject matter.'[94] In addition, a third model (together with a fourth one) is defined, but then rejected, although it is realized in modern narrative literature almost as often as the first and second model. This case is characterized in my system by the fact that here the mediacy of narration is not effected by a teller-character but rather by a reflector-character. If we substitute the concept reflector for that of narrator in Harweg's definition of the third or fourth model, it becomes a definition of the figural narrative situation, in which the reflector-character (Harweg calls him narrator) is actually 'in a relation of simultaneity to the subject matter and in one of anteriority to his receivers,' and is situated 'at the same location as the subject matter but at a different location than the receivers.' If one can also take into account the illusion of immediacy and of the *in actu*-participation of the reader in his own imagination, then Harweg's fourth model coincides to a great extent with the figural narrative situation. In both there exists a relation of simultaneity among subject matter, narrator (= reflector-character) and reader, and all three are situated in one and the same place – according to the imagination.[95] Curiously enough, Harweg does not use this model for his analysis of the narrative situation in 'Tristan,' on which his conclusions are based primarily. He attempts to define the particularity of this story as a deviation from his first two models, the written and oral narrative situation of a personalized narrator.

At the beginning of the story 'Tristan,' a narrative situation prevails which is characterized by a tendency toward reflectorization of a teller-character. The authorial teller first appears to be a figural medium, an imaginary patient at the sanatorium 'Einfried,' but then speaks again in the role of the authorial teller. In effect he combines the points of view and the horizons of knowledge of a reflector-character who is situated at a defined time and place with those of a teller-character who is not bound in time or space. In 'Tristan' this fluctuation between an authorial and a figural situation ultimately develops into a predominantly authorial narrative mode.

The modern reader, who is familiar with the characteristic conventions of both narrative situations, can orient himself without Harweg's somewhat cumbersome explanatory models. These include the 'tourist-guide situation' for the narrative situation of the beginning of the story and the 'visitor-receiver' or the 'nurse-teller' model for the rest of the story.[96] Thomas Mann employs both narrative modes, the teller- and the reflector-mode, with virtuosity here as well as in many of his other stories, such as *Death in Venice* and 'A Weary Hour.' Their use in 'Tristan' can best be illustrated by the first and second references to the main character, the writer Detlev Spinell. Spinell is first introduced by a reflectorized teller-character:

The characters whom Einfried has sheltered! Even a writer is here, an excentric person, who bears the name of some kind of mineral or precious stone and who fritters the Lord's days away here.

Was für Existenzen hat 'Einfried' nicht schon beherbergt! Sogar ein Schriftsteller ist da, ein exzentrischer Mensch, der den Namen irgendeines Minerals oder Edelsteins führt und hier dem Herrgott die Tage stiehlt.[97]

In place of a verb of cognition, it is this first sentence which marks what follows as the inside view of a fictional character. In this sense the passage also approaches free indirect style, which is characteristic of the presentation of characters' thoughts. The subsequent sentence then underscores the internal perspective and the resulting limited point of view: the reflectorized teller, who here approaches the role of a figural medium or a reflector-character, has to admit that he does not know the name of the writer. The next utterance concerning this writer is formulated in a very subjective, personal way and has a similar effect. The second reference to Spinell is entirely different, however. It is made by a teller who narrates in a markedly authorial manner:

Spinell was the name of the writer who had lived in Einfried for several weeks. Detlev Spinell was his name, and his appearance was peculiar.
Imagine a brunet in his early thirties with a portly figure.

Spinell hieß der Schriftsteller, der seit mehreren Wochen in 'Einfried' lebte, Detlev Spinell war sein Name, und sein Äußeres war wunderlich.
Man vergegenwärtige sich einen Brünetten am Anfang der Dreißiger und von stattlicher Statur.[98]

This passage is followed by a very detailed description of Spinell, in which the authorial teller restricts himself to that which could have been observed of Spinell by the patients of Einfried. This foregoing of omniscience and the restriction of the point of view of the authorial teller is the prerequisite for the peculiar fluctuation between a figural and an authorial narrative situation in this story.

One passage in which this fluctuating narrative situation becomes noticeable also plays a role in Harweg's argument,[99] since it cannot easily be subordinated to his explanatory model. It is the *Liebestod* scene, in which Mr Klöterjahn's wife plays a piano excerpt from the second act of the opera *Tristan und Isolde*. The musical *Liebestod* motif is recreated in the narrative and metaphorically enhanced. Here, too, the question remains as to whether the thoughts and feelings reproduced in this passage are those of the figural medium Spinell or those of a reflectorized teller-character, who like Spinell surrenders entirely to the impression of the music. This scene is suddenly interrupted by the entrance of a patient and her nurse into the green salon, where Mrs Klöterjahn and Spinell are sitting at the piano:

Suddenly something startling happened. The woman stopped playing abruptly, putting her hand above her eyes to peer into the gloom, and Mr Spinell turned around quickly in his seat. The door *back there*, which led to the corridor, had opened, and a dark figure came in. [My emphasis]

Plötzlich geschah etwas Erschreckendes. Die Spielende brach ab und führte ihre Hand über die Augen, um ins Dunkel zu spähen, und Herr Spinell wandte sich rasch auf seinem Sitze herum. Die Tür *dort hinten*, die zum Korridor führte, hatte sich geöffnet, und herein kam eine finstere Gestalt.[100]

This unexpected appearance of Mrs Höhlenrauch, who suffers from senility, totally destroys the romantic effect of the *Liebestod* atmosphere. The return of the other patients from a sleigh ride can be heard and Spinell arises to go to his room:

He got up and walked through the room. At the door *back there* he stopped, turned around, and shifted uneasily from one foot to another for a moment. And then it came to pass that, fifteen or twenty steps away from her, he sank upon his knees, silently upon both knees. [My emphasis]

Er stand auf und ging durch das Zimmer. An der Tür *dort hinten* machte er halt, wandte sich um und trat einen Augenblick unruhig von einem Fuß auf den anderen. Und dann begab es sich, daß er, fünfzehn oder zwanzig Schritte von ihr entfernt, auf seine Knie sank, lautlaus auf beide Knie.[101]

Harweg has difficulties with the deictic adverb 'back there' (dort hinten).[102] In the first quotation it very clearly indicates Spinell's point of view. The sentence beginning with 'At the door back there' is free indirect style, reflecting Spinell's perceptions. The recurrence of the deictic adverb 'back there' after Spinell moved from the piano ('here') to the door ('back there') catches the reader's attention. According to text linguistics this second use of the deictic adverb is indeed inconsistent. From a literary point of view, however, the inconsistency has a very definite function: it is supposed to effect a kind of disruption of the reader's spatial orientation. By this device the author is probably pointing to a thematic correspondence between the startling appearance of Mrs Höhlenrauch, and the no less startling genuflection with which Spinell takes his leave. The almost biblical tone of 'And then it came to pass that . . .' reflects the presence of an authorial narrator. From the point of view of this authorial narrator, only 'at the door' would actually be expected as an indication of the place of Spinell's genuflection. The additional 'back there' is an authorial quotation from the figural perspective of perception of the first passage. This detail can be regarded as a result of a temporary reflectorization of the teller-character. We must consider the fact that the perspective of the reflectorized teller approaches that of Mrs Klöterjahn. It cannot be said that it is identical with hers, because here we are given only an outside view of this character. This technique is a very important aspect of the perspectivization of this story, perhaps the most important one of all for an interpretation, yet it is not considered in Harweg's analysis. That is not to say that Harweg's reflections regarding the narrative situation of 'Tristan' are uninteresting or of no use for literary criticism. I am, after all, indebted to him for posing the problem of this interpretation. I have been primarily concerned to show that the findings of text linguistics which reveal, as Harweg himself says with some hesitation, 'inconsistencies in the narrative situation' in Thomas Mann's story,[103] should not be regarded as the last word about the particularity of this passage. Even if text linguistics intentionally abstains from doing 'anything to enhance the artistic–aesthetic effect of the text in question,' the question nevertheless remains, whether its endeavors can actually lead to a 'deepening of our understanding of the structure of texts' and a better understanding of the 'general laws of narration,'[104] as Harweg hopes, without its cooperation with literary criticism. The example discussed here suggests instead that at least for the analysis of fictional texts a close collaboration between both disciplines promises the greatest prospect of success in such an undertaking.

7

THE TYPOLOGICAL CIRCLE: DIAGRAM AND FUNCTION

These elements are so curiously interwoven, the kinds of literature so endlessly varied, that it is very difficult to find a system by which one could arrange them next to or after each other. But one can remedy this situation somewhat by placing the three basic elements in a circle across from each other and looking for examples in which each element exists alone. Then one could collect examples which tend to the one or the other side, until finally the union of all three appears and the whole circle is thus closed.

> (Goethe on 'Natural Forms of Literature'
> in *Noten und Abhandlungen zu besserem
> Verständnis des west-östlichen Divans*)

The typological circle included as a diagram on p. xvi provides an abstract model constructed to facilitate the understanding of the phenomena of narrative theory which have been described in this study. More specifically, it illustrates the following aspects:

1. The three oppositions which form the constitutive basis of the narrative situations – person, perspective, and mode – and their relation to one another in the system of narrative forms. The representation of the three oppositions as poles of the three main axes of the typological circle reveals which element dominates in the determination of a narrative situation and which elements (represented by the directly adjacent poles) play a secondary role.

2. The continuum of forms which results from the variation of the three narrative situations into an infinite number of intermediate and transitional forms. The mobility or dynamics of this continuum are twofold: the system itself has no categorical borders, only transitions; also, the narrative situation of the individual work is not a static condition but a dynamic process of constant modulation or oscillation within a certain sector of the typological circle.

3. The connection between the system of narrative forms and the history of narrative genres. While those areas of the typological circle in the vicinity of the authorial and the first-person narrative situation were inhabited very early in the history of the novel and the short story, the areas on both sides of the figural narrative

situation remained sparsely populated until the turn of the century, but since then have been all the more densely occupied by works of fiction. Most recently there has been a noticeable tendency to fill up the transitional zones between the three narrative situations. A number of novels and shorter tales which experiment with new forms of transmission are appropriately located in these transitional zones. The typological circle as a model of all possible variations of narrative form can therefore be considered a program for all theoretical possibilities of narrative creation which is gradually attaining concrete form in the historical development of the novel and the short story.

This general description of the function of the typological circle must be concluded with a caveat. The typological circle is a model which can be represented by a diagram in its totality without any inconsistencies. The individual work is almost always 'recalcitrant' in respect to its representation in terms of the diagram of the system, and can be incorporated into the system only with difficulty. The dynamics of the system, its openness as a continuum of narrative forms, is *one* dimension which allows for this recalcitrance. The recalcitrance of the individual work, however, is multi-dimensional. The determination of the position to which the individual work is assigned in the circular diagram of the system is, therefore, always tentative, inviting correction or revision in the course of interpretation. The following description of the typological circle, in which we shall traverse the circle in both directions starting from the authorial narrative situation, will also show how the phenomena which were described as isolated phenomena in the course of the systematic presentation often overlap or intersect one another in the individual work. This chapter is thus both a synopsis of those aspects of narrative art which were considered individually in the preceding sections, as well as a catalogue of questions and problems which manifest themselves when the systematic theory confronts the particularity and diversity of the individual narrative work.

7.1 From the authorial to the figural narrative situation: the authorial-figural continuum

If we follow the typological circle, starting from the authorial narrative situation, in the direction of the figural narrative situation, we can recognize some general tendencies in the continuum of the forms which can be summarized as follows:

1. Gradual withdrawal of the person of the authorial narrator up to

and including his (apparent) invisibility in the narrative process.
2. Gradual appearance of a reflector-character (or the reflector-ization of an authorial teller-character) and as a result a change in the reader's orientation system and the spatio-temporal deixis in the fictional reality.
3. Displacement of thought report by free indirect style as a technique of the rendition of dialogue and thought characteristic of the transition between authorial and figural narrative situation.

The first of these three general tendencies is usually a prerequisite for the last two, but overlapping and 'phase shifts' among all three groups are not uncommon: long figural passages appear in the middle of a narrative with a pronounced authorial narrative situation and authorial report becomes audible in an otherwise figural narrative. Finally, authorial and figural perspective also combine in free indirect style.

7.1.1 The withdrawal of the authorial narrator

The consequences of the departure of the personalized narrator from the novel and the short story since the end of the nineteenth century have occupied narrative theory more than any other phenomenon.[1] This tendency is the main starting point of all attempts at ideologizing narrative forms, as Booth discusses in his *Rhetoric of Fiction*.[2] With regard to the continuum of forms of the typological circle, two phenomena result directly from the gradual withdrawal of the personalized narrator. On the one hand, a reduction of the narrative and an increase in the dialogue parts of the narrative text occur; on the other hand, there is a displacement of the authorial reportorial narrative of events of the outer world by figural presentation of events of the inner world, or the reflection of events of the outer world in the consciousness of a figural medium or reflector-character who assumes the transmittal function of the authorial teller-character. These two phenomena appear side by side or successively in the diagram of the typological circle, but in the individual work they often overlap or appear within each other like a Chinese box puzzle. I shall now examine some aspects of these two phenomena more closely.

7.1.2 Authorial dialogue direction

Directing the dialogue with *verba dicendi* like 'he said,' 'she replied' and other introductory verbs of saying is one task of the narrator which is almost exclusively functional and which the reader as a rule does not perceive at all as an utterance of a teller-character. Besides the *verba dicendi* there are also the verbs with which a narrator introduces the thoughts and observations of the characters. Free indirect style, to be discussed in the following section, is a possible alternative for the rendition of dialogue and thought without authorial introduction. While the increased use of free indirect style as a technique for incorporating figural speech and thought reinforces the tendency towards a figural narrative situation, the frequent use of indirect speech and thought report reinforces the tendency towards an authorial narrative situation.[3] Both thought report and indirect speech as 'narrated speech' can reveal different degrees of (authorial) summary and condensation. Speech report and the description of action are often combined, as can be seen in the phrases 'he often said' or 'he would say,' which were very frequently employed by Thackeray and other Victorians to indicate that a certain statement of a character is habitual.[4] Reference to the iterative character of an action or speech is naturally an authorial element, just as every type of narrative summary, condensation, abridgement of action and speech must be considered a manifestation of a teller-character.

An important element related to the withdrawal of the narrator is the increase in dialogue. In an earlier chapter[5] I already pointed out that the quantitative ratio of narrative parts to dialogue, that is, to non-narrative parts in the novel, fluctuates greatly from work to work. In a considerable number of stories and novels, dialogue comprises by far the larger part of the text. Works such as these are located on the typological circle approximately halfway between authorial and figural narrative situation. The presence of the authorial narrator is restricted to brief, impersonal stage directions, but no figural medium appears in them. The presentation ensues strictly from an external perspective. Characteristic works of this kind are the novels *Nothing*, by Henry Green, and those by Ivy Compton-Burnett, for example, *Mother and Son*, which consist primarily of dialogue. Some of Hemingway's stories have their typological *locus* here, too, especially the story 'The Killers.' Since in these works the person of the narrator appears only as a narrative function, that is to say, as an abstract principle, the non-identity of the realms of the characters and of the narrator (or of the narrative function) is realized in them most radically. To the degree to which a narrator assumes personal features, he approaches, although only at some distance, the realm of the characters, for personality is one human characteristic which the narrator and the characters have in common. This fact is one reason why the authorial narrative situation, which always includes the presence of a personalized narrator, must be located at an adequate distance from the non-identity pole of the typological circle.

In most cases the withdrawal of the narrator and the predominance of dialogue also result in a restriction and selection of the objects of the outer world included in the narrative text. Hemingway practiced this 'technique of omission' most consistently. He was guided by the idea 'that you could omit anything if you knew that you omitted, and the omitted part would strengthen the story and make people feel something more than they understood.'[6] The semiotic relevance of the omission or, more precisely, of that which is omitted, is enhanced by the particular narrative situation in Hemingway's stories, in which the absence of the narrator constantly prompts the responsive reader to inquire into the proper significance of all that has not been omitted.

7.1.3 From noun to pronoun

The withdrawal of the authorial narrator is also clearly evident in the reduction and ultimately in the absence of specifically authorial utterances, as, for instance, the references of the authorial narrator to himself, his commentaries on the narrated events, references to the future and to the past, and so on. The purely functional manifestations of the authorial narrator, the direction of dialogue and the naming of the characters, are maintained the longest. The reduction of the authorial element in the reference to a character first of all affects the adjective expressing authorial sympathy ('poor Strether'), then the authorial circumlocution ('our hero'). These are replaced by the simple names of the characters ('Strether,' 'Stephen'), and these, too, are ultimately replaced by the corresponding personal pronouns, as long as a name is not required to avoid ambiguity. The continuous substitution of the personal pronoun for the name is a decisive step in the transition from the authorial to the figural domain. The use of the personal pronoun facilitates the transfer of the reader to the consciousness of the character or the reader's empathy with the character's situation to a greater extent than does the mentioning of the name. This point was already established in the discussion of narrative openings by means of a personal pronoun,[7] and can be demonstrated by a comparison of Joyce's *Stephen Hero* with *A Portrait of the Artist as a Young Man*. *Stephen Hero*, which was discarded by the author, can be considered an early version of a part of *A Portrait of the Artist*.[8] The revision shows a very clear tendency towards the elimination of authorial elements, still numerous in *Stephen Hero*, and towards consistent reinforcing of the figural narrative situation. This tendency is evident in the techniques employed in referring to the main character, Stephen, among other things. *Stephen Hero* still exhibits frequent authorial circumlocutions for the name of the main character with and without adjectives ('this fantastic idealist,' 'the fiery-hearted revolutionary,' 'the youth'[9]) besides the simple mention of his name. Approximately one-third of the references to the hero belong to this group, while the remaining references employ the personal pronoun. In *A Portrait of the Artist* the clearly authorial references to the hero are almost completely eliminated. Simultaneously, however, the number of references by name are reduced. At the same time the frequency of the personal pronoun referring to the main character increases conspicuously. In one passage ten pages in length, for example, the personal pronoun appears ninety times, while the name Stephen does not appear once.[10] These conditions are also reflected at the beginning of the narrative, in which a figural narrative situation, characteristic of this novel, is developed from the very first sentence onwards. The first mention of the name of the hero, who functions as the reflector-character of the novel, does not occur until after the first page, and then, as if incidentally, in the speech of another character.[11]

In Henry James, too, the intensification of the tendency towards a figural narrative situation in the later works or in the later revision of earlier works is reflected in the increase in personal pronoun reference. Chatman cites the results of a comparison of James's early and late styles by Leo Hendrick, revealing an increase of one-third in the number of personal pronouns in the late style.[12]

7.1.4 Free indirect style as a transition from authorial to figural narrative situation

Free indirect style involves a complex of problems which have been extremely controversial ever since the beginning of the discussion of this technique around the turn of the century. It is both a grammatical and a literary phenomenon. It is therefore no coincidence that both linguists and literary critics are involved in its definition. One can also see how the two disciplines try to explain one and the same phenomenon from their own specialized viewpoint. For the grammarian, free indirect style is primarily a phenomenon competing with direct and indirect speech. The differences between these three forms are essentially described in terms of syntax: change of the personal pronoun, transposition of tense, syntactical dependence or independence of the respective sentence or clause. In recent decades the literary explanation of free indirect style has concentrated more and more on its extrasyntactical aspects. Most of the literary explanations of free indirect style today agree in assuming that the essence of free indirect style lies in the dual view of the events from the perspective of the narrator and from that of a fictional character.[13] Again, the dual perspective of free indirect style must be understood as a special form of expression of the mediacy of narration. The opposing tendencies in the narrative medium which were described above, namely, the presence of the narrator as the tangible embodiment of the mediacy of narration, on the one hand, and the illusion of immediacy by the reflection of the fictional reality in the consciousness of a figural medium or a reflector-character, on the other, come together in free indirect style. The figural aspect of this dual perspective is usually more strongly supported by the narrative context than the authorial aspect, however. For this reason, free indirect style appears between the teller-pole and the reflector-pole on the typological circle nearer the figural narrative situation than the authorial narrative situation.

It is essential to the method of literary criticism that the phenomenon of free indirect style be viewed not in an isolated sentence, but in conjunction with other, related phenomena of the narrative mode within a longer text. This approach is even more appropriate when, as in our case, free indirect style is considered to be an aspect of the narrative situation. I shall thus attempt a classification of free indirect style with regard to the authorial-figural continuum of forms while consciously avoiding problems of definition which are treated in great detail in most studies dealing with free indirect style anyway.[14] I shall deal with free indirect style within a first-person narrative situation in the description of the sector of the typological circle between the first-person and figural narrative situations. Consideration of free indirect style within the larger narrative context is also justified from the reader's point of view, since the reader almost never notices free indirect style alone, but always together with several other, related narrative elements. The problem of the definition and delimitation of free indirect style resolves itself under the aspect of the continuum of forms as represented on the typological circle insofar as it becomes evident that free indirect style itself is not to be understood as a homogeneous and inflexible category, but rather as a continuum of forms and their modifications. These modifications can best be presented systematically in the stages of their authorial-figural transition.

7.1.5 The 'contamination' of the narrator's language by the language of the fictional characters

A first stage in the modification of an authorial narrative form in the direction of free indirect style and then towards a figural narrative situation is discernible when the report of the authorial narrator is 'contaminated' by the speech of the fictional characters.[15] The following passage from *Buddenbrooks* is a classic example of this phenomenon. It has already been quoted in earlier studies of free indirect style:

Once again, Mrs Stuht from Bellfounder's Street had the opportunity to associate with the best circles when she helped Mamsell Jungmann and the seamstress with Tony's toilet on the day of the wedding. *She had never, as God was her witness, seen a more beautiful bride*, kneeling, as fat as she was, and attached the little twigs of myrtle to the white antique moiré with her eyes raised in admiration . . . This took place in the breakfast room. [My emphasis]

Frau Stuht aus der Glockengießerstraße hatte wieder einmal Gelegenheit, in den ersten Kreisen zu verkehren, indem sie Mamsell Jungmann und die Schneiderin am Hochzeitstage bei Tony's Toilette unterstützte. *Sie hatte, strafe sie Gott, niemals eine schönere Braut gesehen*, lag, so dick sie war, auf den Knien und befestigte mit bewundernd erhobenen Augen die kleinen Myrtenzweiglein auf der weißen moiré antique . . . Dies geschah im Frühstückzimmer.[16]

A contamination such as this is of the narrator's language by the speech of the fictional characters, a kind of indirect or submerged quotation, can frequently be observed in Victorian novelists such as Dickens, George Eliot and Meredith, who prefer a very pronounced authorial style. As a rule it casts a slightly ironical light on the 'quoted' characters. This narrative element was already employed with virtuosity by Jane Austen, the writer who helped free indirect style to establish itself in the history of the English novel.[17] As an example I shall quote that passage from *Mansfield Park* in which Roy Pascal has identified the words and phrases which echo the speech of the characters by capitals. The italics are Austen's.

The Crawfords . . . were very willing to stay. Mary was satisfied with the parsonage as a present home, and Henry equally ready to lengthen his visit. He had come, intending to spend only a few days with them, but MANSFIELD PROMISED WELL, and there was nothing to call him elsewhere. It DELIGHTED Mrs Grant to keep them both with her, and Dr Grant was EXCEEDINGLY WELL CONTENTED to have it so; A TALKING PRETTY YOUNG WOMAN like Miss Crawford, is always pleasant society to an indolent, stay-at-home man; and Mr Crawford's being his guest was an excuse for drinking claret every day.

The Miss Bertrams' admiration of Mr Crawford was more RAP-TUROUS than any thing which Miss Crawford's habits made her likely to feel. She acknowledged, however, that the Mr Bertrams were VERY FINE YOUNG MEN, that two such young men were not often seen together even in London, and that their manners, particularly those of the eldest, were very good. *He* had been much in London, and had more LIVELI-NESS AND GALLANTRY than Edmund, and MUST, THEREFORE, BE PREFERRED; and, indeed, his being the eldest was another strong claim. She had FELT AN EARLY PRESENTIMENT that she *should* LIKE THE ELDEST BEST. She knew IT WAS HER WAY.[18]

It is an authorial narrator who reports here to the reader how the Crawfords are received as visitors in Mansfield, but in his report the narrator avails himself of numerous flourishes which seem to be characteristic of the speech of the individual characters: 'Most of these "quotations" are both characteristic and ironical, the set attributed to Mary Crawford, for instance, displaying her sophisti-cation, near-cynicism, and sharp self-knowledge.'[19] This inter-mingling of the language of the narrator and of the fictional characters suggests the origin of Jane Austen's use of free indirect style to Pascal. He supposes that it evolved from the way the novelist spoke with members of her family.[20]

7.1.6 Differentiation of the language of the narrator and of the characters

With the greater differentiation of the language of the narrator and of the characters in the modern novel, this narrative element has become perspectivally reinforced, as it were. The quotations from the characters' speech are set off more clearly from the authorial report and attain more prominence, that is, the figural element increases at the expense of the authorial element. Thus Joyce begins his narrative 'The Dead' with an authorial description of the two elderly Morkan sisters as they await the guests for their annual New Year's ball. Their nervousness and their concern about one of the expected guests is expressed in their speech, although the narrator does not quote them either directly or indirectly. Their anxiety is reflected in some idiomatic expressions characteristic of the old ladies which are incorporated into the narrative report:

Of course they had good reason to be fussy on such a night. And then it was long after ten o'clock and yet there was no sign of Gabriel and his wife. Besides they were *dreadfully afraid* that Freddy Malins might turn up screwed. They would *not wish for worlds* that any of Mary Jane's pupils should see him *under the influence*; and when he was like that it was sometimes very hard to manage him. Freddy Malins always came late but they wondered *what could be keeping Gabriel*: and that was what brought them every two minutes to the banisters to ask Lily had Gabriel or Freddy come. [My emphasis][21]

The more frequently such 'quotations' of the characters' speech occur and the more clearly they are distinguished as the language of the characters, the more prominent the figural element in the narrative becomes. Finally, if the quantitative ratio of the speech elements of the narrator to those of the characters is reversed, at first in shorter units of texts, then in longer and longer ones, the figural narrative situation becomes predominant, provided that the other narrative elements (reference to characters by name or personal pronoun, etc) also appear in the figural more often than in the authorial form.

7.1.7 Colloquialization of the narrator's language

Besides the tendency towards differentiation of the language of the narrator and that of the characters, an opposing tendency can also be observed in the modern novel, in the colloquialization of the narrator's language. This technique minimizes the differences between the narrator's speech and the characters' speech. Studies of free indirect style frequently emphasize that the occurrence of free indirect style is stimulated by a stylistic *niveau* which approximates colloquial speech.[22] Through the use of free indirect style 'the written language again' approaches 'the spoken language, which is syntactically simpler.'[23] In conjunction with free indirect style, such a colloquialization has an important semiotic function within the authorial-figural continuum: the register of colloquial language points more towards a figural medium, the register of the literary, standard language more towards an authorial medium. When an author such as Hemingway intentionally forgoes the potential of such a stylistic differentiation, a very specific effect can result: the authorial manner of perception, thought and feeling can approach that of the characters. The internal narrative distance shrinks. This colloquialization of the narrator's language is especially conspicuous in Döblin's novel *Alexanderplatz, Berlin: The Story of Franz Biberkopf*, in which authorial report and figural free indirect style, as Günter Steinberg has already shown, are often no longer distinguishable stylistically:

> She now has her secret with him, now more than ever in fact, the little devil, and she is not a bit afraid as to what her beloved is up to with that Pums gang; she's going to start something herself. She's going to look around on her own and see who's there in the dance-hall or the bowling-alley. Anyhow, Franz doesn't take her along with him, Herbert takes his Eva along, but Franz says: that's no place for you, I don't want you to go with such hell-cats.

> Sie hat jetzt ihr Geheimnis mit dem [Franz], und jetzt mehr als früher, das kleine Biest, und fürchtet sich auch gar nicht, was ihr geliebter Franz da anstellt bei den Pumsleuten: sie wird auch was unternehmen. Sie wird sich mal allein da umsehen, wer da eigentlich ist, aufm Ball oder Kegelfest. Zu die nimmt sie Franz ja nicht mit, Herbert nimmt seine Eva mit, aber Franz sagt: det ist nicht für dich, mit sone Toppsäue will ich dir nicht zusammen-haben.[24]

The beginning of the quotation contains an authorial report which does not essentially differ in style from the free indirect style which starts after the colon. The stylistic downgrading, so to speak, of the authorial language of the narrator, and its assimilation of the speech and thought of the characters can give the reader the impression that a figural narrative situation already predominates here throughout. The authorial narrative parts are no longer perceived as the speech and thoughts of a distant narrator but as those of a contemporary, who experiences the events on the level of the characters. We are dealing with another form of the reflectorization of the teller-character, described above.[25] Döblin's *Alexanderplatz, Berlin*, moreover, presents a very rich spectrum of different degrees of reflectorization of the teller-character.

Exactly the opposite effect can be observed when the speech and thoughts of characters which are rendered in free indirect style are elevated to the level of the literary style of the authorial narrator. This technique occurs very frequently in the early novel, and is especially conspicuous, for example, in Goethe's *Elective Affinities* (*Die Wahlverwandtschaften*). The authorial element is reinforced by the stylistic elevation of the speech or thoughts of the characters which are presented in free indirect style, just as the figural element is reinforced by colloquialization, as observed in Döblin's novel. I shall have to return to this observation in the course of the discussion of first-person narrative situation and its modification in the direction of figural narrative situation, since the level of style there has a similar effect on the narrative situation: a colloquial style, as in Salinger's *The Catcher in the Rye*, tends to limit the narrative perspective to the point of view of the experiencing self.

7.1.8 Authorial-figural problems of demarcation

When not only individual phrases but also arguments, explanations and motivations from the point of view of a fictional character are inserted into the narrative text, a further step has been taken in the direction of the figural narrative situation on the typological circle. Leo Spitzer and, after him, Steinberg have called attention to causal clauses which attach a figural reason to an authorial report. Spitzer speaks of 'pseudo-objective motivation,'[26] but the designation suggested by Steinberg seems more to the point:

The causal clauses with this function of rendering speech indirectly belong to the complex which one could call 'pseudo-authorial' or better 'figural' (sometimes 'neutral') motivation, to use Stanzel's terminology: they are arguments which are to be understood as indirect presentations of utterances or thoughts of the fictional characters. The motivation can follow the report with paratactic '*denn/car*/for,' and is in this case independent and thoroughly normal free indirect style: 'Together with them [the children of the common people] he [little Henri] baked his bread between hot stones and ate it after rubbing it with garlic. *Because garlic made you tall and made you always stay healthy*.' [My emphasis][27]

Although it is not explicitly stated that the reason given in the last sentence of the quotation is not that of the narrator, the reader nevertheless interprets it as the boy's opinion, that is, he assigns it to the horizon of experience and knowledge of the fictional character, not to that of the narrator. As soon as a reflectorization of this kind extends to several sentences or even to an entire paragraph, a figural narrative situation appears and displaces the authorial narrative situation. One could also interpret the last sentence of the quotation as a statement of universal validity, as a gnomic sentence, whose claim to universal validity is called into question by the fact that it is, through the use of past tense characteristic of the free indirect style embedded in a figural consciousness. Here we see the tension-filled relationship between authorial and figural perspective which is difficult to define, but which is very important for the structure of meaning of a narrative. This difficulty was discussed in the chapter on perspective. It is often impossible to determine whether a particular statement is intended as an utterance of opinion of the authorial or of the figural medium. In aperspectival narratives the boundary frequently cannot be drawn at all. Generally speaking, however, it can be said that the number of aperspectival works decreases noticeably when the prevailing narrative situation approaches the figural narrative situation. Narratives with figural narrative situation are as a rule more sharply perspectivized, to be sure, yet an absolutely unambiguous differentiation of the figural and the authorial view is not always possible here either. Sometimes a certain ambiguity in this respect can even be a part of the structure of the work. A definite criterion for the distinction between an authorial and a figural view is provided by two types of the negation of the verb 'to know' (*wissen*). A statement with 'does/did not know that' referring to a fictional character who functions as a figural medium always contains an authorial statement. Statements with 'does/did not know if/why/what,' on the other hand, must, as a rule, be considered figural statements.[28]

In a strictly figural narrative situation, the negation of the verb 'to know' is usually replaced by the direct formulation of the question resulting from the ignorance of the fictional character. *A Portrait of the Artist* contains only a few examples for one of the two uses of the negated verb 'to know' ('It pained him that he did not know well what politics meant'). On the other hand, there are numerous questions in free indirect style such as the following: 'Was it right to kiss his mother or wrong to kiss his mother. What did that mean, to kiss?'; 'What day of the week was it?'; 'Had Cranley not heard him?' Just as frequently appear the words 'He wondered whether/if/which.'[29] The (authorial) statement about the ignorance of the hero is replaced in a figural narrative situation by the presentation of the thoughts which either reveal a lack of knowledge or are evoked by such a lack. Instead of a character's lack of knowledge being communicated by report, the cognitive condition of 'not knowing' is presented in the figural medium.

7.1.9 From free indirect style to figural narrative situation

If the extent of free indirect style in a narrative increases to the point that it largely replaces authorial utterances, a figural narrative situation results. Figural narrative situation can also be understood as the extended use of free indirect style (in the literary rather than strictly grammatical sense of the term) throughout a narrative text. It is better, however, to use the term figural narrative situation for such extended free indirect style, because this designation specifies that the extension of free indirect style over a longer narrative text results for the reader in a new orientation. Since the presence of the authorial narrator is no longer evoked in the reader's imagination, the reader places himself entirely in the Here and Now of the character who functions in the passage as a figural medium or reflector-character. Here, free indirect style actually ceases to be an expression of a 'dual voice,' because the authorial voice in it is for all practical purposes no longer audible. This change is another reason for not speaking of free indirect style but of figural narrative situation when referring to narratives of this kind. This term has already been employed in a number of publications on Kafka's *The Trial* and *The Castle*, Joyce's *A Portrait of the Artist*, and on novels by Virginia Woolf, Hermann Broch, Nathalie Sarraute and others.

7.1.10 The authorial-figural continuum and the reflectorized teller-character

The transition from the authorial to the figural narrative situation can also be considered under the aspect of the gradual transformation of an authorial narrator into an anonymous figural medium. This process, which narrative research has so far all but ignored, was described above as the reflectorization of the teller-character.[30] Now we must define this process according to its position on the formal continuum of the typological circle.

The tendency to displace the authorial narrator from the narrative continues in reflectorization, but with one important difference: reflectorization does not involve the disappearance of the teller-character. Instead he is made similar in spatio-temporal orientation, attitude and stylistic register to the fictional characters, especially to that character who functions as a figural medium. In other words, through his reflectorization the authorial narrator develops the ability to camouflage himself, as it were, not only by positioning himself in the fictional world, but also by assuming the mode of perception and in part even the voice and manner of expression of the fictional characters. A broad scale of possibilities is available here, too, ranging from the appropriation of a single formulation up to the complete observation of a scene or situation in the spirit of the characters.[31] If the latter occurs one must distinguish whether the reflectorized teller functions as a genuine mouthpiece of the characters, perhaps as the voice of their collective experience or philosophy of life, or whether his utterances are ironic because they convey opinions of the characters from which the authorial narrator actually dissociates himself. This distinction, which is important for an interpretation, will not necessarily be easy or unambiguous, as is always the case when irony is involved. Another example from Mansfield's stories will serve to illustrate this point. The example from 'The Garden Party' discussed above[32] was interpreted as an ironic, distanced remark on the part of the implied authorial narrator about the social consciousness of the Sheridans. In the seventh segment of the narrative 'At the Bay,' on the other hand, an observation is rendered by the reflectorized teller in his poetic description of a beach which the characters could also make if they possessed his acuity and his gift of expression.[33] Here the point of view of the reflectorized teller is more figural, in the former case more strongly authorial.

The reflectorization of the teller also implies a shift in the spatio-temporal deixis. The example of a spatio-temporal displacement discussed above[34] – 'There/Here he trudged around the Forum the whole day' – could also be explained with the aid of the concept of reflectorization. 'Here he trudged' expresses the spatial orientation of a reflectorized teller, 'There he trudged' expresses that of an unrestricted authorial teller. In the course of reflectorization, the distant deixis (There/Then), which is characteristic of the authorial narrative situation, is temporarily displaced by the close-up deixis (Here/Now) characteristic of a figural narrative situation. Not every authorial 'now' or 'today' referring to the present time of the action is an indication of reflectorization, however. Thus the 'today again, too' (*auch heute wieder*) at the beginning of Theodor Fontane's *Effi Briest* scarcely modifies the authoriality of the narrator who makes himself known at the beginning of this novel:

The front of the manor house – a slope with pots of aloe and a few garden chairs – was also a pleasant place to be and afforded, at the same time, all kinds of diversions when the sky was cloudy. But on days when the hot sun shone down, everyone preferred the side of the house facing the garden, especially the lady and the daughter of the house, who today again, too, were sitting on the flagstone path which lay in full shade.

Auch die Front des Herrenhauses – eine mit Aloekübeln und ein paar Gartenstühlen besetzte Rampe – gewährte bei bewölktem Himmel einen angenehmen und zugleich allerlei Zerstreuung bietenden Aufenthalt; an

Tagen aber, wo die Sonne niederbrannte, wurde die Gartenseite ganz entschieden bevorzugt, besonders von Frau und Tochter des Hauses, die denn auch heute wieder auf dem im vollen Schatten liegenden Fliesengange saßen.[35]

The frequency and the consistency of the authorial use of deictic adverbs which actually are appropriate for the spatio-temporal orientation of a fictional character, can, on the other hand, bring about a certain reflectorization of the teller-character. A distinct tendency toward the reflectorization of the spatial deixis is discernible at the beginning of Georg Büchner's narrative 'Lenz,' in spite of the authorial narrator:

On the 20th of January Lenz crossed the mountains. The peaks and high slopes in snow, *down* the valleys grey stones, green patches, cliffs and firs. It was wet and cold; the water trickled *down* the rocks and leapt over the path. The branches of the firs sagged heavily in the damp air. Grey clouds drove over the sky, but all so dense – and then the mist came steaming *up*.

Den 20. Januar ging Lenz durch's Gebirg. Die Gipfel und hohen Bergflächen im Schnee, die Täler *hinunter* graues Gestein, grüne Flächen, Felsen und Tannen. Es war naßkalt; das Wasser rieselte die Felsen *hinunter* und sprang über den Weg. Die Äste der Tannen hingen schwer herab in die feuchte Luft. Am Himmel zogen graue Wolken, aber alles so dicht – und dann dampfte der Nebel *herauf*. [My emphasis][36]

As Anderegg has already shown in his interpretation of this passage, both the deictic adverbs and the choice of words and the metaphors in this text allude to the experience of the main character: 'Everything that takes place refers to Lenz and affects him.'[37] Anderegg also calls attention to the fact that the reader's assumption of the spatial orientation of the main character is only possible if the authorial narrator does not define his position.[38] A complete reflectorization, on the other hand, would require that the narrative point of view be fixed in or near the Here and Now of the fictional character.

7.2 From the authorial to the first-person narrative situation

Every story is first-person whether the speaker identifies himself or not. (J. Moffet and K. R. McElheny, *Points of View: An Anthology of Short Stories*)

If we follow the diagram of the typological circle from the authorial narrative situation in the direction of the first-person narrative situation, we soon have to cross the line of demarcation separating the third-person narrative from the first-person narrative in the generally accepted meaning of these two terms. With regard to narrative theory, however, it is also important to note a further change in the narratorial 'I' at this line of demarcation. The ontological basis of the narratorial 'I' changes as this borderline is crossed. The difference is marked by the opposition identity and non-identity of the realms of existence of the narrator and the fictional characters. This change in the ontological basis of the narratorial 'I' has far-reaching consequences. Compared to the bodiless (but not impersonal) authorial 'I,' the person of the first-person narrator increases in embodiment, becomes an embodied narrator in the sense of my definition in Chapter 4.6, to the extent that the position of such a first-person narrative on the typological circle approaches the ideal type of the first-person narrative situation. The increase in embodiment of the first-person narrator results in a restriction of his horizon of knowledge and perception and a linking of the narrative process to the existence of the first-person narrator as a fictional character.

For greater clarity I shall distinguish several stages in this process of the embodiment of the narrator. Closest to the authorial narrator stands the first-person narrator who claims to be the editor or publisher of a manuscript (the fictional editor of *Moll Flanders* or Richard Sympson in *Gulliver's Travels*), the reciter of a story (Douglas in 'The Turn of the Screw'), and the narrator of the frame-story of a cycle of tales ('Chaucer' in *The Canterbury Tales*, the schoolmaster in Theodor Storm's 'Der Schimmelreiter'). Each of these first-person roles, especially that of the narrator of a frame-story can take on a more strongly marked personal and physical presence in the fictional world.[39] In so doing it approaches the next stage in the embodiment of the first-person narrator, that of the periphal first-person narrator. This type of narrator is distinguished from the quasi-autobiographical first-person narrator of the phase that follows next on the typological circle above all by his position in relation to the narrated events. He is located at the periphery of the narrated events and his role is that of an observer, witness, biographer, chronicler, but not that of the hero who stands in the centre of the events. This role also permits the most varied forms of participation in the action, including the entwining of the fates of the narrator and the hero (Overton in *The Way of All Flesh* and Marlow in *Lord Jim*). The last stage is the quasi-autobiographical first-person narrative, in which the narrator and the hero of the story are identical. The majority of first-person narratives are found here. It is necessary, therefore, to differentiate the role of the first-person narrator as main character still further. The relationship between the narrating and the experiencing self can be employed as the criterion of distinction. On our walk along the typological circle we first encounter a first-person narrator whose narrating self presents itself in great detail as narrator (Tristram Shandy, Siggi Jepsen in Siegfried Lenz's novel *The German Lesson*). Next we meet the classic first-person narrator in whom the narrating self and the experiencing self, while not quantitatively balanced, are of equal importance (David Copperfield, Felix Krull). Finally we encounter the first-person narrative in which the experiencing self almost entirely displaces the narrating self in the reader's field of vision (*The Catcher in the Rye*). Epistolary and diary novels belong somewhere in the zone between the two last-mentioned stages of the first-person narrative, according to the emphasis placed on the process of composition and the degree of narrative distance.

7.2.1 The authorial narrator in Pumpernickel

Like all the other boundaries in my narrative theory, the one between the authorial and the first-person narrative situation is open. A tendency towards the embodiment of the narratorial 'I' already begins in the domain of the authorial narrative situation. At the very beginning of *The Brothers Karamazov*, the authorial narrator calls one of the characters of this novel 'one of the most muddle-headed and preposterous fellows of *our* district.'[40] His personal reference here is similar to that of a first-person narrator who tells his own story, as does the narrator of *The Devils*, who begins his story as do most first-person narrators, in the following way: 'Before describing the extraordinary events which took place so recently in our town, hitherto not remarkable for anything in particular . . .'[41] A temporary positioning of the authorial narrator in the world of the characters, which is usually not further developed, was a widespread narrative device in the nineteenth century. It is found in Dickens, George Eliot, Trollope, Jean Paul Richter, and Wilhelm Raabe, but also in Flaubert, who introduces the narrator of *Madame Bovary* as a schoolmate of one of the fictional characters[42] This narrator, quite prominent at the beginning of the novel, later withdraws completely. In most cases this narrative device serves as a means of verification of the story and is therefore part of the rhetoric of dissimulation which aims at obliterating the boundary between the world of the characters and the world not only of the narrator but even the world of the readers. The beginning of Gogol's story 'The Overcoat' furnishes an especially interesting example of this technique because here the crossing of this boundary is expressly retraced. It is through the retraction, however, that the reader first really becomes aware of this boundary. The narrative opening is undertaken twice, as it were, first by a narratorial 'I' who crosses the borderline to the first-person narrative, and then by an authorial narrator who has withdrawn again to his real domain behind the borderline:

In the department of . . . but I had better not mention which department. There is nothing in the world more touchy than a department, a regiment, a government office, and, in fact, any sort of official body. Nowadays every private individual considers all society insulted in his person. I have been told that very lately a complaint was lodged by a police inspector of which town I don't remember, and that in this complaint he set forth clearly that the institutions of the State were in danger and that his sacred name was being taken in vain; and, in proof thereof, he appended to his complaint an enormously long volume of some romantic work in which a police inspector appeared on every tenth page, occasionally, indeed, in an intoxicated condition. And so, to avoid any unpleasantness, we had better call the department of which we are speaking 'a certain department.'

And so, in a *certain department* there was a *certain clerk* . . .[43]

With this, Gogol makes the reader aware of a linguistic distinction which marks this boundary. With reference to the setting and to the characters, the definite article has the effect of concretization, the indefinite article that of generalization. This phenomenon constitutes a parallel to the use of the familiarizing article at the beginning of a narrative with a reflector-character which was discussed above.[44] Here the avoidance of the familiarizing article ('In the department' of the first opening becomes 'in a certain department' in the second opening of the story) is an indication of the authorial external perspective and underscores the separation of the realms of existence of the narrator and the characters.

In addition to the verification of the story, however, there is another reason for the frequency of such crossovers by the authorial narrator in the novel of the nineteenth century. Perhaps one could speak of a desire on the part of the authorial narrator to round off or to complete his personality in the framework of an existence which is also physically determined. This tendency is especially apparent in the elaboration of this narrative convention towards the end of Thackeray's *Vanity Fair*. The narrator, who up to this point had been authorial, suddenly appears among the characters of the novel as one of the visitors in Pumpernickel, the capital of a miniature German principality, as if he were a first-person narrator. In the sixty-second chapter, 'Am Rhein,' the reader is surprised by the information that the narrator saw some of the main characters of the novel personally in his youth, as he was enjoying himself with his peers in Pumpernickel, the spa and capital city ('we young fellows in the stalls').[45] The narrator retains the attitude of the observer, to be sure, but the detail with which this episode is presented forces the reader to note fully the presence of the narrator in the world of the characters. With this transfer of his narrator into the world of Amelia, Becky, Jos Sedley and Dobin, Thackeray invites criticism for inconsistency in the conception of his narrator, since the narrator introduced himself in the preface to the novel ('Before the Curtain') as 'manager of the Performance' and had also fully assumed the traditional privileges of omniscience and the right of disposition over the characters as authorial narrator. The narrator's appearance as a young contemporary and fellow visitor in Pumpernickel would seem to require that he renounce these privileges as Olympian narrator. Thackeray actually makes a gesture in this direction. In Chapter LXXVI the narrator hints that Tapeworm, the British chargé d'affaires at the court of Pumpernickel, is the direct source of his detailed knowledge of Becky's story.[46] The perspective of the presentation is in no way influenced by this suggestion, however. No restriction of the horizon of knowledge of the teller-character corresponding to the reference to his source takes place. We must, therefore, look elsewhere for the reason for this shift of the authorial narrative situation in the direction of a first-person narrative situation.

The actual cause for the shift seems to lie, as I have already indicated, in the need of the authorial narrator to furnish his personality with a physical existence, to transform himself from an abstract functional role into a figure of flesh and blood, a person with an individual history. The young man in Pumpernickel, who many years later will tell Becky's and Amelia's story, does not yet possess the necessary maturity and detachment and, at this age, also lacks the mild cynicism of the adult narrator. In this connection we must not forget that Thackeray makes his authorial narrator at the time of the narrative act older than he, the author Thackeray, was at the actual writing of the novel (Dickens, by the way, very often proceeds very similarly). This observation furnishes a further argument against the identification of author and authorial narrator which is still insinuated by the majority of critics. The *in persona* presence of the narrator as a young man at the scene of one of the last episodes of the novel also provides justification for the numerous authorial commentaries which call the reader's attention to the fact that times have changed very much since the time of the fictional events,[47] and the narrator has changed with them. He, too, was once a person who sought enjoyment at the 'Vanity Fair' of life, and in this sense the Pumpernickel episode contributes to the rounding off of the narrator's personality as a human being similar to you and me, a rounding off which could not have been granted him, or only in a rather circumstantial way, in the domain assigned to an authorial narrator. This is the beginning of an attempt at a history of the development and the education of the authorial narrator. This development is especially relevant for an interpretation, because the suggestion of a developmental history of this kind points out what otherwise would remain completely unnoticed, namely that the truly authorial narrator is not subject to the passing of time. As a rule such a narrator tells the story of his characters from a fixed point in time with a fixed personality, that is, often without personal recollection of his own past. In the first-person narrative situation as it appears in such quasi-autobiographical first-person novels as *David Copperfield* and *Green Henry* it is precisely the linking of the narrative act to the personal experience of the narrator that becomes the main concern of the novel.

7.2.2 The peripheral first-person narrator

To make the demonic strain pass through an undemonic medium . . . (Thomas Mann, *The Story of a Novel: The Genesis of Doctor Faustus*)

In the Pumpernickel episode of *Vanity Fair* we encounter the narratorial 'I' in a role which it retains from beginning to end in many novels and stories: the narrator as eyewitness at the scene of the events, as observer, as the contemporary of the main character, his biographer, etc. In all these cases the narrator himself does not stand at the centre of the events but at the periphery. For this reason I call him the peripheral first-person narrator, thereby distinguishing him from the autobiographical first-person narrator, who is at one and the same time the main character, standing at the centre of the action, and the narrator. The most important function of the peripheral first-person narrator is the mediation or subjectivizing of the narrated events. Mediacy is emphatically overt in this narrative situation. The actual meaning of the narrative lies not in how the main character and his world are in themselves, but rather in how they are perceived at some distance by a narrator who observes, experiences and assesses. This situation impressively reflects 'the epistemological view familiar to us since Kant that we do not apprehend the world in itself, but rather as it has passed through the medium of an observing mind.'[48] Consequently, peripheral first-person narrators differ not only in their temporal and spatial distance from the actual events, but also in the fact that a characteristic feature of their personality is their perception, which is at least in part dependent on their personal relationship with the main character. The role of the peripheral first-person narrator is most frequently that of the paternal friend, the close personal friend or admirer of the main character. This group includes Overton in *The Way of All Flesh*, Marlow in *Lord Jim*, and Zeitblom in *Doctor Faustus: The Life of The German Composer, Adrian Leverkühn, as Told by a Friend*. The thematic goal of such a narrative is the friendly, sympathetic attempt of the narrator to understand the extraordinary main character. From these peripheral first-person narrators we must distinguish those who, because of their typical, representative character, must be interpreted as serving as a contrasting foil, as the antithesis of the hero. As a rule, such narrators are not closely associated with the main characters through a personal, friendly relationship, but are rather subordinated to them as servants (Nelly Dean in *Wuthering Heights*) or as attending companions (Dr Watson in *Sherlock Holmes*). In addition to these peripheral first-person narrators who are sociologically characterized, there are others who are typified chiefly according to their philosophy of life or psychological makeup. They are found, for example, in some of Conrad Ferdinand Meyer's narratives. Friedemann characterized them as follows:

In a letter to Paul Heyse, C. F. Meyer justified his device of having Dante narrate the story of the marriage of the monk by stating that he saw him as the representative of the medieval period. 'My Dante in front of the hearth . . . is a typical figure and simply means middle ages.' In the same way, the author does not present the story of Thomas Becket, the saint who avenged the seduction of his daughter by his king, 'directly, which could easily confuse the reader because the story is so enigmatic, but instead has it narrated by a simple and stouthearted Swiss, who cannot be misled because of his unerring sense of morality.'[49]

Naturally the functions differentiated here often appear in conjunction with each other in individual works. Thus Zeitblom, the peripheral first-person narrator in *Doctor Faustus*, is both a devoted friend and admirer of the great composer Adrian Leverkühn and, as we can infer from Thomas Mann's words quoted in the epigraph to this chapter, a pragmatic type of person who contrasts with the main character in almost every respect.[50] The roles personified by the main character and the narrator, however, are by no means restricted to this distribution of types (hero = complex, demonic; narrator = relatively naive, prosaic). Scholes and Kellogg see the directly opposite distribution of types in this form of the novel:

The old tragic problem of presenting a character with enough crudeness for *hybris* and *hamartia* but enough sensitivity for ultimate discovery and self-understanding has always been a great one for the narrative artist . . . [T]he division of protagonists into the simple, stark actor and the complex, sensitive sharer in the action solves for the novelist a great problem. Marlow can do the understanding for Kurtz or Jim; Carraway can do it for Gatsby; Jack Burden for Willie Stark in *All the King's Men*; and Quentin Compson and Shreve McCannon for Sutpen in Faulkner's *Absalom, Absalom!*[51]

In all narratives with a peripheral first-person narrator, however, the tension between the personality of the narrator and that of the main character(s) is of primary significance for the meaning and must be considered in an interpretation. Booth's concept of reliability can be of help here, as Jacqueline Viswanathan, for one, has shown in her examination of the narrative situation in *Wuthering Heights*, *Under Western Eyes* and *Doctor Faustus*.[52] The problem of the unreliability of the first-person narrator, or, more accurately, of his limited insight into the true state of affairs, is most clearly evident when he avails himself of the privilege of reproducing dialogues of the characters in great detail, as practically all first-person narrators do. Under such circumstances the mediacy of this particular narrative situation is almost completely suppressed. This technique results in an impression of direct scenic presentation, and the reader loses sight of the narrator. The same phenomenon can also be observed, of course, in an autobiographical first-person narrative or in an authorial narrative situation. In a narrative with a peripheral first-person narrator, however, it acquires special significance, since the parts reported by the narrator often contrast with the parts presented directly. In the words of Viswanathan: 'While the narrators' subjective bias is very apparent in the narrative parts, in the scenes they [the peripheral first-person narrators] function as perfect tape-recorders.'[53] In addition, peripheral first-person narrators are often so preoccupied with their function as narrator that they 'forget their part' and temporarily no longer speak 'in character,' but instead like an authorial narrator who is bound neither to a definite personal idiom nor to a definite point of view.[54]

These two tendencies, the emancipation of long passages of dialogue and scenic presentation from the restriction inherent in this narrative situation and the change of narrative style, can be characterized as the authorialization of the peripheral first-person narrator, a phenomenon that moreover can be observed occasionally in the autobiographical first-person narrator, as well. This authorialization of the first-person narrator in a sense provides a counterpart to the reflectorization of the authorial narrator. What both phenomena have in common seems to be a striving for balance between figural and authorial competence. The particularity of characters and narrators as fictional characters strives for the universality of the authorial narrator with external perspective and omniscience, and, inversely, the universality of the authorial narrator seeks to become concrete in the particularity of the fictional characters.

Having established that there is an authorialization of the first-person narrator, the question of the possibility of a reflectorization of the first-person narrative situation arises. The actual reflectorization of the first-person narrator takes place when the first-person narrator withdraws more and more as the teller-character and changes into a reflector-character; this development takes place when the focus of presentation is shifted exclusively to the experiencing self. I shall deal with this process in connection with the further description of the typological circle. It would perhaps be most appropriate to speak of a kind of reflectorization of the peripheral first-person narrator in Conrad, although here the process is more thematic than structural, occurring specifically in those narratives in which a very peculiar relationship exists or is growing between the peripheral first-person narrator and the hero. Conrad scholars have coined the term 'unforeseen partnership' for this relationship. In the course of his endeavors to probe and understand the life of his hero, the narrator discovers an internal affinity between himself and his hero which captivates him more and more and causes him to empathize intensively with the experiences of his hero, to imagine himself so totally in the latter's situation that a psychological or moral identification ensues. This theme is a variation of the *alter-ego* motif, which can also be found in other works by Conrad not in the first-person form, for example, in *The Secret Sharer*. In first-person narratives the motif attains a certain structural significance in addition to its thematic implications. The 'unforeseen partnership' restructures a peripheral first-person narrative situation, which in itself tends towards mediation, towards figural empathy. The first-person narrator seems himself almost compelled to empathize with the hero's situation, which can even lead to the vicarious assumption of the hero's fate by the first-person narrator, as can be seen in Marlow in *Heart of Darkness* and even more so in *Lord Jim*. In this way the peripheral first-person narrator's attitude toward the hero approaches that relationship characteristic of the narrating and the experiencing self in the quasi-autobiographical first-person novel. In the latter case, the 'partnership' is existentially given, which does not prevent the relationship between the narrating and the experiencing self from becoming problematical. One possible cause might be the refusal of the narrating self 'to accept' its experiencing self, as in Frisch's *I'm Not Stiller*, for example. The typical form of the peripheral first-person narrative with predominant empathy ('unforeseen partnership') between the first-person narrator and the main character is, therefore, located closer to the quasi-autobiographical first-person narrative on the typological circle than to the peripheral first-person narrative with a predominantly mediating function.

7.2.3 From the quasi-autobiographical first-person narrative to interior monologue

> A tranquillising spirit presses now
> On my corporeal frame, so wide appears
> The vacancy between me and those days
> Which yet have such self-presence in my mind,
> That, musing on them, often do I seem
> Two consciousnesses, conscious of myself
> And of some other Being.
> (Wordsworth, *The Prelude*)

This sector of the continuum of forms is characterized by the gradual withdrawal of the narrating self and by the increasing emphasis of the presentation on the experiencing self. At first the reader can still recognize the narrator, who is also the main character in the narrative act. At the same time the narrator is spatially and temporally integrated within the fictional reality, that is, he is physically at the scene of the events and participates in their course. The opposition between narrator and hero is replaced here by the opposition between narrating self and experiencing self. Consequently, the existential bond between the narrative act and the experience, described above in Chapter 4.6 as characteristic of the embodied narrator, becomes fully operative. This narrative situation permits any variations and modulations which can again be illustrated as a continuum on the typological circle extending on either side of the ideal type of the first-person narrative situation. The primary principle of classification defining this continuum is the relative distribution of the emphasis either on the narrating or the experiencing self and the field of tension which establishes itself accordingly between the two phases or aspects of the self. In *Moby-Dick*, *Tristram Shandy*, and in Lenz's *The German Lesson*, the reader's attention is attracted more by the narrating self than by the experiencing self. In the classical first-person novel with autobiographical form, the relations are balanced. The experiencing self claims the larger part of the narrative, but because of the continuous presence of the narrating self and the importance of its commentaries, an equilibrium is attained between the experiencing and the narrating self, as in *Moll Flanders*, *David Copperfield*, *Green Henry* and *Felix Krull*. This kind of first-person novel can be considered the classical form, because in it the field of tension between the two selves is always resolved. Some critics of the bourgeois novel of the nineteenth century, such as Jean-Paul Sartre, find this resolution naive and unrealistic.[55] The number of narratives in which the relationship between hero and world is problematic and is not resolved, in fact, seems to be somewhat smaller in this form than in narratives which are directly adjacent to it on the typological circle.

If we proceed from the first-person narrative situation in the direction of the figural narrative situation on the typological circle, we see changes in the forms of the first-person narrative which bear a certain resemblance to the changes in the forms of the third-person narrative between the authorial and the figural narrative situations. The process is multi-layered here, too, and the transition cannot be classified strictly according to a linear scale, because individual phenomena tend to overlap. For the sake of clarity, however, these phenomena will be listed and discussed in the order which comes closest to the system illustrated by the typological circle:

1. The narrating self withdraws more and more; the balance between the narrating and the experiencing self, which is characteristic of the quasi-autobiographical first-person narrative, is abandoned, allowing the experiencing self to dominate. As a result

the embodiment of the narratorial 'I' decreases in importance for the motivation of the narrative process, but not as a physical basis for the state of mind of the experiencing self. The narrative act itself is no longer overt, the reader or listener is addressed less and less.

2. Gradually the focus of presentation is concentrated more clearly in the experiencing self. The accent is on the event *in actu*, on the experience in the momentary Here and Now, which also restricts the horizon of knowledge and perception of the experiencing self. At the same time the main motivation of the action shifts from conscious insight, will and reflection to unconscious or only semi-conscious reaction and, in extreme cases, to mere neurophysiological reflex.

3. The narrative distance, which in the quasi-autobiographical first-person novel constitutes the prerequisite for the well-balanced and judicious attitude of the narrating self to his earlier experiences, almost always decreases with the withdrawal of the narrating self. Holden Caulfield narrates only a few weeks after the 'senseless' experiences of the days he spends in New York; through the confessional character of the narration the narrating self is almost completely displaced by the experiencing self. Beckett's first-person characters vegetate towards their existential disintegration, a disintegration which can also be observed in the absence of distance between the narrating and the experiencing self.

Epistolary and diary novels are located in this sector of the typological circle. It is not the number of correspondents participating in the correspondence which is decisive for the systematic classification of the epistolary novel, but primarily the spatio-temporal and internal, that is, psychological, distance which the correspondent attains from his experience. In this sense the narrative situation must, strictly speaking, be determined separately for each letter. The scale of narrative distance in Richardson's *Pamela*, for example, extends from one week, about which she gives a condensed report, to the 'instantaneous description' of those critical moments in which her pen records the advances of her seducer and tormentor second by second.[56]

4. In analogy to the narratives in dialogue form on the side of the authorial-figural continuum, the narrative in dialogue form on the first-person side of the typological circle is located approximately halfway between the first-person and the figural narrative situation. The predominance of dialogue is only a secondary criterion of classification. Of primary importance is the fact that the narrator has already almost completely withdrawn here, while a reflector-

character has not yet become discernible. This observation also holds for the narrative in dialogue form on the opposite side of the typological circle. Since in both cases the criterion of classification is the absence of distinct features (except for the dialogue form), it is clear that a first-person narrative of this kind, for example, Hemingway's 'Fifty Grand,' is hardly to be distinguished at all from a third-person narrative of a comparable type (for example, 'The Killers'). Besides the dialogue form and the predominance of scenic presentation, both forms are characterized above all by the absence of a teller-character as well as the absence of a reflector-character.

Finally, interior monologue represents the transition between first-person and figural narrative situation. In interior monologue the reader encounters a self which already exhibits the characteristic feature of a reflector-character: it does not narrate or address a listener or reader, but reflects in its consciousness its own momentary situation, including the reminiscences evoked by this situation. The outside world presented in an interior monologue thus appears merely as a reflex in the consciousness of the first-person character. Since the distinction between first-person and third-person reference is unmarked, as was set forth in Chapter 4.8.2,[57] within the context of the rendering of consciousness and in the absence of a teller-character, the transition from the sector of the first-person narrative situation to that of the figural narrative situation on the typological circle takes place inconspicuously. This border is also open. The nature of the typological circle as a continuous system of forms without categorical division is confirmed here again.

Some problems arising in the first-person sector of the typological circle which has just been described will be analyzed in somewhat greater detail in the following section.

7.2.4 The relationship between the two selves in the quasi-autobiographical narrative situation

I hope that I am a wiser and more charitable man now than I was then – I am certainly a happier man – and that the light of wisdom falling upon a fool can reveal, together with folly, the austere outline of truth. (Iris Murdoch, *The Black Prince*, Preface of the first-person narrator, Bradley Pearson)

The characteristic feature of the quasi-autobiographical first-person narrative situation is the internal tension between the self as hero and the self as narrator. In an earlier book, I suggested the terms 'experiencing self' and 'narrating self' for these two phases in the life of the narratorial 'I.'[58] The narrative distance separating the two phases of the narratorial 'I' temporally, spatially and psychologically, is generally a measure of the intensity of the process of experience and education to which the narrating self was subjected before it began the narration of its story. The narrative distance (between the narrating and the experiencing self) is, therefore, also one of the most important points of departure for the interpretation of the quasi-autobiographical first-person novel. The variety of its forms extends from identification to complete estrangement between the narrating and the experiencing self. The earlier quasi-autobiographical first-person novel frequently ends with a total change in the moral personality of the first-person character. Estrangement is dominant here in the form of a turning away from the earlier self, as in Hans Jakob Christoph von Grimmelshausen's *The Adventurous Simplicissimus*[59] and Defoe's *Moll Flanders*. Often, however, little consideration is given in these novels to the continuity of the psychological development of the personality of the first-person narrator. The numerous commentaries which the morally transformed Moll Flanders makes on her earlier life as a thief, prostitute and bigamist, for example, create the impression that Defoe has yoked together in a single person Moll Flanders's experiencing self and the reflections of the authorial 'I,' an entirely different person.[60] The history of the quasi-autobiographical first-person novel is the history of the more and more convincing psychological integration of the experiencing and the narrating self.

In the quasi-autobiographical first-person narrative, the narrative process itself also becomes an essential part of the story, but in a different way than in an authorial narrative. These two narrative situations are similar in the varying degree of detail which can characterize the narrative process. If a scale were constructed to represent this aspect it would extend from detailed presentation (in the vicinity of the junction with the peripheral first-person narrative situation) to the almost complete suppression of the narrative process at the transition to interior monologue. More essential, however, are the dissimilarities between those two narrative situations. In the first-person narrative situation, the narrative act is a form of continuation of the experiences of the self which results in an existential motivation to narrate foreign to the authorial narrative situation. The quasi-autobiographical first-person narrator remains bound to his earlier self by numerous existential threads despite his manifold transformations. If he or she looks back at the mistakes and confusion of his or her former life from the distance of mellow age, as do Moll Flanders or Felix Krull, the narrator usually can recognize some kind of pattern; if, on the other hand, he or she has not yet attained this distance from the experiencing self of the surveyed life or has attained it only partially (like Holden Caulfield or Oskar Mazerath) then confusion and the lack of orientation of experience will also become part of the narrative process. The shorter the narrative distance, the closer the narrating self stands to the experiencing self. The horizon of knowledge and perception of the experiencing self becomes narrower and the effect of memory as a catalyst capable of clarifying the substance of experience is correspondingly limited.[61] Here the close connection between the delimitation of the horizon of knowledge and the effect of memory in the first-person narrative becomes clearly apparent.

7.2.5 Point of view and memory in the first-person narrative

A minimum of memory is indispensible, if one is to live really. (Beckett's Malone in *Malone Dies*)

The delimitation of the horizon of knowledge and experience frequently occurs as a theme in works of fiction characterized by the opposition of the two selves of the first-person narrator. Contrary to a common belief, such a restriction results in more advantages than disadvantages for the novelist. The disadvantages, or what are traditionally considered to be disadvantages, are almost always the consequence of some awkward use of the first-person narrative situation or of a too-literal adherence to the point of view of the first-person narrator. A number of conventions, such as eaves-dropping and the mirror monologue,[62] are also commonly used to avoid such difficulties. But what can be an artful means of perspectivization and ironization on the stage, however, as in *Love's Labour's Lost*, is almost always an awkward solution in the novel. Nevertheless, the eavesdropping or keyhole scene has always enjoyed a certain popularity in the first-person novel. It can already be found in a very striking form, for example, in one of the first first-person novels, Thomas Nashe's *The Unfortunate Traveller*: looking through a crack in the wall, the first-person narrator witnesses how a bandit rapes a virtuous matron while she lies prone on the corpse of her murdered husband.[63] Most of the Victorian authors employ this device: Dickens uses it in *David Copperfield*,[64] for example. The long stairway and the partially open door of the room which serves as a temporary lodging for

Martha and as Emily's place of refuge offer very favourable conditions for such a scene, and Dickens makes the best possible use of them. But even the great narrative skill of a Dickens cannot entirely hide the fact that an eavesdropping scene like this is a makeshift solution. Such solutions result in the final analysis from too narrow an understanding of the perspectival necessities and possibilities of the first-person narrative situation. This misunderstanding also constitutes the basis for many critical discussions of the first-person form. I must agree with Hamburger when she contradicts Georg Misch's view that 'the vividness of creative representation' can be attained 'more freely and pleasurably as first-person presentation' than when the imagination must be transferred into a third person.[65] Even if we conceded the gift of 'perfect memory' to the first-person narrator, making him capable, among other things, of reproducing lengthy dialogues verbatim from days long past, such a convention would still not cover everything that is presented by first-person narrators in the great first-person novels of the eighteenth and nineteenth centuries.

The role of the first-person narrator, as conceived by a large number of critics and even theorists of the first-person novel, is just as much in need of deschematization as is the role of the authorial narrator. The tendency to schematization stems from the various realistic and naturalistic programs in which the narrator is for the most part understood as being occupied with the presentation of circumstances which have come to his knowledge through his own experience and first-hand observations or through investigations which he has carried out himself. In literary practice, however, the first-person narrator has never bothered very much with these programs and prescriptions and was often not content with the function of the conscientious reporter but also claimed privileges to which actually only the author as creator of the narrative is entitled. Many first-person narrators go far beyond transcribing that which they have experienced themselves by letting the narrative arise anew from their imagination. During this process the boundary between recollection and creation is often suspended. Reproductive memory and productive imagination prove to be two different aspects of one and the same process.[66] The function of memory in the first-person narrative far exceeds the ability which is conventionally attributed to memory, namely the ability to visualize and vividly present that which is past. Remembering itself is a quasi-verbal process of silent narration by which the story receives an aesthetic form, primarily as a result of the selection and structuring inherent in recollection.[67] Another difference between first-person narration and authorial narration is evident here. For the authorial narrator, the creative power of memory will never be operative in the narrative process to the same extent as it is for a first-person narrator who evokes his story in an act of recollection. The first-person narrator David Copperfield thus deviates only in a very superficial sense from the restrictions imposed on him by his personal horizon of knowledge and perception, for example, when he gives such a detailed description of his mother's condition immediately before his birth, as if he himself had observed it:

My mother was sitting by the fire, but poorly in health, and very low in spirits, looking at it through her tears, and desponding heavily about herself and the fatherless little stranger, who was already welcomed by some grosses of prophetic pins in a drawer upstairs, to a world not at all excited on the subject of his arrival; my mother, I say, was sitting by the fire, that bright, windy March afternoon, very timid and sad, and very doubtful of ever coming alive out of the trial that was before her, when, lifting her eyes as she dried them, to the window opposite, she saw a strange lady coming up the garden.

My mother had a sure foreboding at the second glance, that it was Miss Betsey. The setting sun was glowing on the strange lady, over the garden-fence, and she came walking up to the door with a fell rigidity of figure and composure of countenance that could have belonged to nobody else.[68]

It is not necessary to declare the first-person narrator an authorial narrator here.[69] The scene is a thoroughly authentic product of the imaginative empathy of the first-person narrator who has no difficulties evoking this particular image of his mother in his imagination from his general memory of her character. The justification which appears in the second sentence of the novel ('as I have been informed and believe') is, therefore, not at all necessary.

When an equilibrium is achieved between the commentaries of the narrating self and the actions of the experiencing self, the presentation of the relationship of the two selves approaches the ideal type of the first-person narrative situation. The imagination of the reader is equally aware of both positions of the self. Naturally one position can temporarily gain superiority, but in the course of extensive reading an equilibrium is usually restored. The first half of *David Copperfield* corresponds to this model to a large degree; in the second half, the experiencing self declines somewhat in importance, since the narrative deals in great detail with characters who do not stand at the centre of the action. These include Mr Peggotty, Betsey Trotwood, Wickfield, Uriah Heep, Mr Micawber.

For this reason the following two quotations, which illustrate the predominance first of the narrating and then of the experiencing self, have been taken from the first part of the novel. The first passage describes David's taking his leave from Dr Strong and his school in Canterbury at the beginning of the nineteenth chapter:

I am doubtful whether I was at heart glad or sorry, when my school-days drew to an end, and the time came for my leaving Doctor Strong's. I had been very happy there, I had a great attachment for the Doctor, and I was eminent and distinguished in that little world. For these reasons I was sorry to go; but for other reasons, unsubstantial enough, I was glad. Misty ideas of being a young man at my own disposal, of the importance attaching to a young man at his own disposal, of the wonderful things to be seen and done by that magnificent animal, and the wonderful effects he could not fail to make upon society, lured me away. So powerful were these visionary considerations in my boyish mind, that I seem, according to my present way of thinking, to have left school without natural regret. The separation has not made the impression on me that other separations have. I try in vain to recall how I felt about it, and what its circumstances were; but it is not momentous in my recollection. I suppose the opening prospect confused me. I know that my juvenile experiences went for little or nothing then; and that life was more like a great fairy story, which I was just about to begin to read, than anything else.[70]

This part of the narrative consists only of report and reflections on the part of the *narrating self*. Several elements underscore the retrospective character, which shift the narrated event into the past in the reader's imagination, too. The present time of the narrating self forms the point of temporal orientation and is clearly marked, not least of all by the repeated occurrence of the present tense and the present perfect in verbs referring to the narrative act ('I am doubtful,' 'I seem,' 'has not made,' 'I try,' 'I suppose,' 'I know'); other indications are the narrative distance, signaled by the 'then' and the 'now' which it implies, the summarizing characterization of the situation as it presented itself to the hero at the time, and last but not least the reference to the attempted act of recollection with its characteristic course, 'I try in vain to recall how I felt about it . . . I suppose . . . I know . . .' Here we see how recollection overcomes the barrier of the temporal remoteness of the fictional events inserting at least a general explanation where a gap of memory leaves things uncertain. There can be no doubt that the reader imagines clearly the narrating self while reading the beginning of this chapter, but is only vaguely aware of the experiencing self in the background.

A scene with a dialogue in which David himself participates is best suited to illustrate a passage in which the experiencing self stands in the foreground. David Copperfield contains many such passages. We can also cite a scene which exhibits the point of view of the experiencing self. Towards the end of Chapter XVII part of the action is reported entirely from the point of view of the experiencing self. Mr and Mrs Micawber's departure from Canterbury takes David completely by surprise. The day after the grand dinner invitation to the Micawbers, David receives a letter from Mr Micawber informing him that the latter is compelled to leave the city as quickly as possible because of financial difficulties and in order to await the unavoidable, that is, the confinement to debtors' prison in London:

I was so shocked by the contents of this heart-rending letter, that I ran off directly towards the little hotel with the intention of taking it on my way to Doctor Strong's, and trying to soothe Mr Micawber with a word of comfort. But, half-way there, I met the London coach with Mr and Mrs Micawber up behind; Mr Micawber, the very picture of tranquil enjoyment, smiling at Mrs Micawber's conversation, eating walnuts out of a paper bag, with a bottle sticking out of his breast pocket. As they did not see me, I thought it best, all things considered, not to see them. So, with a great weight taken off my mind, I turned into a by-street that was the nearest way to school, and felt, upon the whole, relieved that they were gone; though I still liked them very much, nevertheless.[71]

Although this is a reportorial narrative form, the reader visualizes not the narrating self but the experiencing self. This orientation towards the Here and Now of the narrated event is facilitated by the fact that no explicit reference is made to the narrative process itself. The reader, however, finds himself even more directly transferred to the scene by the restriction of the point of view to that of the naive, gullible young David. The inexplicably contented look of Mr Micawber upon his allegedly urgent departure causes David to be mildly astonished, to be sure, but the narrating self fails to interpose an explanatory comment. The story is not yet enough advanced for such an explanation. A first-person narrator is similar to an authorial narrator in that he, too, tries to arouse suspense while telling his story and to maintain it as long as possible.

7.2.6 The first-person narrative situation and free indirect style

For a long time the discussion of the concept free indirect style was almost exclusively restricted to examples from so-called third-person narratives, because these most clearly exhibit one of the distinctive features of free indirect style, namely the combination of the speech, the perception or the thought of a fictional character with the voice of the narrator as the teller. This emphasis created the impression that free indirect style could be found only in third-person texts.[72] Hamburger even advanced the thesis that in the first-person novel free indirect style could occur 'neither with reference to the third-person characters nor to the first-person narrator himself.'[73] A significant number of examples contradict this thesis. Cohn has most emphatically and convincingly demonstrated the existence of free indirect style or narrated monologue, as she prefers to call it when mental events rather than verbal utterances are represented in this mode of discourse, in first-person narratives.[74] She cites the following quotation from Hermann Hesse's *Steppenwolf*:

Oh, yes, I had experienced all these changes and transmutations that fate reserves for her difficult children, her ticklish customers. I knew them only too well . . . Was I really to live through all this again? All this torture, all this pressing need, all these glimpses into the paltriness and worthlessness of my own self, the frightful dread lest I succumb, and the fear of death. Wasn't it better and simpler to prevent a repetition of so many sufferings and to quit the stage? Certainly, it was simpler and better . . . No, in all conscience, there was no power in the world that could prevail with me to go through the mortal terror of another encounter with myself, to face another reorganization, a new incarnation . . . There was an end of it!

Ach ja, ich kannte diese Erlebnisse, diese Wandlungen, die das Schicksal seinen Sorgenkindern, seinen heikelsten Kindern bestimmt hat, allzu gut kannte ich sie . . . Sollte ich all dies nun wirklich noch einmal durchleben? All diese Qual, all diese irre Not, all diese Einblicke in die Niedrigkeit und Wertlosigkeit des eigenen Ich, all diese furchtbare Angst vor dem Erliegen, all diese Todesfurcht? War es nicht klüger und einfacher, die Wiederholung so vieler Leiden zu verhüten, sich aus dem Staub zu machen? Gewiß, es war einfacher und klüger . . . Nein, bei allen Teufeln, es gab keine Macht in der Welt, die von mir verlangen konnte, nochmals eine Selbstbegegnung mit ihren Todesschauern und nochmals eine Neugestaltung, eine neue Inkarnation durchzumachen . . . Genug und Schluß damit![75]

Kafka's *The Castle* contains much free indirect style, in accordance with the figural narrative situation prevailing in this novel. By means of a comparison with the corresponding passages from the manuscript version of the first chapters of the novel, written in first-person form, Cohn also shows that free indirect style can be found in the same passages of the first-person version as in the final, third-person version. Cohn establishes further that 'free indirect style is found in the first-person novel only when the emphasis is entirely on the experiencing self, when the narrating self is thus unstressed, indeed not presented . . . This empathy with the past stage of the self is in my opinion one of the prerequisites for free indirect style in the first-person novel.'[76] This observation illuminates also one of the reasons why free indirect style as a form of rendering thought occurs relatively seldom in the first-person novel as a form for rendering thought. (Free indirect style as a form for rendering speech must be disregarded for the moment.) The narrating self often forces itself so strongly into the foreground precisely in the most common forms of the first-person narrative, namely in the quasi-autobiographical ones, that empathy, which is a prerequisite for the appearance of free indirect style, can no longer really arise, as was shown above. The narrating self with its Here and Now in the narrative act determines the orientation of the reader.

Steinberg has called attention to the fact that grammatical differences also exist between free indirect style as it occurs within a first-person narrative situation, on the one hand, and within authorial or figural narrative situation, on the other. The transposition of the personal reference from 'I' to 'he,' naturally does not take place when a narrating self reproduces the thoughts of the experiencing self by means of free indirect style. If the transposition of verb forms also fails to occur, for example in a contrary-to-fact form or an infinitival phrase, then the free indirect style in a first-person narrative situation can become indistinguishable from direct speech. 'Free indirect style in the first person overlaps (in a first-person narrative . . .) more frequently with direct speech than does free indirect style in a third-person narrative.'[77] At the same time Steinberg attempts to explain in general why so little attention has been given to free indirect style in the first-person form by pointing out that there are fewer first-person than third-person narratives: 'The preponderance of free indirect style in the third person . . . is not due to any characteristic of free indirect style, but simply to the quantitative superiority of the . . . third-person narrative.'[78] This quantitative factor which Steinberg suggests is of only secondary importance, however. The lower frequency of free indirect style in first-person narratives results primarily from the structural conditions created by the first-person narrative situation. If the dual perspective of the narrator and the fictional character is accepted as the essential feature of free indirect style, as was set forth in section

7.1.2, then the explanation for the lower frequency of free indirect style in first-person narratives lies in the lesser frequency with which such dual perspectives occur in first-person narratives than in third-person narratives. The difference reflects the fact that here a dual perspective does not result in a true doubling of the perspective because the narrating self ultimately retains an existential link with his earlier, experiencing self.

Up until now free indirect style in the first-person narrative has been considered only as a means of rendering thoughts and perceptions. It can also occur, however, as a technique for the rendering of speech. As we turn to the difference between free indirect style as a technique for the reproduction of thought on the one hand and for the incorporation of figural speech on the other, we must remember that, within a first-person narrative situation, only the narrator's own thoughts can be reproduced by this method. In contrast, free indirect style within a first-person narrative situation can also be used to reproduce the speech of other characters, since the horizon of knowledge of the first-person narrator is not restricted with regard to the rendering of speech. It is important, however, that in a first-person narrative situation the reproduction of thoughts and that of speech by means of free indirect style are capable of producing entirely different effects.

When David Copperfield one day tries to tell his 'doll wife' gently that he is now completely without means, Dora simply cannot believe the news:

But I looked so serious, that Dora left off shaking her curls, and laid her trembling little hand upon my shoulder, and first looked scared and anxious, then began to cry. That was dreadful. I fell upon my knees before the sofa, caressing her, and imploring her not to rend my heart; but, for some time, poor little Dora did nothing but exclaim Oh dear! Oh dear! And oh, she was so frightened! And where was Julia Mills! And oh, take her to Julia Mills, and go away, please! until I was almost beside myself.[79]

The words Dora blurts out in her crying fit and with which she enjoins her fiancé to leave her alone and to take her to her girlfriend are in free indirect style. The actual mixture of direct exclamation and reported speech or free indirect style in this passage and in a very similar context again two pages later [80] lends Dora's words a very special sound in the ears of the reader. Free indirect style makes the hysteria of the reaction of the immature and spoiled Dora more clearly audible than would direct speech, because the voice of the narrating self, David, can also be heard through it as he remembers this scene years later with a certain bemusement, perhaps, but surely no longer with the astonishment he experienced at the time. The effect of rendering Dora's hysterical outcry in indirect style clearly creates distance and irony. Fritz Karpf interpreted this passage differently. Karpf believes that free indirect style has a stronger effect here than direct speech would have: 'not only does the lamentation of the spoiled child-wife Dora touch the reader's ear more movingly, it seems to me that this form of speech reproduction also couches a reproach of the narrator against himself, a later reproach directed against his previous folly.'[81] Karpf does not take sufficiently into account the fact that free indirect style appears here in a first-person narrative situation and that, therefore, whatever effect Dora's words may have had on David's experiencing self, they are ultimately viewed here from the more mature perspective of his narrating self.

With the aid of a longer quotation from Richardson's epistolary novel *Clarissa Harlowe*, I shall now show that the characteristic intonation and sound of the speech of a fictional character can be expressed by means of free indirect style not only more precisely than in indirect speech, but also more clearly than in direct speech. In her second letter to her friend Miss Howe, Clarissa (Clary) reports the visit of a certain Mr Lovelace to the home of her sister Arabella. Arabella informed her the next day about her conversation with Mr Lovelace, who was generally regarded as a suitor of Arabella. The following passage from Clarissa's letter to Miss Howe begins with a reproduction of Arabella's words to Clarissa in free indirect style, which Richardson himself has put in quotation marks. The quotation can be identified as free indirect style by the transposition of 'O my beloved Clary!' to 'O her beloved Clary!', just as Arabella's 'I' is always replaced thereafter by 'she' and the 'you' referring to Clarissa always by 'I' or 'me': 'let her tell me' thus stands for 'let me [Arabella] tell you [Clarissa]' in direct speech:

'So handsome a man! – O her beloved Clary!' (for then she was ready to love me dearly, from the overflowings of her good humour on his account!) 'He was but *too* handsome a man for *her*! – Were she but as amiable as *somebody*, there would be a probability of *holding* his affections! – For he was wild, she heard; *very* wild, very gay; loved intrigue. But he was young; *a man of sense*: would see his error, could she but have patience with his faults, if his faults were not cured by marriage.'

Thus she ran on; and then wanted me 'to see the charming man,' as she called him. Again concerned, 'that she was not handsome enough for him'; with, 'a sad thing, that the man should have the advantage of the woman in that particular!' – But then, stepping to the glass she complimented herself,

'That she was very *well*: that there were many women deemed passable who were inferior to herself: that she was always thought comely; and comeliness, let her tell me, having not so much to lose as Beauty had, would hold, when that would evaporate or fly off. Nay, for that matter' (and again she turned to the glass), 'her features were not irregular; her eyes not at all amiss.' And I remember they were more than usually brilliant at that time. – 'Nothing, in short, to be found fault with, though nothing very engaging, she doubted – was there, Clary?'[82]

The effect of free indirect style, which expands in this passage to direct as well as to indirect speech, is further reinforced in its specific effect – here especially revealing – by the use of italics for individual words and phrases in the original in an attempt to make visible, or rather, audible, the emphatic accentuation by the original speaker, Arabella. At the same time that Clarissa so accurately transcribes Arabella's enthusiastic intonation, she comments on it as well. It becomes clear that Clarissa does not share her sister Arabella's enthusiasm. The reduction of Arabella's speech to stereotypical gushing by the use of free indirect style produces the same impression. This passage from *Clarissa Harlowe* is consequently an interesting parallel to the passage from *Mansfield Park* quoted in section 7.1.5. In both examples the speech of the fictional characters is reproduced in free indirect style and the *manner* of speech is especially characterized, in Jane Austen principally by the choice of words, in Richardson by the choice of words and the intonation. In both instances the choice of free indirect style furthermore indicates a certain detachment on the part of the transmitter of the speech with regard to the actual speakers. The passage from *Clarissa Harlowe* is also very revealing in this context, because Clarissa herself explains immediately afterwards that her main concern in the preceding report was to present the 'air and manner in which things are spoken':

Excuse me, my dear, I never was thus particular before . . . You will always have me give you minute descriptions, nor suffer me to pass by the air and manner in which things are spoken that are to be taken notice of; rightly observing that air and manner often express more than the accompanying words.[83]

If we consider this passage together with the one from *Mansfield Park* quoted in section 7.1.5, it does not seem unwarranted to conclude that free indirect style as a technique for the rendition of speech offers a very subtle possibility of characterization and indirect commentary on the intonation of this speech. One can also conclude that in this regard there do not seem to be any differences between the third-person and the first-person form of narration. The situation is somewhat different when free indirect style is used to render thoughts. The dual perspective characteristic of free indirect style arises between the teller and the fictional character who is thinking, feeling or perceiving in an authorial or an authorial-figural narrative situation. This dual perspective involves two persons with different points of view, opinions, judgements, and so on. The situation is different in a first-person narrative situation. Here, free indirect style is only possible for the thoughts, feelings and perceptions of the first-person narrator. The dual perspective arises here, as Cohn has already explained, between the narrating self and the experiencing self: 'Just as free indirect style occurs in the third-person novel only when the teller *completely* disappears behind his fictional character and the narrative act itself is unstressed, free indirect style is found in the first-person novel only when the emphasis is *entirely* on the experiencing self, when the narrating self is thus unstressed, *indeed not presented*.'[84] This view should perhaps be modified and the emphasis indicated by my italics omitted, in order to weaken somewhat Cohn's criterion of exclusion. For the first-person narrative, the use of free indirect style to render thoughts actually does effect a narrowing of the focus of the presentation on the experiencing self in its Here and Now. The narrating self is suppressed but its presence is not completely denied; otherwise one would have to speak not of free indirect style but of a silent monologue.

Free indirect style as a form for rendering thought in a first-person narrative situation creates a latitude of expression for the subjectivity of experience of the experiencing self in which it can develop undisturbed, although often only temporarily so, by the other 'persona' of its person, the narrating self. In a first-person narrative situation, therefore, free indirect style promotes the reader's empathy with the experiencing self much more frequently than it ironizes or creates distance between the experiencing self and the narrating self. On the other hand, in an authorial (not figural!) narrative situation, free indirect style very often distances the reader from the fictional characters, because this distance is already inherent in the dual perspective of narrator and fictional character. Consequently, free indirect style must also be regarded as a means of directing the reader's sympathy, but its effect in this sense is dependent ultimately upon the narrative situation in which it appears.

7.3 From the first-person narrative situation to the figural narrative situation

Contract full intimacy with the stranger within thee. (Edward Young to Samuel Richardson, *Conjectures on Original Composition*)

As the emphasis on the experiencing self increases, internal perspective and the restriction of the fictional reality to the inner world become dominant features of the first-person narrative. We are approaching the pole of internal perspective on the perspective axis of the typological circle. The narrative forms which manifest themselves here are just as diverse as they are artful and are often difficult to appreciate. Aside from the epistolary novel, this sector of the typological circle was consequently not occupied very densely before the emergence of modern fiction.

Naturally the withdrawal of the narrating self and the simultaneous concentration of the focus of presentation on the experiencing self can also be observed in the quasi-autobiographical first-person novel, although only temporarily. The shift of the focus of presentation from the narrating self to the experiencing self and back again to the narrating self is even a structural feature of this first-person form, which could also be described as a sequence of passages with the focus of presentation alternately in the narrating and in the experiencing self. In first-person novels such as *Huckleberry Finn*, *The Catcher in the Rye* and Iris Murdoch's *Under the Net*, the narrating and the experiencing self can hardly be distinguished, since the presentation is focused here almost entirely on the self in its Here and Now of experience.

The diary novel (Sartre's *Nausea* (*La Nausée*)) anticipates one aspect of interior monologue: the diary self does not address a 'you' but soliloquizes, speaks to itself. In the novel in the second person (Michel Butor's *A Change of Heart* (*La Modification*)) the 'you' is really a self-dramatization of the 'I,' and the form of the monologue prevails here, too.[85] Finally, in the dramatic monologue the soliloquizing first person does indeed speak to a 'you,' but this 'you' remains an indeterminate area which the reader can concretize only approximately and in an indirect way. In the dramatic monologue the listener never has the opportunity to make his answer heard, but his reactions to what has been said or his objections are sometimes recorded indirectly in the speech of the speaker. In a sense, the dramatic monologue is non-narrative, because it consists only of directly quoted speech. In this respect it approaches the first-person narratives in which the narrative act is colloquially coloured, such as

Huckleberry Finn and *The Catcher in the Rye*, which of course belong without reservation to the narrative genre. For generic theory the difference lies in the fact that the second person implied in *The Catcher in the Rye* and in similar colloquial first-person narratives is an implicit reader, while the second person implied in the dramatic monologue is an implicit fictional character. The spontaneity of the self-expression of the narratorial 'I' is common to both forms, the colloquial first-person narrative and the dramatic monologue. This spontaneity also occurs in conjunction with interior monologue. Prior to the twentieth century, dramatic monologue was almost completely restricted to poetry (e.g., Robert Browning's 'My Last Duchess'). In more recent fiction, it appears more often as a short narrative form for which Mansfield's 'A Lady's Maid,' Sinclair Lewis's 'Travel Is So Broadening' or Dorothy Parker's 'Lady With a Lamp' may serve as illustrations.

If we go one step further along the typological circle, we come to interior monologue proper ('direct interior monologue').[86] The monologue self does not write down its experiences and thoughts, nor does it strive for verbal communication with a counterpart (be it another person or, as in most diary novels, its own self). Rather, it reveals the content of its consciousness unwittingly, as it were. Therefore, while the self of a diary novel (Roquentin in *Nausea*) is still a teller-character, the self of an interior monologue (Gustl in Schnitzler's 'Leutnant Gustl') is best understood as a reflector-character. The borderline between the narrator's realm and that of the reflector on the typological circle lies between these two narrative forms on the first-person side of the circle. This boundary is also open. The 'I' in Beckett's *Malone Dies*, for example, is a reflector-character as long as the interior monologue refers to the present state of consciousness of Malone, who is lying in bed waiting for death. This 'I' transforms itself again and again into a teller-character in order to pass the time, as it were, until the complete extinction of his life's functions by telling the stories of Saposcat, Macmann and others. These stories are narrated in the past tense, while the interior monologues of the novel are in the present tense. Even this division is not absolute, however. Memories from his own life force themselves into Malone's interior monologue and are reported consistently in the past tense.

It is evident, therefore, that interior monologue, too, is an open form.[87] Many modifications of this form are possible and can be accommodated in the pertinent, rather large, sector of the typological circle. Apart from the 'depth' of the rendering of consciousness in the individual interior monologue, which is a criterion of content and hence cannot be taken into account in my system, there are several degrees of disengagement from the first-person model of narrative transmission. The two most important degrees are marked by the transition of tense from the past to the present and by the displacement of the uniform first-person pronominal reference by a variation from first- to third-person reference, or from 'I,' 'he' and the impersonal pronoun 'one,' leading ultimately to the complete absence of a clear reference to the category of person. The displacement of the first-person pronominal reference facilitates the transition from the realm of the first-person narrative situation to the realm of the figural narrative situation in which third-person pronominal reference dominates.

In longer narrative works in which interior monologue prevails, more than one of these variations of the form of interior monologue usually occur. For this reason different passages or sections of a longer work often occupy different positions on the typological circle. In Faulkner's *The Sound and the Fury*, the first three of the four large segments consist of interior monologues of three different characters. All three monologues are in the past tense. Much of the outer world and the external events in the household of the Compson family are presented in them. Together these factors create the impression in the reader that the first-person characters are occupied with a silent narrative act, which of course is not directed to any listener or reader. In several segments of Faulkner's *As I Lay Dying* the past tense is replaced by the present. The use of the present tense for the rendition of the momentary state of consciousness emphasizes the reflector-mode of this kind of presentation of the monologue self. It also facilitates a clear separation of the momentary content of consciousness from reminiscences, for which the past tense continues to be used. These reminiscences in the past tense impart in turn a narrative element to the interior monologue. An example of the very consistent use of this technique is the interior monologue of Molly Bloom in *Ulysses*.

In *Ulysses*, especially in the first chapters (for example 'Proteus' and 'Lestrygonians') longer passages devoted to the rendition of consciousness occur in which the reference to the bearer of consciousness alternates between 'I' and 'he'. This change indicates that the opposition person has become unmarked in the zone of transition between first-person narrative situation and figural narrative situation on the typological circle. This change is also apparent in the frequency of the impersonal pronoun 'one,' which is non-distinctive in regard to the opposition person, and in the prevalence of infinitival and participial constructions and sentence fragments lacking a verb in its finite form. Such usages do not permit any conclusions about the category person.

Cohn has raised doubts about my assumption that the transition from first-person pronominal reference to third-person pronominal reference does not imply an absolute distinction. What I consider a zone of transition appears to her a 'closed border.'[88] The idea of open borders and zones of transition is so central to my concept of the typological circle, however, that such a modification would vitiate the whole system. Cohn also would like to replace my triadic system by a division of the typological circle into four quadrants. It is precisely the triadic foundation, however, which makes clear that there are no categorical or impassable boundaries within my system. Even the first-person/third-person boundary, which also some other critics consider a categorical one – a narrative text, they believe, must either be written in the grammatical form of the first or the third person[89] – is not an impassable borderline, as I was able to demonstrate above by means of the continuum of forms in the vicinity of the teller pole between the authorial third-person form and the first-person form of the narrative situation. The transitions between third- and first-person reference in the vicinity of the reflector pole marking the divison between the figural and the first-person narrative situations are similarly fluid. One must keep in mind that these boundary crossovers occur especially in narratives of innovative character, for example in Joyce's *Ulysses*. Thus in the first paragraph of the 'Lestrygonians' episode, the question of first- or third-person reference remains unanswered because no explicit pronominal or nominal reference is made by the bearer of consciousness, Leopold Bloom; verbs occur only in the infinite form, so that both person (first and third) and tense (present or past) remain undetermined:

Pineapple rock, lemon platt, butter scotch. A sugarsticky girl shovelling scoopfuls of creams for a christian brother. Some school treat. Bad for their tummies. Lozenge and comfit manufacturer to His Majesty the King. God. Save. Our. Sitting on his throne, sucking red jujubes white.[90]

A text such as this, in which a third-person as well as a first-person reference is latent ('Bad for their tummies [he thought/I believe]'), would be located exactly on the transition point between figural (third-person) narrative situation and first-person narrative situation (interior monologue), if the text were longer and this manner of presentation extended throughout the text. What is decisive is that the reflector-mode, marked by Bloom's presence as reflector-character on the scene, prevails here, that is to say, all external and internal processes presented must be interpreted as part of the content of the consciousness of Leopold Bloom. Interior mono-logue and figural narrative situation meet and join without a seam in the fulfillment of this narrative function, as if it were no longer relevant for the reader to ask whether narration is taking place in the first- or in the third-person form.

7.3.1 Dying in the first-person form

I'm flying . . . I'm dreaming . . . I'm sleeping . . . I'm drea . . . drea – I'm fly . . . (Arthur Schnitzler, the end of 'Fräulein Else')

The difficulties arising from the presentation of the death of a narratorial 'I' have not deterred authors from selecting the first-person form for the fictional presentation of this extreme situation. The earlier novel employed mainly the epistolary form for this subject. It permits the author to carry the intimate self-presentation of the thoughts and feelings of the dying person on up to the threshold of life. After the death an authorial narrator in the role of the editor of the letters usually appears as in *The Sufferings of Young Werther* (*Die Leiden des jungen Werthers*), in order to complete the story; or the other correspondents round off the narrative, sometimes with the fictional editor of the letters intruding in the narrative, as in *Clarissa Harlowe*. In all these cases the narrative is continued by other narrators after the death of the first-person narrator. The internal perspective of presentation is re-placed by an external perspective. This solution to the problem is still found in more recent novels, such as Murdoch's *The Black Prince*, where the death of the first-person narrator, Bradley Pearson, is announced by a fictional editor of the autobiography. Other modern authors have not been content to use this conven-tional form of the presentation of the death of the first-person narrator. By making the narratorial 'I' a reflector-character, they try to present dying itself without relinquishing the internal perspective. An intense death scene such as this, which forces the reader, as it were, to experience the last moments of the dying person, can be very effective. The possibilities for doing justice to the individuality of the first-person character in this decisive moment are limited, however. The gradual fading away of consciousness easily assumes somewhat stereotyped features in such a presentation. A certain uneasiness about this situation seems to have been the cause of Booth's criticism of the conclusion of Schnitzler's interior monologue 'Fräulein Else': 'The mistake of Schnitzler in *Fräulein Else* is not, of course, in entering a character's mind but in entering it at the wrong time for the wrong purpose.'[91] Booth contradicts himself, however, in a footnote (which was probably added later) with a very positive comment on Katherine Anne Porter's short story 'The Jilting of Granny Weatherall,' in which the consciousness of the main character is also presented up to the moment of death. It is more probable that Porter's declining 'to be literal and realistic in the heroine's language' constitutes the real difference between the two death scenes.[92] A comparison of the last fragments of consciousness of Fräulein Else, quoted as the epigraph of this section, with those of Malone from Beckett's *Malone Dies*, reveals that Schnitzler's procedure is more comparable to the scene of Beckett than to that of Porter:

> . . .
> or light light I mean
> never there he will never
> never everything
> there
> any more[93]

As characters Fräulein Else and Malone have practically nothing in common. The form of interior monologue, which presents their dying, makes the two characters similar in a way which does not seem to agree with their personality. This problem was taken up here, because it discloses an important difference between the first- and the third-person forms used to render consciousness. This difference exists despite the fact that the distinction between first- and third-person reference is unmarked, as was established in the preceding section. The difference does not lie primarily in the first-/third-person reference itself, but rather in the various possibilities offered by these forms for embedding the passage into a larger narrative context. Interior monologue is compatible only with an internal perspective and for this reason is less flexible than is the presentation of consciousness within a figural narrative situation. In a figural narrative situation the internal perspective can be transformed at any time into a neutral-objective or an authorial external perspective. When the death of a fictional character functioning as a figural medium is presented, an (authorial) narrator can thus lend assistance wherever necessary. In this way the danger of stereo-typing the final utterances, thoughts and perceptions of the dying person can be avoided. A large number of examples could be cited here. Tolstoy's 'The Death of Ivan Ilych' is therefore very illumin-ating in this context, because in this story about the life, illness and death of the main character, the narrative profile clearly develops from a predominantly authorial to a predominantly figural narrative situation. In the end, however, the narrator does not deny the dying man his authorial assistance.

'And death . . . where is it?'
He sought his former accustomed fear of death and did not find it. 'Where is it? What death?' There was no fear because there was no death.
In place of death there was light.
'So that's what it is!' he suddenly exclaimed aloud. 'What joy!'
To him all this happened in a single instant, and the meaning of that instant did not change. For those present his agony continued for another two hours. Something rattled in his throat, his emaciated body twitched, then the gasping and rattle became less and less frequent.
'It is finished!' said someone near him.
He heard these words and repeated them in his soul.
'Death is finished,' he said to himself. 'It is no more!'
He drew in a breath, stopped in the midst of a sigh, stretched out, and died.[94]

Thomas Mann proceeds very similarly in *Death in Venice*, as does H. G. Wells in 'The Country of the Blind.' Gerald's lonely death in the snow of the Tyrolean mountains in *Women in Love* is also rendered in a similar figural-authorial way. I showed elsewhere by means of Faulkner's presentation of Hightower's death that per-spectival problems can result from this kind of presentation, specifically from the transition from figural internal perspective to authorial external perspective.[95]

Porter's narrative 'The Jilting of Granny Weatherall' combines both elements under discussion here, the alternation of third- and first-person reference and the authorial assistance given to the dying woman. The story about the illness and the death of Granny Weatherall is presented in a predominantly figural narrative situation with Granny Weatherall as the figural medium. Granny is very resolute up to the final hour, and the rendition of her thoughts alternates several times between the figural third-person form and the first-person form of the interior monologue. This change of pronominal reference even occurs in the last paragraph. But the authorial narrator has the last word. Through his laconic report,

231

Granny's dying turns into a gesture which sheds light once more on her whole personality:

For the second time there was no sign. Again no bridegroom and the priest in the house. She could not remember any other sorrow because this grief wiped them all away. Oh, no, there's nothing more cruel than this – I'll never forgive it. She stretched herself with a deep breath and blew out the light.[96]

William Golding's novel *Pincher Martin* must be considered a narrative *tour de force* in the presentation of this subject. The death by drowning of the main character, who has been shipwrecked and is clinging to a rocky reef washed by the ocean waves, is rendered directly from the viewpoint of the drowning man by means of a predominantly figural narrative situation, in which, however, short sections of interior monologue appear again and again. In addition to this alternation between third- and first-person reference, it is especially interesting in our context that the last phase of death is rendered exclusively by means of a figural narrative situation.[97]

This comparison of death scenes in the first- and third-person forms revealed that the choice between first-person and third-person is less important for the rendering of the consciousness of dying persons than for the embedding of the death scene into a larger narrative context. From this aspect, the figural-authorial form of presentation proves superior to the use of interior monologue, at least insofar as the former allows more latitude for the presentation of the dying person's individuality than does the strict internal perspective of interior monologue.

7.3.2 'Camera eye'

I am a camera with its shutter open, quite passive, recording, not thinking. (Christopher Isherwood, *Goodbye to Berlin*)

The self-characterization of the first-person narrator in Christopher Isherwood as a camera does not go beyond a program; his narrative style is hardly influenced by it all. Norman Friedman uses this term in a technical sense and defines it in the manner in which it also is understood here: 'the ultimate in authorial exclusion. Here the aim is to transmit, without apparent selection or arrangement, a "slice of life" as it passes before the recording medium.'[98] Friedman considers the 'camera' essentially as the completion of his scale of point-of-view techniques, but does not seem to ascribe great importance to it. But since the time when Friedman published his article (1955), authors have made frequent use of the camera-eye technique. Its use in the *nouveau roman* has been more influential than any of the other characteristic innovations of that genre. For this reason a short analysis of this technique is necessary. Perhaps this purpose can be served best by a comparison with interior monologue, which is in some respect related. Proceeding from a study of the function of the present tense in both forms, Casparis has done some very important preparatory work for a comparison of this kind.[99] He takes as his point of departure the close affinity between interior monologue and the camera-eye technique. Together they constitute a continuum of forms in such a way that a sharp delimitation of the two phenomena is impossible.[100] The classification of the two narrative forms in my system reveals a distinction, however, which is also implied by Casparis. To begin with I shall arrange the most important characteristic features of the two forms in parallel columns:

	Interior monologue	Camera eye
Person:	First-person reference	First-person/third-person reference is indistinguishable
Tense of presentation:	Present	Present
Tense of memory:	Past	Non-existent
Perspective:	Internal perspective Inner world Inside view	Internal perspective Outer world No inside view
Mode:	Reflector-character (personal) Full presentation of consciousness	Reflector-character (impersonal) Reduced presentation of consciousness
Structuring of the content:	By perception, association, memory (predominantly metaphorical)	Only by perception (predominantly metonymic)

This juxtaposition calls attention to a number of relevant aspects of the two techniques.

The first point deals with the opposition person. The camera-eye technique does not permit a distinction between first- and third-person reference. This situation might be explained as a consequence of the fact that the opposition person is unmarked in the rendering of consciousness, the cause of which is to be found in the depersonalization of the consciousness which the camera eye reflects, so to speak. For the same reason the camera-eye consciousness is not capable of remembering, but is limited merely to perceiving the outer world, the elements of which present themselves essentially metonymically, that is to say, objects are not arranged by association, but by their contiguity in space, by the configuration in which they can be perceived. According to Casparis the camera eye presents a 'reflection of the retina, but not the reflection in the mind,' but he at once adds an important restriction. The depersonalization of the process of presentation by means of the camera-eye technique can never be carried as far in literature as in film: 'There can be no pretence of reflecting like a mirror. Camera-eye technique is linked to "humanity" physiologically in terms of *Gestalt* perception, not to speak of its dependence on human language. It can merely *aspire* to present sensation detached from cognition, mental reflection, evaluation, emotion within the limits of language.'[101] Nevertheless, the real reason for the frequency of the camera-eye technique in modern fiction lies in its ability to create an illusion of impersonal or dehumanized perception.[102]

One must, however, distinguish various functions of this technique. The camera-eye technique can be regarded as the ultimate consequence of those programs of realism and objectivity which have been so important for the novel since the nineteenth century and which have found abundant literary expression in the novels of Joyce to Döblin and Sartre. It was the ideology of the *nouveau roman* of Robbe-Grillet, Sarraute and others, however, which first lent the camera-eye technique an anthropological and psychological meaning. This technique is especially suited for presenting man as a 'figure without depth' and for expressing 'his internal muteness' in language.[103] Hence we find this technique in a moderate form in Meursault's self-presentation in Camus's *The Stranger* and in a radical form in Robbe-Grillet's *Jealousy*, where one assumes that the (camera) eye peering through the Venetian blind is that of a jealous husband. The reification of reality captured by the camera eye is carried so far here that inferences drawn about the perceiving consciousness, which must be assumed at the location of the camera, are as a rule idle. It does not seem out of place to speak here of an indeterminate area in Ingarden's sense.[104] The indeterminacy of this area, which is so important for the process of narrative transmission, goes so far that it is by no means certain whether in *Jealousy* we 'are dealing with a text which is narrated in the first person,' as Gerda Zeltner-Neukomm believes.[105] Bruce Morrissette is more cautious when he speaks of a 'suppressed first person [narration],' in this novel.[106] Doubts also arise about this statement, however, because occasionally the camera eye records things in an aperspectival manner which usually indicates the prevalence of the authorial over the figural medium:

As it [the noise] fades in time, its likelihood diminishes. Now it is as if there had been nothing at all. Through the chinks of the blinds – a little later – it is, of course, impossible to see anything at all. All that can be done is to close the blinds by manipulating the cord at the side.

A mesure qu'il s'éloigne dans le passé, sa vraisemblance diminue. C'est maintenant comme s'il n'y avait rien eu du tout. Par les fentes d'une jalousie entrouverte – un peu tard – il est évidemment impossible de distinguer quoi que ce soit. Il ne reste plus qu'à refermer, en manoeuvrant la baguette latérale qui commande un groupe de lames.[107]

The information about the mechanism which opens and closes the Venetian blind can certainly be interpreted as either authorial or figural. Again, the camera eye of this novel is by no means always entirely depersonalized. Sometimes it entertains assumptions, tentative conclusions, as in the following quotation:

A . . . must have just washed her hair, otherwise she would not be bothering to brush it in the middle of the day. She has interrupted her movements, having finished this side perhaps.

A . . . doit venir de se laver les cheveux, car elle ne serait pas, sans cela, occupée à les peigner au milieu du jour. Elle a interrompu ses mouvements, ayant peut-être fini avec ce côté-là.[108]

If the camera-eye technique serves Robbe-Grillet first of all for the reification and depersonalization of perception and of the presentation of reality, then Beckett employs it mainly to reduce the personality of the character, whom we must assume to be located where the camera is, to a few functions of existence. One of these functions seems to be the ability to perceive the continuity and the causal relations in the course of an event. The image of the camera eye is thus actually no longer quite applicable to Beckett's late prose writings published under the title *Residua*.[109] The camera of these prose writings no longer takes pictures continuously, but rather seems to string picture upon picture together in the manner of a kaleidoscope. Consequently the syntactical connections between the parts of speech are omitted for the most part. The radicalness of the reduction which already had increased novel by novel in the trilogy *Molloy*, *Malone Dies*, *The Unnamable*, escalates by leaps and bounds in the late fragments from 'Enough' to 'Imagination Dead Imagine' to 'Ping.' In the apparently meaningless word sequence 'Ping,' which is only punctuated by the

constantly recurring acoustical signal 'Ping,' all three basic oppositions of my system are left undetermined: first- or third-person
reference? internal or external perspective? teller-character or
reflector-character? the total reduction of the narrative process
corresponds to the equally total reduction of the personality of the
bearer of consciousness to whom this sequence of words might be
attributed. Lodge's description of the situation of this reduced
being seems to confirm this explanation with regard to its content: 'I
suggest that "Ping" is the rendering of the consciousness of a person
confined in a small, bare, white room, a person who is evidently
under extreme duress, and probably at the last gasp of life. He has
no freedom of movement: his body is "fixed." '[110] Taken in this
sense, 'Ping' is the expression of a reduction in terms of content as
well as of form, that is to say, a regression from an ontogenetic as
well as literary point of view. No place can be found for it in the
diagram of my typological circle, unless it were a point near the
centre of the circle where the axes of the three determinants of the
narrative process, i.e., person, perspective and mode intersect.
Narrative texts which have to be located close to this zero point of
our typology generally reveal a very low degree of intelligibility.

Beckett's 'Ping' was introduced at the end of the description of
the typological circle in order to complete the continuum of forms
presented by the typological circle, and thus to close it, while at the
same time, opening it up again and calling it into question. We
cannot say yet what will happen when all the possibilities of the
typological circle have been exhausted. Will a narrative literature
arise – provided this term is still applicable – whose centre of gravity
will centrifugally or – as in the case of 'Ping' – centripetally break
out of the typological circle to find new means of expression?

7.4 Final observations

The most important observations resulting from our circuit along
the typological circle can be summarized as follows: All boundaries
between the realms marked by the three opposition axes are open.
Narrative works can be found at each boundary in which elements
from both sides of the boundary are combined.

Because each of the three narrative situations is capable of
modulation in both directions, there are innumerable ways in
which the act of narration can be performed. The circular form of
the typological diagram is a schematic expression of both the

continuity of the sequence of narrative forms and of the totality of the theoretical system.

The continuum of forms on the typological circle can also be understood as a theoretical program encompassing the various possibilities of narration which are gradually being realized in the historical development of the novel and the short story. At this point literary history and literary theory encounter each other. This theory of narration was conceived with the intention of providing a comprehensive system of the conceivable as well as of the historical narrative forms. It may also serve as a frame of conceptual reference for practical criticism.

NOTES

Introduction

1. Franz K. Stanzel, *Die typischen Erzählsituationen im Roman: Darge-stellt an 'Tom Jones', 'Moby-Dick', 'The Ambassadors', 'Ulysses' u.a.*, (Vienna and Stuttgart, 1955). This work was published in English as *Narrative Situations in the Novel: 'Tom Jones', 'Moby-Dick', 'The Ambassadors', 'Ulysses'* (Bloomington, 1971).
2. See Robert Petsch, *Wesen und Formen der Erzählkunst* (Halle/Saale, 1934), p. 331; and Wolfgang Kayser, *Entstehung und Krise des modernen Romans*, 2nd edn (Stuttgart, 1955), p. 34.
3. 'Auswahlbibliographie zur Erzählforschung,' in *Erzählforschung I*, ed. Wolfgang Haubrichs (Göttingen, 1976).
4. Stanzel, *Typische Formen des Romans*, 10th edn (Göttingen, 1981), has also received critical attention.
5. Thomas A. Sebeok (ed.), *The Tell-Tale Sign: A Survey of Semiotics* (Lisse, Netherlands, 1975), p. 60.
6. Sebeok, *The Tell-Tale Sign*, p. 17.

1. Mediacy of presentation as the generic characteristic of narration

1. Manfred Pfister, *Das Drama: Theorie und Analyse* (Munich, 1977), pp. 20ff., contrasts the communicative models of narrative and dramatic texts. In addition to those differences between narrative and drama involving the manner of presentation, there are some features which both genres have in common, especially the fictionality of plot, setting and characters. See Pfister, especially pp. 221ff.
2. Käte Friedemann, *Die Rolle des Erzählers in der Epik* (1910; rpt. Darmstadt, 1965), p. 26.
3. An exception is narratology, an approach derived from the works of Vladimir Propp, *Morphology of the Folktale*, 2nd edn (Austin, 1968), and Claude Lévi-Strauss, *The Savage Mind* (Chicago, 1966). This approach is mainly concerned with the deep structure of narrative. It is characteristic of narratology's 'disregard for the surface structure of the text' (Elisabeth Gülich), for example, that in William O. Hendricks's narratological analysis of Ambrose Bierce's story 'Oil of Dog' the only reference to the narrative situation of this story is

relegated to a footnote. See William O. Hendricks, 'The structural study of narration: sample analysis,' *Poetics*, 3 (1972), 112; and Elisabeth Gülich, 'Erzähltextanalyse,' *Linguistik und Didaktik*, 15 (1973), 326. A comprehensive overview of the narrative text models with a linguistic (and narratological) basis is to be found in Elisabeth Gülich and Wolfgang Raible, *Linguistische Textmodelle* (Munich, 1977), pp. 192–314.

4. Käte Hamburger, *The Logic of Literature*, 2nd, revised edn (Bloomington, 1973).

5. Johannes Anderegg, *Fiktion und Kommunikation: Ein Beitrag zur Theorie der Prosa*, 2nd edn (Göttingen, 1977). (The English translation of Anderegg's terms is taken from Dorrit Cohn, 'The encirclement of narrative. On Franz Stanzel's *Theorie des Erzählens*,' *Poetics Today*, 2 (1981), 170. Translator's note.)

6. Seymour Chatman, 'The structure of narrative transmission,' in *Style and Structure in Literature: Essays in the New Stylistics*, ed. Roger Fowler (Oxford, 1975), pp. 213–57.

7. R. Fowler, *Linguistics and the Novel* (London, 1977), pp. 12–13.

8. See Roman Jakobson, *Fundamentals of Language* (The Hague, 1956), pp. 55–82.

9. Victor Shklovsky, 'Sterne's *Tristram Shandy*: stylistic commentary,' in Lee T. Lemon and Marion J. Reis (eds.), *Russian Formalist Criticism: Four Essays* (Lincoln, Nebraska, 1965), p. 27.

10. See Bernhard Fabian, 'Laurence Sterne: *Tristram Shandy*,' in *Der englische Roman*, ed. Stanzel (Düsseldorf, 1969), I, pp. 232–69; Stanzel, '*Tristram Shandy* und die Klimatheorie,' *Germanisch-Romanische Monatsschrift*, NS 21 (1971), 16–28; and Robert Scholes, *Structuralism in Literature* (New Haven, 1974), pp. 84–5.

11. Scholes, *Structuralism*, p. 185.

12. George Steiner, 'A Preface to *Middlemarch*,' *Nineteenth-Century Fiction*, 9 (1955), 275.

13. See Stanzel, *Typische Formen des Romans*, p. 8.

14. Max Weber, *Gesammelte Aufsätze zur Wissenschaftslehre* (Tübingen, 1922), pp. 190–1.

15. For a discussion of the concept of deviation and for criticism of the deviation theory see Jan Mukařovský, 'Standard language and poetic language,' in *A Prague School Reader on Esthetics, Literary Structure, and Style*, ed. Paul L. Garvin, 3rd edn (Georgetown, 1964), pp. 17ff.; Yury Lotman, *The Structure of the Artistic Text* (Ann Arbor, 1977), pp. 69–75; Michael Riffaterre, *Essais de Stylistique Structurale* (Paris, 1971); Chatman, *Linguistics and Literature: An Introduction to Literary Stylistics* (London, 1973); and Wolfgang Iser, *The Act of Reading: A Theory of Aesthetic Response* (Baltimore, 1978), pp. 87–8.

16. See Bernard Bergonzi, *The Situation of the Novel* (Harmondsworth, 1972), p. 26.

17. Kristin Morrison, 'James's and Lubbock's differing points of view,' *Nineteenth-Century Fiction*, 16 (1961), 245–55.

18. 'Free indirect style' is perhaps the most widely used English term for the concept of *erlebte Rede*. Others are 'free indirect speech/discourse' and 'narrated monologue' (Dorrit Cohn). For a definition see Paul Hernadi, 'Dual perspective: free indirect discourse and related techniques,' *Comparative Literature* 24 (Winter 1972), 32–43; also Roy Pascal, *The Dual Voice: Free Indirect Speech and its functioning in the nineteenth-century European novel* (Manchester, 1977); and Dorrit Cohn, *Transparent Minds: Narrative Modes for Presenting Consciousness in Fiction* (Princeton, 1978). Of interest are also Brian McHale, 'Free indirect discourse: a survey of recent accounts,' *PTL: A Journal for Descriptive Poetics and Theory of Literature*, 3 (1979), 249–87; and Stanzel, 'Zwei erzähltechnische Termini in komparatistischer Sicht: *Erlebte Rede* und *Erzähler* im Deutschen und Englischen,' *Sprachkunst*, 10 (1979), 192–200. Translator's note.

19. See Bertil Romberg, *Studies in the Narrative Technique of the First-Person Novel* (Stockholm, 1962); and Françoise van Rossum-Guyon, 'Point de vue ou perspective narrative,' *Poétique*, 1 (1970), 476–97.

20. Gérard Genette, *Narrative Discourse* (Ithaca, New York, 1980); Boris A. Uspensky, *A Poetics of Composition: The Structure of the Artistic Text and Typology of a Compositional Form* (Berkeley, 1973); Lubomír Doležel, 'The typology of the narrator: point of view in fiction,' in *To Honor Roman Jakobson* (The Hague, 1967), I, pp. 541–52; Chatman, 'Structure,' pp. 213–57.

21. Boris Eikhenbaum, 'Die Illusion des "skaz," ' in *Russischer Formalismus: Texte zur allgemeinen Literaturtheorie und zur Theorie der Prosa*, ed. Yury Striedter (Munich, 1971), pp. 161–7; and Irwin R. Titunik, 'Das Problem des "skaz": Kritik und Theorie,' in *Erzählforschung II*, ed. Wolfgang Haubrichs (Göttingen, 1977), pp. 114–40.

22. Shklovsky, 'Art as technique,' in *Russian Formalist Criticism*, eds. Lemon and Reis, p. 12.

23. See Uspensky, *Poetics*, p. 131.

24. Friedmann, *Die Rolle*, p. 26.

25. See Philip Collins, *A Critical Commentary on 'Bleak House'* (London, 1971), p. 30.

26. See Ian Watt, *The Rise of the Novel: Studies in Defoe, Richardson and Fielding* (London, 1957), pp. 98–9 and 115–18.

27. George Orwell, *The Collected Essays, Journalism and Letters of George Orwell* (Harmondsworth, 1970), IV, p. 478: 'One difficulty I have never solved is that one has masses of experience which one

passionately wants to write about . . . and no way of using them up
except by disguising them as a novel.'

28. Wolfdietrich Rasch, 'Erinnerung an Robert Musil,' as quoted by Uwe
Baur, 'Musils Novelle "Die Amsel," ' in *Vom 'Törless' zum 'Mann
ohne Eigenschaften*,' ed. Uwe Baur and Dietmar Goltschnigg
(Munich and Salzburg, 1973), p. 269.
29. See Anderegg, *Fiktion*, p. 118.
30. Norman Friedman, 'Point of view in fiction,' *PMLA*, 70 (1955), 1167.
31. Thus in Stanzel, *Narrative Situations*, the English translation of the
original German version which was published in 1955, the terms
'author' and 'narrator or author' occasionally occur in place of
'authorial narrator' (pp. 21, 23 *et passim*), and reference is made to
'the author's presence in the figure of the authorial narrator' (p. 27).
This lack of precision in terminology is clarified at the start, however,
by the observation that 'the figure of the authorial narrator is not
simply identical with the personality of the author' (p. 24). (It must be
noted, however, that English and American critics have not been as
quick as German speaking critics to adopt this distinction. See
Stanzel, 'Zwei erzähltechnische Termini,' pp. 192–200. Translator's
note.)
32. Wolfgang Kayser, 'Wer erzählt den Roman?', in his *Die Vortragsreise: Studien zur Legende* (Bern, 1958), pp. 82–101; rpt. in *Zur
Poetik des Romans*, ed. Volker Klotz (Darmstadt, 1965), pp.
197–216.
33. Thomas Mann, *Der Erwählte* (Frankfurt am Main, 1951), pp. 10–11.
(Most of Thomas Mann's works were translated into English by H. T.
Lowe-Porter. Unfortunately, Lowe-Porter's translations are quite
imprecise, and for this reason useless for the examination of narrative
technique. When no page reference is given to the English version of a
work by Thomas Mann, the translation is my own. Translator's note.)
34. Reinhard Klesczewski, 'Erzähler und "Geist der Erzählung": Diskussion einer Theorie Wolfgang Kaysers und Bemerkungen zu
Formen der Ironie bei Th. Mann,' *Archiv für das Studium der
Neueren Sprachen und Literaturen*, 210 (1973), 126–31.
35. See Hamburger, *Logic*, pp. 178 and 339; and Kayser, 'Wer erzählt?,'
in *Poetik*, ed. Klotz, p. 171.
36. Kayser, 'Wer erzählt?', in *Poetik*, ed. Klotz, pp. 213–14.
37. See Kayser, *Entstehung und Krise des modernen Romans*, 2nd edn
(1954; rpt. Stuttgart, 1955), p. 17.
38. Hamburger, *Logic*, pp. 139–40.
39. Ibid., p. 140.
40. Ibid., p. 141.
41. Ibid., p. 136. According to Hamburger, the situation is different in the
first-person novel: the first-person narrator is a figure created by the

author; the relationship between the two is characterized by a genuine statement structure. See *Logic*, pp. 136, 139–40, 311–41.

42. Hamburger, *Logic*, p. 339. See also pp. 178–9.

43. Wolfgang Haubrichs recently introduced a new aspect into the discussion of the passage from Thomas Mann's *The Holy Sinner* which was quoted above. Haubrichs related the two layers of narration and their counterparts in the passage – the abstract 'spirit' and the concrete Irish monk – to the opposition *fable* and *sujet* or *histoire* and *discours* employed by the Russian formalists and the French structuralists. See *Erzählforschung I*, ed. Haubrichs (Göttingen, 1976), pp. 11–12.

44. One of the many nuances which this term assumes is characterized by the following statement: 'the chief value to which *this* implied author is committed . . . is that which is expressed by the total form.' See Wayne C. Booth, *The Rhetoric of Fiction* (Chicago, 1961), pp. 73–4.

45. Hamburger, *Logic*, p. 83.

46. Hamburger herself approaches this explanation in her essay 'Noch einmal: Vom Erzählen,' *Euphorion*, 59 (1965), 70, when she assigns the concept of the 'personalized narrator' to the 'stylistic basis of examination of language theory,' and the concept of the 'narrative function' to the 'structural basis.'

47. See Booth, *Rhetoric*, p. 44.

48. Hamburger, *Logic*, pp. 136ff.

49. See Hamburger, *Die Logik der Dichtung* (Stuttgart, 1968), pp. 72–114, and *Logic* (1973), pp. 134–94.

50. Kayser, *Entstehung*, p. 34.

51. Joseph Warren Beach, *The Twentieth-Century Novel: Studies in Technique* (New York, 1932), p. 14.

52. See Hamburger, *Logic*, p. 139.

53. Stanzel, *Narrative Situations*, pp. 25–7.

54. Booth, *Rhetoric*, Chapters II and III.

55. John R. Frey, 'Author-intrusion in the narrative: German theory and some modern examples,' *Germanic Review*, 23 (1948), 274–89.

56. Dan Jakobson, 'Muffled Majesty,' *Times Literary Supplement*, 26 October 1967, 1007.

57. Bergonzi, *Situation*, pp. 84–5 and 225.

58. N. Friedman, 'Point of view,' 1167. See my p. 12 for the entire quotation.

59. Helmut Winter, *Literaturtheorie und Literaturkritik* (Düsseldorf, 1975), p. 14.

60. Friedemann, *Die Rolle*, p. 26.

61. On the other hand, the inclusion of the reader in the discussion by Cordula Kahrmann, Gunter Reiß and Manfred Schluchter in *Erzähltextanalyse: Eine Einführung in Grundlagen und Verfahren*,

2nd edn (Königsstein/Taunus, 1981), I, stresses the communicative aspect.

62. Stanislaw Eile outlines possible ideological connections between the choice of one of the narrative situations described here and the world view of the author in 'The novel as an expression of the writer's vision of the world,' *New Literary History*, 9 (1977–8), 116–28. Eile touches upon a broad field which still is in need of intensive work.

63. Robert Weimann, 'Erzählerstandpunkt und "Point of View". Zur Geschichte und Ästhetik der Perspektive im englischen Roman,' *Zeitschrift für Anglistik und Amerikanistik*, 10 (1962), 379.

2. Zero grades of mediacy: synopsis, chapter heading, outline

1. The first 'Western' reference to the *fable–sujet* opposition of the Russian formalists occurred in 1949 in René Wellek and Austin Warren, *Theory of Literature* (Harmondsworth, 1970), pp. 218ff. References to more recent works on *fable–sujet* and *histoire–discours* can be found in Wilhelm Füger, 'Zur Tiefenstruktur des Narrativen: Prolegomena zu einer generativen "Grammatik" des Erzählens,' *Poetica*, 5 (1972), 268–92, and in Thomas M. Scheerer and Markus Winkler, 'Zum Versuch einer Erzählgrammatik bei Claude Bremond,' *Poetica*, 8 (1976), 1–24, especially 11ff. See also Emile Benveniste *Problèmes de linguistique générale* (Paris, 1966), especially p. 250; Tzvetan Todorov, 'Les catégories du récit littéraire,' *Communications*, 8 (1966), 126ff.; Lubomír Doležel, 'Toward a structural theory of content in prose fiction,' in *Literary Style: A Symposium*, ed. Chatman (London, 1971), pp. 95–110; Gérard Genette, *Narrative Discourse* (Ithaca, New York, 1980); Karlheinz Stierle, 'Geschehen, Geschichte, Text der Geschichte,' in *Geschichte – Ereignis und Erzählung*, ed. Reinhart Koselleck and Wolf-Dieter Stempel, *Poetik und Hermeneutik* 5 (Munich, 1973), pp. 530–4; rpt. in Stierle, *Text als Handlung: Perspektiven einer systematischen Literaturwissenschaft* (Munich, 1975), pp. 49–55; Jochen Schulte-Sasse and Renate Werner, *Einführung in die Literaturwissenschaft* (Munich, 1977), pp. 147–50; Chatman, *Story and Discourse: Narrative Structure in Fiction and Film* (Ithaca, New York, 1978).

2. I intentionally avoid contrasting the novel to the drama, the most common way of demonstrating the mediacy of narrative. Klaus Kanzog recently showed, however, that this method can also yield interesting results. Kanzog proceeds from dramatic texts which Brecht, for example, had rewritten in the form of narrative in order to help the actors understand their roles. Such texts by Brecht deserve a more thorough analysis on the basis of narrative theory than Kanzog is able to devote to them in his introduction. See *Erzählstrategie* (Heidelberg, 1976), pp. 39–46.

3. Wellek and Warren, *Theory*, p. 140.

4. For a discussion of the pedagogical aspects of the summary as a paraphrase, see Bettina Hurrelmann, 'Erzähltextverarbeitung im schulischen Handlungskontext,' in *Erzählen im Alltag*, ed. Konrad Ehlich (Frankfurt am Main, 1980), pp. 308ff.

5. One of the few exceptions is the discussion about the function of the present tense in summaries which was sparked by Hamburger, *Logic*, p. 64 *et passim*.

6. Winter, p. 14.

7. *A Student's Guide to 50 British Novels*, ed. Abraham H. Lass (New York, 1966); and Wolfgang Karrer and Eberhard Kreutzer, *Daten der englischen und amerikanischen Literatur von 1890 bis zur Gegenwart* (Munich, 1973).

8. Hamburger, *Logic*, p. 109.

9. Pascal, 'Tense and novel,' *Modern Language Review*, 57 (1962), 8.

10. Harald Weinrich, *Tempus. Erzählte und besprochene Welt*, 2nd edn (Stuttgart, 1971), pp. 33 and 43.

11. See also Christian Paul Casparis, *Tense Without Time. The Present Tense in Narration* (Bern, 1975), p. 127, where Casparis, agreeing essentially with Weinrich's view, explains: 'The purpose of any summary is to attract attention to *what* is being summarized not to *how* it is done,' and p. 143, where he states that the discussing tenses, to which the synoptic present tense belongs, have in common the fact 'that the "world" is *not* narrated.'

12. Stierle supports his distinction between 'systematic' and 'narrative' texts, which he derived from Louis Hjelmslev, by referring to a very instructive example of a tense alternation in Gotthold Ephraim Lessing's 'Abhandlungen über die Fabel.' See *Text*, pp. 20ff. Note that the two pairs of concepts 'systematic/narrative' and 'synopsis/narrative' are not identical, although they share the opposition of tense. In every narrative with a personalized teller-character there are always systematic passages in addition to narrative ones. *Diegesis* and *narratio* in the sense of classical rhetoric always belong together in a story related by a personalized narrator.

13. Doris Lessing, *The Golden Notebook* (New York, 1972), pp. 76–7.

14. Ibid., p. 308.

15. David Lodge, *The Novelist at the Crossroads and Other Essays on Fiction and Criticism* (London, 1971), p. 28.

16. *Student's Guide*, p. 41.

17. *Reclams Romanführer*, 5th edn (Stuttgart, 1974), pp. 338–9.

18. *Student's Guide*, p. 110.

19. Weinrich, *Tempus*, p. 229.

20. *Kindlers Literaturlexikon* (Zurich, 1965) has always been unique in that its summaries include information on literary history and critical commentaries.

21. *Student's Guide*, p. 118.

22. Ibid. My emphasis.
23. Henry James, *The Notebooks of Henry James*, ed. F. O. Matthiessen and Kenneth B. Murdock (New York, 1947), p. 87.
24. Ibid., p. 179.
25. Ibid., pp. 61–2.
26. Ibid., pp. 370.
27. Ibid., p. 370.
28. Ibid., p. 226.
29. Todorov, 'Les catégories du récit littéraire,' *Communications* 8 (1966), 143.
30. James, *Notebooks*, pp. 226–7.
31. See Hamburger, *Logic*, p. 77 and note 66.
32. See Stanzel, *Narrative Situations*, pp. 39–40.
33. See Flann O'Brien, *At Swim-Two-Birds* (Harmondsworth, 1960), pp. 100–2, 150, 164–208, 215–16.
34. James, *Notebooks*, pp. 241–2.
35. Ibid., pp. 88, 94, 201, 231, 243–4 and 274.
36. In his interpretation of 'The Turn of the Screw,' Edmund Wilson interpreted the vacillation in the meaning of the 'I' in the passage from the *Notebooks* quoted above as a 'reflection of James's doubts, communicated unconsciously by James himself.' Such an explanation is not entirely convincing. The cause of this phenomenon is not so much the uncertainty of the author as the fact that the process of composition is not yet completed. 'The Ambiguity of Henry James,' in *A Casebook on Henry James's 'The Turn of the Screw*,' ed. G. Willen, 2nd edn (New York, 1969), p. 146.
37. See James, *Notebooks*, pp. 386, 389, 390 *et passim*.
38. Ibid., p. 386.
39. Ibid., p. 381.
40. See Weinrich, *Tempus*, pp. 44ff.
41. See James, *Notebooks*, p. 372.
42. Ibid., pp. 381, 390 *et passim*.
43. See James, *The Art of the Novel. Critical Prefaces*, ed. Richard P. Blackmur (New York, 1950), pp. 320ff.
44. Chapter headings such as these are 'meta-narrative texts' in Gülich's sense, since they emphasize the narrative process. See Gülich, 'Ansätze zu einer kommunikationsorientierten Erzähltextanalyse,' in *Erzählforschung I*, ed. Haubrichs, pp. 234ff.
45. After completion of the manuscript I became aware of Ernst-Peter Wieckenberg, *Zur Geschichte der Kapitelüberschriften im deutschen Roman vom 15. Jahrhundert bis zum Ausgang des Barock* (Göttingen, 1969). Wieckenberg's conclusions confirm my thesis in a number of points.
46. Pascal, 'Tense,' 6.
47. In an epistolary novel the first-person pronominal reference of the

letter writer is sometimes transposed into third-person reference in chapter or letter headings. An example from Samuel Richardson:

LETTER XI. *To her Mother.* – Cannot find her letter; so recites her master's free behaviour to her in the summer-house. Her virtuous resentment. Refuses his offers of money. He injoins her to secrecy, pretending he only designed to try her. (*Pamela or, Virtue Rewarded* [London, 1801], Vol. I, Contents VI.)

Wolfgang Zach notes that 'Richardson adheres here essentially to Pamela's perspective, but interprets the events in part authorially.' See 'Richardson und der Leser: *Pamela–Shamela–Pamela II,' Arbeiten aus Anglistik und Amerikanistik*, 1 (1976), 80. Strictly speaking, this synoptic heading contains a narrative element, namely an incipient interpretation by the author-editor.

48. Casparis, *Tense Without Time*, p. 128.
49. See Hamburger, *Logic*, pp. 59ff. and 311ff.; and Weinrich, pp. 26ff.
50. According to Ludwig, there is a direct connection between what the picture portrays and the tense used in the caption. What is depicted in the picture and can thus be perceived by the reader is described in the present tense. What is not depicted and therefore has to be supplemented (i.e. *added to the picture*) by the narrator is referred to in the past tense. In texts of this type the past tense, therefore, indicates the appearance of a narrator *in the story*. Otto Ludwig, 'Thesen zu den Tempora im Deutschen,' *Zeitschrift für deutsche Philologie*, 91 (1972), 58–81; see especially p. 68.
51. Heinrich Hoffmann, 'Die gar traurige Geschichte mit dem Feuer-zeug,' in his *Der Struwwelpeter*, 1st edn (Frankfurt am Main, n.d.), p. 4.
52. Ludwig, 'Thesen,' p. 69.
53. Ibid., p. 74.
54. See W. J. M. Bronzwaer, *Tense in the Novel: An Investigation of Some Potentialities of Linguistic Criticism* (Groningen, 1970), pp. 120–1.
55. Several of Hamburger's observations on the use of tense in the lyric genre, *Logik*, 1st edn, p. 194, were deleted in the second edition, on which the English translation, *Logic*, is based.

3. A new approach to the definition of the narrative situations

1. The last two, more extensive critical discussions of *Narrative Situations* (almost a quarter century after its original publication!) could not be dealt with here in detail. Some of the objections raised in them, however, have been anticipated in my *Theory*. See Jürgen H. Petersen, 'Kategorien des Erzählens: Zur systematischen Deskription epischer Texte,' *Poetica*, 9 (1977), 167–95; Albrecht Staffhorst,

Die Subjekt–Objekt–Struktur: Ein Beitrag zur Erzähltheorie (Stuttgart, 1979), especially pp. 17–22.

2. Some of the considerations included here were outlined several years ago, but were published only recently as 'Zur Konstituierung der typischen Erzählsituationen,' in *Zur Struktur des Romans*, ed. Bruno Hillebrand (Darmstadt, 1978), pp. 558–76.

3. The dynamization of the narrative situations, that is, the adaptation of the theoretical concepts to the flowing character of the narrative text, is in a way diametrically opposed to the procedure of structuralist and linguistic narratology, which, through 'rewriting' (Ihwe) or 'normalization' (Hendricks), strives to formalize the narrative text, that is, to adapt the text to the conceptual model of the analysis. See Ihwe, 'On the foundations of a general theory of narrative structure,' *Poetics*, 3 (1972), 7; and Hendricks, 'The structural study of narration,' *Poetics*, 3 (1972), 101.

4. The question of how thorough this analysis of the constitutive elements must be in order to arrive at categories which are not laden with typological generalities but which are as detailed as possible is not just a methodological question. It also depends on the aim of the particular theory of narration. Baur, for example, favours a more analytical and purely descriptive procedure. See 'Deskriptive Kategorien des Erzählverhaltens,' in *Erzählung und Erzählforschung im 20. Jahrhundert*, ed. Rolf Kloepfer and Gisela Janetzke-Dillner (Stuttgart, 1981), pp. 31–9.

5. See Otto Ludwig, 'Formen der Erzählung,' in his *Epische Studien: Gesammelte Schriften*, ed. A. Stern (Leipzig, 1891), VI, pp. 202ff.; Percy Lubbock, *The Craft of Fiction*, (New York, 1947), p. 67; N. Friedman, 'Point of view,' 1161ff.; Stanzel, *Narrative Situations*, p. 22.

6. See N. Friedman, 'Point of view,' 1169–78.

7. See Eduard Spranger, 'Der psychologische Perspektivismus im Roman,' rpt. in *Poetik*, ed. Klotz, pp. 217–38.

8. Erwin Leibfried, *Kritische Wissenschaft vom Text: Manipulation, Reflexion, transparente Poetologie*, 2nd edn (Stuttgart, 1972), p. 244. The new approach to the definition of the narrative situations on the basis of person, perspective and mode has, I hope, made it clear that the term narrative situation does not merely mean perspective, as Leibfried implies.

9. See Jean Pouillon, *Temps et roman* (Paris, 1946), pp. 74–114; Todorov, 'Les catégories,' 125–59; Genette, *Narrative Discourse*, Ithaca, New York, 1980, pp. 185–98, where perspective and focalization are subordinated to the aspect of mood.

10. A partial list of such works is given in Stanzel, 'Zur Konstituierung,' pp. 568ff.

11. See Hamburger, *Logic*, pp. 3ff. and 311ff.; Anderegg, *Fiktion*, pp.

43ff.; Leibfried, *Kritische Wissenschaft*, pp. 244–5; Cleanth Brooks and Robert Penn Warren, *Understanding Fiction*, New York, 1943, pp. 659ff.; Genette, *Narrative Discourse*, pp. 30–2; Doležel, 'Typology,' pp. 541–52. Doležel further develops his typology in the introduction to his *Narrative Modes in Czech Literature* (Toronto, 1973).

12. See Cohn, 'The encirclement of narrative. On Franz Stanzel's *Theorie des Erzählens*,' *Poetics Today*, 2 (Winter 1981), 174ff. and 179–80.

13. Note how the forms in the dyadic system suggested by Cohn are located in clearly differentiated sectors or quadrants, while the individual forms in my typological circle with a triadic basis can always be located on one of the continua linking two narrative situations. See Cohn, 'Encirclement,' 163, Chart II, and 179, Figure 2.

14. For the meaning of the binary oppositions for linguistics and also for structuralistically oriented literary theory see Jonathan Culler, *Structuralist Poetics: Structuralism, Linguistics, and the Study of Literature* (Ithaca, New York, 1978), pp. 14–16. An introduction to this and other structuralistic terms can be found in Jürgen Link, *Literaturwissenschaftliche Grundbegriffe. Eine programmierte Einführung auf strukturalistischer Basis* (Munich, 1974).

15. Doležel, 'Typology,' pp. 541–52. In Doležel's further development of this typology he employs a circular model in addition to the linguistic tree diagram. See especially the Introduction to his *Narrative Modes*.

16. See Leibfried, *Kritische Wissenschaft*, pp. 245ff.

17. Ibid., p. 243.

18. Ibid., p. 247.

19. Ibid., p. 244.

20. See also Stanzel, 'Zur Konstituierung,' pp. 574–5.

21. Füger, 'Zur Tiefenstruktur,' pp. 268–92.

22. Chatman, 'Structure,' pp. 213–57.

23. John Austin, *How to Do Things With Words* (New York, 1962).

24. Chatman, 'The structure of narrative transmission,' in *Style and Structure in Literature: Essays in the New Stylistics*, ed. R. Fowler, Oxford, 1975, p. 233.

25. Ibid., p. 229.

26. Ibid., pp. 238–9.

27. Ibid., p. 235.

28. Chatman, *Story and Discourse: Narrative Structure in Fiction and Film* (Ithaca, New York, 1978), has been published in the meantime. This narrative theory contains a revised version of Chatman's essay which I cited above. His discussion of my *Narrative Situations* does not appear in the book.

29. The principal objections to my typology on a triadic basis can be divided into four groups. One group demands a reduction of the three constitutive elements to the third-/first-person opposition

(Hamburger), to which the teller/reflector opposition is then sub-ordinated (Lockemann, Staffhorst). The other group demands the reduction of the three constitutive elements to the teller-reflector opposition, to which the third-/first-person opposition is then sub-ordinated (Anderegg, Herbert Kraft, and others). A third group wants to subordinate person and mode to perspective (Leibfried, Füger). The fourth group suggests abandoning the constitutive element perspective (Cohn, Lockemann, Staffhorst and others). Considering the incompatibility of the objections and the suggestions for change, it seems to me that it remains to be a real advantage of my approach that it embodies all three constitutive elements without postulating an order of rank for them. See Staffhorst, *Die Subjekt–Objekt-Struktur*, pp. 17–22, and Herbert Kraft, *Um Schiller betrogen* (Pfullingen, 1978), pp. 48–58.

30. David Goldknopf, *The Life of the Novel* (Chicago, 1972), p. 33.
31. J. D. Salinger, *The Catcher in the Rye* (Harmondsworth, 1958), p. 5.
32. In order to better facilitate an overview of these fundamental considerations, I shall not discuss the possibility of transposing a first-person narrative into narrative with a peripheral first-person narrator, who would refer to the central character in the third-person (see Samuel Butler's *The Way of All Flesh*).
33. James Joyce, *A Portrait of the Artist as a Young Man* (Harmonds-worth, 1963), p. 143.
34. Cohn subjected this passage to a more extensive transposition experiment which yielded significant results, especially in relation to the presentation of inner world with the aid of free indirect style. See 'Narrated monologue: definition of a fictional style,' *Comparative Literature*, 18 (1966), 98ff.
35. Joyce, *Ulysses* (Harmondsworth, 1969), pp. 38–9.
36. Jürgen Landwehr and others maintain that there can be no ahistoric constant in the humanities, but Landwehr's argument is not con-vincing. He asserts that ahistoric constants must also be valid for the future, which would mean that they permit a prediction which could be proved incorrect at any time by the intentional production of a work which disproves the constants. In this context, however, a single work has no relevance and the intentional mass production of works to disprove these constants is unlikely. It can be expected, however, that drawing attention to constants such as these by describing them could cause a reaction among authors. The anti-constants which might then arise would in all likelihood be located once again on the typological circle. Such a development has been noticeable at least since Joyce. This phenomenon does not invalidate the ahistoricity of the narrative situations as they have been described here. It is not the ideal types as theoretical constructs of characteristic possibilities of narrative presentation, but rather the historical forms,

which more or less approach the ideal types, which are subject to historical change. See *Text und Fiktion: Zu einigen literaturwissenschaftlichen und kommunikationstheoretischen Grundbegriffen* (Munich, 1975), pp. 24–5.

37. See Stanzel, 'Wandlungen des narrativen Diskurses in der Moderne,' in *Erzählung und Erzählforschung im 20. Jahrhundert*, ed. R. Kloepfer and G. Janetzke-Dillner (Stuttgart, 1981), pp. 371–83.

38. Jacques Dubois *et al.*, *Rhétorique générale* (Paris, 1971), pp. 187ff.

39. Link's distinction between a 'normal type of epic discourse', and an 'epic discourse defamiliarized by dialogue' is also based on the deviation model, Link, pp. 293–304. Strictly speaking, this distinction comprises several oppositions: third-/first-person narration, reflector-/teller-character, and Anderegg's narrating/reporting text. At one point Link specifically equates the 'normal type' with a figural narrative situation (see p. 367). Like any 'normalization' of a *single* type of the possible narrative situations, this seems problematic.

40. See Thomas S. Kuhn, *The Structure of Scientific Revolutions*, 2nd edn, (Chicago, 1970), pp. 84ff; Hans Robert Jauss (ed.), *Nachahmung und Illusion* (Munich, 1969); and Anderegg, *Literaturwissenschaftliche Stiltheorie* (Göttingen, 1977) for the background of this change.

41. James, Preface to 'The Tragic Muse,' in his *Art*, p. 84.

42. Valentina Zavarin and Susan Wittig, Translators' Preface, *Poetics*, by Uspensky, p. xvi.

43. In this context it is especially interesting to note that Johannes Holthusen has found that in the Russian novel the figural narrative situation never occurs completely independently of the authorial narrative situation. See 'Erzählung und auktorialer Kommentar im modernen russischen Roman,' *Welt der Slaven*, 8 (1963), 252–67; and Wolf Schmid, 'Zur Erzähltechnik und Bewußtseinsdarstellung in Dostoevskijs "Večnyj Muž," ' *Welt der Slaven*, 13 (1968), 305–6.

44. See Jean Ricardou, 'Nouveau Roman, Tel Quel,' *Poétique*, 1 (1970), 433–54; and John Barth, *Lost in the Funhouse* (Garden City, New York, 1968), p. 38.

45. Eberhard Lämmert, *Bauformen des Erzählens* (Stuttgart, 1955).

46. Robert Petsch, *Wesen und Formen der Erzählkunst* (Halle/Saale, 1934).

47. See Helmut Bonheim, 'Theory of narrative modes,' *Semiotica*, 14 (1975), 329ff. Bonheim has now elaborated his distinction of the four modes in *The Narrative Modes. Techniques of the Short Story* (Cambridge, 1982).

48. See also Klaus W. Hempfer, *Gattungstheorie* (Munich, 1973), especially pp. 156ff.; and Paul Hernadi, *Beyond Genre: New Directions in Literary Classification* (Ithaca and London, 1972), especially pp. 55ff., 155–6, and 187ff.

49. This does not, of course, mean that the dialogue cannot be integrated

into the narrative context. See Michał Głowiński, 'Der Dialog im Roman,' *Poetica*, 6 (1974), 1–16. Doležel, after all, defines a narrative text as a sequence of segments of 'narrator's discourse' and 'characters' discourse.' See Doležel, *Narrative Modes*, p. 4. Such a definition draws attention to the fact that many of the especially interesting phenomena of narrative discourse are located right at the borderline between these two types of discourse.

50. Chatman, 'Structure,' p. 237. See also Genette, *Narrative Discourse*, pp. 162–4.

51. Hamburger, *Logic*, p. 176.

52. Narrative parts are the segments of a narrative text in which the mediacy of narration is expressed. The term in this sense must be distinguished from the meaning of the word in Link's concept of 'narrative text,' which means 'all texts based on a plot.' For Link, narrative texts include films, radio plays, comics, etc., besides the novel and drama. Link, *Grundbegriffe*, p. 272.

53. Stanzel, *Narrative Situations*, Chapter II.

54. See Werner Günther, *Probleme der Rededarstellung. Untersuchungen zur direkten, indirekten und erlebten Rede im Deutschen, Französischen und Italienischen* (Marburg, 1928), pp. 81–2.

55. See Hamburger, *Logic*, pp. 178–80.

56. See Winfried Kudszus, 'Erzählperspektive und Erzählgeschehen in Kafkas "Prozeß," ' *Deutsche Vierteljahrsschrift für Literaturwissenschaft und Geistesgeschichte*, 44 (1970), 106–17; and Walter H. Sokel, 'Das Verhältnis der Erzählperspektive zum Erzählgeschehen und Sinngehalt in "Vor dem Gesetz," "Schakale und Araber" und "Der Prozeß," ' *Zeitschrift für deutsche Philologie*, 86 (1967), especially 267–76.

57. See Hernadi, *Beyond Genre*, pp. 161ff.

58. See Wolfgang Wickardt, *Die Formen der Perspektive in Charles Dickens' Romanen, ihr sprachlicher Ausdruck und ihre strukturelle Bedeutung* (Berlin, 1933), pp. 37ff.

59. See Dickens, *Dombey and Son* (Harmondsworth, 1977), Chapter XVI, and Section 2.4.

60. See Fred W. Boege, 'Point of view in Dickens,' *PMLA*, 65 (1950), 90–105.

61. Joyce, *A Portrait of the Artist*, pp. 59–60.

62. See Stanzel, '*Tristram Shandy* und die Klimatheorie,' *Germanisch-Romanische Monatsschrift*, NS 21 (1971), 16.

63. See Bonheim, 'Theory,' 329–44, and his 'Mode markers in the American short story,' in *Proceedings of the Fourth International Congress of Applied Linguistics* (Stuttgart, 1976), pp. 541–50.

64. Stanzel, 'Die Komplementärgeschichte. Entwurf zu einer leserorientierten Romantheorie,' in *Erzählforschung II*, ed. Haubrichs, p. 258.

**4. The opposition person: identity and non-identity of the
realms of existence of the narrator and the fictional characters
(first- and third-person reference)**

1. Egon Werlich, *A Text Grammar of English* (Heidelberg, 1976).
2. Fowler, *Linguistics and the Novel*, London, 1977, p. 5.
3. Ibid., p. 17.
4. Ferdinand de Saussure, *Course in General Linguistics*, ed. Charles Bally and Albert Sechehaye (New York, 1959), p. 121.
5. Friedrich Spielhagen, 'Der Ich-Roman,' in *Poetik*, ed. Klotz, p. 128.
6. Kurt Forstreuter, *Die deutsche Ich-Erzählung: Eine Studie zu ihrer Geschichte und Technik* (Berlin, 1924), p. 44.
7. This is at least true for the general discussion. In his afterword to the reprint of Spielhagen's works on the theory of the novel, Hellmuth Himmel has drawn attention to the fact that several persons had noted the 'non-identity of the author and the narrator' even before Spielhagen. See Hellmuth Himmel, Afterword, *Beiträge zur Theorie und Technik des Romans*, by Spielhagen (Göttingen, 1967), pp. 354–5.
8. Kayser, 'Wer erzählt den Roman?' in *Poetik*, ed. Klotz, p. 209.
9. Ibid., pp. 208–9.
10. See Stanzel, *Typische Formen des Romans*, Göttingen, 1981, pp. 34–5. See also Romberg, *Studies in the Narrative Technique of the First-Person Novel*, Stockholm, 1962, p. 84.
11. It is no coincidence that Gerhart von Graevenitz pays much attention to just this novel. In his otherwise very exhaustive analyses he, like Booth and Kayser, attributes very little importance to the first-/third-person opposition. See *Die Setzung des Subjekts* (Tübingen, 1973), pp. 68–73.
12. See Lothar Cerny, *Erinnerung bei Dickens* (Amsterdam, 1975), Chapter III. 3, 'Erinnerung als dichterische Vergegenwärtigung,' especially pp. 106ff.
13. Booth, *Rhetoric*, p. 150.
14. Ibid., pp. 150ff.
15. See my comment on Booth in 'Second thoughts on *Narrative Situations in the Novel*: Towards a "Grammar of Fiction," ' *Novel: A Forum on Fiction*, 11 (1978), 254–5.
16. This prejudice is especially crass in Booth's essay 'Distance and point of view,' *Essays in Criticism*, 11 (1961), 60–79. It is also evident here that Booth associates that systematic study of literature which he regards so scornfully mainly with critical works in the German language.
17. See Joyce Cary, *Art and Reality* (Cambridge, 1958), pp. 97–8.
18. James, *Art*, pp. 320–1. See also his *Notebooks*, p. 130, where, in his first draft for *The Golden Bowl*, he considers the first-person form for a moment, but immediately rejects it. In his *Tales*, on the other hand,

James chose the first-person form relatively often. Krishna Baldev Vaid discusses James's reasons for choosing the first-person form and provides a complete list of the tales, identifying the first-person narratives in *Technique in the Tales of Henry James* (Cambridge, Mass., 1964).

19. See Richard Stang, *The Theory of the Novel in England, 1850–1870* (New York, 1959); Kenneth Graham, *Criticism of Fiction in England 1865–1900* (Oxford, 1965); Miriam Allott, *Novelists on the Novel* (London, 1959); Reinhold Grimm (ed.), *Deutsche Romantheorie: Beiträge zu einer historischen Poetik des Romans in Deutschland* (Frankfurt am Main, 1968); Lämmert (ed.), *Romantheorie: Dokumentation ihrer Geschichte in Deutschland seit 1880* (Cologne, 1975).

20. Margit Henning, *Die Ich-Form und ihre Funktion in Thomas Manns 'Doktor Faustus' und in der deutschen Literatur der Gegenwart* (Tübingen, 1966).

21. See Hugh Kenner, *Samuel Beckett: A Critical Study* (London, 1962).

22. P. F. Botheroyd, *Ich und Er: First and Third Person Self-Reference and Problems of Identity in Three Contemporary German-Language Novels* (The Hague and Paris, 1976). Dieter Meindl has shown that there has also been a renaissance of the first-person novel in the American novel. See Meindl's interesting article 'Zur Renaissance des amerikanischen Ich-Romans in den fünfziger Jahren,' *Jahrbuch für Amerikastudien*, 19 (1974), 201–18.

23. Botheroyd, *Ich und Er*, p. 126.

24. See Dostoevsky, *The Devils*, pp. 287–99.

25. See Herbert Marshall McLuhan, *The Gutenberg Galaxy: The Making of Typographic Man* (Toronto, 1962).

26 William Jinks, *The Celluloid Literature: Film in the Humanities* (Beverly Hills, 1974); Helmut Schanze, *Medienkunde für Literaturwissenschaftler* (Munich, 1974), with a detailed bibliography; Adam J. Bisanz, 'Linearität versus Simultaneität im narrativen Zeit-Raum-Gefüge: Ein methodisches Problem und die medialen Grenzen der modernen Erzählstruktur,' in *Erzählforschung I*, ed. Haubrichs, pp. 184–223; Horst Meixner, 'Filmische Literatur und literarisierter Film,' in *Literaturwissenschaft–Medienwissenschaft*, ed. Helmut Kreuzer (Heidelberg, 1977), pp. 32–43. The beginnings of a clarification of the relationship between literary and cinematic narrative on the basis of literary theory can be found in Susanne Langer, *Feeling and Form: A Theory of Art Developed From 'Philosophy in a New Key*,' 4th edn (London, 1967), pp. 411ff.; and in Hamburger, *Logic*, pp. 218–30.

27. For a discussion of the historical development of the first-person form compared to the third-person form see Głowiński, 'On the first-person novel,' *New Literary History*, 9 (1977), 103–14.

28. See Wolfgang Lockemann, 'Zur Lage der Erzählforschung,'

Germanisch-Romanische Monatsschrift, NS 15 (1965), 63–84.
29. See Booth, *Rhetoric*, p. 158 *et passim*.
30. Lockemann, 'Zur Lage,' p. 81.
31. The concept of reliability used here is partially equivalent to Günter Waldmann's 'believing somebody something' as a basic element of every communicative process. Waldmann assigns one variant to each of the three narrative situations. See *Kommunikationsästhetik: Die Ideologie der Erzählform* (Munich, 1976), pp. 185–97.
32. The English translation 'embodied narrator' for Stanzel's term *Ich mit Leib* is taken from Cohn, 'Encirclement,' 164. Translator's note.
33. Thomas Mann, *Confessions of Felix Krull, Confidence Man: The Early Years*, trans. Denver Lindley (New York, 1955), p. 3; *Die Bekenntnisse des Hochstaplers Felix Krull* (Frankfurt am Main, 1955), p. 9.
34. In his analysis of Iris Murdoch's first-person novel *The Italian Girl*, Bronzwaer employs a slightly different system of reference and other terms, but nevertheless arrives at similar conclusions. Bronzwaer writes as follows about the opening sentence of the novel, 'I pressed the door gently,' which refers to the first-person narrator's return to the house of his childhood after a long absence:

In the first analysis, the I here refers to the implied author or the narrator. It is a purely instrumental pronoun, which can for that reason function as the initiator of the narrative. With the definite article in 'the door,' however, the I's involvement in the story is suddenly brought about: he is now talking about a door that is familiar to him. His response to the door . . . is not that of a narrator; it is that of a character, a human being who has known this door from childhood and cannot help responding to it emotionally.' (See Bronzwaer, *Tense in the Novel*, p. 90.)

35. 'Tristram Shandy . . . as a novel about the impossibility of writing a novel,' Fabian, 'Laurence Sterne: *Tristram Shandy*,' in *Der Englische Roman*, ed. F. K. Stanzel, (Düsseldorf, 1969), I, p. 240.
36. Karl Bühler, *Sprachtheorie*, 2nd edn (Stuttgart, 1965), p. 138.
37. Hamburger, *The Logic of Literature*, 2nd revised edn, Bloomington, 1973, p. 129.
38. The problem of deixis in narration is still very far from a definitive solution, but some very interesting works have recently been published on it. Note especially Reinhold Winkler, 'Über Deixis und Wirklichkeitsbezug in fiktionalen und nicht-fiktionalen Texten,' in *Erzählforschung I*, ed. Haubrichs, pp. 156–74, who provides further references.
39. Laurence Sterne, *The Life and Opinions of Tristram Shandy, Gentleman*, ed. J. A. Work (New York, 1940), VII, p. 1. See also Stanzel, '*Tom Jones* und *Tristram Shandy*,' in *Henry Fielding und der englische Roman des 18. Jahrhunderts*, ed. Wolfgang Iser (Darmstadt, 1972), p. 446.

40. James, *The Complete Tales of Henry James*, ed. Leon Edel (London, 1963), VIII, pp. 236–7.
41. James, *Complete Tales*, VII, pp. 422–3.
42. See Vaid, 'Chronology of Tales,' in his *Technique in the Tales of Henry James*, pp. 264–5.
43. James, *Complete Tales*, VII, p. 284.
44. Ibid.
45. Goldknopf, *The Life of the Novel*, pp. 38–9. My emphasis in lines 2–5.
46. See Goldknopf, *The Life of the Novel*, p. 39.
47. W. Somerset Maugham, *Cakes and Ale* (Harmondsworth, 1963), pp. 143–4.
48. See the discussion of the question of whether it is the function of the narrative present tense to present an event as if it were taking place at the present moment, or whether it has another function: Hamburger, *Logic*, pp. 98–110; Casparis, *Tense without Time*, pp. 17ff.; Cerny, *Erinnerung*, pp. 95ff.; Manfred Markus, *Tempus und Aspekt: Zur Funktion von Präsens, Präteritum und Perfekt im Englischen und Deutschen* (Munich, 1977), pp. 36ff.
49. Dickens, *David Copperfield* (Harmondsworth, 1975), pp. 691–5.
50. Longer segments (of several chapters) with a predominantly authorial narrative situation alternate regularly with segments of the same length in which a first-person narrator appears in Dickens's *Bleak House* (1852–3), which was written at nearly the same time. Since the authorial narrator and the first-person narrator (Esther Summerson) are two different persons who see things from different points of view and in quite different ways, however, we are actually dealing here with two different narratives on one and the same topic, not with a change of reference.
51. Thackeray, *Henry Esmond* (Harmondsworth, 1972), p. 203.
52. Geoffrey Tillotson, *Thackeray the Novelist* (Cambridge, 1954).
53. See James Sutherland, *Thackeray at Work* (London, 1974), pp. 66ff.
54. See John Loofbourow, *Thackeray and the Form of Fiction* (Princeton, 1964), p. 119.
55. See Iser, *The Implied Reader: Patterns of Communication in Prose Fiction from Bunyan to Beckett* (Baltimore, 1974), pp. 130ff.
56. Ibid., pp. 206–7.
57. The detachment of an autobiographical self from the earlier stages of his life history is one of Philippe Lejeune's two explanations of autobiography in the third person. The other explanation refers to so-called 'fictive fictions,' in which the autobiographical self is transferred to another person, from whose imaginative point of view it looks at itself, for example Gertrude Stein's *Autobiography of Alice B. Toklas*. See 'Autobiography in the third person,' *New Literary History*, 9 (1977), 26–50.
58. Thackeray, *Henry Esmond*, pp. 193 and 313–34.

59. Ibid., pp. 439–40.
60. See Stanzel, *Narrative Situations*, pp. 61–2. My explanation at that time, namely, that the change from 'he' to 'I' always occurs where strong emotions are presented, is too general and must be revised; an essential prerequisite for the return from third-person to first-person reference is the reflectorization of the narrative situation.
61. See Sutherland, *Thackeray at Work*, p. 66.
62. See Botheroyd, *Ich und Er*, especially pp. 118ff.; Henning, *Die Ich–Form*, especially pp. 156ff.; and Walter Jens, *Deutsche Literaturgeschichte der Gegenwart* (Munich, 1961), pp. 93–4, where transition from first person to third person is termed an attempt at objectifying a first-person narrative.
63. Max Frisch, *Mein Name sei Gantenbein* (Frankfurt am Main, 1964), p. 20.
64. Kurt Vonnegut, Jr, *Slaughterhouse-Five, or the Children's Crusade* (New York, 1969), pp. 85–6.
65. See the references provided by Botheroyd, *Ich und Er*, especially in his introduction, pp. 1–27, and 132–40.
66. Saul Bellow, *Herzog* (Harmondsworth, 1965), pp. 157–9.
67. D. H. Lawrence, *Women in Love* (Harmondsworth, 1973), p. 471.
68. Compare the last quotation from *Henry Esmond* and the quotation from *Herzog* above.
69. For a discussion of the term 'gnomic present tense' see Günter Steinberg, *Erlebte Rede. Ihre Eigenart und ihre Formen in neuerer deutscher, französischer und englischer Erzählliteratur* (Göppingen, 1971), pp. 225ff.
70. Frisch, *Montauk* (New York, 1976), p. 113; *Montauk* (Frankfurt am Main, 1975), p. 165.
71. See Shklovsky, 'Art as Technique,' in *Russian Formalist Criticism*, eds. Lemon and Reis, pp. 3–24; and Renate Lachmann, 'Die "Verfremdung" und das "Neue Sehen" bei Viktor Šklovskij,' *Poetica*, 3 (1970), 226–49.
72. Frisch, *Montauk* (New York), p. 104; (Frankfurt), p. 152.
73. Frisch, *Montauk* (New York), p. 72; (Frankfurt), p. 107. My emphasis.
74. Frisch, *Montauk* (New York), p. 94; (Frankfurt), p. 138. My emphasis.
75. Frisch, *Montauk* (New York), p. 110; (Frankfurt), p. 82.
76. Samuel Beckett, *Molloy, Malone Dies, The Unnamable* (London, 1959), p. 345.

5. The opposition perspective: internal perspective–external perspective

1. Brooks's and Warren's opposition 'internal analysis of events'– 'outside observation of events' closely approaches my opposition

internal perspective–external perspective, while their second distinction 'narrator as a character in the story' and 'narrator not a character in the story' largely coincides with my opposition person. However, the opposition mode is lacking in their scheme. See *Understanding Fiction*, p. 660.

2. See Section 1.1.

3. See Joyce, *Ulysses*, pp. 42ff. and 150ff.

4. For a thorough and critical comparison of Genette's *Narrative Discourse* with my *Theory of Narrative*, see Cohn, 'Encirclement,' especially 160ff. and 174ff. Genette's narrative theory, essentially the result of his research on Proust's novel, was originally published as 'Discours du récit' in *Figures III* (Paris, 1972), pp. 65–282.

5. Mieke Bal has convincingly demonstrated that Genette's 'zero focalization' and 'external focalization' are merely variants of one and the same presentation with external perspective. See 'Narration et focalisation,' *Poétique*, 29 (1977), 113 and 119.

6. Genette, *Narrative Discourse*, pp. 186 and 212ff.

7. See Lockemann, 'Zur Lage', pp. 81–2.

8. See Leibfried, *Kritische Wissenschaft*, p. 244, and Lockemann, 'Zur Lage', p. 82.

9. Of course, the theoretical distinction between person and perspective is not a condition *sine qua non* for the understanding of these phenomena, but it sharpens the perception of them and facilitates their discussion. Thus Françoise van Rossum-Guyon, *Critique du roman* (Paris, 1970), arrives at some very interesting and well founded insights into what she terms 'La Perspective narrative,' (Chapter III), without distinguishing the concepts person and perspective. Her main interest, however, is the second-person (*vous*) narrative form in Michel Butor's *A Change of Heart* (*La Modification*), whose classification in my opposition of first-person and third-person form would cause difficulty if one did not consider it a variant of the first-person form, albeit a very significant one.

10. Gotthold Ephraim Lessing, *Laocoön: An Essay on the Limits of Painting and Poetry* (Indianapolis, 1962), p. 78 (Chapter XVI).

11. As early as 1945 Joseph Frank recognised the tendency toward spatial form as an innovative deviation from the temporally dominated form of the conventional narrative, 'Spatial form in modern literature: an essay in three parts,' *Sewanee Review*, 53 (1945), 221–240. This essay sparked an exhaustive discussion, especially in American criticism. See Jeffrey R. Smitten and Ann Daghistany, *Spatial Form in Narrative* (Ithaca, New York, 1981). German works on the presentation of space in the novel are primarily oriented towards content and theme. (See Hermann Meyer, 'Raum und Zeit in Wilhelm Raabes Erzählkunst,' *Deutsche Vierteljahrsschrift für Literaturwissenschaft und Geistesgeschichte*, 27 (1953), 237–67; Bruno Hillebrand, *Mensch*

und Raum im Roman (Munich, 1971); Alexander Ritter (ed.), *Landschaft und Raum in der Erzählkunst* (Darmstadt, 1957); and Gerhard Hoffmann, *Raum, Situation, erzählte Wirklichkeit* (Stuttgart, 1978).) What remains to be done is to relate both aspects of spatial presentation to each other, as Hoffmann has already attempted in his very broadly based book.

12. See Roman Ingarden, *The Cognition of the Literary Work of Art* (Evanston, 1973), and *The Literary Work of Art: An Investigation on the Borderlines of Ontology, Logic and Theory of Literature* (Evanston, 1973), pp. 246–54. Ingarden's seminal concept of the 'indeterminate areas' or 'gaps' in the narrative presentation of fictional worlds has been elaborated in reader response theories of narrative. The most prominent exponent of this approach is Wolfgang Iser, whose main studies are available in English: *The Implied Reader* (Baltimore, 1974), and *The Act of Reading* (Baltimore, 1978). For a critical evaluation of Iser's theory see *Diacritics*, June and Winter issues 1980, and most recently Brooks Thomas 'Reading Wolfgang Iser or responding to a theory of response,' *Comparative Literature Studies*, 19 (1982), 54–66. A short summary of the main concepts of Iser's theory and a comparison with Stanley Fish and Walter J. Slatoff, the American exponents of the theory of response or reception theory, is to be found in Catherine Belsey, *Critical Practice. New Accents* (London, 1980), pp. 34f.

13. Daniel Halpern and John Fowles, 'A sort of exile in Lyme Regis,' *London Magazine*, March 1971, 46–7. See also Stanzel, 'Komplementärgeschichte,' p. 245.

14. See Uspensky, *Poetics*, pp. 76–80.

15. See Ernest Hemingway, *A Moveable Feast* (Harmondsworth, 1966), p. 58: 'my new theory that you could omit anything if you knew that you omitted, and the omitted part would strengthen the story and make people feel something more than they understood.' See also Winkler, *Lyrische Elemente in den Kurzgeschichten Ernest Hemingways* (Erlangen 1967), pp. 72ff.

16. Aldous Huxley, *The Doors of Perception* (Harmondsworth, 1963), p. 20. Huxley first refers to the related theories of C. D. Broad and then continues:

To make biological survival possible, Mind at Large has to be funneled through the reducing valve of the brain and nervous system . . . To formulate and express the contents of this reduced awareness man has invented and endlessly elaborated those symbol-systems and implicit philosophies that we call languages.

Huxley is not interested here in the literary–historical consequences of this state of affairs, however, but rather in the question of how consciousness could be expanded by avoiding the 'reducing valve' by means of 'bypasses.'

17. See Robert E. Ornstein, *The Psychology of Consciousness* (San Francisco, 1972), pp. 19–42.
18. E. M. Forster has already drawn attention to this point: 'Well, in what senses do the nations of fiction differ from those of the earth? . . . they need not have glands, for example, whereas all human beings have glands.' *Aspects of the Novel* (Harmondsworth, 1974), p. 81.
19. Joyce, *A Portrait of the Artist*, pp. 154–5.
20. Ibid., p. 160.
21. Dickens, *Bleak House*, pp. 663 and 669.
22. Anthony Trollope, *Barchester Towers*, in his *Barchester Towers and The Warden* (New York, 1950), pp. 234–5.
23. The English translation is by Marilyn J. Rose in Hamburger, *Logic*, p. 131; Thomas Mann, *Die Buddenbrooks* (Berlin, 1930), p. 12.
24. Hamburger, *Logic*, p. 131.
25. Like every stylistic trend, this, too, has numerous causes. The striving for the most objective presentation possible and for a sharper perspectivization in the novel which took place just before and at the turn of the century is only one aspect of that complex process in the history of literature which Lothar Hönnighausen convincingly relates to its larger context in the intellectual history. See 'Maske und Perspektive: Weltanschauliche Voraussetzungen des perspektivischen Erzählens,' *Germanisch-Romanische Monatsschrift*, NS 26 (1976), 287–307.
26. See E. H. Gombrich, *Art and Illusion: A Study in the Psychology of Pictorial Representation*, 3rd edn (London, 1968), pp. 24–5, 55–78 *et passim*. Iser integrated Gombrich's thesis into his theory of literary reception in modified form. See Iser, *Act*, pp. 90–2.
27. Booth aptly terms perspectivism or, in his terminology, the new 'consistent treatment of point of view' the fourth fundamental unity which joins the three unities of place, time and plot in the novel. See Booth, *The Rhetoric of Fiction*, Chicago, 1961, p. 64.
28. Forster, *Aspects*, p. 54.
29. See W. J. Harvey, *The Art of George Eliot* (London, 1961), and *Character and the Novel* (London, 1970); and Barbara Hardy, *The Novels of George Eliot*, 2nd edn (London, 1963). A good portion of Dickens criticism after Edmund Wilson and Humphry House could also be mentioned here.
30. Barbara Hardy, *The Appropriate Form: An Essay on the Novel* (London, 1964), p. 8.
31. See Robert Scholes and Robert Kellogg *The Nature of Narrative* (London, 1971), pp. 271–2.
32. See Section 1.2 and note 63.
33. See Jean-Paul Sartre, *Qu'est-ce que la littérature?* (Paris, 1948), p. 174: 'Ainsi l'aventure est un bref désordre qui s'est annulé. Elle est racontée du point de vue de l'expérience et de la sagesse, elle est

écoutée du point de vue de l'ordre. L'ordre triomphe, l'ordre est partout . . . D'ailleurs y eut-il même jamais trouble? L'évocation d'un brusque changement effrayerait cette société bourgeoise.'

34. Lodge, *The Novelist*, pp. 120–1.

35. See also Winfried Wehle's discussion of this aspect of the *nouveau roman* in his *Französischer Roman der Gegenwart: Erzählstruktur und Wirklichkeit im Nouveau Roman* (Berlin, 1972), especially pp. 102ff.

36. See Füger, 'Das Nichtwissen des Erzählers in Fieldings *Joseph Andrews*: Baustein zu einer Theorie des negierten Wissens in der Fiktion,' *Poetica*, 10 (1978), 188–216.

37. Hamburger, *The Logic of Literature*, 2nd, revised edn, Bloomington, 1973, p. 83.

38. If Cohn's book had been available at the time of writing of the original German edition of my *Theory*, I could have formulated several observations, especially those dealing with the forms of interior monologue and free indirect style, more precisely.

39. For the history of the presentation of consciousness and inside view in the novel, see Stanzel 'Innenwelt: Ein Darstellungsproblem des englischen Romans,' *Germanisch-Romanische Monatsschrift*, NS 12 (1962), 273–86, and 'Gedanken zur Poetik des Romans,' in *Der englische Roman*, ed. Stanzel, I, pp. 19–20.

40. See Margaret Drabble, *The Needle's Eye* (Harmondsworth, 1973), pp. 374–5.

41. During a conversation with Margaret Drabble I learned that a conscious attempt by the author to control the reader's sympathy is unlikely in the case cited. This finding, however, only increases the significance of this aspect, since it permits conclusions about the author's attitude to the individual characters during the process of writing for which the author himself frequently does not or cannot account.

42. See for example the analyses of Shakespeare's imagery by Catherine Spurgeon, *Shakespeare's Imagery and What It Tells Us* (Cambridge, Mass., 1961), and Wolfgang Clemen, *Shakespeares Bilder: Ihre Entwicklung und ihre Funktionen im dramatischen Werk* (Bonn, 1936).

43. Tony Tanner, Introduction, *Sense and Sensibility*, by Jane Austen (Harmondsworth, 1974), p. 17.

44. See Jane Austen, *Sense and Sensibility* (London, 1962), pp. 351ff.

45. For a discussion of the revision of the narrative form of this novel see Frederick B. Pinion, *A Jane Austen Companion* (London, 1973), p. 84; and A. Walton Litz, *Jane Austen: A Study of Her Artistic Development* (London, 1965), pp. 72ff.

46. To explain this state of affairs it is also of interest that Jane Austen devoted more and more room to the presentation of consciousness

and inside view in her later novels. See Wolfgang Müller, 'Gefühls-darstellung bei Jane Austen,' *Sprachkunst*, 8 (1977), 87–103.

47. The information about this case is from Jauss, *Literaturgeschichte als Provokation der Literaturwissenschaft* (Konstanz, 1967), pp. 67ff., who also cites the sources.

48. Jauss, *Literaturgeschichte als Provokation der Literaturwissenschaft*, (Konstanz, 1967), pp. 67–8.

49. The term 'fingierte direkte Rede' (simulated direct speech) has been in common usage since Otto Funke's article 'Zur "erlebten Rede" bei Galsworthy,' *Englische Studien*, 64 (1929), 450–74.

50. Gustave Flaubert, *Madame Bovary* (New York, n.d.), p. 186; French as quoted in Jauss, *Literaturgeschichte*, p. 68. Jauss's emphasis. (See also Harmondsworth edn, 1950, p. 175.)

51. Flaubert, *Madame Bovary* (New York), p. 302; (Paris, 1966), p. 287. (Also Harmondsworth edn, pp. 273–4.)

52. Roy Pascal, *The Dual Voice: Free indirect speech and its functioning in the nineteenth-century European novel* (Manchester, 1977), p. 107: 'Flaubert's aesthetic interest has overcome his artistic, he indulges his own response to the city landscape instead of constructing Emma's.'

53. See C. H. Rolph (ed.), *The Trial of Lady Chatterley: Regina vs. Penguin Books Limited* (Harmondsworth, 1961), pp. 101–2 *et passim*.

54. N. Friedman, 'Point of view in Fiction. The development of a critical concept,' *PMLA* 70 (1955), 1167.

55. Jauss, *Literaturgeschichte*, p. 69.

56. H. G. Wells, *The Short Stories of H. G. Wells* (London, 1927), pp. 198–9.

57. Ibid., pp. 218–19.

58. Thackeray, *The Memoirs of Barry Lyndon, Esq., Written by Himself* (London, 1844).

59. It is significant that it was the readers of the popular serialization of the novel who voiced their displeasure and finally moved Thackeray to add this authorial footnote to Barry's first-person narrative. Thackeray deleted part of this commentary for the first edition in book form. See Gordon N. Ray, *Thackeray: The Uses of Adversity* (London, 1955), pp. 346 and 487 (note), and G. Tillotson, *Thackeray the Novelist* (Cambridge, 1954), p. 214, who find the deletion of this commentary regrettable.

60. Thackeray, *Barry Lyndon*, p. 496.

61. Ibid., p. 613.

62. See Boege, 'Point of view in Dickens,' *PMLA* 65 (1950), 101ff.

63. Louis Cazamian, *The Social Novel in England 1830–1850* (London and Boston, 1973), pp. 117ff.

64. Dickens, *The Christmas Books* (Harmondsworth, 1975), I, pp. 81–2.

65. Ibid., p. 131.

66. Ibid., p. 129.

67. Ibid., pp. 131ff.

6. The opposition Mode: teller-character–reflector-character

1. A condensed version of this chapter was published as Stanzel, 'Teller-characters and reflector-characters in narrative theory,' *Poetics Today*, 2 (1981), 5–15.
2. See Plato, *The Republic*, trans. and ed. Raymond Larson (Arlington Heights, Illinois, 1979), esp. Book 3.
3. See N. Friedman, 'Point of View,' 1162–3, note 3.
4. See Otto Ludwig, 'Formen der Erzählung,' in *Epische Studien. Gesammelte Schriften*, ed. A. Stern, Leipzig, 1891, VI, pp. 202ff. It is significant that he also acknowledges a hybrid.
5. Stanzel, *Narrative Situations*, pp. 22–3.
6. See Percy Lubbock, *The Craft of Fiction*, New York, 1947, pp. 62ff. *et passim*; N. Friedman, 'Point of view,' 1161–5 *et passim*.
7. The term 'narrating model' (*Erzählmodell*) for a type of narrative process in which scenic presentation or a figural narrative situation, not reportorial narration, is predominant, can easily lead to misunderstandings. Note that Anderegg himself distinguishes his use of the terms 'reporting' and 'narrating' from their use by Lämmert and by me. See Anderegg, *Fiktion und Kommunikation: Ein Beitrag zur Theorie der Prosa* (1973), 2nd edn, Göttingen, 1977, p. 170, note 2.
8. Anderegg, *Fiktion*, p. 54.
9. See Wilhelm Worringer, *Abstraction and Empathy: A Contribution to the Psychology of Style*, trans. Michael Bullock (New York, 1953), and Gombrich, *Art and Illusion*, pp. 76, 99ff. *et passim*.
10. Anderegg, *Fiktion*, p. 45.
11. See Section 3.2.1.
12. In *Narrative Situations* the term 'neutral narrative situation' was used to refer to the first type of scenic presentation. Because of its ambiguity, this term will not be used any more. See *Narrative Situations*, pp. 23 and 28–9.
13. Joseph Conrad's marked preference for the teller-mode, especially in the Marlow narratives, is probably connected with the Eastern tradition of oral narrative (Russian *skaz*, Polish *gawęda*). See Frederick R. Karl, *Joseph Conrad: The Three Lives* (London, 1979), pp. 30 and 942.
14. Ann Banfield distinguishes between 'reflective' and 'non-reflective consciousness.' Reflector-characters can function on both levels of consciousness. Emma Bovary, for example, exhibits predominantly a non-reflective consciousness: ' "during much of the narrative" she "is nothing more than bodily surfaces and intense sensations." On the other hand, Virginia Woolf's novels show a preponderance of reflective consciousness,' as do the later novels of Henry James, as well, one could add. Ann Banfield, 'Reflective and non-reflective

consciousness in the language of fiction,' *Poetics Today*, 2 (1981), 75.
15. N. Friedman, 'Point of View,' 1169.
16. For a discussion of the term 'narrative strategy' see Kanzog, *Erzählstrategie* (Heidelberg, 1976), pp. 104ff.
17. Jane Austen, *Emma* (Harmondsworth, 1977), p. 194.
18. Ibid., p. 195.
19. Muriel Spark, *The Prime of Miss Jean Brodie* (Harmondsworth, 1974), pp. 27-31.
20. Joyce, *The Dubliners: Text, Criticism, and Notes*, ed. Scholes and Litz (New York, 1969), p. 248 and p. 14.
21. See Stanzel, 'Die Personalisierung des Erzählaktes im *Ulysses*,' in *James Joyces 'Ulysses': Neuere deutsche Aufsätze*, ed. Therese Fischer-Seidel (Frankfurt am Main, 1977), pp. 286 and 289.
22. Romberg, *Studies* p. 100, is of the opinion that the first-person narrative situation is suspended in interior monologue. This is only true, however, when a first-person reflector-character replaces the first-person teller-character.
23. Beckett, *Molloy*, pp. 305, 309, 397 *et passim*.
24. Booth, *Rhetoric*, pp. 158–9.
25. As narrators Booth lists 'Cid Hamete Benengeli, Tristram Shandy, the "I" of *Middlemarch*, and Strether,' *Rhetoric*, pp. 149–50. Genette, *Narrative Discourse*, p. 188, criticizes this classification of Strether.
26. Booth, *Rhetoric*, pp. 152–3.
27. Ibid., p. 164.
28. For a discussion of areas of indeterminacy, see Ingarden, *Literary Work of Art*, pp. 246–54, and his *Cognition*, pp. 13, 51 *et passim*.
29. See Rainer Warning (ed.) *Rezeptionsästhetik: Theorie und Praxis* (Munich, 1975), esp. pp. 42–70.
30. I described this phenomenon in a previously published article with reference to the first-person and the authorial narrative situations, on the one hand, and to the figural narrative situation, on the other. See Stanzel, 'Komplementärgeschichte,' pp. 240–59.
31. See Ingarden, *Cognition*, p. 292; and Warning, *Rezeptionsästhetik*, p. 60.
32. See Ingarden, *Cognition*, pp. 56f; and Warning, *Rezeptionsästhetik*, p. 50.
33. Stanzel, 'Komplementärgeschichte,' p. 250.
34. Cohn, 'K. enters *The Castle*: on the change of person in Kafka's manuscript,' *Euphorion*, 62 (1968), 36.
35. Lothar Fietz has already called attention to the connection between figural narrative situation and the principle of selection in this novel. See 'Möglichkeiten und Grenzen einer Deutung von Kafkas Schloß-Roman,' *Deutsche Vierteljahrsschrift für Literaturwissenschaft und Geistesgeschichte*, 37 (1963), 73.

36. Tobias Smollett, *The Adventures of Peregrine Pickle* (London, 1964).

37. Austen, *Emma*, p. 37.

38. Dickens, *Great Expectations* (Harmondsworth, 1955), p. 35.

39. See Stanzel, *Typische Formen des Romans*, 10th edn (Göttingen, 1981), p. 36.

40. James, 'The Aspern Papers,' in *Complete Tales*, VI, p. 275.

41. William Faulkner, 'Honor,' in *Collected Stories* (New York, 1943), p. 551.

42. Charles C. Fries, *The Structure of English* (New York, 1952), p. 242.

43. See Joseph M. Backus, ' "He came into her line of vision walking backward": Nonsequential sequence-signals in short story openings,' *Language Learning*, 15 (1965), 67–8.

44. Nathaniel Hawthorne, 'Egotism; or The Bosom Serpent,' in *The Complete Novels and Selected Tales of Nathaniel Hawthorne* (New York, 1937), p. 1106.

45. Joyce, 'A Little Cloud,' in *Dubliners* (Harmondsworth, 1974), p. 68.

46. Maugham, 'The Force of Circumstance,' in *The Complete Short Stories of W. Somerset Maugham* (London, 1963), I, p. 481.

47. Katherine Mansfield, 'Mr and Mrs Dove,' in *The Garden Party and Other Stories* (Harmondsworth, 1976), p. 120.

48. O. Henry, *Complete Works* (Garden City, 1953), II, p. 973.

49. Godfrid Storms, *The Origin and the Functions of the Definite Article in English* (Amsterdam, 1961), p. 13; and Bronzwaer, *Tense in the Novel*, p. 90.

50. Bronzwaer, *Tense in the Novel*, p. 90.

51. James, *Complete Tales*, VI, p. 383.

52. Winkler, 'Über Deixis,' pp. 166–7.

53. Hemingway, 'The Gambler, the Nun, and the Radio,' in *The Short Stories of Ernest Hemingway* (New York, 1953), p. 468.

54. Mansfield, 'The Daughters of the Late Colonel,' in *The Garden Party*, p. 88.

55. Mansfield, 'The Garden Party,' in *The Garden Party*, p. 65.

56. Chatman, 'The Structure of Narrative Transmission,' in *Style and Structure in Literature: Essays in the New Stylistics*, ed. Roger Fowler (Oxford, 1975), p. 255.

57. Backus, 'Nonsequential sequence-signals,' 69.

58. See Karl Boost, *Neue Untersuchungen zum Wesen und zur Struktur des deutschen Satzes* (Berlin, 1955).

59. Roland Harweg, *Pronomina und Textkonstitution* (Munich, 1968).

60. Kenneth L. Pike, *Language in Relation to a Unified Theory of the Structure of Human Behavior* (Glendale, 1954).

61. Harweg, *Pronomina*, p. 152.

62. Ibid., p. 163.

63. Heinrich von Kleist, *Michael Kohlhaas: From an Old Chronicle* (London, 1967), p. 1; 'Michael Kohlhaas,' in his *Sämtliche Werke*

(Leipzig, 1883), I, p. 137.

64. Harweg, *Pronomina*, p. 319.
65. Thomas Mann, *Stories of a Lifetime* (London, 1961), I, p. 325; *Der Tod in Venedig und andere Erzählungen* (Frankfurt am Main, 1954), p. 181..
66. Maugham, *Complete Short Stories*, I, p. 481.
67. I have already published a study of the reflectorization of the teller-character in *Ulysses*. The results are briefly summarized in this section. See Stanzel, 'Personalisierung.'
68. Harweg, 'Präsuppositionen und Rekonstruktion: Zur Erzählsituation in Thomas Manns *Tristan* aus textlinguistischer Sicht,' in *Textgrammatik*, ed. Schecker and Wunderli (Tübingen, 1975), pp. 166–85.
69. The negation of the verb 'to know' (*wissen*) is an important criterion in narrative theory in general. 'He doesn't know that . . .' can only be said by an (authorial) teller-character about a character in a narrative; on the other hand, 'he doesn't know whether/how . . .' can also occur as the statement of a reflector-character. See Stierle, *Text als Handlung*, Munich, 1975, pp. 127ff.
70. Mansfield, *Garden Party*, pp. 76–7.
71. Ibid., pp. 28, 36, 76–7, 92–3.
72. Chatman draws attention to a passage at the beginning of *Mrs Dalloway* in which a 'communal or sympathetic mode' is expressed. This mode corresponds to the reflectorization of the teller-character in my terminology. See Chatman, 'Structure,' p. 254.
73. See Spark, pp. 61, 68, 79 *et passim*.
74. This was set forth at length in my article 'Personalisierung.'
75. See *Narrative Situations*, pp. 123–6.
76. See Fischer-Seidel, 'Charakter als Mimesis und Rhetorik: Bewußtseinsdarstellung in Joyces *Ulysses*,' in *James Joyce*, esp. p. 316 *et passim*, and *Bewußtseinsdarstellung im Werk von James Joyce. Von 'Dubliners' zu 'Ulysses'* (Frankfurt am Main, 1973), pp. 121ff.
77. Joyce, *Ulysses*, pp. 254–6.
78. In *Narrative Situations*, pp. 130–1, I tried to show how a new structure of meaning emerges when for example, several of the word- and sound-motifs of the 'Sirens' episode form the motif sequence of a morning song in the prelude.
79. See Stanzel, 'Personalisierung,' pp. 291–300.
80. Joyce, *Ulysses*, pp. 218–23.
81. Ibid., pp. 218–19.
82. Ibid., p. 219.
83. Ibid., p. 220.
84. Steinberg terms it 'free indirect style,' *Erlebte Rede*, pp. 166, 236 and 272.
85. Stimulated by C. G. Jung, I first presented this hypothesis in *Narrative*

Situations and then in the essay 'Personalisierung.' See *Narrative Situations*, pp. 141–2, and 'Personalisierung,' pp. 292–4 and 298–9.

86. Francis Bulhof, *Transpersonalismus und Synchronizität: Wiederholung als Strukturelement in Thomas Manns 'Zauberberg'* (Groningen, 1966).
87. Ibid., p. 168.
88. Ibid., p. 188.
89. Harweg, 'Präsuppositionen,' p. 166.
90. Ibid., p. 183.
91. See Harweg, 'Präsuppositionen,' p. 168, note 3. For the modification of Hamburger's thesis see my essay 'Episches Präteritum, erlebte Rede, historisches Präsens,' *Deutsche Vierteljahrsschrift für Literaturwissenschaft und Geistesgeschichte*, 33 (1959), 1–12, rpt. in *Poetik*, ed. Klotz, pp. 319–38; and the discussion of Hamburger's *Logic* in Section 1.2 of this book, as well as in *Narrative Situations*, pp. 22–37.
92. Harweg, 'Präsuppositionen,' p. 168.
93. Casparis provides a detailed analysis of the use of the present tense as the narrative tense in more than a dozen English novels in which the 'relation of simultaneity between the sender and the subject matter' is almost always a subordinate aspect of this unusual use of tense. (In the English translation of Franz Werfel's novel, *The Song of Bernadette*, trans. Ludwig Lewisohn (New York, 1964), the present tense of narration is not retained after Chapter X. Translator's note.)
94. Harweg, 'Präsuppositionen,' p. 169.
95. Ibid., p. 169, points 3 and 4.
96. Ibid., pp. 178–9.
97. Thomas Mann, *Der Tod in Venedig*, p. 65.
98. Ibid., p. 69.
99. Harweg, 'Präsuppositionen,' pp. 182–3.
100. Thomas Mann, *Der Tod in Venedig*, p. 86 (see also note 33 on p. 242).
101. Ibid.
102. Harweg, 'Präsuppositionen,' pp. 182–3.
103. Ibid., pp. 184–5.
104. Ibid., p. 185.

7. The typological circle: diagram and function

1. See Section 1.2.
2. See especially Chapters II through V of *Rhetoric*, pp. 23–144, in which Booth discusses the demand for realism, objectivity, 'Pure Art' and 'The Role of Belief' in narrative theory.
3. For a discussion of the term 'thought report' see Stanzel, *Narrative Situations*, pp. 146–7. Günther terms indirect speech 'narrated speech.' See Günther, *Probleme der Rededarstellung* (Marburg, 1928), pp. 3, 55 and 81.

4. See John A. Lester, Jr, 'Thackeray's narrative technique,' *PMLA*, 69 (1954), 404–5.
5. See Section 3.2.1.
6. Hemingway, *A Moveable Feast*, p. 58. See also the explanation in Winkler, *Lyrische Elemente,* pp. 72ff, and 'Über Deixis,' p. 167.
7. See Section 6.4.
8. See Theodore Spencer, 'Introduction to the First Edition,' in Joyce, *Stephen Hero*, ed. John J. Slocum and Herbert Cahoon (London, 1969), pp. 13–16.
9. Joyce, *Stephen Hero* (London, 1969), pp. 39, 84, 40 *et passim*.
10. Joyce, *A Portrait of the Artist*, pp. 216–25.
11. Ibid., p. 8.
12. See Leo Hendrick, 'Henry James: the late and early styles,' Diss. Univ. of Michigan 1953, pp. 32ff., as cited by Chatman, *The Later Style of Henry James* (Oxford, 1972), p. 57. Chatman establishes here that also during the revision of the earlier novel *The American* James frequently replaced the name of the main character with a personal pronoun.
13. For example, Albrecht Neubert, *Die Stilformen der 'Erlebten Rede' im neueren englischen Roman* (Halle/Saale, 1957), pp. 13ff.; Steinberg, *Erlebte Rede*, pp. 85–6; Hernadi, *Beyond Genre*, p. 193; and Pascal, *Dual Voice*, p. 25.
14. Steinberg, *Erlebte Rede*, pp. 55–118, gives a thorough overview of the problem of definition.
15. For a discussion of the concept 'contamination' see Leo Spitzer, 'Sprachmischung als Stilmittel und als Ausdruck der Klangphantasie,' *Germanisch-Romanische Monatsschrift*, NS 11 (1923), 193–216; and Pascal, *Dual Voice*, pp. 54–7. Graham Hough speaks of 'coloured narrative' in his 'Narrative and dialogue in Jane Austen,' *Critical Quarterly*, 12 (1970), 204.
16. Quotation and emphasis from Steinberg, *Erlebte Rede*, p. 1. See also Werner Hoffmeister, *Studien zur erlebten Rede bei Thomas Mann und Robert Musil* (London/The Hague/Paris, 1965).
17. See Willi Bühler, *Die 'Erlebte Rede' im englischen Roman. Ihre Vorstufen und ihre Ausbildung im Werke Jane Austens* (Zurich and Leipzig, 1937), pp. 81ff.
18. As quoted by Pascal, *Dual Voice*, p. 56.
19. Ibid., p. 56.
20. Ibid., pp. 56–7.
21. Joyce, *Dubliners* (Harmondsworth, 1974), p. 173.
22. See Neubert, *Stilformen*, p. 14.
23. Steinberg, *Erlebte Rede*, p. 61.
24. Alfred Döblin, *Alexanderplatz, Berlin: The Story of Franz Biberkopf* (New York, 1931), pp. 466–7; *Berlin Alexanderplatz: Die Geschichte von Franz Biberkopf* (Munich, 1977), p. 303.

25. See Section 6.4.
26. As quoted by Steinberg, *Erlebte Rede*, p. 101, note 51.
27. Ibid., p. 101. The German quotation from Heinrich Mann, *Die Jugend des Königs Henri Quatre*, was also taken from Steinberg with his emphasis.
28. See Stierle, *Text*, pp. 127–8. Stierle draws attention to Kleist's novella *The Marquise of O–*, in which the negation 'did not know if/what' predominates: '[Kleist] narrates in such a way that the reader adopts the ignorance of the heroine,' which corresponds to the orientation of the reader in a figural narrative situation. See also my note 69 to Section 6.4.
29. Joyce, *A Portrait of the Artist*, pp. 17, 15, 177, 232 and 195.
30. See Section 6.4.
31. Compare the examples from *Ulysses* to those from 'The Garden Party' in Section 6.4.
32. See Section 6.4.
33. Mansfield, *Garden Party*, p. 36.
34. See Section 4.5.
35. Theodor Fontane, *Effi Briest*, in *Sämtliche Werke* (Munich, 1959), VII, p. 171.
36. Georg Büchner, 'Lenz,' as translated into English by Pascal, *Dual Voice*, p. 62; *Werke und Briefe* (Wiesbaden, 1958), p. 85.
37. Anderegg, *Leseübungen* (Göttingen, 1970), p. 24. See also the interpretation of this text in Pascal, *Dual Voice*, pp. 62ff.
38. Andereggg, *Leseübungen*, p. 29.
39. Cohn argues that frame-narrators and fictional editors of manuscripts narrate from a different level than first-person and authorial narrators. We must remember, however, that many of these frame-narrators and editors present themselves as contemporaries of the characters whose story they are narrating in that they allege to have heard about the event or have received the manuscript from precisely these characters. The editor of Moll Flanders's memoirs, for example, claims to have received this life history from Moll Flanders herself. He also was forced to revise her confessions stylistically, in order to avoid any offensiveness. With this explanation the character of the editor moves a bit closer along the typological circle to the location of the peripheral first-person narrator, with whom he shares the narrative level as well as the existential level. Editors and frame-narrators, on the other hand, who have no personal contact with the characters of their stories cannot be placed in the sector between authorial and first-person narrative situation. Cohn's objection is applicable to these narrators only. See Cohn, 'Encirclement,' pp. 165–6 and 180.
40. Dostoevsky, *The Brothers Karamazov* (Baltimore, 1958), p. 3. My emphasis.
41. Dostoevsky, *The Devils*, p. 21.

42. Flaubert, *Madame Bovary*, pp. 33ff.
43. Nikolai Gogol, 'The Overcoat,' in *The Collected Tales and Plays of Nikolai Gogol*, ed. Leonard J. Kent (New York, 1964), pp. 262–3.
44. See Chapter 6.3.
45. Thackeray, *Vanity Fair*, p. 722.
46. Ibid.
47. See Heinz Reinhold, *Der englische Roman des 19. Jahrhunderts* (Düsseldorf, 1976), p. 94.
48. Friedemann, *Die Rolle des Erzählers in der Epik*, rpt. Darmstadt, 1965, p. 26.
49. Ibid., p. 39.
50. The narrative situation in Mann's *Doctor Faustus* is, of course, much more differentiated. For a thorough analysis of the first-person narrative situation of this novel see Henning, pp. 34–153.
51. Scholes and Kellogg, *The Nature of Narrative*, London, 1971, pp. 261–2. Hönnighausen, 'Maske und Perspektive,' p. 294, views the role of the peripheral first-person narrator in relation to the delight of the authors of the turn of the century in concealing their personality, in disguising themselves: 'Besides the theatrical masks of Wilde and Nietzsche, there is an attitude of ostentatious inconspicuousness and bourgeois ordinariness in Pater, Henry James, T. S. Eliot and Thomas Mann – a cloak of invisibility and an anti-mask which is ironically incarnated in Mann's Zeitblom and his prototype, Stevenson's Mackellar.'
52. Jacqueline Viswanathan, 'Point of view and unreliability in Emily Brontë's *Wuthering Heights*, Conrad's *Under Western Eyes* and Mann's *Doktor Faustus*,' *Orbis Litterarum*, 29 (1974), 42–60.
53. Ibid., p. 43.
54. Viswanathan refers to appropriate passages in the novels she analyzed, 'Point of View,' 48ff.
55. See Section 5.4, note 33.
56. See Richardson, *Pamela* (London, 1955), I, pp. 125, 158–9 *et passim*. The term 'instantaneous description' occurred in Richardson's 'Preface' to *The History of Clarissa Harlowe* (London, 1932). For a discussion of the narrative distance in the epistolary novel see Natascha Würzbach, *The Novel in Letters* (London, 1969), pp. xvff.
57. See Section 4.8.2. See also Kathleen Tillotson, *The Novel of the 1840s* (Oxford, 1954), p. 192, where she asserts that the death scene of Paul Dombey in *Dombey and Son*, which is presented in the authorial-figural third-person form, approaches the first-person form.
58. See Stanzel, *Narrative Situations*, p. 61. These two terms were coined before Spitzer's essay 'Zum Stil Marcel Prousts' came to my attention. In this essay Spitzer makes a similar distinction when he speaks of the 'mysterious duality of the two "I's," the superior narrating "I" and the benumbed, dully experiencing "I" ' in Proust. *Stilstudien II* (Munich,

1928), p. 478. See also Romberg, *Studies in the Narrative Technique of the First-Person Novel* (Stockholm, 1962), pp. 95–6.

59. See Clemens Heselhaus, 'Grimmelshausen, *Der abenteuerliche Simplicissimus,*' in *Der deutsche Roman*, ed. Benno von Wiese (Düsseldorf, 1963), I, pp. 28ff.

60. Attempts to reconcile the resulting interpretative difficulties by treating Moll's authorially-coloured comments as ironic have not been very successful. This incongruity presents a problem for any interpretation of this novel, as Watt pointed out, *The Rise of the Novel* (London, 1957), pp.115–18.

61. Even relatively small changes in the relationship between the selves can have implications for an interpretation, as is the case in *David Copperfield* and *Great Expectations*. See Kurt Tetzeli von Rosador, 'Charles Dickens: *Great Expectations.* Das Ende eines Ich-Romans,' *Die Neueren Sprachen*, NS 18 (1969), 399–408, where the problem of the two conclusions of this novel is related to the handling of the relationship of the selves in a very revealing manner. Robert B. Partlow, Jr, 'The moving I: a study of the point of view in *Great Expectations,*' *College English*, 23 (1961), 122–31, arrives at similar results without referring to my theory of the first-person narrative. It is especially interesting that Partlow equates the effect of the detachment of the narrating self from the experiencing self with a transition from first-person to third-person reference: 'There is often such a great difference between the two I's that the latter, the "I-as-I-was" becomes virtually "he," ' p. 124.

62. The mirror monologue is also found occasionally in narratives with a figural narrative situation – for the same reasons as in the first-person narrative situation. In the figural narrative situation, the function of the mirror can also be assumed by a subordinate character, who temporarily becomes the reflector of the image of the main character. See James, *Ambassadors*, p. 6.

63. See Stanzel, 'Thomas Nashe: *The Unfortunate Traveller,*' in *Der englische Roman*, ed. Stanzel, I, pp. 71–2.

64. Dickens, *David Copperfield*, pp. 784ff.

65. Misch, as cited in Hamburger, *Logic*, p. 316.

66. See Cerny's analysis of Dickens's first-person novels, *Erinnerung bei Dickens* (Amsterdam, 1975), especially pp. 59ff., 144ff. and 204ff. Cerny also attempts to distinguish characteristic forms of memory in the individual first-person narrators on the basis of the particular memory process. These characteristic forms are largely identical to narrative stances.

67. Ibid., pp. 95ff. For a discussion of this topic in general see Frances A. Yates, *The Art of Memory* (London, 1969).

68. Dickens, *David Copperfield*, pp. 51–2.

69. As Cerny does, for example, *Erinnerung*, p. 107.

70. Dickens, *David Copperfield*, p. 330.
71. Ibid., p. 322.
72. See for example Hoffmeister, *Studien*, pp. 22ff., and Neubert, *Stilformen*, pp. 6–7 *et passim*.
73. Hamburger, *Logic*, p. 316.
74. Cohn, 'Erlebte Rede im Ich-Roman,' *Germanisch-Romanische Monatsschrift*, NS 19 (1969), 303–13. See also Bronzwaer, pp. 53ff.
75. Hermann Hesse, *Steppenwolf* (New York, 1929), pp. 93–5; Hesse, *Der Steppenwolf*, in his *Gesammelte Dichtungen* (Frankfurt am Main, 1952), IV, pp. 255–6.
76. Cohn, 'Erlebte Rede,' pp. 308–9.
77. Steinberg, *Erlebte Rede*, p. 293.
78. Ibid., p. 271.
79. Dickens, *David Copperfield*, p. 603.
80. Ibid., p. 605.
81. Fritz Karpf, 'Die erlebte Rede im Englischen,' *Anglia*, 45 (1933), 242–3. This essay is one of the first works of an Anglicist on free indirect style which is still useful today as a critical collection of material.
82. Richardson, *Clarissa Harlowe*, p. 5.
83. Ibid.
84. Cohn, 'Erlebte Rede,' p. 308. My emphasis.
85. This point is an oversimplification, but it characterizes the second-person narrative adequately in this context. Referring essentially to this novel van Rossum-Guyon demonstrated very convincingly the complex function which the second-person (*vous*) can assume. See her analysis of *La Modification* in *Critique du roman*.
86. The term 'indirect interior monologue,' which English and American critics have taken from Larbaud and Dujardin, corresponds essentially to the presentation of inner world with the aid of the figural narrative situation in my terminology.
87. Cohn, *Transparent Minds: Narrative Modes for Presenting Consciousness in Fiction*, Princeton, 1978, gives a detailed description of the various forms of interior monologue. It would also be wise to adopt her distinction between 'autonomous (interior) monologue' ('Leutnant Gustl,' the Penelope episode of *Ulysses*) and 'quoted (interior) monologue,' that is, short passages with interior monologue which are embedded in an authorial or figural narrative situation. Yet Cohn's view that the autonomous monologue has no legitimate place on my typological circle because it is an autonomous form, that is, it is free of the mediacy of narration is, at least with respect to Molly's monologue in the Penelope episode, not convincing. See Cohn, *Transparent Minds*, pp. 257–61, and 'Encirclement,' 170.
88. Cohn, 'Encirclement,' 174.
89. See for example Staffhorst, *Die Subjekt–Objekt Struktur. Ein Beitrag zur Erzähltheorie*, Stuttgart, 1979, pp. 20–1.

90. Joyce, *Ulysses*, p. 150.
91. Booth, *Rhetoric*, p. 61.
92. Ibid., pp. 61–2.
93. Beckett, *Malone Dies*, p. 289.
94. Leo Tolstoy, 'The Death of Ivan Ilych,' in his *Short Novels* (New York, 1966), II, p. 62.
95. Stanzel, *Narrative Situations*, pp. 56–8.
96. Katherine Anne Porter, *The Collected Stories of Katherine Anne Porter* (New York, 1965), p. 89.
97. See William Golding, *Pincher Martin* (London, 1956), p. 201. In their comparison of the presentation of shipwrecked characters in *Robinson Crusoe* and *Pincher Martin*, Mark Kinkead-Weekes and Ian Gregor come across a contrast in the structure of these two works which is essentially identical to the opposition teller-character/reflector-character:

> Where Defoe's passage is dominated by the personal pronoun, in Golding it is not the beholder but what is beheld that takes all our attention. He works to make us experience as directly as possible what is being described . . . We are never, as in Defoe, an audience for a narrator. We are inside a head, we are a pair of eyes, a consciousness aware of fear and pain. (Mark Kinkead-Weekes and Ian Gregor, *William Golding: A Critical Study* (London, 1967), pp. 123–4.)

98. N. Friedman, 'Point of View,' 1178–9. See also Leon Edel, 'Novel and camera,' in *The Theory of the Novel. New Essays*, ed. John Halperin (New York, 1974), pp. 177–88.
99. See Casparis, *Tense Without Time*, pp. 49–62.
100. Ibid., pp. 58–9.
101. Ibid., p. 53.
102. Recently authors have also been utilizing the form of the filmscript, including directions for the camera, etc., as a form of literary narrative. It is to the credit of Viswanathan that she brought this interesting attempt to the attention of narrative research in her article 'Le roman-scénario: étude d'une forme romanesque,' *Journal Canadien de Recherche Sémiotique* (1980), 125–49. With the aid of an analysis of three examples of the roman-scénario – H. Aquin, *Neige noire*, K. Gangemi, *Pilote de Chasse*, and William Burroughs, *The Last Words of Dutch Schulz* (all published in 1975) – she draws some conclusions which are very revealing in their implications for narrative theory, for example, 'According to the classification of Benveniste who distinguishes *histoire* and *discours* as regards the usage of tense and pronouns, one can say that the filmscript follows the temporal system of *discours* but that it adapts the pronominal system of *histoire*. One finds the same combination in Robbe-Grillet's *Jealousy*, for example. This combination produces an effect of emotional detachment (pronominal system) accompanied by immediate attention to the diegesis (tense of *discourse*).'

103. Gerda Zeltner-Neukomm, *Das Wagnis des französischen Gegen-wartsromans: Die neue Welterfahrung in der Literatur* (Hamburg, 1960), pp. 56 and 72.

104. See Section 5.2, note 12, and Section 6.2, notes 28 and 29.

105. Zeltner-Neukomm, *Wagnis*, pp. 87–8.

106. Bruce Morrissette, 'The evolution of narrative viewpoint in Robbe-Grillet,' *Novel: A Forum on Fiction*, 1 (1967), 28–9.

107. Alain Robbe-Grillet, *Jealousy* (New York, 1959), p. 116; *La Jalousie* (Paris, 1957), p. 171.

108. Robbe-Grillet, *Jealousy*, p. 43; *La Jalousie*, p. 36.

109. Beckett, *Residua: Prosadichtungen in drei Sprachen* (Frankfurt am Main, 1970).

110. Lodge, 'Samuel Beckett: Some Ping Understood,' in his *Novelist*, pp. 174–5.

BIBLIOGRAPHY

1. Primary literature

Aquin, H., *Neige noire*, Montreal, 1975.

Austen, Jane, *Emma*, Harmondsworth, 1977.

—— *Mansfield Park*, Harmondsworth, 1972.

—— *Sense and Sensibility*, London, 1962.

Balzac, Honoré de, *Père Goriot*, Paris, 1968.

Barth, John, *Lost in the Funhouse*, Garden City, N.Y., 1968.

Beckett, Samuel, *Molloy, Malone Dies, The Unnamable*, London, 1959.

—— *Residua. Prosadichtungen in drei Sprachen*, Frankfurt am Main, 1970.

Bellow, Saul, *Herzog*, Harmondsworth, 1965.

Broch, Hermann, *Death of Virgil*, London, 1981.

Brontë, Charlotte, *Shirley*, London, 1911.

Brontë, Emily, *Wuthering Heights*, Harmondsworth, 1956.

Büchner, Georg, *Werke und Briefe*, ed. Fritz Bergemann, Wiesbaden, 1958.

Burroughs, William, *The Last Words of Dutch Schulz*, N.Y., 1975.

Butler, Samuel, *The Way of All Flesh*, London, 1961.

Butor, Michel, *La Modification*, Paris, 1973.

Camus, Albert, *L'Etranger*, Paris, 1957.

—— *Carnets 1935–1942*, Paris, 1962.

Cary, Joyce, *Mister Johnson*, London, 1947.

—— *A Prisoner of Grace*, London, 1954.

Cervantes Saavedra, Miguel de, *Don Quixote*, Harmondsworth, 1951.

Chaucer, Geoffrey, *The Canterbury Tales*, in *The Works of Geoffrey Chaucer*, ed. F. N. Robinson, London, 1957.

Compton-Burnett, Ivy, *Men and Wives*, London, 1931.

—— *Mother and Son*, London, 1955.

Conrad, Joseph, *Lord Jim. A Tale*, Harmondsworth, 1962.

—— 'The Secret Sharer,' in *Three Tales from Conrad*, ed. Douglas Brown, London, 1960.

—— *Under Western Eyes*, London, 1963.

—— *Youth, Heart of Darkness, The End of the Tether*, London, 1967.

Crane, Stephen, *The Red Badge of Courage. An Episode of the American Civil War*, N.Y., 1951.

Defoe, Daniel, *Moll Flanders*, London, 1963.

Dickens, Charles, *Bleak House*, Harmondsworth, 1974.

—— *The Christmas Books*, I, Harmondsworth, 1975.

—— *David Copperfield*, Harmondsworth, 1975.

—— *Dombey and Son*, Harmondsworth, 1977.

—— *Great Expectations*, Harmondsworth, 1955.

—— *Hard Times*, Harmondsworth, 1975.

—— *The Mystery of Edwin Drood*, London, 1972.

—— *The Old Curiosity Shop*, London, 1966.

—— *Our Mutual Friend*, Harmondsworth, 1975.

—— *The Posthumous Papers of the Pickwick Club*, London, 1948.

Döblin, Alfred, *Alexanderplatz, Berlin: The Story of Franz Biberkopf*, N.Y., 1931.

—— *Berlin Alexanderplatz. Die Geschichte von Franz Biberkopf*, Munich, 1977.

Dostoevsky, Fyodor, *The Brothers Karamazov*, Baltimore, 1958.

—— *The Devils*, London, 1953.

Doyle, Arthur Conan, *Tales of Sherlock Holmes*, Washington, 1932.

Drabble, Margaret, *The Needle's Eye*, Harmondsworth, 1973.

—— *The Waterfall*, London, 1970.

Edgeworth, Maria, *Letters of Julia and Caroline* (1795), in *Tales and Novels*, VIII, N.Y. 1967, pp. 463-86.

Eliot, George, *Middlemarch*, London, 1963.

Faulkner, William, *Absalom, Absalom!*, N.Y., 1951.

—— *As I Lay Dying*, Harmondsworth, 1972.

—— 'Honor', in *Collected Stories*, N.Y., 1943, pp. 551–64.

—— *The Sound and the Fury*, Harmondsworth, 1964.

Fielding, Henry, *The History of Tom Jones*, London, 1966/67.

Flaubert, Gustave, *Madame Bovary*, Paris, 1966.

—— *Madame Bovary*, N.Y., n.d. (Also see Harmondsworth edn, 1950.)

Fontane, Theodor, *Effi Briest*, in *Sämtliche Werke*, VII, Munich, 1959.

Forster, Edward Morgan, *A Passage to India*, London, 1968.

Fowles, John, *The French Lieutenant's Woman*, N.Y., 1970.

Frisch, Max, *Montauk*, N.Y., 1976.

—— *Montauk. Eine Erzählung*, Frankfurt am Main, 1975.

—— *Mein Name sei Gantenbein*, Frankfurt am Main, 1964.

—— *Gantenbein*, London, 1982.

—— *Stiller. Roman*, Frankfurt am Main, 1975.

—— *I'm Not Stiller*, N.Y., 1958.

Gangemi, K., *Pilote de chasse*, Paris and Montreal, 1975.

Goethe, Johann Wolfgang von, *Die Leiden des jungen Werthers*, Berlin and Weimar, 1974.

—— *The Sufferings of Young Werther*, London, 1970.

—— 'Noten und Abhandlungen zu besserem Verständnis des west–östlichen Divans,' in *West–östlicher Divan*, Munich, 1961, pp. 121–254.

—— *West–Eastern Divan*, London, 1974.

—— *Die Wahlverwandtschaften*, Munich, 1963.

—— *Elective Affinities*, London, 1976.

—— *Wilhelm Meisters Lehrjahre*, Berlin and Weimar, 1974.

—— *Wilhelm Meister: The Years of Apprenticeship*, Dallas, 1979.

Gogol, N., 'The Overcoat,' in *The Collected Tales and Plays of Nikolai Gogol*, ed. Leonard J. Kent, N.Y., 1964.

Golding, William, *Pincher Martin*, London, 1956.

Grass, Günter, *Die Blechtrommel*, Frankfurt am Main, 1963.

—— *The Tin Drum*, London, 1971.

Green, Henry, *Nothing*, London, 1950.

Greene, Graham, *Brighton Rock*, London, 1947.

Grimmelshausen, H. J. C. von, *Simplicissimus Teutsch*, Halle/Saale, 1938.

Handke, Peter, *Die linkshändige Frau. Erzählung*, Frankfurt am Main, 1976.

—— *The Left-Handed Woman*, N.Y., 1978.

Hardy, Thomas, *The Return of the Native*, London, 1961.

—— *Tess of the D'Urbervilles*, London, 1928.

—— *The Woodlanders*, London, 1958.

Hawthorne, Nathaniel, 'Egotism; or, The Bosom Serpent,' in *The Complete Novels and Selected Tales of Nathaniel Hawthorne*, N.Y., 1937, pp. 1106–15.

Hemingway, Ernest, 'Fifty Grand' and 'The Killers,' in *Men Without Women*, Harmondsworth, 1955.

—— 'The Gambler, the Nun, and the Radio,' in *The Short Stories of Ernest Hemingway*, N.Y., 1953, pp. 468–87.

—— *A Moveable Feast*, Harmondsworth, 1966.

Henry, O., 'The Marionettes,' in *The Complete Works*, II, Garden City, N.Y., 1953.

Hesse, Hermann, *Der Steppenwolf*, in *Gesammelte Dichtungen*, IV, Frankfurt am Main, 1952.

—— *Steppenwolf*, N.Y., 1929.

Hoffmann, Heinrich, *Der Struwwelpeter*, Frankfurt am Main, n.d.

James, Henry, *The Ambassadors*, N.Y., 1948.

—— *The Art of the Novel. Critical Prefaces*, ed. Richard P. Blackmur, N.Y., 1950.

—— *The Complete Tales of Henry James*, ed. Leon Edel, London, 1963.

—— *The Notebooks of Henry James*, ed. F. O. Mathiessen, and K. B. Murdock, N.Y., 1947.

Johnson, Uwe, *Das dritte Buch über Achim. Roman*, Frankfurt am Main, 1961.

—— *The Third Book About Achim*, N.Y., 1967.

Joyce, James, *Dubliners*, Harmondsworth, 1974.

—— *The Dubliners, Text, Criticism, and Notes*, ed. R. Scholes and A. W. Litz, N.Y., 1969.

Bibliography

—— *A Portrait of the Artist as a Young Man*, Harmondsworth, 1963.

—— *Stephen Hero*, London, 1969.

—— *Ulysses*, Harmondsworth, 1969.

Kafka, Franz, *Der Prozess*, Frankfurt am Main, 1970.

—— *The Trial*, N.Y., 1937.

—— *Das Schloss*, Frankfurt am Main, 1974.

—— *The Castle*, London, 1954.

—— *Die Verwandlung. Erzählung*, Wiesbaden, 1958.

—— *The Metamorphosis*, N.Y., 1968.

Keller, Gottfried, *Der grüne Heinrich*, 2 vols., Stuttgart, 1912.

—— *Green Henry*, London, 1960.

—— *Die Leute von Seldwyla*, Basel, 1942.

—— *The People of Seldwyla and 7 Legends*, N.Y., 1929.

Kesey, Ken, *One Flew Over the Cuckoo's Nest*, London, 1976.

Kleist, Heinrich von, *Michael Kohlhaas: From an Old Chronicle*, London, 1967.

—— *Sämtliche Werke*, Leipzig, 1883.

Lawrence, David Herbert, *Lady Chatterley's Lover*, London, 1960.

—— *The Rainbow*, London, 1961.

—— *Sons and Lovers*, N.Y., 1968.

—— 'The Spirit of Place,' in *Studies in Classic American Literature*, N.Y., 1969, pp. 1–8.

—— *Women in Love*, Harmondsworth, 1973.

Lenz, Siegfried, *Deutschstunde*, Munich, 1977.

—— *The German Lesson*, N.Y., 1973.

Lessing, Doris, *The Golden Notebook*, N.Y., 1972.

Lessing, Gotthold Ephraim, *Laokoon*, Zurich, 1965.

—— *Laocoön: An Essay on the Limits of Painting and Poetry*, Indianapolis, 1962.

Mann, Thomas, *Die Bekenntnisse des Hochstaplers Felix Krull*, Frankfurt am Main, 1955.

—— *Confessions of Felix Krull, Confidence Man: The Early Years*, trans. Denver Lindley, N.Y., 1955.

—— *Die Buddenbrooks*, Berlin, 1930.

—— *The Buddenbrooks*, N.Y., 1961.

—— *Doktor Faustus*, Frankfurt am Main, 1960.

—— *Doctor Faustus*, N.Y., 1971.

—— *Die Entstehung des Doktor Faustus. Roman eines Romans*, Amsterdam, 1949.

—— *Der Erwählte*, Frankfurt am Main, 1951.

—— *The Holy Sinner*, London, 1952.

—— *Stories of a Lifetime*, London, 1961.

—— *Der Tod in Venedig und andere Erzählungen*, Frankfurt am Main, 1954.

—— 'Tristan,' in *Sämtliche Erzählungen*, Frankfurt am Main, 1963.

—— *Der Zauberberg*, Frankfurt am Main, 1960.

—— *The Magic Mountain*, N.Y., 1969.

Mansfield, Katherine, *The Garden Party and Other Stories*, Harmondsworth, 1976.

Maugham, W. Somerset, *Cakes and Ale*, Harmondsworth, 1963.

—— 'The Force of Circumstance,' in *The Complete Short Stories of W. Somerset Maugham*, I, London, 1963, pp. 481–505.

Melville, Herman, *Moby-Dick*, N.Y., 1952.

Mitchell, Julian, *The Undiscovered Country*, London, 1968.

Murdoch, Iris, *The Black Prince*, Harmondsworth, 1977.

—— *The Italian Girl*, London, 1964.

—— *Under the Net*, London, 1954.

Musil, Robert, *Der Mann ohne Eigenschaften*, Hamburg, 1958.

—— *The Man Without Qualities*, N.Y., 1965.

Nashe, Thomas, *The Unfortunate Traveller*, Elizabethan Fiction, ed. R. Ashley and M. Moseley, N.Y., 1953.

O'Brien, Flann, *At Swim-Two-Birds*, Harmondsworth, 1960.

Orwell, George, *The Collected Essays, Journalism and Letters of George Orwell*, IV, Harmondsworth, 1970.

Paltock, Robert, *The Life and Adventures of Peter Wilkins* (1750), London, 1973.

Pater, Walter, *Marius the Epicurean*, London, 1939.

Plato, *The Republic*, trans. and ed. Raymond Larson, Arlington Heights, Illinois, 1979.

Porter, Katherine Anne, *The Collected Stories of Katherine Anne Porter*, N.Y., 1965.

Rabelais, François, *Pantagruel*, Paris, 1955.

Richardson, Dorothy, *Pilgrimage*, London, 1915.

Richardson, Samuel, *The History of Clarissa Harlowe*, London, 1932.

—— *Pamela or, Virtue Rewarded*, London, 1801; *Pamela*, London, 1955.

—— 'Preface,' *Clarissa Harlowe*, London, 1932.

Richter, Johann Paul Friedrich (Jean Paul), *Flegeljahre*, Berlin, 1841.

—— *Siebenkäs*, Berlin, 1841.

—— *Flower, Fruit and Thorn Pieces; or, the married life, death and wedding of the advocate of the poor, Firmian Stanislaus Siebenkäs*, London, 1845.

Robbe-Grillet, Alain, *La Jalousie*, Paris, 1957.

—— *Jealousy*, N.Y., 1959.

—— *Le Voyeur*, Paris, 1955.

—— *The Voyeur*, N.Y., 1958.

Salinger, J. D., *The Catcher in the Rye*, Harmondsworth, 1958.

Sarraute, Nathalie, *Le Planétarium*, Paris, 1959.

Sartre, Jean-Paul, *La Nausée*, Paris, 1948.

—— *Nausea*, N.Y., 1964.

Schnitzler, Arthur, 'Fräulein Else,' in *Die Erzählenden Schriften*, II, Frankfurt am Main, 1970, pp. 324–81.

—— *Fräulein Else*, London, 1925.

—— *Leutnant Gustl und andere Erzählungen*, in *Ausgewählte Werke*, II, Frankfurt am Main, 1962.

—— 'None but the Brave' ['Leutnant Gustl'] in *Viennese Novelettes*, N.Y., 1931.

Scott, Sir Walter, *Ivanhoe*, London, 1960.

Shakespeare, William, *Love's Labour's Lost*, ed. R. David, London, 1956.

Smollett, Tobias, *The Adventures of Peregrine Pickle*, ed. James L. Clifford, London, 1964.

Spark, Muriel, *The Prime of Miss Jean Brodie*, Harmondsworth, 1974.

Stein, Gertrude, *Autobiography of Alice B. Toklas*, N.Y., 1955.

Steinbeck, John, *The Pearl*, N.Y., 1957.

Sterne, Laurence, *The Life and Opinions of Tristram Shandy, Gentleman*, ed. J. A. Work, N.Y., 1940.

Stifter, Adalbert, *Nachsommer*, Augsburg, 1954.

Storm, Theodor, *Der Schimmelreiter*, in *Werke*, IV, Frankfurt am Main, 1967.

—— 'The Rider on the White Horse', in *Three Eerie Tales from 19th Century Germany*, N.Y., 1975.

Swift, Jonathan, *Gulliver's Travels*, London, 1960.

Thackeray, William Makepeace, *Henry Esmond* (1852), Harmondsworth, 1972.

—— *The History of Pendennis*, Leipzig, 1849–50.

—— *The Memoirs of Barry Lyndon, Esq., Written by Himself*, London, 1844.

—— *The Newcomes*, Leipzig, 1855.

—— *Vanity Fair*, Harmondsworth, 1968.

Tolstoy, Leo, *Anna Karenina*, N.Y., 1978.

—— 'The Death of Ivan Ilych,' in *Short Novels*, II, N.Y., 1966.

—— *War and Peace*, N.Y., 1976.

Trollope, Anthony, *Barchester Towers*, N.Y., 1963.

—— *Phineas Finn*, London, 1973.

Twain, Mark, *The Adventures of Huckleberry Finn*, N.Y., 1957.

Vonnegut, Kurt, Jr, *A Breakfast of Champions*, N.Y., 1973.

—— *Slaughterhouse-Five, or the Children's Crusade*, N.Y., 1969.

Warren, Robert Penn, *All the King's Men*, N.Y., 1964.

Wells, H. G., 'The Country of the Blind,' in *The Short Stories of H. G. Wells*, London, 1927.

Werfel, Franz, *Das Lied von Bernadette*, Stockholm, 1942.

—— *The Song of Bernadette*, trans. Ludwig Lewisohn, N.Y., 1964.

Wieland, Christoph Martin, *Agathon*, Berlin, 1937.

Woolf, Virginia, *Mrs Dalloway*, Harmondsworth, 1975.

—— *To the Lighthouse*, London, 1932.

Wordsworth, William, *The Prelude*, in *The Poetical Works of W. Wordsworth*, London, 1956.

2. Secondary literature

Allott, Miriam, *Novelists on the Novel*, London, 1959.

Anderegg, Johannes, *Fiktion und Kommunikation: Ein Beitrag zur Theorie der Prosa* (1973), Göttingen, ²1977.

—— *Leseübungen*, Göttingen, 1970.

—— *Literaturwissenschaftliche Stiltheorie*, Göttingen, 1977.

Austin, John, *How to Do Things With Words* (1955), New York, 1962.

Backus, Joseph, M., ' "He came into her line of vision walking backward:" Nonsequential sequence-signals in short story openings,' *Language Learning* 15 (1965), 67–83.

Bakhtin, Mikhail M., *Die Ästhetik des Wortes,* ed. R. Grübel, Frankfurt am Main, 1979.

Bal, Mieke, 'Narration et focalisation. Pour une théorie des instances du récit,' *Poétique* 29 (1977), 107–27.

Banfield, Ann, 'Reflective and non-reflective consciousness in the language of fiction,' *Poetics Today* 2, Winter 1981, 61–76.

Baur, Uwe, 'Deskriptive Kategorien des Erzählverhaltens,' in *Erzählung und Erzählforschung im 20. Jahrhundert*, ed. R. Kloepfer and G. Janetzke-Dillner, Stuttgart, 1981, pp. 31–9.

—— 'Musils Novelle "Die Amsel," ' in *Vom 'Törless' zum 'Mann ohne Eigenschaften,'* ed. U. Baur, and D. Goltschnigg, Munich and Salzburg, 1973, pp. 237–92.

Beach, Joseph Warren, *The Twentieth-Century Novel: Studies in Technique*, N.Y., 1932.

Belsey, Catherine, *Critical Practice. New Accents*, London, 1980.

Benveniste, Emile, *Problèmes de linguistique générale*, Paris, 1966.

Bergonzi, Bernard, *The Situation of the Novel*, Harmondsworth, 1972.

Bisanz, Adam J., 'Linearität versus Simultaneität im narrativen Zeit-Raum-Gefüge. Ein methodisches Problem und die medialen Grenzen der modernen Erzählstruktur,' in *Erzählforschung I*, ed. W. Haubrichs, Göttingen, 1976, pp. 184–223.

Boege, Fred W., 'Point of view in Dickens,' *PMLA* 65 (1950), 90–105.

Bonheim, Helmut, 'Mode markers in the American short story,' in *Proceedings of the Fourth International Congress of Applied Linguistics*, Stuttgart, 1976, pp. 541–50.

—— *Submodes of Speech*, Kölner Anglistische Papiere, Cologne, 1981.

—— *The Narrative Modes. Techniques of the Short Story*, Cambridge, 1982.

—— 'Theory of narrative modes,' *Semiotica* 14 (1975), 329–34.

Boost, Karl, *Neue Untersuchungen zum Wesen und zur Struktur des deutschen Satzes*, Berlin, 1955.

Booth, Wayne C., 'Distance and point of view,' *Essays in Criticism* 11 (1961), 60–79.

—— *The Rhetoric of Fiction*, Chicago, 1961.

Botheroyd, P. F., *Ich und Er. First and Third Person Self-Reference and Problems of Identity in Three Contemporary German-Language Novels*, The Hague and Paris, 1976.

Bremond, Claude, *Logique de récit*, Paris, 1973.

Bronzwaer, W. J. M., *Tense in the Novel. An Investigation of Some Potentialities of Linguistic Criticism*, Groningen, 1970.

Brooks, Cleanth and Warren, R. P., *Understanding Fiction*, N.Y., 1943.

Bühler, Karl, *Sprachtheorie* (1934), Stuttgart ²1965.

Bühler, Willi, *Die 'Erlebte Rede' im englischen Roman. Ihre Vorstufen und ihre Ausbildung im Werke Jane Austens*, Zurich and Leipzig, 1937.

Bulhof, Francis, *Transpersonalismus und Synchronizität. Wiederholung als Strukturelement in Thomas Manns 'Zauberberg,'* Groningen, 1966.

Cary, Joyce, *Art and Reality*, Cambridge, 1958.

Casparis, Christian Paul, *Tense Without Time. The Present Tense in Narration*, Bern, 1975.

Cazamian, Louis, *The Social Novel in England 1830–1850*, London and Boston, 1973.

Cerny, Lothar, *Erinnerung bei Dickens*, Amsterdam, 1975.

Chatman, Seymour, *The Later Style of Henry James*, Oxford, 1972.

—— *Linguistics and Literature. An Introduction to Literary Stylistics*, London, 1973.

—— *Story and Discourse: Narrative Structure in Fiction and Film*, Ithaca, N.Y., 1978.

—— 'The structure of narrative transmission,' in *Style and Structure in Literature: Essays in the New Stylistics*, ed. Roger Fowler, Oxford, 1975, pp. 213–57.

Chatman, Seymour (ed.), *Literary Style. A Symposium*, London, 1971.

Clemen, Wolfgang, *Shakespeares Bilder. Ihre Entwicklung und ihre Funktionen im dramatischen Werk*, Bonn, 1936.

Clissmann, Anne, *Flann O'Brien. A Critical Introduction to His Writings*, Dublin, 1975.

Cohn, Dorrit, 'The encirclement of narrative. On Franz Stanzel's *Theorie des Erzählens*,' *Poetics Today* 2 (Winter 1981), 157–82.

—— 'Erlebte Rede im Ich-Roman,' *Germanisch-Romanische Monatsschrift*, NS 19 (1969), 303–13.

—— 'K. enters *The Castle*: On the change of person in Kafka's manuscript,' *Euphorion* 62 (1968), 28–45.

—— 'Narrated monologue: definition of a fictional style,' *Comparative Literature* 18 (1966), 97–112.

—— *Transparent Minds: Narrative Modes for Presenting Consciousness in Fiction*, Princeton, N.J., 1978.

Collins, Philip, *A Critical Commentary on 'Bleak House,'* London, 1971.

Culler, Jonathan, *Structuralist Poetics: Structuralism, Linguistics, and the Study of Literature*, Ithaca, N.Y., 1978.

Doležel, Lubomír, *Narrative Modes in Czech Literature*, Toronto, 1973.

—— 'Toward a structural theory of content in prose fiction,' in *Literary Style. A Symposium*, ed. S. Chatman, London, 1971, pp. 95–110.

—— 'The typology of the narrator: point of view in fiction', in *To Honor Roman Jakobson*, I, The Hague, 1967, pp. 541–52.

Dubois, Jacques et al., *Rhétorique générale*, Paris, 1971.

Edel, Leon, 'Novel and camera,' in *The Theory of the Novel. New Essays*, ed. J. Halperin, N.Y., 1974, pp. 177–88.

Eikhenbaum, Boris, 'Die Illusion des "skaz," ' in *Russischer Formalismus. Texte zur allgemeinen Literaturtheorie und zur Theorie der Prosa*, ed. Yury Striedter, Munich, 1971, pp. 161–7.

Eile, Stanisław, 'The novel as an expression of the writer's vision of the world,' *New Literary History* 9 (1977–8), 116–28.

Fabian, Bernhard, 'Laurence Sterne: *Tristram Shandy*,' in *Der englische Roman*, ed. F. K. Stanzel, Düsseldorf, 1969, I, pp. 232–69.

Fietz, Lothar, 'Möglichkeiten und Grenzen einer Deutung von Kafkas Schloß-Roman,' *Deutsche Vierteljahrsschrift für Literaturwissenschaft und Geistesgeschichte* 37 (1963), 71–7.

Fischer-Seidel, Therese, *Bewußtseinsdarstellung im Werk von James Joyce. Von 'Dubliners' zu 'Ulysses,'* Frankfurt am Main, 1973.

—— 'Charakter als Mimesis und Rhetorik. Bewußtseinsdarstellung in Joyces *Ulysses*,' in *James Joyces 'Ulysses.' Neuere deutsche Aufsätze*, ed. Fischer-Seidel, Frankfurt am Main, 1977, pp. 309–43.

Fischer-Seidel, Therese (ed.), *James Joyces 'Ulysses.' Neuere deutsche Aufsätze*, Frankfurt am Main, 1977.

Forster, Edward Morgan, *Aspects of the Novel* (1927), Harmondsworth, 1974.

Forstreuter, Kurt, *Die deutsche Ich-Erzählung: Eine Studie zu ihrer Geschichte und Technik*, Berlin, 1924.

Fowler, Roger, *Linguistics and the Novel*, London, 1977.

Fowler, Roger (ed.), *Style and Structure in Literature: Essays in the New Stylistics*, Oxford, 1975.

Frank, Joseph, 'Spatial form in modern literature: an essay in three parts,' *Sewanee Review* 53 (1945), 221–40, 433–56, 643–53.

Frey, John R., 'Author-intrusion in the narrative: German theory and some modern examples,' *Germanic Review* 23 (1948), 274–89.

Friedemann, Käte, *Die Rolle des Erzählers in der Epik*, rpt. Darmstadt, 1965.

Friedman, Melvin, *Stream of Consciousness: A Study in Literary Method*, New Haven, 1955.

Friedman, Norman, 'Point of view in fiction. The development of a critical concept,' *PMLA* 70 (1955), 1160–84.

Fries, Charles C., *The Structure of English*, N.Y., 1952.

Füger, Wilhelm, 'Das Nichtwissen des Erzählers in Fieldings *Joseph Andrews*,' *Poetica* 10 (1978), 188–216.

—— 'Zur Tiefenstruktur des Narrativen. Prolegomena zu einer generativen "Grammatik" des Erzählens,' *Poetica* 5 (1972), 268–92.

Funke, Otto, 'Zur "Erlebten Rede" bei Galsworthy,' *Englische Studien* 64 (1929), 450–74.

Genette, Gérard, *Narrative Discourse (Figures III)*, trans. Jane E. Lewis, Ithaca, N.Y., 1980.

Głowiński, Michał, 'Der Dialog im Roman,' *Poetica* 6 (1974), 1–16.

—— 'On the first-person novel,' *New Literary History* 9 (1977), 103–14.

Goldknopf, David, *The Life of the Novel*, Chicago, 1972.

Gombrich, E. H., *Art and Illusion. A Study in the Psychology of Pictorial Representation* (1960), London ³1968.

Graevenitz, Gerhart von, *Die Setzung des Subjekts*, Tübingen, 1973.

Graham, Kenneth, *Criticism of Fiction in England 1865–1900*, Oxford, 1965.

Grimm, Reinhold (ed.), *Deutsche Romantheorie: Beiträge zu einer historischen Poetik des Romans in Deutschland*, Frankfurt am Main, 1968.

Gülich, Elisabeth, 'Ansätze zu einer kommunikationsorientierten Erzähltextanalyse,' in *Erzählforschung I*, ed. W. Haubrichs, Göttingen, 1976, pp. 224–56.

—— 'Erzähltextanalyse (Narrativik),' *Linguistik und Didaktik* 15 (1973), 325–8.

Gülich, E., and Raible, W., *Linguistische Textmodelle*, Munich, 1977.

Günther, Werner, *Probleme der Rededarstellung. Untersuchungen zur direkten, indirekten und erlebten Rede im Deutschen, Französischen und Italienischen*, Marburg, 1928.

Habermas, Jürgen, 'Der Universalitätsanspruch der Hermeneutik,' in *Hermeneutik und Ideologiekritik*, ed. J. Habermas, D. Henrich and J. Taubes, Frankfurt am Main, 1971, pp. 120–59.

Habicht, Werner and Schabert, I. (eds.), *Sympathielenkung in den Dramen Shakespeares*, Munich, 1978.

Halperin, John (ed.), *The Theory of the Novel. New Essays*, N.Y., 1974.

Halpern, Daniel and Fowles, John, 'A sort of exile in Lyme Regis,' *London Magazine*, March 1971, 34–46.

Hamburger, Käte, *The Logic of Literature*, 2nd, revised edn, Bloomington, 1973.

—— *Die Logik der Dichtung* (1957), Stuttgart ²1968.

—— 'Noch einmal: Vom Erzählen,' *Euphorion* 59 (1965), 46–71.

Hardy, Barbara, *The Appropriate Form: An Essay on the Novel*, London, 1964.

—— *The Novels of George Eliot*, London ²1963.

Harvey, W. J., *The Art of George Eliot*, London, 1961.

—— *Character and the Novel*, London, 1970.

Harweg, Roland, 'Präsuppositionen und Rekonstruktion. Zur Erzählsituation in Thomas Manns *Tristan* aus textlinguistischer Sicht,' in *Textgrammatik*, ed. Schecker and Wunderli, Tübingen, 1975, pp. 166–85.

—— *Pronomina und Textkonstitution*, Munich, 1968.

Haubrichs, Wolfgang (ed.), *Erzählforschung I*, Göttingen, 1976.

—— *Erzählforschung II*, Göttingen, 1977.

Hempfer, Klaus, *Gattungstheorie*, Munich, 1973.

Hendrick, Leo, 'Henry James: the late and early styles,' Univ. of Michigan Diss. 1953.

Hendricks, William O., 'The structural study of narration: sample analysis,' *Poetics* 3 (1972), 100–23.

Henning, Margit, *Die Ich-Form und ihre Funktion in Thomas Manns 'Doktor Faustus' und in der deutschen Literatur der Gegenwart*, Tübingen, 1966.

Hernadi, Paul, *Beyond Genre: New Directions in Literary Classification*, Ithaca and London, 1972.

—— 'Dual perspective: Free indirect discourse and related techniques,' *Comparative Literature* 24 (1972), 32–43.

Heselhaus, Clemens, 'Grimmelshausen, *Der abenteuerliche Simplicissimus*,' in *Der deutsche Roman*, ed. B. v. Wiese, Düsseldorf, 1963, I, pp. 15–163.

Hillebrand, Bruno, *Mensch und Raum im Roman*, Munich, 1971.

Hillebrand, B. (ed.), *Zur Struktur des Romans*, Darmstadt, 1978.

Hoffmann, Gerhard, *Raum, Situation, erzählte Wirklichkeit*, Stuttgart, 1978.

Hoffmeister, Werner, *Studien zur erlebten Rede bei Thomas Mann und Robert Musil*, London/The Hague/Paris, 1965.

Holthusen, J., 'Erzählung und auktorialer Kommentar im modernen russischen Roman,' *Welt der Slaven* 8 (1963), 252–67.

Hönnighausen, Lothar, 'Maske and Perspektive. Weltanschauliche Voraussetzungen des perspektivischen Erzählens,' *Germanisch-Romanische Monatsschrift*, NS 26 (1976), 287–307.

Hough, Graham, 'Narrative and dialogue in Jane Austen,' *Critical Quarterly* 12 (1970), 201–29.

Hurrelmann, B., 'Erzähltextverarbeitung im schulischen Handlungskontext,' in *Erzählen im Alltag*, ed. K. Ehlich, Frankfurt am Main, 1980, pp. 296–334.

Huxley, Aldous, *The Doors of Perception*, Harmondsworth, 1963.

Ihwe, Jens, 'On the foundations of a general theory of narrative structure,' *Poetics* 3 (1972), 5–14.

Ingarden, Roman, *Vom Erkennen des literarischen Kunstwerks*, Tübingen, 1968.

—— *The Cognition of the Literary Work of Art*, Evanston, 1973.

—— *Das literarische Kunstwerk*, Tübingen [4]1972.

—— *The Literary Work of Art: An Investigation on the Borderlines of Ontology, Logic and Theory of Literature*, Evanston, 1973.

—— 'Konkretisation und Rekonstruktion,' in *Rezeptionsästhetik*, ed. R. Warning, Munich, 1975, pp. 42–70.

Bibliography

Iser, Wolfgang, *Der Akt des Lesens*, Munich, 1976.

—— *The Act of Reading: A Theory of Aesthetic Response*, Baltimore, 1978.

—— *Der implizite Leser*, Munich, 1972.

—— *The Implied Reader: Patterns of Communication in Prose Fiction from Bunyan to Beckett*, Baltimore, 1974.

Jakobson, Dan, 'Muffled Majesty,' *Times Literary Supplement*, 26 October, 1967, 1007.

Jakobson, Roman, *Fundamentals of Language*, The Hague, 1956.

James, Henry, *The Art of the Novel. Critical Prefaces*, ed. Richard P. Blackmur, N.Y., 1950.

Janik, Dieter, *Die Kommunikationsstruktur des Erzählwerkes. Ein semiologisches Modell*, Bebenhausen, 1973.

Jauss, Hans Robert, *Literaturgeschichte als Provokation der Literaturwissenschaft*, Konstanz, 1967.

Jauss, Hans Robert (ed.), *Nachahmung und Illusion*, Munich, 1969.

Jens, W., *Deutsche Literaturgeschichte der Gegenwart*, Munich, 1961.

Jinks, William, *The Celluloid Literature. Film in the Humanities*, Beverly Hills, 1974.

Kahrmann, C., Reiß, G., and Schluchter, M., *Erzähltextanalyse: Eine Einführung in Grundlagen und Verfahren*, Königsstein/Taunus [2]1981, I.

Kanzog, Klaus, *Erzählstrategie*, Heidelberg, 1976.

Karl, F. R., *Joseph Conrad: The Three Lives*, London, 1979.

Karpf, Fritz, 'Die erlebte Rede im Englischen,' *Anglia* 45 (1933), 225–76.

Karrer, Wolfgang and Kreutzer, Eberhard, *Daten der englischen und amerikanischen Literatur von 1890 bis zur Gegenwart*, Munich, 1973.

Kayser, Wolfgang, *Entstehung und Krise des modernen Romans*, rpt. Stuttgart, (1954) 1955.

—— *Die Vortragsreise. Studien zur Legende*, Bern, 1958.

—— 'Wer erzählt den Roman?' in *Zur Poetik des Romans*, ed. V. Klotz, Darmstadt, 1965, pp. 197–216.

Kenner, Hugh, *Samuel Beckett. A Critical Study*, London, 1962.

Kimpel, Dieter and Wiedemann, Conrad, *Theorie und Technik des Romans im 17. und 18. Jahrhunderts*, 2 vols., Tübingen, 1970.

Kindlers Literaturlexikon (1964), Zurich, 1965.

Kinkead-Weekes, Mark and Gregor, Ian, *William Golding, a critical study*, London, 1967.

Klesczewski, R., 'Erzähler und "Geist der Erzählung." Diskussion einer Theorie Wolfgang Kaysers und Bemerkungen zu Formen der Ironie bei Th. Mann,' *Archiv für das Studium der Neueren Sprachen und Literaturen* 210 (1973), 126–31.

Klotz, Volker (ed.), *Zur Poetik des Romans*, Darmstadt, 1965.

Kraft, Herbert, *Um Schiller betrogen*, Pfullingen, 1978.

Kudszus, Winfried, 'Erzählperspektive und Erzählgeschehen in Kafkas

"Prozeß",' *Deutsche Vierteljahrsschrift für Literaturwissenschaft und Geistesgeschichte* 44 (1970), 106–17.

Kuhn, Thomas, *The Structure of Scientific Revolutions*, Chicago [2]1970.

Kunz, Josef, *Die deutsche Novelle im 20. Jahrhundert*, Berlin, 1977.

Kunze, Christoph, 'Die Erzählperspektive in den Romanen Alain Robbe-Grillets,' Diss. Regensburg, 1975.

Lachmann, Renate, 'Die "Verfremdung" und das "Neue Sehen" bei Viktor Šklovskij,' *Poetica* 3 (1970), 226–49.

Lamb, Charles and Mary, *Tales from Shakespeare*, ed. A. Hämel-Würzburg, Vienna, 1926.

Lämmert, Eberhard, *Bauformen des Erzählens*, Stuttgart, 1955.

Lämmert, E. (ed.), *Romantheorie: Dokumentation ihrer Geschichte in Deutschland seit 1880*, Cologne, 1975.

Landwehr, J., *Text und Fiktion: Zu einigen literaturwissenschaftlichen und kommunikationstheoretischen Grundbegriffen*, Munich, 1975.

Langer, Susanne, *Feeling and Form: A Theory of Art Developed From 'Philosophy in a New Key'*, London [4]1967.

Lass, Abraham (ed.), *A Student's Guide to 50 British Novels*, N.Y., 1966.

Leibfried, Erwin, *Kritische Wissenschaft vom Text. Manipulation, Reflexion, transparente Poetologie* (1970), Stuttgart [2]1972.

Lejeune, Philippe, 'Autobiography in the third person,' *New Literary History* 9 (1977), 26–50.

Lester, John A., Jr, 'Thackeray's narrative technique, *PMLA* 69 (1954), 392–409.

Lévi-Strauss, Claude, *The Savage Mind*, Chicago, 1966.

Lewandowski, Theodor, *Linguistisches Wörterbuch*, Heidelberg, 1975.

Link, Jürgen, *Literaturwissenschaftliche Grundbegriffe. Eine programmierte Einführung auf strukturalistischer Basis*, Munich, 1974.

Litz, A. Walton, *Jane Austen: A Study of Her Artistic Development*, London, 1965.

Lockemann, Wolfgang, 'Zur Lage der Erzählforschung,' *Germanisch-Romanische Monatsschrift*, NS 15 (1965), 63–84.

Lodge, David, *The Novelist at the Crossroads and Other Essays on Fiction and Criticism*, London, 1971.

Loofbourow, John, *Thackeray and the Form of Fiction*, Princeton, N.J., 1964.

Lotman, Yury, *Die Struktur literarischer Texte*, Munich, 1972.

—— *The Structure of the Artistic Text*, Ann Arbor, 1977.

Lubbock, Percy, *The Craft of Fiction*, N.Y., 1947.

Ludwig, Otto, 'Formen der Erzählung,' in *Epische Studien. Gesammelte Schriften*, ed. A. Stern, Leipzig, 1891, VI.

Ludwig, O., 'Thesen zu den Tempora im Deutschen,' *Zeitschrift für deutsche Philologie* 91 (1972), 58–81.

McHale, Brian, 'Free indirect discourse: a survey of recent accounts,' *PTL:*

A Journal for Descriptive Poetics and Theory of Literature 3 (1979), 249–87.

McLuhan, Herbert Marshall, *The Gutenberg Galaxy: The Making of Typographic Man*, Toronto, 1962.

Markus, Manfred, *Tempus und Aspekt. Zur Funktion von Präsens, Präteritum und Perfekt im Englischen und Deutschen*, Munich, 1977.

Meindl, Dieter, 'Zur Problematik des Erzählerbegriffs,' in *Zur Terminologie der Literaturwissenschaft und Literaturkritik*, ed. W. Erzgräber, Göttingen, 1978, pp. 207–13.

—— 'Zur Renaissance des amerikanischen Ich-Romans in den fünfziger Jahren,' *Jahrbuch für Amerikastudien* 19 (1974), 201–18.

Meixner, Horst, 'Filmische Literatur und literarisierter Film,' in *Literaturwissenschaft–Medienwissenschaft*, ed. Helmut Kreuzer, Heidelberg, 1977, pp. 32–43.

Meyer, Hermann, 'Raum und Zeit in Wilhelm Raabes Erzählkunst,' *Deutsche Vierteljahrsschrift für Literaturwissenschaft und Geistesgeschichte* 27 (1953), 237–67.

Moffet, J. and McElheny, K. R., *Points of View. An Anthology of Short Stories*, N.Y. and London, 1966.

Morrison, Kristin, 'James's and Lubbock's differing points of view,' *Nineteenth-Century Fiction* 16 (1961), 245–55.

Morrissette, Bruce, 'The evolution of narrative viewpoint in Robbe-Grillet,' *Novel. A Forum on Fiction* 1 (1967), 24–33.

Mukařovský, Jan, 'Standard language and poetic language,' in *A Prague School Reader on Esthetics, Literary Structure, and Style*, ed. Paul L. Garvin, Georgetown [3]1964, pp. 17–30.

Müller, Wolfgang, 'Gefühlsdarstellung bei Jane Austen,' *Sprachkunst* 8 (1977), 87–103.

Neubert, Albrecht, *Die Stilformen der 'Erlebten Rede' im neueren englischen Roman*, Halle/Saale, 1957.

Neuhaus, Volker, *Typen multiperspektivischen Erzählens*, Cologne, 1971.

Ornstein, Robert, *The Psychology of Consciousness*, San Francisco, 1972.

Partlow, R. B., Jr, 'The moving I: a study of the point of view in *Great Expectations*,' *College English* 23 (1961), 122–31.

Pascal, Roy, *The Dual Voice: Free indirect speech and its functioning in the nineteenth-century European novel*, Manchester, 1977.

—— 'Tense and novel,' *Modern Language Review* 57 (1962), 1–11.

Peper, Jürgen, 'Über transzendentale Strukturen im Erzählen,' *Sprache im technischen Zeitalter* 34 (1970), 136–57.

Petersen, Jürgen, H., 'Kategorien des Erzählens: Zur systematischen Deskription epischer Texte,' *Poetica* 9 (1977), 167–95.

Petsch, Robert, *Wesen und Formen der Erzählkunst*, Halle/Saale, 1934.

Pfister, M., *Das Drama: Theorie und Analyse*, Munich, 1977.

Pike, Kenneth L., *Language in Relation to a Unified Theory of the Structure of Human Behavior*, Glendale, 1954.

Pinion, F. B., *A Jane Austen Companion*, London, 1973.

Pouillon, Jean, *Temps et roman*, Paris, 1946.

Propp, Vladimir, *Morphology of the Folktale*, Austin ²1968.

Ray, Gordon N., *Thackeray: The Uses of Adversity*, London, 1955.

Reclams Romanführer, Stuttgart ⁵1974.

Reinhold, Heinz, *Der englische Roman des 19. Jahrhunderts*, Düsseldorf, 1976.

Ricardou, Jean, 'Nouveau Roman, Tel Quel,' *Poétique* 1 (1970), 433–54.

Richardson, Samuel, 'Preface' to *Clarissa Harlowe*, London, 1932.

Riehle, Wolfgang, '*Coriolanus*: Die Gebärde als sympathielenkendes Element,' in *Sympathielenkung in den Dramen Shakespeares*, ed. W. Habicht and I. Schabert, Munich, 1978, pp. 132–41.

Riffaterre, Michael, *Strukturale Stilistik*, Munich, 1973.

Ritter, Alexander (ed.), *Landschaft und Raum in der Erzählkunst*, Darmstadt, 1957.

Rolph, C. H. (ed.), *The Trial of Lady Chatterley: Regina vs. Penguin Books Limited*, Harmondsworth, 1961.

Romberg, Bertil, *Studies in the Narrative Technique of the First-Person Novel*, Stockholm, 1962.

Rossum-Guyon, Françoise van, *Critique du roman*, Paris, 1970.

—— 'Point de vue ou perspective narrative,' *Poétique* 1 (1970), 476–97.

Sartre, Jean-Paul, *Qu'est-ce que la littérature?*, Paris, 1948.

—— *What is Literature?*, London, 1950.

Saussure, Ferdinand, *Course in General Linguistics*, ed. Charles Bally and Albert Sechehaye, N.Y., 1959.

Schanze, Helmut, *Medienkunde für Literaturwissenschaftler*, Munich, 1974.

Scheerer, Thomas M. and Winkler, Markus, 'Zum Versuch einer Erzählgrammatik bei Claude Bremond,' *Poetica* 8 (1976), 1–24.

Schmid, Wolf, 'Zur Erzähltechnik und Bewußtseinsdarstellung in Dostoevskijs "Večnij muž," ' *Welt der Slaven* 13 (1968), 294–306.

Schober, Wolfgang Heinz, *Erzähltechniken in Romanen. Eine Untersuchung erzähltechnischer Probleme in zeitgenössischen deutschen Romanen*, Wiesbaden, 1975.

Scholes, Robert, *Structuralism in Literature*, New Haven, 1974.

Scholes, R. and Kellogg, R., *The Nature of Narrative*, London, 1971.

Schulte-Sasse, J. and Werner, R., *Einführung in die Literaturwissenschaft*, Munich, 1977.

Sebeok, Thomas A. (ed.), *The Tell-Tale Sign. A Survey of Semiotics*, Lisse, Netherlands, 1975.

Seidler, Herbert, *Die Dichtung. Wesen, Form, Dasein*, Stuttgart, 1965.

Shklovsky, Victor, 'Sterne's *Tristram Shandy*: stylistic commentary,' in Lee T. Lemon and Marion J. Reis (eds.), *Russian Formalist Criticism: Four Essays*, Lincoln, Nebraska, 1965.

—— 'Art as technique,' in Lee T. Lemon and Marion J. Reis (eds.),

Russian Formalist Criticism: Four Essays, Lincoln, Nebraska, 1965.

Smitten, Jeffrey R. and Daghistany, Ann, *Spatial Form in Narrative*, Ithaca, N.Y., 1981.

Sokel, Walter H., 'Das Verhältnis der Erzählperspektive zu Erzähl-geschehen und Sinngehalt in "Vor dem Gesetz," "Schakale und Araber" und "Der Prozeß," ' *Zeitschrift für deutsche Philologie* 86 (1967), 267–300.

Spencer, Theodore, 'Introduction to the First Edition,' in *Stephen Hero*, ed. J. Slocum and H. Cahoon, London (1944), 1969, pp. 13–24.

Spielhagen, Friedrich, *Beiträge zur Theorie und Technik des Romans*, Göttingen, 1967.

—— 'Der Ich-Roman,' in *Zur Poetik des Romans*, ed. Volker Klotz, Darmstadt, 1965, pp. 66–161.

Spitzer, Leo, 'Sprachmischung als Stilmittel und als Ausdruck der Klang-phantasie,' *Germanisch-Romanische Monatsschrift*, NS 11 (1923), 193–216.

—— *Stilstudien II*, Munich, 1928.

Spranger, Eduard, 'Der psychologische Perspektivismus im Roman,' rpt. in *Zur Poetik des Romans*, ed. V. Klotz, Darmstadt, 1965, pp. 217–38.

Spurgeon, C., *Shakespeare's Imagery and What It Tells Us* (1953), Cambridge, Mass., 1961.

Staffhorst, Albrecht, *Die Subjekt–Objekt-Struktur: Ein Beitrag zur Erzähl-theorie*, Stuttgart, 1979.

Stang, R., *The Theory of the Novel in England 1850–1870*, N.Y., 1959.

Stanzel, F. K., 'Episches Präteritum, erlebte Rede, historisches Präsens,' *Deutsche Vierteljahrsschrift für Literaturwissenschaft und Geistesgeschichte* 33 (1959), 1–12; rpt. in *Zur Poetik des Romans*, ed. V. Klotz, Darmstadt, 1965, pp. 319–38.

—— 'Gedanken zur Poetik des Romans,' in *Der englische Roman*, ed. F. K. Stanzel, Düsseldorf, 1969, I, pp. 9–20.

—— 'Innenwelt. Ein Darstellungsproblem des englischen Romans,' *Germanisch-Romanische Monatsschrift*, NS 12 (1962), 273–86.

—— 'Die Komplementärgeschichte. Entwurf zu einer leserorientierten Romantheorie,' in *Erzählforschung II*, ed. Wolfgang Haubrichs, Göttingen, 1977, pp. 240–59.

—— 'Zur Konstituierung der typischen Erzählsituationen,' in *Zur Struktur des Romans*, ed. B. Hillebrand, Darmstadt, 1978, pp. 558–76.

—— *Narrative Situations in the Novel: 'Tom Jones,' 'Moby-Dick,' 'The Ambassadors,' 'Ulysses,'* trans. J. Pusack, Bloomington, 1971.

—— 'Die Personalisierung des Erzählaktes im *Ulysses*,' in *James Joyces 'Ulysses.' Neuere deutsche Aufsätze*, ed. T. Fischer-Seidel, Frankfurt am Main, 1977, pp. 284–308.

—— 'Second Thoughts on *Narrative Situations in the Novel*: Towards a "Grammar of Fiction," ' *Novel. A Forum on Fiction* 11 (1978), 247–64.

—— 'Teller-characters and reflector-characters in narrative theory,' *Poetics Today* 2 (Winter 1981), 5–15.

—— 'Thomas Nashe: *The Unfortunate Traveller*,' in *Der englische Roman*, ed. F. K. Stanzel, Düsseldorf, 1969, I, pp. 54–84.

—— '*Tom Jones* und *Tristram Shandy*,' in *Henry Fielding und der englische Roman des 18. Jahrhunderts*, ed. W. Iser, Darmstadt, 1972, pp. 437–73.

—— '*Tristram Shandy* und die Klimatheorie,' *Germanisch-Romanische Monatsschrift*, NS 21 (1971), 16–28.

—— *Typische Formen des Romans*, Göttingen [10]1981.

—— *Die typischen Erzählsituationen im Roman. Dargestellt an 'Tom Jones,' 'Moby-Dick,' 'The Ambassadors,' 'Ulysses,' u.a.*, Vienna and Stuttgart, 1955.

—— 'Die typischen Formen des englischen Romans und ihre Entstehung im 18. Jahrhundert,' in *Stil- und Formprobleme in der Literatur*, ed. Paul Böckmann, Heidelberg, 1959, pp. 243–8.

—— 'Wandlungen des narrativen Diskurses in der Moderne,' in *Erzählung und Erzählforschung im 20. Jahrhundert*, ed. R. Kloepfer and Gisela Janetzke-Dillner, Stuttgart, 1981, pp. 371–83.

—— 'Zwei erzähltechnische Termini in komparatistischer Sicht: *Erlebte Rede* und *Erzähler* im Deutschen und Englischen,' *Sprachkunst* 10 (1979), 192–200.

Stanzel, F. K. (ed.), *Der englische Roman*, 2 vols., Düsseldorf, 1969.

Steinberg, Günter, *Erlebte Rede. Ihre Eigenart und ihre Formen in neuerer deutscher, französischer und englischer Erzählliteratur*, Göppingen, 1971.

Steiner, G., 'A Preface to *Middlemarch*,' *Nineteenth-Century Fiction* 9 (1955), 262–79.

Stierle, Karlheinz, 'Geschehen, Geschichte, Text der Geschichte,' in *Geschichte – Ereignis und Erzählung*, ed. R. Koselleck and W.-D. Stempel, *Poetik und Hermeneutik* 5, Munich, 1973, pp. 530–4; rpt. in K. Stierle, *Text als Handlung*, Munich, 1975, pp. 49–55.

—— *Text als Handlung. Perspektiven einer systematischen Literaturwissenschaft*, Munich, 1975.

Storms, Godfrid, *The Origin and the Functions of the Definite Article in English*, Amsterdam, 1961.

Sutherland, James, *Thackeray at Work*, London, 1974.

Tanner, Tony, Introduction to *Sense and Sensibility*, Harmondsworth, 1974, pp. 7–34.

Tetzeli von Rosador, Kurt, 'Charles Dickens: *Great Expectations*. Das Ende eines Ich-Romans,' *Die Neueren Sprachen*, NS 18 (1969), 399–408.

Thomas, Brooks, 'Reading Wolfgang Iser or responding to a theory of response,' *Comparative Literature Studies* 19 (1982), 54–66.

Tillotson, Geoffrey, *Thackeray the Novelist*, Cambridge, 1954.

Tillotson, Kathleen, *The Novel of the 1840s*, Oxford, 1954.

Titunik, Irwin R., 'Das Problem des "skaz." Kritik und Theorie,' in *Erzählforschung II*, ed. Wolfgang Haubrichs, Göttingen, 1977, pp. 114–40.

Todorov, Tzvetan, 'Les catégories du récit littéraire,' *Communications* 8 (1966), 125–51.

—— *Poétique de la prose*, Paris, 1971.

Ulich, Michaela, *Perspektive und Erzählstruktur von 'The Sound and the Fury' bis 'Intruder in the Dust,'* Heidelberg, 1972.

Uspensky, Boris A., *A Poetics of Composition: The Structure of the Artistic Text and Typology of a Compositional Form*, trans. Valentina Zavarin and Susan Wittig, Berkeley, Calif., 1973.

Vaid, Krishna Baldev, *Technique in the Tales of Henry James*, Cambridge, Mass., 1964.

Viswanathan, Jacqueline, 'Point of view and unreliability in Emily Brontë's *Wuthering Heights*, Conrad's *Under Western Eyes* and Mann's *Doktor Faustus*,' *Orbis Litterarum* 29 (1974), 42–60.

—— 'Le roman-scénario: étude d'une forme romanesque,' *Journal Canadien de Recherche Sémiotique*, 1980, 125–49.

Waldmann, Günter, *Kommunikationsästhetik: Die Ideologie der Erzählform*, Munich, 1976.

Warning, Rainer (ed.), *Rezeptionsästhetik: Theorie und Praxis*, Munich, 1975.

Watt, Ian, *The Rise of the Novel: Studies in Defoe, Richardson and Fielding*, London, 1957.

Weber, Dietrich, *Theorie der analytischen Erzählung*, Munich, 1975.

Weber, Max, *Gesammelte Aufsätze zur Wissenschaftslehre*, Tübingen, 1922.

Wehle, Winfried, *Französischer Roman der Gegenwart. Erzählstruktur und Wirklichkeit im Nouveau Roman*, Berlin, 1972.

Weimann, Robert, 'Erzählerstandpunkt und "Point of View". Zur Geschichte und Ästhetik der Perspektive im englischen Roman,' *Zeitschrift für Anglistik und Amerikanistik* 10 (1962), 369–416.

Weinrich, Harald, *Tempus. Erzählte und besprochene Welt* (1964), Stuttgart ²1971.

Wellek, René and Warren, Austin, *Theory of Literature* (1949), Harmondsworth, 1970.

Welzig, Werner, *Der deutsche Roman im 20. Jahrhundert*, Stuttgart ²1970.

Werlich, Egon, *A Text Grammar of English*, Heidelberg, 1976.

Wickardt, Wolfgang, *Die Formen der Perspektive in Charles Dickens' Romanen, ihr sprachlicher Ausdruck und ihre strukturelle Bedeutung*, Berlin, 1933.

Wieckenberg, Ernst-Peter, *Zur Geschichte der Kapitelüberschriften im deutschen Roman vom 15. Jahrhundert bis zum Ausgang des Barock*, Göttingen, 1969.

Wilson, Edmund, 'The Ambiguity of Henry James,' in *A Casebook on Henry James's 'The Turn of the Screw,'* ed. G. Willen, N.Y. [2]1969.

Winkler, Reinhold, 'Lyrische Elemente in den Kurzgeschichten Ernest Hemingways,' Diss. Erlangen 1967.

—— 'Über Deixis und Wirklichkeitsbezug in fiktionalen und nicht-fiktionalen Texten,' in *Erzählforschung I*, ed. W. Haubrichs, Göttingen, 1976, pp. 156–74.

Winter, Helmut, *Literaturtheorie und Literaturkritik*, Düsseldorf, 1975.

Worringer, Wilhelm, *Abstraktion und Einfühlung*, Berlin, 1908.

Würzbach, Natascha, *The Novel in Letters*, London, 1969.

—— 'Die Struktur des Briefromans und seine Entstehung in England,' Diss. Munich, 1964.

Yates, F. A., *The Art of Memory*, London, 1969.

Young, E., 'Conjectures on Original Composition – in a Letter to the Author of Sir Charles Grandison (1759),' in *English Critical Essays*, ed. E. D. Jones, London, 1968, pp. 270–311.

Zach, Wolfgang, 'Richardson und der Leser. *Pamela–Shamela–Pamela II*,' *Arbeiten aus Anglistik und Amerikanistik* 1 (1976), 65–105.

Zeltner-Neukomm, Gerda, *Das Wagnis des französischen Gegenwartsromans. Die neue Welterfahrung in der Literatur*, Hamburg, 1960.

INDEX

INDEX OF AUTHORS

Reference to footnotes is given only if these supply more than merely biblio-graphical information about works and authors already mentioned in the main body of the text.

The abbreviation TC stands for the diagram of the typological circle on p. xvi.

Index

SUBJECT INDEX

300